THE NATIONAL INSTITUTE OF
ECONOMIC AND SOCIAL RESEARCH

=1995

=1660

NIESR Students' Edition

5

THE EVOLUTION OF
GIANT FIRMS IN BRITAIN

250137

THE EVOLUTION OF
GIANT FIRMS IN BRITAIN

A Study of the Growth of Concentration
in Manufacturing Industry in Britain
1909–70

BY

S. J. PRAIS

Second Impression
with a new preface on
Developments in 1970–6

CAMBRIDGE UNIVERSITY PRESS

CAMBRIDGE

LONDON   NEW YORK   NEW ROCHELLE
MELBOURNE   SYDNEY

Published by the Press Syndicate of the University of Cambridge
The Pitt Building, Trumpington Street, Cambridge CB2 1RP
32 East 57th Street, New York, NY 10022, USA
296 Beaconsfield Parade, Middle Park, Melbourne 3206, Australia

First published 1976
Second Impression, with new preface 1981

Printed in Great Britain at the
University Press, Cambridge

Library of Congress Cataloguing in Publication Data
Prais, S. J.
The evolution of giant firms in Britain
(National Institute of Economic and Social Research. Economic and social studies; 30;
Students' Edition; 5)
Bibliography: p.
1. Great Britain – Manufactures. 2. Industrial concentration – Great Britain – History
3. Industries, Size of. 4. Industrial concentration – History
I. Title. II. Series
HD9731.5.P72   338.6′ 44′ 0941   76–18410
ISBN 0 521 28273 X paperback
(First Impression ISBN 0 521 21356 8 hard covers)

For
MICHELLE
and
DAVID
and
SARAH
and
JUDITH

CONTENTS

[vii]

LIST OF TABLES

LIST OF CHARTS

PREFACE TO THE SECOND IMPRESSION

In preparing a fresh impression of this book it has not been found necessary to introduce any revisions, apart from some remarks in this preface on trends in the most recent years and some observations on recent research studies.

According to tabulations now prepared annually by the Business Statistics Office from the Censuses of Production, the share in net output of the hundred largest enterprises in private manufacturing rose from 39·8 per cent in 1970 to 41·8 per cent in 1976 (the latest year for which these data are available). Their rise in the share of sales has been very similar, from 45·0 per cent to 47·0 per cent.[1] The pace at which these largest firms have recently increased their share of industrial activity has thus been rather lower than the rise of almost 1 percentage point a year observed in the decade or so before 1970 (see table 1.1 in the main text, page 4). Their share in employment has hardly risen at all, as we shall discuss further in a moment.

A pause in the rise in aggregate concentration has previously been observed, in the period covering the Second World War. It would thus be a mistake to infer that the long-term rising trend in concentration observed over a number of decades had fundamentally changed – or was on the verge of coming to an end – on the basis of what may well be merely a few years' change in tempo.

Many factors may readily be suggested as accounting for a slowing-down in 1970–6, though it is clearly not possible to say how important each might have been: for example, the high levels of concentration already reached may have made it more difficult for concentration to rise further; the exceptionally rapid rises in the 1960s may have required a period of consolidation; domestic anti-monopoly legislation and scrutiny of large mergers probably became gradually more effective; and EEC anti-monopoly legislation put an end to market-sharing arrangements affecting a number of large international companies. It is also possible that the increasingly heavy strikes experienced by the very largest manufacturing plants in this country have had a significant part in restraining the growth of the very largest enterprises. This last development is of wider significance for the efficiency of Britain's manufacturing industry, and some further words of explanation are in order.

The number of *man–days* lost a year due to strikes in manufacturing has quadrupled from 180 days a year per thousand employees in 1964–6 (the period examined by the Donovan Commission[2]) to 850 in

1976–8. (It is to be hoped that the further approximate quadrupling to over 3000 days in 1979 will prove to be an aberration rather than an intensification of that trend.) The *number of strikes* nearly doubled in the same period, from twelve a year per 100,000 employees in 1964–6 to twenty in 1976–8. These figures are based on records compiled by the Department of Employment; however, a more comprehensive survey of strikes based on plant records (carried out by the Industrial Relations Research Unit at the University of Warwick) has concluded that by omitting 'small' strikes the official figures cover probably only a quarter of the total number.[3] These small 'wildcat' strikes may not account for the loss of many man–days, but they contribute heavily to the great proportion of their efforts that British managers have to devote to preserving the running of their plants. From the point of view of the present book, the important feature of strikes in Britain is that the chance of a plant suffering a strike is very nearly proportional to its total size (for example, a plant with 1000–2000 employees has about ten times as many strikes as a plant with 100–200 employees, and it loses about seven times as many days per employee).[4] With the general rise in strike-proneness over time, it may be inferred that the net advantages of large-scale manufacturing operations have progressively been reduced in this country.

It is thus perhaps not surprising that in terms of employment the share of the hundred largest has advanced less than in terms of output; over the period 1970–6 the share of the hundred largest employers rose from 36·7 per cent only to 37·0 per cent, and the share in manufacturing employment of the hundred enterprises with the largest net output (which is of course not quite the same group as the hundred largest employers) was virtually unchanged (35·7 per cent in 1970, 35·6 per cent in 1976).[5] An increase in the degree of subcontracting by the largest enterprises, and an increase in their capital intensity, would account for these differential movements.

Changes in merger-rates clearly also influence the rate of increase in concentration, and the number of mergers has fluctuated considerably from year to year. But on taking averages over five years – which is more relevant when looking at these changes in trends – it does not appear that much can be attributed to recent changes in the rate of mergers. Expenditures on acquisitions and mergers by quoted industrial and commercial companies reached a peak in 1965–9 (£900 million a year); but in both the subsequent quinquennia, 1970–4 and 1975–9, expenditures on mergers were at least as great (annual rates of £500 million and £800 million) as in the two quinquennia before the peak (£350 million in 1960–4, and £150 million in 1955–9).[6] Adjusting for inflation by using an index of ordinary share prices does not alter this conclusion.

The view reached in this book is that, while the very largest mergers need to be supervised in the interests of promoting a thriving and competitive economy, it is mistaken to attach sole, or even over-riding, importance to mergers as the source of the historical growth in concentration. They have probably accounted for a third, or a half, of the rise since the 1950s. Studies based on unrepresentative sampling can lead to higher proportions being mistakenly attributed to mergers; for example, if an undue proportion of companies are included in a sample because they came to a researcher's notice in the 'mergers column' of newspapers, one can obviously not draw conclusions that are valid for the economy as a whole.[7]

Another error that occasionally arises in sample studies of mergers may be exemplified by a finding of the type that, in over half the sample, profitability was lower after the merger than before. There are two difficulties in drawing any practical policy conclusions from such a finding. The first is that some mergers are undertaken precisely in order to avoid a bad patch lying ahead: two firms together may hope to weather the storm better than if they are separate, or the shareholders in one of them may be keen to 'sell out in good time'. It would not need many mergers of this sort for a sample to show lower profitability in relation to its pre-merger experience, or in relation to another 'control' sample of companies not involved in mergers. The second difficulty arises from the usually very skew distribution of business risks: that is, typically there are only a very few large 'winners', but these are large enough to more than offset the very many small 'losers'. If the variability of the outcomes of mergers was similar to that of the general growth-rates of firms,[8] then one would expect two-thirds of mergers to show less than the arithmetic average outcome (and if, as seems plausible, the risks attached to mergers were twice or thrice as great as business risks in general, then three-quarters or nine-tenths, respectively, would lie below the arithmetic average).[9] The various studies that have appeared showing that more than half the firms engaged in mergers have done less well than, for example, the average for their industry are therefore entirely compatible with the possibility that the group of mergers as a whole yielded a positive return.

As far as I know the studies available so far on the successes of mergers do not permit any very clear conclusion on these matters. In the present state of knowledge I believe that any blanket discouragement of mergers would be misconceived; but there is much to be said for an increasingly severe scrutiny of mergers as the size of the companies concerned rises, and where competition is likely to suffer.

In summary, while on balance the forces making for greater sizes of enterprises and for a greater concentration of industry have recently moderated, the need for a proper understanding of the underlying factors remains as strong as ever. The previous government's consultative documents on policies relating to monopolies, mergers and restrictive practices are thus very much to be welcomed;[10] as also are the recent strengthening of the powers of the Office of Fair Trading, and the revisions in tax treatment proposed by the present government in its 1980 budget to facilitate the de-merging of large companies.

LONDON   SJP
March 1980

Notes to Preface to the Second Impression (pages xv–xviii)

1 As suggested in footnote *c* to table 1.1, about 1 per cent needs to be deducted from earlier figures (or added to the new figures) to put them on to a comparable basis. The percentage shares in net output of the hundred largest enterprises, ranked according to their net output, were as follows in the years 1970–6: 39·8, 40·3, 41·0, 42·0, 42·2, 41·7, 41·8. The shares in sales of the hundred enterprises with the largest sales were as follows in the same years: 45·0, 45·0, 44·4, 45·7, 46·6, 47·0, 47·0 (the figure for 1970 is approximate).

2 Royal Commission on Trade Unions and Employers' Associations 1965–68, *Report*, Cmnd 3623, London, HMSO, 1968.

3 This relates to plants with over 50 employees. I am indebted to Mr P. K. Edwards, of the University of Warwick, for showing me his forthcoming article on this subject (to appear in the *Oxford Bulletin of Economics and Statistics*). International rankings of strike-proneness are obviously heavily dependent on this adjustment which is particularly important for Britain, but less important in countries such as the United States where 'wildcat' strikes are subject to legal sanctions.

4 S. J. Prais, 'The strike-proneness of large plants in Britain', *Journal of the Royal Statistical Society* (series A), vol. 141, part 3, 1978, pp. 368–84, especially p. 384

5 The percentage shares in manufacturing employment of the hundred largest enterprises, ranked according to their employment, moved as follows in 1970–6: 36·7, 37·3, 37·0, 38·0, 37·3, 37·5, 37·0.

6 Department of Industry, *Business Monitor, Miscellaneous series: M3, company finance*, and *M7, acquisitions and mergers of industrial and commercial companies*.

7 See the interchange in the *Journal of Industrial Economics*, 1980, between L. Hannah, J. A. Kay, P. E. Hart and the present writer.

8 That is, if the outcomes followed a log-normal distribution with a standard deviation measured over a decade of 0·6 (see p. 205 below).

9 These proportions are conveniently tabulated in the penultimate column in the table prepared by J. Aitchison and J. A. C. Brown, *The Lognormal Distribution*, Cambridge University Press, 1957, pp. 154–5.

10 Department of Prices and Consumer Protection, *A Review of Monopolies and Mergers Policy*, Cmnd 7198, London, HMSO, 1978, and *A Review of Restrictive Trade Practices Policy*, Cmnd 7512, London, HMSO, 1979.

PREFACE TO THE FIRST IMPRESSION

I undertook this study believing that it would be useful to make a fresh attempt at a long-term view of the development of the sizes of industrial firms. It seemed to me that the news of mergers of great enterprises that were filling our newspapers should be understood not merely as isolated steps towards increased market power in particular products – which might be controlled in the public interest by the *ad hoc* recommendations of a Monopolies Commission – but as part of a deeper general process gradually transforming the nature of our economy. A study setting out – as precisely as available statistics permitted – the trends in the size of manufacturing firms in the past half century, and a consideration of the forces at work, I hoped would be found helpful in leading to a reconsideration of the kind of industrial structure that society desired and of the ways in which it might be obtained.

A great many empirical studies have been carried out in recent years of particular aspects of industrial structure related to firm-size, ranging from the costs of capital to discounts on bulk advertising; these needed to be brought together so that their implications for the growth of industrial concentration could be systematically assessed. I also thought that the Censuses of Production, those vast repositories of statistics concerning our industrial structure, could be made to yield helpful indicators of long-term trends in concentration, despite the many difficulties that arise because of changes in the methods of compiling the Censuses. These are the hopes that led to the present book.

It is always difficult to know at what level of exposition to write a book. The compromise I have attempted – and I am conscious that it may not always seem a happy one – is to write the main text as simply as I could, putting into notes and appendices such technical matters as I thought might be of interest only to the specialist or research worker; on those technical matters I have attempted to be brief and have restricted references to those works that I thought would positively assist the reader. The headings on the pages of notes are intended to help the reader link notes and text quickly. Full references to other books are given in the notes the first time they occur; on subsequent occasions they are abbreviated and given in brackets in the text. I have not attempted to be comprehensive in references to the literature: a task that is difficult because of its great growth, nor always useful since so much of it is controversial. The recent appearance of two massively learned American works in this field by Professor F. M. Scherer (1970) and Professor J. M. Blair (1972), each of over 500 closely printed pages, has made my conscience easier; the student who wishes to look further than is indicated in the references here will find adequate guidance there – I have learnt much from these books. My greatest debt, however, is to that unduly neglected work of Alfred Marshall, *Industry and Trade* (1919; 4th edition, 1923), the publication of which Pigou described in his review (*Economic Journal*, vol. 29, December 1919, p. 443) as 'a very important event'; I believe that no one who wishes to understand what is happening to the structure of modern industry can, even today, do better than invest his time in a study of that great work.

I should like to express my deep thanks to the National Institute, especially to Mr David Worswick (Director) and Mrs K. Jones (Secretary) for allowing, encouraging and helping me to carry out this study; also to the Social Science Research Council which financed it. Many of the ideas in this study go back to my earlier work at the National Institute in 1955–9 (embodied in a paper published in the *Economic Journal* of 1957, and in a joint paper with Peter Hart published in the *Journal of the Royal Statistical Society* of 1956); I regard it as a great privilege to be allowed to continue my researches in this area after a gap of nearly twenty years, of which ten were spent in industry. It was a pleasure to find that my friend Professor Peter Hart was also again at the Institute, and working on recent developments in industrial concentration, joined by Michael Utton, Grahame Walshe and Roger Clarke; I have benefited immensely from the 'teamwork' that this permitted and am grateful to them for their immense help.

I was ably assisted in my researches, successively, by Miss Barbara Stephenson, Mrs Caroline Reid, Mr D. E. Allen and Miss Alice Knight; Miss Janet Laraway acted as my personal assistant and secretary for the greater part of the project, Miss G. Little prepared the book for the press and, together with Mrs A. Cowen, compiled the index. To all of them, my thanks.

I am indebted to many persons who have offered guidance on detailed aspects of the work, or have commented on earlier drafts of particular chapters. I should particularly like to thank the following: G. Bannock, Professor R. A. Brealey, Professor Sir Alec Cairncross, A. D. Chesher, A. H. Cowley, Professor J. S. Cramer, M. Fessey, Professor P. Sargant Florence, J. D. Gribbin, Professor Colin Harbury, C. D. Jones, R. Marris, B. Mitchell, A. Quinn, G. F. Ray, Professor J. M. Samuels, V. Schetgen, H. C. Stanton, C. Sutcliffe, M. Tamari, Professor B. Tew, Sir Hugh Weeks, Professor G. Whittington and the Research Department of the Bank of England. I am also much indebted to the Business Statistics Office and the Department of Trade and Industry for providing a number of special tabulations based on the Census of Production and answering a great many of my questions, so permitting me to improve the empirical basis of this work.

Earlier versions of parts of chapters 2 and 6 appeared, respectively, as an article in *Oxford Economic Papers* (1974) and as a contribution to a conference volume (A. P. Jacquemin and H. W. de Jong (eds.), *Markets, Corporate Behaviour and the State*, The Hague, Nijhoff, 1976). I am grateful to the editors for permission to reproduce in a revised form the findings which they were good enough to publish.

SJP

LONDON
March 1976

Symbols in the tables

.. = not available

n.a. = not applicable

— = nil or negligible

CHAPTER I

THE GROWTH OF INDUSTRIAL CONCENTRATION

There were giants in the earth in those days
Genesis 6: 4

SCOPE OF THE STUDY

The growth of large industrial enterprises of a size undreamt of in earlier centuries is a modern phenomenon, the progress of which is traced before our eyes almost day by day. The cumulative effect of this evolutionary process has been the creation of a new world of giant businesses which, as many have noted, bears little resemblance to earlier ideas of a competitive world – one which was peopled by a myriad of small firms, contriving to produce goods in the right quantities at the right prices guided by the 'invisible hand' of market forces. The process of concentration is a continuing one; how far it has already gone, what are the factors determining its rate of increase and what are the prospects for the future form the subject matter of the present study.

It is a study in 'economic statistics'; and in several senses. First, it is based on statistics collected by the Censuses of Production and related statistical sources; in other words, it aims as far as possible to be an empirical and quantitative study, rather than a mainly speculative exercise in economic theorising. Secondly, it is a statistical study in the sense that it is concerned not with the fate of individual firms, but with the changing balance of the distribution of firm-sizes regarded as a whole, and with the forces that have led to those observed and systematic changes. Thirdly, the properties of a particular theoretical statistical distribution, known as the log-normal distribution, will be seen to be of much help in understanding how varying and irregular economic forces may combine to produce a size-distribution of firms, the concentration of which rises as time proceeds, and at a predictable rate.

The subject matter of the study is centred on the sizes of manufacturing firms in the United Kingdom (together with a number of limited comparisons with other countries, of which the United States is considered in most detail). The period covered is from the beginning

Notes to this chapter will be found on pp. 225–30.

[1]

of this century till 1970, although it must be said that for the earlier years the information is rather sparse. For the most part manufacturing industry is considered as a whole, but at certain points we consider also the major industrial groups into which manufacturing can be divided.

The scope of the study was determined by the following considerations. The changes in the economy with which we are concerned are of a long-term nature, and do not always stand out with adequate clarity in comparisons over short periods, such as those between two adjacent Censuses. Taking a longer view is more difficult, and in some ways less precise (because Census definitions and coverage are modified over time, partly in response to changes in the economy), but for manufacturing sufficient information is now available to make an attempt at a longer view worthwhile, although outside manufacturing this is still not so. The more detailed picture to be obtained from examining changes in individual trades between adjacent Censuses has been set out in a number of earlier Institute studies; the present, mainly aggregative, long-term study may be regarded as a development from, and a complement to, those studies.[1]

This introductory chapter is concerned to set out the factual background. First, it traces the development in this century of the share of the very largest manufacturing firms. Secondly, the associated decline of the smallest firms is described. Thirdly, our findings on aggregate concentration are compared with previous studies of concentration in individual trades; we shall see that the growth of holding companies with diversified interests spread over a number of trades has made it more necessary to consider aggregate concentration. This is followed by an outline of the book's central theme, together with a warning to the reader of certain reservations that he should keep in mind.

THE SHARE OF THE HUNDRED LARGEST MANUFACTURING FIRMS

There are many possible ways of measuring the growth in importance of the largest firms, but we have chosen one simple measure: the share of the hundred largest enterprises in the country's net output in manufacturing. The definitions used in arriving at this measure follow those of the Census of Production. An enterprise is defined as a parent company including all its subsidiary companies, but where no confusion is likely to arise we shall continue to use the simpler term 'firm'. The importance of a firm is measured by its net output, which, roughly speaking, is the value of the work done by the firm, that is the total value of the goods made during the year less the cost of the materials used and of certain bought-in services; it is equal to the total income generated by the firm, that is the sum of wages, salaries, rent, taxes and profits (gross of depreciation, plus some minor items such as selling expenses).[2]

This measure serves as our main indicator of the level of aggregate concentration in the economy. It provides a convenient quantitative summary of the changes in a significant aspect of the industrial structure. It is also a measure that can be estimated without too much difficulty over a fairly long period of time from the available sources. Other measures corresponding to those used elsewhere might also have been quoted here, such as the share of the 200 largest firms in capital employed (as in the classical study of the United States by Berle and Means),[3] or of the hundred or the fifty largest firms in profits (Prais, 1957; Hart, 1960; Bannock, 1971);[4] but alternative measures of aggregate concentration can be expected to move in much the same way, and it may be doubted whether anything of value would emerge from an extended consideration of a multiplicity of alternative measures. It is important, however, to ensure that *precisely* the same measure is compared at various dates; this is not always easy (and complex adjustments are often required) because the sources of information are limited, especially for earlier years.

Today it may seem self-evident that knowledge of the share of the hundred largest firms and the trend in that share is important in guiding public policy relating to monopolies and mergers, as well as for more general reasons; this no doubt follows from the large size of that share today. In earlier years, however, when giant firms were not quite so gigantic, and their share in the economy was smaller, the relevance of that share for economic policy may well have been less obvious;[5] that stage has long been passed. Of course no single measure can fully reflect the complexities of changes in market power or concentration in the host of markets that make up the economic system; nor can any very exact correspondence be expected between one summary measure of average tendencies and another. It may also be said, by way of qualification, that if a fuller analysis were possible it would take account of the consequences for competition of the reduction in transport costs over time, and the growth of internal and international trade. But while those matters must be kept in mind, it will perhaps be agreed that they do not really detract from the primary importance of observing the movements in some aggregate measure of concentration. The intimate connection between aggregate and market concentration has been made clear in a recent examination of market concentration in a representative sample of detailed product-groups for 1963.[6] This indicated that the hundred largest firms in

Table 1.1. *Share of the hundred largest enterprises in manufacturing net output, United Kingdom, 1909–70*

	1909	1924	1935	1949	1953	1958	1963	1968	1970
Share (%)	16[a]	22[a]	24	22	27	32	37[b]	41	40/41[c]

SOURCES: see appendix A.

[a] Approximate figures.

[b] Includes steel companies; reduced to 36½ per cent approximately if steel companies are excluded.

[c] Provisional estimate; the higher figure includes steel and the lower one excludes it. This estimate is artificially low (perhaps by 1 per cent) compared to previous years because of the increased Census coverage of smaller firms (see p. 177).

manufacturing as a whole were precisely those firms that contributed to the high level of concentration in at least half those product-groups, and very often one of these giant enterprises was the leader in a number of products.

In the present study considerable effort has been devoted to examining as long a period as possible, and to making the many adjustments – even if they are approximate – required to ensure that the estimates for the various dates (shown in table 1.1) may properly be compared. The detailed basis of the estimates is set out in appendix A, which also discusses the size of the differences that arise between different measures of concentration. The general reader perhaps need only note that the estimates are more reliable for those years in which they are based directly on Censuses of Production, namely 1935 and from 1958 onwards. These have been used as benchmarks, on to which have been linked estimates for other years relying mainly on movements in gross profits taken from company accounts. A margin of error of roughly 1 percentage point should be kept in mind as being attached to estimates for years before 1953. Finally, the estimates derived for the two earliest years, 1909 and 1924, should be treated with somewhat more reserve because of the limited information available; it does not seem likely, however, that further research would yield any improvement in their accuracy.[7]

The results of our computations are illustrated in chart 1.1; from this and table 1.1 the following inferences may be drawn. First, taking the long view, there has been a strong tendency for concentration to increase, the share of the hundred largest enterprises in manufacturing output having risen from some 16 per cent in 1909 to about 41 per cent in 1970. This rise is obvious today; but it is worth noting that it differs from the conclusion that might have been, and often was, drawn

Chart 1.1. *Share of the hundred largest enterprises in manufacturing net output, United Kingdom, 1909–70*

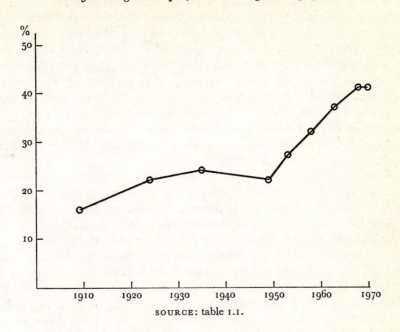

SOURCE: table 1.1.

some twenty years ago. At that time fewer observations were available, and those that were available were less precise. To an observer standing in the early 1950s and looking backwards at the data then available, it would not be entirely clear that there had been any marked trend. Consequently many economists were then prepared to take it as a working assumption that, if concentration was increasing at all, it was doing so at only a moderate pace. The statistical information now available is both fuller and more reliable, and there can be little doubt today that the long-term trend is one of increasing concentration.

Secondly, comparing the post-war with the pre-war period, it appears that the rate of increase in concentration has accelerated; the proportionate rate of increase (that is the increase in percentage points per annum divided by the average level of concentration during the period) in the period 1949–70 was about half as great again as that in the period 1909–35. At the time of writing it is difficult to speak with any confidence on changes since 1968, partly because the coverage of the Census has increased slightly (see appendix A), and partly because there are Census results for only a further two-year period during which – allowing for errors of measurement – one cannot expect to observe much of the long-term effect.

Thirdly, the long-term rising trend in concentration was interrupted during the period 1935–49 which spanned the Second World War. A decline during the war-period had been suspected from the results of two earlier studies: these had examined the fifty largest firms' share in profits between 1938 and 1950 (Hart, 1960, p. 52) and the dispersion of sizes of quoted companies between 1939 and 1950.[8] The present estimates support those earlier suspicions, in that our first post-war estimate, for 1949, lies some 2 percentage points below that for 1935. Bearing in mind the margin of error attached to our estimates, it may however be more prudent to speak of a freezing of the industrial structure during the war-period.

A number of factors probably accounted for the anomalous experience of this period. Small firms are basically more adaptable (they have a greater proportion of entrepreneurial to other inputs) and would have enjoyed a comparative advantage in adapting to the great changes required by the war economy and in improvising in the face of wartime shortages. The system of wartime controls and raw-material quotas would also have acted at least to stabilise the industrial structure. Further, the change to a full-employment economy on the outbreak of war and the practice of subcontracting government orders on a cost-plus basis to smaller firms would both have been to the advantage of small firms. Finally, the control, and at times complete prohibition of capital issues (more especially issues over £50,000) exercised through the Capital Issues Committee would have had a differential effect in holding back the progress of larger companies in this period. It would need a very full study, going much beyond our resources, to establish the contribution these factors made to the changes in concentration at that time and, indeed, whether other important factors were at work. In this study we restrict ourselves to recording the evidence, which suggests that a mild decline in concentration probably took place during the war-period, and noting a number of exceptional factors that may have contributed to that result.

As we shall see in more detail in chapter 6, comparable statistics for the United States suggest a remarkably parallel development: there was a decline in concentration during the war-period which ran contrary to an otherwise generally upward movement in aggregate concentration.

Finally, the rise in concentration in the twenty years since 1949 has been at a fairly steady rate. In chapter 2 below predictions are made on the basis of a somewhat 'sophisticated' model of the size-distribution of enterprises, but it is already clear that if we were naively to extend the trend of the period 1949–68 forward in chart 1.1 we would deduce that the hundred largest enterprises in manufacturing would be responsible for about two-thirds of manufacturing net output before another twenty years had elapsed. If we assumed the rise was at a constant proportionate (rather than a constant absolute) rate – as might appear reasonable – that stage would be reached by the mid-1980s. Government intervention may, however, prevent large-scale mergers continuing at the previous pace (in 1973, at a time when preliminary results of this study were attracting public comment, it was often said that it was now in the public interest to prevent a further reduction in the number of independent large enterprises); any prediction is thus a matter of conjecture. Nevertheless, it is helpful to have a notion of where present trends would lead if left to themselves.

Given that today nearly half of all manufacturing output is produced by the hundred largest enterprises, it seems of interest to ask what number of enterprises in earlier years accounted for half of total output. Though we do not wish to burden the reader with a multiplicity of measures of the same phenomenon, and though the available long-term statistics on this measure are less satisfactory than for our main measure, it is worth spending a moment with this alternative way of examining the transformation in the scale of industry during this century. The particular feature of this measure is that it is in terms of a varying *number* of enterprises and this may indicate more directly the change in what can loosely be called the 'competitive tone' of industry. For the most recent period of twelve years for which we have Census information, the number of largest enterprises accounting for half the output in manufacturing has fallen from 420 in 1958 to 240 in 1963, to 160 in 1968 and to 140 in 1970. If we wish to go back to before the Second World War, and are prepared to make some fairly strong assumptions in order to derive a rough estimate, we would conclude that in 1935 it was necessary to total the output of the 800 largest enterprises in order to reach half of total output in manufacturing. Before the First World War, under the same assumptions, we would estimate that the output of the 2000 largest enterprises would have to be totalled to reach half of total output.[9]

These figures indicate very clearly how large-scale industry has progressively become more concentrated; if we consider the implications of these figures for the change in the number of suppliers of individual products, it will be apparent that there will now often be only a handful of suppliers of those products that are made on a large scale, where previously there were perhaps twenty times as many. Of course small firms still abound in great numbers (as will be seen later in this chapter) and, to the extent that they continue to provide competition for their larger brethren, the cataclysmic decline in the numbers of large firms mentioned in the previous paragraph gives an exaggerated impression of the decline in the competitiveness of the industrial structure. But the exaggeration is not necessarily very great. It will be recognised that, when firms of vastly varying sizes co-exist in what is called the same trade, and are classified in the same industrial group by Census authorities, they are often not really competing or producing a recognisably similar good; in the car industry, for example, 700 small enterprises with an average of ten employees each were classified in 'motor vehicle manufacturing' in the 1968 Census, but they produced or processed small parts and were not in any real sense competing with the three main car manufacturers, who had an average of 80,000 employees each.

Table 1.2. *Estimated shares[a] of the hundred largest enterprises in total private sector manufacturing by Industrial Order, 1958, 1963 and 1968*

Percentages[b]

	Employment			Net output 1968
	1958	1963	1968	
Food, drink and tobacco	28	49	51	57
Chemicals and allied industries	34	37	36	46
Metal manufacture[c]	55	47	40[d]	..
Engineering and electrical goods	32	34	39	37
Shipbuilding and marine engineering	18	30	41	28
Vehicles	69	65	69	73
Metal goods n.e.s.[c]	4	13	18	16
Textiles	9	12	27	35
Leather, leather goods and fur	—	—	2	1
Clothing and footwear	6	7	15	10
Bricks, pottery, glass, cement, etc.	11	13	20	25
Timber and furniture	—	—	4	3
Paper, printing, publishing	16	22	31	36
Other manufacturing	24	28	26	29
Total manufacturing	27	32	37	41

SOURCES: *Census 1963*, vol. 132, tables 13 and 15; *Census 1968*, vol. 158, tables 42 and 42A; special tabulations by the Business Statistics Office.

[a] Methods of estimation described in note 10 on pp. 226–7.

[b] Percentages of total employment or output in each industry attributable to the hundred largest enterprises in the whole private sector.

[c] Changes in employment in metal manufacture should be ignored; the comparisons are affected by steel renationalisation in 1968, also possibly some enterprises classified there in 1958 were reclassified in metal goods n.e.s. in 1963.

[d] Excludes nationalised steel; estimate is approximate, based on ratio of 114,000 employees in the hundred largest enterprises to 300,000 employees in the whole private sector.

So much on manufacturing industry considered as a whole. As a next step it is useful to examine whether large firms are to be found in particular sectors of industry, or whether they are widely distributed over the various manufacturing industries. A convenient test is to ask what fraction of the output or employment in each industry is accounted for by the hundred largest firms. Table 1.2 sets out the results of a special tabulation relating to the hundred largest in 1968, together with estimates of the changes in the preceding decade. The estimated changes are not as precise as we should like, but they probably provide an adequate indication of what happened. (For the sake of clarity, it may be emphasised that this table is concerned not with the hundred largest in each industry, but with the hundred largest firms in all manufacturing; the table shows the share of those same hundred firms in each of the fourteen industries distinguished.)

It will be seen that in 1968 the hundred largest firms accounted for three-quarters of the output of vehicles, for about half of the output of food, drink and tobacco and of chemicals, for about a third of engineering, of textiles and of paper and printing, and for lower but not negligible proportions of all other Industrial Orders apart from leather and timber, which are still the preserve of smaller concerns. The hundred largest firms have increased their share of employment during the decade examined in virtually all industry groups (but see note c to table 1.2). Their rise in importance in the food, drink and tobacco industries is particularly marked. We may note here (in anticipation of the discussion in chapter 4) that advertising and marketing economies have become rather more important in this period, and may be expected particularly to affect the organisation of those trades that produce for final sale to the broad mass of the consuming public.

It is apparent also that large firms tend to predominate in those industries which are capital-intensive, and are less important where capital per person employed is lower.[11] Because of the higher capital intensity of large firms, the share of the hundred largest in net output is higher than their share in employment (41 per cent as compared with 37 per cent in 1968). Their share in capital expenditure is higher still (47 per cent in 1968).

The extent to which large firms are relatively capital-intensive is shown more directly in table 1.3: the hundred largest firms spend about half as much again on capital per person employed as do the remaining smaller firms. The relation between the supply of capital, financial economies of scale and the evolution of large firms is apparently an important one, and forms the theme of the detailed investigations reported in chapter 5 below.

Table 1.3. *Capital expenditure per employee by the hundred largest manufacturing enterprises and all other enterprises, 1963 and 1968*

£s per head

	1963	1968
Hundred largest enterprises	183	243
All other enterprises	103	160

SOURCE: *Census 1968*, tables 42 and 45.

NOTE: Capital expenditure is defined as expenditure on fixed assets (land, buildings, machinery and vehicles), and excludes expenditure on acquisitions of the shares of other companies.

THE DECLINE OF THE
SMALL MANUFACTURING FIRM

So far we have examined the largest firms and the great changes in their share of the economy during this century. The underlying causes of those changes will, of course, have had a pervasive influence throughout the whole range of firm sizes. While an examination of various intermediate size-groups would be both laborious and difficult (the statistical sources for long-term comparisons being extremely limited), it is worth examining what has been happening to the very smallest firms. In this way we shall obtain a view of developments at both extremes of the size-distribution of manufacturing firms, and that may be adequate to encompass most of the significant features of the story.

Given the ever-growing share of the largest firms, it is hardly surprising to find that the scope for smaller manufacturing firms has been reduced. Chart 1.2 shows a continuous and sharp decline between 1930 and the mid-1960s in the number of establishments recorded in the Census as having ten employees or less: the decline was from 93,000 establishments in 1930 to 35,000 establishments in 1968, that is by about two-thirds.[12] To set this decline in perspective, it is as well to keep in mind that there was a total of only 62,000 manufacturing enterprises of all sizes returned in the 1968 Census, and that, during this period of forty years when the number of small establishments fell so very rapidly, the (human) population in Britain increased by a sixth and real national product doubled.

Many of the smallest 'manufacturing' firms typically used to sell – and still do – directly to the public; for example, the small tailor both makes up and sells his clothes, and the small baker both bakes and sells his bread. Whether the greater part of such an establishment is engaged in manufacturing or in distribution is often not entirely clear. It seems likely that with the passage of time there has been an increasing

Chart 1.2. *Establishments with ten employees or less,*
United Kingdom, 1930–68

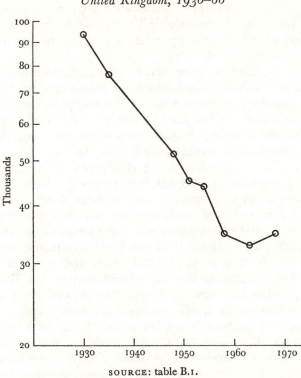

SOURCE: table B.1.

specialisation of activities – the smaller firm concerning itself more with selling, while manufacturing activities have migrated to larger firms which provide the smaller with its supplies. These changes in the balance of activities of small firms have posed great problems to the compilers of Censuses of Production, who have found it convenient progressively to restrict the industrial coverage of such Censuses by excluding certain trades of the kind just mentioned, with the intention of including them in due course in surveys of distribution and services. In order to bring the available statistics as far as possible on to a constant definitional basis, we have therefore made a number of adjustments which are described in appendix B.1. (The Census figures as originally published showed a very much steeper decline, starting from 160,000 establishments in 1930 instead of the figure of 93,000 firms that we have adopted for that year.) These adjustments inevitably incorporate a certain amount of judgement and, though we believe the overall downward trend is correctly shown, it is not possible to speak with much confidence on changes in that rate of decline. Nevertheless, some stabilisation in the number of small firms in the most recent decade, 1958–68, seems likely (see chart 1.2 which, it may be noted, has been drawn on a ratio-scale).[13] The rate of decline taken over the whole period averaged some 3 per cent a year (equivalent to a decline of about a quarter in a decade).

This great decline has not occurred without discomfort to the small-firm sector, nor without occasioning wide public concern;[14] one of the important questions has been whether the number of small firms has been reduced to such a low level that they have ceased to provide an adequate 'seedbed' for a new generation of entrepreneurs. But with as many as 30,000 small manufacturing firms still in existence, accounting for about half of all manufacturing enterprises by number, it is not obvious that any critical level has been reached. Of course, although there are very many such small firms in terms of numbers, they do not account for very much of total activity – a bare 2 per cent of total employment in 1968 as compared with 7 per cent in 1930. And, as will be seen in chapter 6, the role of small manufacturing firms is now smaller in Britain than in the United States and in major European countries. This underlines the recommendation by the Bolton Committee (1971) that the trend in the number of small firms is a matter that will warrant careful public attention in coming years.

In terms of the fourteen broad Industrial Orders into which manufacturing is partitioned by the Census, table 1.4 shows that in 1968 small establishments accounted for about a third of the number of all establishments, with surprisingly little variation amongst industries;[15] however great the pressures that led to the shift in economic activity towards larger enterprises, it would appear that there is still opportunity in all sectors of industry for certain activities to be carried out on a small scale. The least scope for the small firm is in textiles, but even there one in six of all establishments has fewer than ten employees. A more detailed examination of the Census indicates that these small establishments are found relatively frequently in certain specialised smaller textile trades, such as rope, twine and net, canvas goods and sacks, household textiles and handkerchiefs, and lace; but they are also to be found in certain of the more substantial trades, such as woollens and worsteds, and hosiery and knitted goods. In vehicles also the proportion of small establishments is relatively low but, surprisingly, only just lower than in clothing and footwear. In the former trade small establishments are producers only of parts and may be engaged in some form of repairing (though not predominantly in repairing, for then they would lie outside the scope of the Census); in the latter it is notable that a relatively high proportion of small

Table 1.4. *Small establishments^a as a proportion of all establishments by number and employment, 1968*

Percentages

	By number	By employment
Food, drink and tobacco	23	1·0
Chemicals and allied industries	30	1·1
Metal manufacture	22	0·7
Engineering and electrical goods	35	1·8
Shipbuilding and marine engineering	39	1·3
Vehicles	22	0·4
Metal goods n.e.s.	37	4·0
Textiles	19	1·0
Leather, leather goods and fur	44	7·0
Clothing and footwear	23	2·0
Bricks, pottery, glass, cement, etc.	45	3·8
Timber and furniture	47	7·8
Paper, printing, publishing	47	3·7
Other manufacturing	36	2·5
Total manufacturing	34	2·0

SOURCE: *Census 1968*, analysis of manufacturing industries by employment-size of establishment (special publication supplementary to the main Census *Reports*).

^{a} Ten employees or less.

firms is to be found in the more fashion-conscious sections of the trade (dresses, etc.).

The greatest scope for the small firm seems to be in leather, leather goods and fur, in building materials, in timber and furniture, and in paper, printing and publishing. (But small metal goods – metal goods not elsewhere specified – should perhaps also be mentioned as providing fair scope for the small firm.) In these industries small establishments form about 45 per cent of the total; nevertheless, even in these four industries, small establishments are substantially outweighed by their bigger brethren in terms of total activity and account for under a tenth of total employment in these Industrial Orders.

An examination of the list of trades showing the greatest declines in numbers of small firms in the past generation is of some interest. Table 1.5 sets out ten trades which account for over half the total fall between 1935 and 1968 (a fall of 29,000 establishments out of a fall of 42,000 establishments in all manufacturing). This list of trades in which the small firm is rapidly disappearing has an old-fashioned, almost nursery-rhyme, charm about it: we find here the miller, the baker, the tailor and dressmaker, the shoemaker, the cabinet-maker and upholsterer (the candlestick-maker had lost his importance in earlier years); all are trades that cater for the basic necessities of human

Table 1.5. *Trades[a] showing substantial declines in the number of small establishments, 1935–68*

No. of establishments

	1935	1958	1963	1968	Decline 1935–68
Grain milling	2,150	320	230	110	2,040
Bread and flour confectionery	1,750	800	430	210	1,540
Soft drinks, etc.	1,170	360	210	150	1,020
Perambulators, hand trucks	3,070	190	70	50[b]	3,020
Jewellery	1,280	440	460	200	1,080
Leather goods	1,550	380	280	270	1,280
Clothing	8,150	1,870	1,600	1,500	6,650
Footwear	970	180	150	130	840
Timber, miscellaneous wood and cork	9,220	2,720	2,240	2,330	6,890
Furniture, upholstery, bedding[c]	6,380	1,740	1,640	1,620	4,760
Total of above[d]	35,690	9,000	7,310	6,570	29,120

SOURCES: Censuses of Production.

[a] Extracted from the division of all manufacturing into 118 minimum list headings.
[b] Approximate estimate (merged with toys, etc. in the 1968 Census).
[c] Includes shop and office fittings.
[d] Not shown in this table are the declines in miscellaneous metal goods due to doubts as to definitional comparability over time; a decline of 5000 small establishments for this group seems possible over the period 1935–68.

life. The demand for the products of these trades as a whole has certainly grown over this long period with the rise in the general standard of living – but not as fast as productivity, so that total employment in these trades (considering establishments of all sizes) has fallen by 11 per cent over this period, that is by 0·3 per cent a year. (This figure is based on the Census employment for eight of these trades only – baking and clothing have been omitted because changes in Census coverage would make the results somewhat arbitrary.) And in the last ten years of this period, that is from 1958 to 1968, the fall in employment in these trades was at a rate of 0·6 per cent a year (based on all ten trades, since satisfactory figures are available for this decade).

Our central interest in this book is in the consideration of the various factors responsible for the shift towards larger firms, that is in studying to what extent technological, marketing and financial factors have been responsible. Many of the small-firm activities mentioned above, such as baking and clothes-making, were typically carried out at home not so very long ago. The early stages of industrialisation moved them to small workshops, where use could be made of basic equipment (to take

Table 1.6. *Trades showing substantial rises in the*
number of small establishments, 1958–68

No. of establishments

	1958	1963	1968	Rise 1958–68
Miscellaneous non-electrical machinery	460	680	1,000	540
Scientific, surgical and photographic instruments	610	740	940	330
Radio and other electronic apparatus	120	270	410	290
Miscellaneous electrical goods	280	370	410	130
Shipbuilding and marine engineering	410	480	510	100
Iron castings	200	330	300	100
Miscellaneous building materials	1,400	1,450	1,840	440
Printing and publishing of newspapers and periodicals	110	250	280	170
General printing, publishing, bookbinding and engraving etc.	3,450	3,850	4,310	860
Plastics moulding and fabricating	320	510	670	350
Total of above	7,360	8,930	10,670	3,310

SOURCES: Censuses of Production.

those trades again) such as larger ovens and mixing machines, and sewing and cutting machines; that is to say, technological developments were then paramount. But it would be wrong to infer from this that the emergence of ever-larger firms is equally to be attributed to technological advance; marketing factors may well be more important. In baking, for example, although three firms now account for three-quarters of the nation's output of bread, it appears that there is little to be gained by way of production economies once a size accounting for 2 per cent of the market has been reached; and in clothes-making the sewing machine and its operator remain the basic unit of production, 'outworkers' still persist, and the growth of giant clothing firms (especially for wholesale bespoke tailoring in the inter-war period) depended to an important extent on marketing techniques.[16]

There are certain trades in which small firms have been growing in number in contrast to the general trend. Table 1.6 lists the ten trades accounting for the greater part of the rise in numbers in the decade 1958–68. Unfortunately it is not possible to take this table back to 1935 since many of these trades were then not separately distinguished in the Census. It will be noticed that many of these trades are 'modern', in that they include scientific instruments, electronic apparatus, plastics fabrication and printing (where new 'offset' methods have helped smaller concerns). Technological developments thus remain of importance in promoting small firms.

At this preliminary stage in our study we do not need to go beyond noting that there has been a very great flux, and a net decline, in the small-firm sector; and that the growth of the very largest firms may be attributable to factors altogether different from those responsible for the decline in the smallest firms.

CHANGES IN CONCENTRATION IN INDIVIDUAL TRADES AND INCREASING DIVERSIFICATION

That a change of very great dimensions in the size-structure and concentration of British industry has taken place in recent decades will be clear from the figures considered so far in this chapter. Readers familiar with earlier studies of the growth of industrial concentration in Britain may find a change of such dimensions surprising; our object in this section is therefore to provide a survey of the results of those earlier studies for comparison with those arrived at here.[17] The earlier studies related to a selection of trades, in each of which the change in the concentration ratio, that is the change in the share of the three (or occasionally more) largest firms in the employment or output of an individual trade or the sales of its main products, was calculated on the basis of successive Censuses; some average was then taken of these individual concentration ratios to provide a summary indication of the change in the economy as a whole (sometimes only a judgement as to the central tendency was made, without explicitly calculating an average). Our first concern is with consistency: to what extent are the implications of the present study, which is based on a single aggregative concentration ratio for the whole manufacturing sector, consistent with the movements that have previously been observed in the averages of the concentration ratios of a selection of individual trades?

There is a second, but associated, reason for such a comparison. If, for example, we look simply at the share of the three largest firms in two trades, any possible overlap between those two sets of largest firms is ignored. Perhaps they were distinct initially, but at a subsequent date one or more of the three largest firms in one trade may also be one of the three largest in a second trade. As is well known, one of the accompaniments of the merger waves of recent years has been the growth of cross-interests between trades in the form of industrial holding companies and 'conglomerates'. The growth of such cross-interests is not apparent on looking at the concentration ratios of each trade separately, but of course it affects the aggregate level of concentration, and this is reflected in a measure such as the share of the hundred largest firms in manufacturing considered in total. In other words, if diversification has increased one might expect the aggregate concentration ratio to rise more rapidly than the average of a selection of individual trade concentration ratios.[18]

Studies of changes in the concentration of individual trades are subject to a general difficulty which needs to be mentioned at the outset of our survey–voyage, and this may help to explain (and so alleviate) some tedious moments. Industrial products and product-mixes change over time, with the consequence that successive Censuses are often not quite comparable in their industrial classifications. No single unambiguous summary measure can therefore be derived in practice for the average change from one Census to the next in the concentration ratios of individual trades. It may seem sensible to confine comparisons to those trades which have remained strictly unchanged in their definitional scope in the two Censuses, but the difficulty is that such trades may form a minority. Further, new trades (those not yet born or not separately distinguished in the earlier Census, but which are large enough to be given a separate heading in the later Census) may well have a different average concentration from those that have survived unchanged throughout; and corresponding considerations apply to trades that disappear from the Census. It is therefore often thought useful, in addition to a measure based on *comparable* trades, to have regard also to the average concentration in *all* trades at both dates, even if the lists of trades compared are in some respects no more alike than the proverbial chalk and cheese.

During the first period, 1935–51, for which movements in aggregate concentration and in the average concentration of individual trades can be compared, the share of the hundred largest firms changed very little on balance; our estimates suggest (see chart 1.1) that there was initially a mild decline in that share, followed by a post-war rise which brought the 1951-level close to that of 1935. The exact timing and depth of the wartime oscillation in aggregate concentration cannot be established precisely from the available information, and perhaps it does not matter too much. As far as individual trades are concerned one must suppose that they would not all have shared the same timing; consequently the precise selection of trades compared in this period may be expected to affect not merely the size of any measured average change, but perhaps also its direction.

With this background in mind we may now look at the figures. At first sight the concentration ratios for individual trades that have been calculated for this period suggest an increase in average concentration. Evely and Little, in their well known study of this period (1960, p. 152), selected forty-one trades that were comparable in definition in 1935 and 1951, and calculated the concentration ratio for the sales of the principal products of each trade. The weighted average share of the three largest firms in each trade rose from 29 to 32 per cent. However, these forty-one trades accounted for as little as 9 per cent of employment in all trades covered by the Census of Production in 1951, and it is not obvious that an entirely definite conclusion can be drawn from such a small sample.[19] If we take a wider view and look at the broader selection of trades – irrespective of the comparability of their definitions – for which employment concentration ratios have been calculated for each year, a fairly similar rise is found in the average level of concentration – from a weighted average of 26 per cent in 1935 to 29 per cent in 1951. The average for the former year is based on 249 trades and for the latter year on 220 trades (Evely and Little, 1960, p. 9).

The end of the story has not however been reached; even these broader selections did not cover the whole of industry, as there were certain trades for which concentration ratios were not available (mainly due to the omission of residual, ill-defined categories). No ratio was calculated for trades accounting for 14 per cent of industrial employment in 1935, nor for as much as 36 per cent of industrial employment in 1951. This rise in the proportion of omitted or 'non-comparable' trades is unfortunate, since one cannot exclude the possibility of their having a different average change in concentration. Unsatisfactory as it may seem, Evely and Little found it prudent to come to an agnostic conclusion with regard to this period; they said: 'It is impossible, therefore, to reach any definite or clear-cut conclusion about the change in the level of concentration in British industry between 1935 and 1951' (ibid. p. 10). Possibly that was too cautious an assessment, given that the two comparisons quoted here both suggest some rise, but taking into account that a sixteen-year interval is involved in this comparison, there can be little doubt that if there was any rise in the period 1939–51 it must have been very slow, at least in comparison with later developments. The impression given by our estimates of the movement in the share of the hundred largest firms, as already said, is one of no very substantial change over the period as a whole; given the possible errors of measurement, there is probably no real inconsistency with the conclusion of Evely and Little. The prudent conclusion for this period, as already suggested, is to regard it as one during which the industrial structure was substantially frozen.

In longer retrospect it is now apparent that the time-span studied by Evely and Little was unfortunately not a representative one: the development of concentration in the period 1935–51 was atypical in relation both to what had happened previously and to what has happened subsequently. That is in the nature of an 'accident of history', and does not, of course, detract from the valuable examination in that study of the relations between concentration and other aspects of industrial structure.

For the next period, 1951–8, our estimates of the share of the hundred largest enterprises show a very sharp rise, from about 24 or 25 per cent to 32 per cent. In their study of the concentration of individual trades in this period, Armstrong and Silberston selected a sample of sixty-three trades as comparable in their definitional scope;[20] the weighted average employment concentration ratio that we have calculated for these trades rose, however, by merely 1 point, from 28·3 to 29·2 per cent. The trades included in this sample accounted for no more than 40 per cent of employment in all manufacturing; further (as the authors note on page 403), those trades were smaller than the average Census trade and it might be questioned how far they were representative. A broader comparison of trades for this period – irrespective of their definitional scope – has been set out by Shepherd, who tabulated concentration ratios for 134 trades in 1951 and 120 trades in 1958;[21] the weighted average employment concentration ratios on this broader comparison showed the rather greater rise of $3\frac{1}{2}$ points – from 28·3 to 31·8 per cent. The proportion of all manufacturing employment covered by the trades in this comparison was 84 per cent in 1951 and 99 per cent in 1958; these proportions seem satisfactorily high, although the rise in coverage perhaps suggests that some caution is in order. Whilst the average level of concentration has clearly risen in the years 1951–8 whichever way we measure that average, it is also apparent that the proportionate rise on the aggregate approach (the share of the hundred largest) is much steeper than would appear from an examination of individual trades.

Taken by itself that difference may not warrant too much attention, but it acquires more weight when considered together with the similar story for the two ensuing quinquennial periods. Our estimates of the share of the hundred largest firms rose between 1958 and 1963 by 5 points, from 32 to 37 per cent. For individual trades in this period there have been two studies yielding broadly consistent results. First, the sales of the principal products of 214 trades, accounting for about three-quarters of all manufacturing sales, indicate a rise in the weighted average concentration ratio (calculated in respect of the share of the five largest firms) from 54·4 to 58·8 per cent; in proportionate terms this rise is only about half that suggested by our aggregate measure.[22] A second study is available with a wider coverage: Sawyer calculated employment concentration ratios for the four largest firms on the basis of virtually all the 120 industries into which the Census divided manufacturing industry for these two years; their weighted average rose from 29 to 32 per cent – a proportionate rise slightly larger than that in sales concentration ratios, but again rather lower than shown by our measure of aggregate concentration.[23]

For the final five-year period, 1963–8, for which comparisons of this kind are possible, our measure of aggregate concentration (after excluding the effects of steel nationalisation) rose from 37 to 41 per cent. Sales concentration ratios relating to the five largest firms in each product-group were compared in respect of 295 product-groups (again excluding steel products) accounting for about 60 per cent of all sales. The rise in their unweighted average was from 62·0 to 66·0 per cent; the weighted average of a substantially similar group rose from 63·4 to 67·8 per cent.[24] Both of these rises are proportionately only about two-thirds of that in our measure of aggregate concentration.

Taken together, the comparisons for the three periods since 1951 that we have looked at may suggest that increasing diversification has probably contributed to the faster rise in the share of the hundred largest enterprises. But there have no doubt been other contributing factors, such as the changing industrial balance of national output, or the differing rates of growth of the giant firms in the economy as a whole and the largest in each trade (which in many trades, such as furniture, will not be amongst the giants). A precise analysis and reconciliation would be difficult and is perhaps not necessary here. Before leaving the question of diversification it is, however, worth noting that a more direct measure of its growth can be obtained from special tables prepared by the Census authorities for 1958 and 1963, showing the number of industrial groups (out of a total of fifty-one industrial groups distinguished) in which the largest enterprises operate. The published information does not relate to the hundred largest enterprises, but to something which is fairly similar for the present purpose, namely manufacturing enterprises with employment in excess of 5000; there were 180 such large enterprises in 1958 and 210 in 1963. In 1958 these enterprises owned establishments in an average of 6·6 industrial groups, and within only five years this average had risen to 7·5 industrial groups. That is to say, in the course of this short period these large enterprises had, on average, taken a substantial interest in one industrial group that was new to them (to the extent of having at least one establishment with that its major activity).[25] It is also worth noting that in 1958 there were sixteen large enterprises active in (that is, with establishments classified in) ten or more industrial groups, and in 1963 this had doubled to thirty-two. On the other hand, the number of large specialised enterprises – those active in only a single industrial group – had fallen from thirty-eight to nineteen.[26]

The growth of concentration in individual trades and the growth of the share of giant enterprises in the economy as a whole are thus distinct (but obviously not unrelated) phenomena; that must be the main conclusion to be drawn from the above survey and comparisons. In the past twenty years giant manufacturing enterprises have increased their share of activity at a pace rather faster than might have been inferred from previous studies of concentration of individual trades; the need to understand the forces determining aggregate concentration has thus become a matter of practical importance and not merely one of academic interest. It will also be apparent that a long-term view is required if one is to see with any clarity the cumulative effect of what has been happening to the industrial structure, and it seems somewhat easier to distinguish the wood from the trees on using an aggregate measure of concentration than on using comparisons based on individual trades; however, the two kinds of study should properly be regarded as complementary rather than competing.

A GUIDE TO THE BOOK (AND SOME RESERVATIONS)

This chapter has attempted to summarise the main features of the very radical changes of the last half century or so in the size-structure of manufacturing firms in this country. The remainder of this study is concerned to elucidate the factors contributing to those changes. In examining them our concern has been to describe and analyse what has been happening in as precise a way as possible, in the hope that this may contribute towards a better judgement of the likely benefits and costs to society as a whole. The central question is: has concentration increased as a result of the 'invisible hand' of market forces guiding the economy to a more efficient industrial structure? Or are those forces leading the economy to ever-increasing concentration of a kind that can usefully be counteracted by government intervention in such a way that the economic and social benefits would outweigh the costs of interference and possible losses in technical efficiency?

In effect, we reach the same question as posed by Marshall eighty years ago. He contrasted the advantages to society of, on the one hand, large firms who were able to carry out extensive programmes of research and, on the other hand, a mass of small firms each exercising their inventive ability in a competitive environment. He put his views on the alternatives as follows:

It has always been recognized that large firms have a great advantage over their smaller rivals in their power of making expensive experiments; and in some of the modern 'scientific' industries they use part of their resources in hiring specialists to make experiments for them in the technical applications of science. But on the whole observation seems to show, what might have been anticipated *a priori*, that these advantages count for little in the long run in comparison with the superior inventive force of a multitude of small undertakers. There are but few exceptions to the rule, that large private firms...are...inferior to private businesses of a moderate size in that energy and resource, that restlessness and inventive power, which lead to the striking out of new paths. And the benefits which the world reaps from this originality are apt to be underrated. For they do not come all at once like those gains which a large business reaps by utilizing existing knowledge and well proven economies; but they are cumulative, and not easily reckoned up.

I believe that the importance of considerations of this kind is habitually underrated in the world at large; and that the older economists though fully conscious of them, did not explain with sufficient clearness and iteration the important place which they take in the claims of industrial competition on the gratitude of mankind.[27]

With industrial concentration today at a level unimaginably higher than when that passage was written, the debate still continues. Does the balance of advantage lie in encouraging more small firms, or in encouraging more amalgamations? If the industrial progress of this country has lagged in relation to other countries, is it perhaps partly because concentration here is greater?

In considering the consequences of monopoly in Marshall's time, it was the 'simple' economic aspect that was the foremost aspect of practical significance. Concentration today has however reached such levels that wider political and social aspects come into issue. If the greater part of the investment policy of the country is in relatively few hands, and if the greater part of the country's employment is controlled by relatively few employers, then the market mechanism is increasingly by-passed and replaced – ultimately by the administrative decisions of a few powerful men, whose aims and responsibilities are often not clear, and on whom the impact of market forces may be as a gnat's bite on the tail of a dinosaur. The spectre of the concentration of economic *power* has of course been raised by earlier writers; so long as concentration was at the level of twenty years ago (say, a quarter of output in the hands of the hundred largest firms) and was not increasing too rapidly that spectre could be dismissed from the scene (if necessary, by intoning the words 'countervailing power'). But the statistics on concentration set out above are such that those older fears now seem on the point of acquiring new substance. It is in the hope of providing some relevant facts for the public debate on these many-sided and difficult issues that the present book has been written.

The order of discussion in the remainder of this book is as follows. We first deal with an issue that requires some theoretical development. The unconstrained growth of firms may by itself be sufficient to result in an ineluctable tendency towards increasing concentration; this complex, and in the past not well understood, idea has probably been at the back of the mind of many previous writers; but it is only recently, with a better understanding of the mathematical logic of probability-growth processes, that it has proved possible to describe explicitly how the fortunes of individual firms may be of the greatest diversity and yet the distribution of firm-sizes as a whole be subject to a systematic and progressive change in its balance. Chapter 2 gives an elementary account of this process, and examines to what extent it may explain the generally rising trend of concentration in this country during this century.

Economies of scale provide a more familiar explanation of the rise in size of firms, and in the number and sizes of the plants they own. Scale-economies of production may be expected to show themselves more particularly in an increasing plant-size, and the contribution of this element to the rise in enterprise-concentration is examined in chapter 3. The following chapter considers the number of plants owned by the average giant enterprise, and how the rise in that number has been affected by factors that may broadly be put under the head of 'marketing economies of scale'.

Changes in the financial organisation of the economy, such as the growth of the Stock Exchange, the rise of the institutional investor and the reduction of risk by building up large and diversified company groupings, have perhaps been the most important of recent influences bearing on the optimum size of businesses. Chapter 5 deals with some new aspects of these very complex matters.

The industrial structure of the United States presents a number of interesting parallels, which are set out in chapter 6. Comparisons of concentration with other countries are also attempted there, but it will be seen that no very precise comparisons can be made because of the very poor official statistics so far compiled on the sizes of European enterprises.

The final chapter offers some reflections on possible government policies.

In concluding this introductory chapter, it is right to warn the reader of three reservations he should keep in mind which are associated with the Census statistics that form our principal empirical material. First, this study has been confined to manufacturing and its conclusions do not necessarily extend to the rest of the economy. One might suppose that concentration in manufacturing is higher than in other sectors of the economy. This may well be so. However, there is little precise information except for retailing, where the Monopolies Commission has recently estimated that 28·5 per cent of all retail sales

in 1971 were in the hands of the twenty-five largest retail businesses
– a degree of aggregate concentration that, surprisingly enough, is
similar to that in manufacturing.[28] On the other hand, by looking
exclusively at manufacturing we have left out of account the growing
links between manufacturing and other sectors of the economy,
especially distribution; to that extent our measure of the growth of
aggregate concentration represents an understatement.

The second limitation is of a similar nature and relates to interests
abroad. If a foreign enterprise operates here it is counted as if it were
a local enterprise, but only to the extent that it has local manufacturing
establishments (that is, its foreign operations are ignored for the purposes of the Census – and hence of this study – and its British establishments are treated as a separate enterprise). Similarly, if a British
enterprise has foreign subsidiaries the latter are ignored. Thus we are
concerned with manufacturing enterprises in so far as they operate in
this country. This conventional limitation is only to be defended on the
grounds of practicality in the compilation of statistics; taking a broader
view of the development of international associations amongst giant
enterprises, we are again omitting an element in the general growth
of concentration.

Finally, it should be remembered that this is a study of concentration
and not an assessment of the state of competition. Concentration has
an important influence on competition, but the lowering of transport
costs and the growth in the extent of markets, both nationally and
internationally, are also relevant in coming to a final conclusion on
the state of competition.

But every study must have its boundaries and, if they are somewhat
arbitrary, time and the help of others will no doubt improve matters.

CHAPTER 2

SPONTANEOUS DRIFT AS A CAUSE OF CONCENTRATION

as sheep which have no shepherd
Numbers 27: 17

INTRODUCTION

The long-term growth of the share of the hundred largest enterprises in the net output of British manufacturing industry, from some 16 per cent in 1909 to 41 per cent in 1970, has been described in the previous chapter. The object of the present chapter is to show how this rise in concentration is related to the pattern of growth-rates of individual firms. It will be seen that, under certain simple but realistic assumptions, we must expect concentration to rise – and to rise at a predictable pace – simply as a result of there being some variability in the growth-rates of individual firms; further, this rise in concentration takes place without larger firms expanding on average any faster than smaller firms.

To put it more precisely, our object is to analyse the observed rise in concentration in terms of two aspects of the growth-patterns of individual firms: the degree of *dispersion* of the growth-rates of firms (sometimes termed the size-mobility of firms) and the *Regression* of the sizes of firms (these terms will be explained later in this chapter). The application of these concepts to the analysis of industrial concentration was developed in an earlier study at the National Institute of industrial companies which had shares quoted on the Stock Exchange (Hart and Prais, 1956). Sufficient data are now available to try out this tool-kit on the broader sector of all manufacturing firms (both quoted and unquoted), and for a reasonably long period of time, during which concentration changed substantially.

The discussion below involves difficult ideas, and it has been set out at some length and with simplifications in the hope that it may be more widely understood. For expositional convenience it is set out in two parts: first, a simplified Special theory, which is helpful in explaining the broad development over the period as a whole; secondly, a General theory (involving the notion of Regression), which permits a better understanding of the recent acceleration in the pace of concentration.[1]

Notes to this chapter will be found on pp. 230–6.

THE SPECIAL THEORY AND ITS APPLICATION

It is convenient to begin by explaining simply, and without the burden of theoretical rigour, the relevance of the dispersion of the growth-rates of firms to the analysis of concentration (readers familiar with the theory of stochastic processes may omit this and the next two paragraphs). The essential point is that, if a group of firms is subject to varying rates of growth unconstrained in any way, the concentration of the group inevitably increases as time proceeds. This fundamental, and at first sight surprising, theorem may be understood with the help of a simple example. Suppose an economy is started with a group of, say, 128 firms, initially all of equal size and each employing a hundred persons, and every year they are subject to the following simple growth-process: half the firms remain unchanged in size, a quarter increase in size by ten employees and a quarter decrease in size by ten employees. At the end of the first year the firms will, of course, no longer all be of equal size: there will be thirty-two firms with 90 employees, sixty-four with 100 employees and thirty-two with 110 employees. Total employment in the economy is unchanged, but it is redistributed amongst the firms.

In the second year we suppose the growth-process to continue and to apply again to each size-group precisely as it did in the first year. In the example: of the thirty-two firms with 90 employees at the end of the first year, sixteen remain unchanged in size, eight rise in size to 100 employees and eight fall in size to 80 employees; similar changes apply to the other groups. The result will be a greater dispersion of sizes; table 2.1 shows what happens. As each year passes, firms of ever-increasing size emerge, though, of course, only small numbers of firms will be in the highest and lowest size-groups. The dispersion of the distribution thus grows inexorably as time proceeds as a result of spontaneous drift (the sizes of firms follow a random walk, 'as sheep which have no shepherd'); and this increase in dispersion is to be seen whether it is measured in familiar statistical terms, such as the range of sizes or their standard deviation, or whether it is measured in terms of the share of total activity in the hands of a particular number of largest firms. In the above example, if we took the proportion employed by the ten largest firms as our measure of concentration, it can be calculated that this measure grew from an initial 7·81 per cent to 8·59 per cent in the first year and to 9·22 per cent in the second year (and, for the third year, if the same procedure is followed through, it will be found that the measure rises to 9·53 per cent).

Whether concentration grows slowly or fast depends on how variable the growth-rates of firms are. In the above example the possible change

Table 2.1. *Size-dispersion of firms illustrated under*
'law of absolute growth'

No. of firms

	Size of firm					All firms
	80 employees	90 employees	100 employees	110 employees	120 employees	
Year 0	—	—	128	—	—	128
Year 1	—	32	64	32	—	128
Year 2	8	32	48	32	8	128

in the size of a firm in a year was limited to only ten employees (up or down), but if the change in a year was limited to one employee concentration would obviously rise only a tenth as rapidly. In general, the wider the variation in the annual growth-rates of firms the more rapid the rise in concentration. It is also important to notice – and this is part of the novelty of the process described here – that large and small firms are all subject to the same chances of growth and decline, but concentration nevertheless increases. In other words, the process of increasing concentration is entirely consistent with 'fair chances' for firms of all sizes, and with economists' ideas of constant long-run returns to scale; we have no need to look to increasing returns to scale to provide an explanation of growing concentration.

As a next step one may alter the above example slightly to allow those firms that change their size to do so not by the same absolute amount of employees but in the same proportion, say by 10 per cent (or, to put it more precisely, by the same factor, in this example 11/10, used as a multiplier or divisor). Proportionate growth may be accepted as being intuitively a more realistic assumption,[2] equi-proportionate changes at different sizes representing steps of more closely equal difficulty and likelihood. In other respects the assumptions are unchanged (for the sake of clarity: each year half the firms remain unchanged in size, a quarter increase to 11/10 of their original size and a quarter decline to 10/11 of their original size). Following through the same arithmetic, it will be found that the rate of increase in concentration is similar to that in the previous example of absolute growth, but under the assumptions made it turns out to be slightly more rapid (in the third year, for example, the ten largest firms would have 9·58 per cent of total employment, as against 9·53 per cent in the previous example).

The distinguishing feature of a size-distribution governed by such a 'law of proportionate growth' is that it loses its symmetry as time proceeds, since large firms can now grow by greater absolute amounts than small firms, whereas in the previous example, governed by a 'law of absolute growth', the distribution retains its symmetry.[3] Eventually the distribution consists of ever-fewer very large firms, accompanied by a preponderant number of ever-smaller firms. In addition to the increasing disparity of firm-sizes there is also, in the case of proportionate growth, a characteristic increase in the asymmetry or skewness of the distribution.

The same result would follow if the growth-process was not of the very restricted kind adopted in the above numerical example, but was more general, in that it permitted various possible proportional rates of growth, each with given probabilities, to apply to all firms in each period. The distribution would in due course assume the smooth regular form known as the log-normal distribution which, as has been recognised for some time, provides a fairly satisfactory mathematical representation of the distribution of firm-sizes, and of which the formal properties are now well understood.[4]

Before introducing further complications it is of interest to examine to what extent this very simple model might account for the observed rise in industrial concentration in this century. To put it more precisely: whilst it may be sufficiently clear from the above discussion that *some* increase in concentration is to be expected as time proceeds merely as a result of a random inequality in the growth-rates of individual firms, it has yet to be shown that the *amount* of increase in concentration from that source is at all substantial in relation to the total increase. The final results of a somewhat elaborate calculation designed to examine this correspondence in relation to British manufacturing are set out in chart 2.1, in which the theoretical curve shows the rise in the share of the hundred largest enterprises to be expected during this century on the basis of the above Special model.

Only two pieces of empirical information were required to draw this theoretical curve:

(i) the distribution of enterprises by size for some particular year during the period, which determines its level;

(ii) a measure of the dispersion of the growth-rates of enterprises during the period, which can be regarded as determining its slope.

It may be emphasised that the slope, which is our main concern here, has not been determined merely by deriving a curve of best fit to the empirical observations shown in that diagram, but has been derived independently (that is by applying a transformation, as will be explained, to observations on the dispersion of growth-rates). On the other hand, no credit can be taken by our theory for the level of the curve which, so to speak, is fitted to the observations shown in the figure. However that should not be regarded as too much of a

Chart 2.1. *Actual and theoretical (Special model) shares of the hundred largest enterprises in manufacturing net output, United Kingdom*

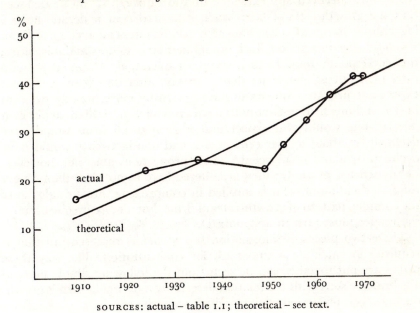

SOURCES: actual – table 1.1; theoretical – see text.

deficiency: it is difficult to conceive that theoretical reasons alone would be sufficient to predict that a particular level of concentration would be reached by a particular year in the twentieth century; it is sufficient that the theory helps us in understanding the rate of change in concentration from any particular level that may have been reached.

The way in which the theoretical curve was constructed must now be described in more detail. First, its level was determined so that it passed through the observed share of the hundred largest in 1963, shown by the Census of Production for that year as having been 37 per cent (see table 1.1 above). To apply the present theory we require also an alternative measure of the inequality of firm-sizes, namely the standard deviation of their logarithms; this is the important characteristic value of the corresponding theoretical log-normal distribution. Measuring size again in terms of net output, that value was estimated from the same source as $\sigma = 2.65$. In what follows, the technical side of the argument has to be conducted in terms of such values of σ, which have then to be translated back into 'commonsense' terms of the share of the hundred largest.[5]

Next, for the dispersion of the growth-rates of firms we can turn to

a number of previous empirical studies by various authors which together cover the extensive period 1896 to 1969. From these studies
(which are surveyed and extended in appendix D), it can be deduced
that the growth-rates of firms when measured over a decade have a
logarithmic standard deviation which may be put at an average of about
$s = 0.82$ over this period. In more immediately understandable terms,
this corresponds roughly to a standard deviation of annual growth-
rates of about 25 per cent: that is to say, after one year one would
expect one firm in about six to have grown by more than 25 per cent
in size and one firm in twenty to have grown by more than 50 per cent
in size; one would also expect that a sixth of all firms would have
declined by about 25 per cent in size and one in twenty would have
declined by about 50 per cent.[6] These proportions must not, however,
be treated too precisely; they are offered here as no more than a very
rough indication of what is implied in compressing into a single figure
the complex pattern of growth-rates of firms. For a more precise account
the reader must turn to appendix D.

These two pieces of information (on σ and s) represent all that is
required to calculate a time-path for concentration. The way these
pieces are put together can be seen from the following simple piece of
algebra. We start with the relation describing a particular firm's growth
during a certain period of time, which we write as

$$x_1 = x_0 + \epsilon_1 \tag{1}$$

where x_1 denotes the logarithm of a firm's size (measured as a deviation
from the mean of the logarithms of size) at the end of year 1, x_0 is the
corresponding value in the previous year and ϵ_1 is the logarithmic
growth-rate of the firm (for example, if a particular firm grew by
5 per cent, ϵ would be $\log_e 1.05 = 0.049$). The variance of the sizes of
all firms in the population at the two dates can then be found as usual
by squaring and taking expectations, which yields

$$\sigma_1^2 = \sigma_0^2 + s^2 \tag{2}$$

It has been assumed here that the growth-rate is independent of the
initial size – an assumption that is relaxed in the latter part of this
chapter.

After t periods of time, during each of which the same relation held,
we would have

$$\sigma_t^2 = \sigma_0^2 + ts^2 \tag{3}$$

This is the basic equation governing the variance of firm-sizes at two
dates t periods of time apart. It will be noticed that it is the growth
in the variance that is directly proportional to the time-interval; the

growth in other measures of dispersion or concentration will, of course, not follow such a simple time-path.

It may be helpful to outline the main steps in the calculation of an example (fuller details are given in appendix C). We start with the observed value noted above for 1963 of $\sigma_{63} = 2\cdot65$, and calculate the value to be expected for 1993 – that is three decades later – as $3\cdot01$ (since $3\cdot01^2 = 2\cdot65^2 + 3 \times 0\cdot82^2$). Similarly, if we wished to look backward to 1903, again starting from the observed value for 1963 we would calculate a theoretical value for 1903 of $1\cdot73$ (since $1\cdot73^2 = 2\cdot65^2 - 6 \times 0\cdot82^2$).

To make everyday sense of these figures one has to translate them into theoretical shares of the hundred largest firms, so that they can be compared with the corresponding actual observations. It is found, on consulting tables of the normal probability function (assuming that the firms are log-normally distributed with the above variances) that they correspond to theoretical shares of the hundred largest firms for 1903 of 11 per cent and for 1993 of 52 per cent. Similar theoretical calculations have been made for other years and are shown in the chart by the smooth theoretical curve.

Before commenting on the correspondence (and the divergences) between this theoretical curve and the actual one, a final qualification has to be considered. It is assumed in the above calculations that the total number of firms remains constant over time (at 66,000, the observed value in 1963), even though we know – at least for recent years – that the total number of firms has been declining. Fortunately, however, this limitation does not seem to be of much practical consequence for the present calculations. From a formal point of view it might be supposed that firms that have disappeared from Census coverage continue in hypothetical existence while being of some arbitrary but negligible size, so that their influence on total output and on the calculated share of the hundred largest firms can be virtually ignored. This way of looking at things is not as unrealistic as might at first appear. The coverage by the Census of the smallest firms has probably never been very exhaustive, and this deficiency is not very important from most points of view, since the smallest firms never make a great contribution to total activity. In 1963, for example, the 18,000 manufacturing establishments with five or fewer employees, which probably belonged to about a quarter of all manufacturing enterprises by number, accounted for a mere 1 per cent of manufacturing employment. It should therefore be a requirement of any mathematical representation of reality that it should not be sensitive to 'errors in observation' at the lowest end of the size-range, nor should it be sensitive to the total number of firms covered. In fact trial calculations have confirmed that the log-normal distribution in the present application is robust in the face of even very large errors of this sort. To quote an extreme example, if the true total number of enterprises had been double the number assumed above (that is double the number recorded in 1963), but the additional firms were of negligible size in that year, the theoretical share of the hundred largest firms calculated for 1903 would have emerged at 13 per cent, instead of 11 per cent as in the preceding paragraph. It may be inferred that much the same theoretical predictions for the share of the hundred largest firms would be made on this approach within an extremely wide range of values for the total number of firms.

TWO EXERCISES IN EXTRAPOLATION

The remarkable feature of the calculations illustrated in chart 2.1 is that they suggest that a great deal of the long-term upward trend in concentration observed in this century could have been anticipated; while in reality there must have been a great many other contributory factors, it is also remarkable that so much of the rise is explicable in terms of as simple and apparently innocuous a process as the unconstrained variability in the growth-rates of firms. The type of constraint that would have been necessary to prevent an increase in concentration is considered below, but we may first pause to consider what happens if this Special model is extrapolated into the far future and, as proves to be equally of interest, what is to be learnt from an extrapolation into the distant past. Extrapolations greatly outside the period of observation always have to be treated with reserve and these exercises should, of course, not be taken too seriously. They are included here as much to illustrate the properties of this scheme of thought as for the curious air of verisimilitude that they possess.

If the model continued to apply in future decades, the dispersion of the size-distribution of firms would, of course, continue to grow. The tendency towards increasing concentration is in one sense an asymptotic one, that is to say the rate of increase in the share of the hundred largest firms would eventually tail-off. Even in a century's time the model suggests that the hundred largest firms would account for (only!) 80 per cent of total activity, which is, after all, only about double the present share (see appendix C, example 2, for details of the calculation). But it may be a cause of greater worry to know that the model also predicts that the ten largest of those firms would then account for nearly two-thirds, and the single largest of those firms for over a third, of total activity. The tendency for any given share of economic activity to fall into the hands of an ever-smaller number of giants would be limitless, but there would be a degree of continuing change in their composition.

Looking backwards, before the beginning of this century, it becomes clear that the model could not have applied for very long, and certainly not throughout the whole of history. The rise in concentration from a (hypothetically) primeval state of equality would have been at a very slow rate according to the mathematics embodied in the model, but it would have had a definite beginning. That beginning is dated by the model as being in the 1850s. In that decade the variance as calculated from equation (3) reduces to zero; this represents the point at which all firms are of equal size, so that this simple scheme of thought cannot be carried further back in time. We cannot become more equal if we are equal already.

The full evolutionary path of concentration embodied in this approach is thus of the sigmoid type – a slow rise initially, followed by a period of acceleration, which is finally succeeded by a period of tailing-off. The theoretical curve in chart 2.1 gives only the slightest indication of such a sigmoid shape. Calculations put the early flat part mainly in the nineteenth century and the latter-day flat part in the late twenty-first century; if, however, one were to look rather precisely at that curve (more precisely than is warranted by the underlying statistical data), it would be seen that the fastest rate of rise in the share of the hundred largest happened to fall – curiously enough – precisely in the decade of the 1960s that has just elapsed.[7]

If, in the spirit of an academic explorer, one were to search for some single initiating development in the middle of the nineteenth century which had a crucial influence on the evolution of concentration, one might well point to the fact that limited liability first became generally available under the Companies Act of 1856 (before that date incorporation with limited liability had indeed been possible, but it was a difficult and restricted process). One would also recall Marshall's thought-provoking analogy between the dynamic equilibrium of the sizes of businesses and the sizes of 'trees in the forest'; according to his later views (6th edition of the *Principles*, 1910) this analogy held only 'before the great recent development of vast joint-stock companies which often stagnate but do not readily die'.[8] Not long afterwards (1919) he wrote:

There might have seemed to be nothing to prevent the concentration in the hands of a single firm of the whole production of the world, except in so far as it was closed by tariff barriers. The reason why this result did not follow was simply that no firm ever had a sufficiently long life of unabated energy and power of initiative for the purpose. It is not possible to say how far this position is now changed by the expansion of joint stock companies with a potentially perpetual life: but every recent decade has contained some episodes which suggest that it may probably be greatly changed.[9]

Marshall thought this applied only to those goods produced 'under the law of Increasing Return' where 'each step that the firm took forwards ...would make the next step surer, longer and quicker' (ibid., p. 315). But, as we have seen, the force making for higher concentration has a wider applicability: the unconstrained growth of firms leads to that end provided enough time is allowed to elapse – that is if firms have a sufficiently long life.

It is perhaps accidental that our simple model should point precisely to the decade of the 1850s for the commencement of this process; other values of the variables that have been tried, and that may be quite as realistic, point to perhaps a decade or so earlier. These are small matters. The important point rather is to recognise Marshall's insight that the appearance of the limited liability company as an easily available form of business organisation had fundamentally upset the equilibrium of the size-distribution; as far as can be seen today no new equilibrium is in sight.[10]

THE GENERAL REGRESSION MODEL

We must next examine more precisely the rate at which concentration has grown, and the apparent change in the trend at about the end of the war. The rate of increase in concentration for the period up to, say, 1950 was somewhat lower than would be expected from the theoretical curve in chart 2.1; indeed, as already mentioned, an observer standing in the mid-1950s might have been forgiven for concluding that the actual level of concentration had substantially stabilised. Since 1950 the appearance of the situation has changed radically: not only has there been a marked further increase in concentration but, as will be noted from the chart, the rate of increase in concentration has been greater than might have been anticipated from the Special theory.

If concentration is governed by the type of process outlined above, it may be asked, first, in what way it is consistent with such a process for there to be a break of the kind seen at the end of the war. Secondly, and more generally, it may be asked whether it is at all consistent with such a process for concentration ever to cease growing short of the limit when one firm has absorbed all activity. Answers to these questions require a more precise and more general analysis, which basically is the same as Galton's theory of Regression.[11] According to this theory, stability in the dispersion of a size-distribution is possible, notwithstanding continuous changes in the sizes of its constituents, provided that as part of those changes there is a *systematic* tendency for extreme values to Regress towards the centre. So modified, the growth in a firm's size can be considered as consisting of two parts: a random part which has the effects described in the previous section, and a systematic part which is negatively related to its size – that is, large firms *on average* tend to decline in size (or show a lower rate of growth) in comparison with small firms, but individual firms may show substantial variations in either direction about that average tendency. This systematic tendency thus acts as an offsetting factor in relation to the inherent pressure towards growing dispersion arising from the random part. This is precisely the process that was thought to operate in Galton's classic studies of the inheritance of human characteristics, the theory of which has remarkable analogies with the present topic. A son's height depends partly on his father's height and is partly a matter of chance; tall fathers tend to have tall sons, but the sons are not quite as tall as the fathers were – that is, in Galtons's language, they Regress towards the mean. If there was no such Regression we would have the impossible situation in which, to quote Galton, 'the giants (in any mental or physical particular) would become more gigantic, and the dwarfs more dwarfish, in each successive generation'.[12]

It is likely that Marshall had closely related ideas in mind when discussing the size-distribution of firms; he drew attention to the limited 'length of life during which a business of any kind is likely to retain its full vigour'. So long as there is some limit to the size of firms, whether that limit is governed by the length of human life and the limitations of the inheritance of exceptional ability and wealth, or whether it is governed by technical optima beyond which diseconomies of scale eventually become effective, it is possible for the distribution of firm-sizes to retain a stable degree of inequality over time.[13]

The tendency towards Regression can be examined empirically by dividing a sample of firms into size-groups and seeing how the average rate of growth over a period of time for each size-group varies with initial size; if large firms grow less rapidly on average than small firms, then Galtonian Regression is present. But that Regression must be of adequate strength if stability is to be preserved; to discover how much is 'adequate' requires the following piece of algebra. The strength of the Regression effect is conveniently measured in terms of the gradient, b, of the relationship between the sizes of firms at two dates,

$$x_1 = bx_0 + \epsilon_1 \qquad (4)$$

where, as before, x is the logarithm of the size of the firm (measured from its mean), b is a constant which is less than unity in the usual case of Regression, and ϵ is the component of the firm's growth independent of its opening size. It will be apparent that the theory presented in the earlier sections of this chapter was based on the Special assumption that b was equal to unity.

The growth in the dispersion of firm-sizes between two adjacent periods is now governed by the relationship

$$\sigma_1^2 = b^2\sigma_0^2 + s^2 \tag{5}$$

and, provided b is sufficiently less than unity, it is possible for the dispersion to remain constant over time (this is in contrast with equation (2) above, where the dispersion necessarily increases over time).

To find the critical amount c by which b must fall below unity, it is convenient to transform equation (4) and express the change in the size of a firm as

$$x_1 - x_0 = cx_0 + \epsilon_t \tag{6}$$

where $c = b - 1$; cx is what has been termed above the systematic part of the change in size over the time-period considered. A criterion for the constancy of the dispersion of the distribution over time is that the actual value of c should be at least equal to a certain critical value, which we may term Galton's contant c_g, and which is given approximately[14] by

$$c_g = -\tfrac{1}{2}s^2/\sigma^2 \tag{7}$$

It will be seen that the critical degree of Regression required to stabilise the concentration of the distribution at the particular level reached varies directly with the variability of growth-rates and inversely with the level of concentration – that is, for a given variability of growth, we need less Regression if we are satisfied to maintain a high level of concentration than if we wish to maintain a low level of concentration. If the actual value of the Regression c is greater than this critical value, that is if the Regressive forces are stronger, concentration will decrease; if they are weaker concentration will increase. The required critical values have been calculated for various dates in this century on the basis of the values of s and σ adopted in the earlier section of this chapter and lie in the range $-0\cdot10$ to $-0\cdot05$. The higher values correspond to the beginning of the century when σ was smaller; the lower values correspond to present circumstances. It may again be noted that the amount of Regression, and hence the values of s and c, depends on the length of time-period considered; the values quoted here are all in terms of a decade.

To interpret these values of Galton's constant in more everyday terms one may, by way of illustration, consider what they would imply for the expected rate of growth of an enterprise that is at the upper quartile of the distribution in relation to the rate of growth of the median enterprise. We would like to know, in other words, whether the requirement of a constant level of concentration necessitates a large relative retardation in the growth of larger firms, or whether a mild retardation would be adequate. For 1963 it emerges from calculations that a Regression of -0.05 would imply a relative fall in the size of the upper quartile firm in relation to the median firm of about 0.9 per cent a year. The same difference arises whether we are considering the quartile in terms of the number of firms or in terms of the number of employees, provided that the median is defined correspondingly; this holds precisely only if the distribution is log-normal. Larger firms would require to show a greater relative fall: for example, the firm at the upper decile of the distribution would show a relative fall of 1.7 per cent a year (again considered in relation to the median firm). Firms below the median would show corresponding relative increases in size; that is firms at the lowest quartile and decile would show relative rises in size of 0.9 and 1.7 per cent a year respectively. These do not seem unreasonably large magnitudes, especially when considered in relation to the general growth of the economy; if the median firm were growing at 5 per cent a year, concentration would remain stable if firms at the lowest decile grew at 6.7 per cent and firms at the upper decile at 3.3 per cent (with corresponding variations for other firms according to their distance from the median).

The actual values of c observed in studies of quoted companies before the war (over the period 1885–1939) were not as great as required by Galton's constant and averaged only -0.02. Thus a certain degree of Regression probably applied in this period (that is, larger firms on average grew slightly less rapidly than smaller firms), but the magnitude of the Regression was insufficient to prevent concentration increasing. For the war-period, 1939–50, we found – exceptionally – that there was a very strong Regression of -0.23, and this was adequate to ensure de-concentration in that period.[15] These estimated values of c are subject to sampling error, as well as to the reservation that they are based on changes in the sizes of quoted companies only; no studies of smaller concerns are available for that period. They may therefore be accepted as indicative of the general mechanism at work, but they cannot strictly be regarded as providing an entirely adequate indication of what happened to the whole size distribution, though of course they represent a large part of it.

The results of similar studies for the post-war years stand in substantial contrast to those for the pre-war period. For 1951–60 a sample of quoted industrial companies studied by Samuels yielded a positive value of $c = +0.12$;[16] for the partially overlapping period 1954–65 a study by Utton of all quoted manufacturing companies yielded the very similar value, $c = +0.08$.[17] The perverse positive sign in both

Chart 2.2. *Actual and theoretical (General and Special models) shares of the hundred largest enterprises in manufacturing net output, United Kingdom*

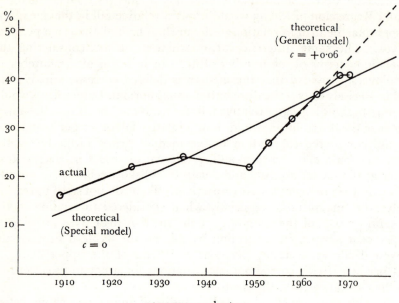

SOURCES: as chart 2.1.

studies should be noted; positive values are inconsistent with any possibility of stability of the size-distribution.

These positive values have been confirmed by an analysis of some hitherto unpublished statistics based on a wider coverage of firms from the Censuses of Production for 1951 and 1958. This new information relates to manufacturing enterprises with over twenty-five employees, and allows their growth in terms of employment to be traced between these two Census years. It is a particularly important body of statistics from the point of view of this study, both because unquoted (that is to say, smaller) enterprises are included as well as quoted enterprises, and because size is measured in terms of employment (and not in terms of balance-sheet values or market valuations as in other studies). The Regression for the period 1951–8 calculated from these figures was $c = +0.12$.[18]

It appears, therefore, that in recent years a new balance of forces has established itself which favours the growth of the larger concern. The result has been an exceptionally rapid rise in concentration in recent years, a rise that is greater than could have been anticipated from the general diffusion process envisaged under the Special theory.

Chart 2.2 shows how very important such dispersive (or anti-

Regressive) elements can be in hastening the growth of concentration. A further theoretical line has been drawn on this chart showing the expected rise in concentration if $c = +0·06$; it has been drawn through the actual observation for 1963, and seems to describe very closely the post-war course of events. The value of c chosen is slightly lower than suggested by the studies just surveyed, but even this conservative value has very strong implications as outlined in the next section.

From the point of view of policy it is helpful to divide the total rise in concentration into two parts with the help of this chart. The observed rise of 19 percentage points in the share of the hundred largest firms in the period 1949–70 (from 22 to 41 per cent) may be divided into a portion to be expected from the general diffusion process (represented by the Special theory) and amounting to some 10 percentage points or half of the total rise, and the remaining half to be attributed to the systematic factors which have particularly favoured the growth of large concerns in this period.

IMPLICATIONS OF THE RECENT TREND

If a positive value of $c = +0·06$ were to persist, concentration must be expected to rise very rapidly. By 1983 the hundred largest enterprises would produce 60 per cent of net output (instead of the 47 per cent implied by the Special theory) and by the turn of the century their share would rise to 80 per cent. More disconcerting still is that half of all manufacturing net output could then be produced by no more than the seven largest enterprises![19] It must, of course, be anticipated that society will intervene in various ways before such extreme levels of concentration are reached, and there are indeed signs that public policy is moving in that direction. The calculations presented here should thus not be taken as predictions of what will happen, but rather as warnings that, on recent trends, the time left for manoeuvre is limited.

A sceptic may well say that the change to a positive Regression in the post-war period from the slightly negative value before the war is only a complicated and formal way of saying that there has been an acceleration in the process governing concentration. Even so the present analysis is helpful in showing how much concentration would rise under conditions which may be characterised as corresponding to constant returns to scale (the Special theory) and how much is to be attributed to factors favouring large size.[20] It is the task of later chapters to examine to what extent the break in the process may be attributed to apparently beneficial elements, such as increased production economies of scale, and to what extent to changes in factors where the benefit is less clear, for example changes in the supply of capital to large-scale industry associated with the growth of insurance companies and pension funds. Even if we cannot unambiguously isolate the contribution of each causative factor, it may be sufficient to form a view of the preponderant element. This may enable one to decide whether any corrective pressure is appropriate, and if so what type.

SYNOPSIS

The numerical results set out in this chapter must not, of course, be taken too precisely, nor should the extrapolations be regarded as much more than rough indications of what is implied by current trends. Perhaps, by way of a summary of the argument and at the obvious risk of naive simplification, the following broad division of the history of industrial concentration over the past 150 years may be offered. Three periods may be distinguished.

The first is that before limited liability became widely available in the middle of the nineteenth century, when the concentration of industrial power was generally at a low level. The extent of concentration was limited by factors such as the span of human life, the amount that a man could accumulate in a lifetime together with a few partners, and the role of heredity which limited the span of family dynasties to a few generations.

Following the introduction of general limited liability in the 1850s a second period ensued, during which concentration increased at a mild rate, more or less as might be predicted by the Special theory; this period is characterised by the emergence of ever-larger firms and is reflected in questionings amongst economists of the possible ultimate limits to the size of a firm. During this period, which must not of course be supposed to have been entirely uniform, closer examination shows that large firms probably grew on average slightly less rapidly than small firms, but it had not been realised that this was consistent with an inherent rise in concentration due to the logic of the general diffusion process described here. This period lasted for about a century; its end may be set at about 1950.[21]

In the current, third, period it appears that factors systematically favouring a relatively faster rate of growth by large firms have become dominant; these have combined with the general diffusion process to make for an unprecedented rate of increase in concentration, to which no limit can be seen at present.

CHAPTER 3

CHANGES IN PLANT-SIZES

behold, his bedstead was a bedstead of iron; ... nine
cubits was the length thereof, and four cubits the breadth
of it

Deuteronomy 3: 11

STANDARDISATION, SPECIALISATION AND THE RANGE OF PLANT-SIZES

In trying to understand why concentration has increased it is easy
enough to point to various examples of modern products, such as aircraft, strip steel and synthetic fibres, where present-day production
techniques very clearly demand a large-scale plant. Production on
a small scale is so uneconomical that in practice it would not be undertaken. For this reason small countries have tended to be at a disadvantage in the production of such products; but with the growth of
international trade that disadvantage has diminished, so that today
we find aircraft produced in Holland, steel in Luxembourg and synthetic fibres in Switzerland. If products of this type have become more
typical, that is if technological progress has favoured production of
standardised commodities in large-scale plants, it might be concluded
that large and dominating plants were inevitable, and that it was the
progress of technology that was responsible for the general tendency
towards rising industrial concentration.

But, together with the evolution of production possibilities on an
ever-larger scale, the need has grown for specialist producers who work
on a smaller scale, and whose activities in various ways complement
those of large-scale producers. The small or medium-sized specialist
buys from the large-scale producer and, for example, turns mass-
produced raw steel into specialist alloys and then into cutlery; or, to
take another example, artificial textile fibres produced on a massive
scale in huge chemical plants are converted by small firms into cloth
and, eventually, by other small firms into individual items of clothing.
The small specialist also sells to the large mass-producer, whether it is
specialist tools required for the production of raw materials, or small
parts or components such as carburettors or sun-visors, for assembly
into complex products such as motor cars; or specialist services such as

Notes to this chapter will be found on pp. 236–42.

electroplating. The evolution of large-scale production processes for raw materials, or for the assembly of complex new commodities, leads to a restructuring of the existing industrial pattern, and opportunities for small specialists seem to be created by technology almost hand-in-hand with the growth of large-scale producers.

Further, as technology advances, the saving of labour on those goods made by large-scale producers might occur at a rate so much greater than amongst smaller specialists that a reduced fraction of the total labour force might eventually be found in the larger plants; that is to say, there might be a shift in employment towards smaller plants. It is equally conceivable that there might be a similar shift towards small plants in the value of output measured in terms of current relative values.[1]

The advance of technology has no doubt led to an increase in production in plants of all sizes. But whether it has on balance led to a relative shift towards large- or small-scale employers cannot be known from abstract reflection and can only be ascertained from the statistics. It is the task of this chapter to assess the available statistics on plant-sizes from this point of view, together with their implications for the rise in concentration. Questions affecting multi-plant operation, and the rise of large managerial and financial units of control, are deferred to the following two chapters.

Any explanation of the rise in concentration in terms of technology, to the extent that it may be sustained by the facts, would supplement that advanced in the preceding chapter. The explanation put forward there, it will be remembered, was in terms of the effect of 'the slings and arrows of outrageous fortune' which, even if they affect firms of all sizes equi-proportionately, would cumulate over time and lead to an ever-increasing dispersion, and thereby to an increasing concentration, of the resources available to the economy. It was concluded that an explanation on these lines might be sufficient to account for the general trend in concentration up to about 1950, but since then an acceleration in concentration has taken place. If technical economies of scale had become particularly important in this last period, we might have had a valuable adjunct to our previous explanation; and, of course, if it proved an important part of the total explanation in this period, public policy might favour growing industrial concentration rather more strongly than if it was shown that larger plant-sizes had little to do with rising concentration.

To clarify our ideas it is helpful next to consider at a general level the possible ways in which economies of scale may manifest themselves over time in the observed size-distributions of plants. If economies of scale have become more important over time, one would primarily expect to observe a rise in the average size of plants, but the range of sizes about that average (due to the host of individual factors that determine the precise size of a particular plant) might well remain unchanged. If the rise in the average were more rapid than that required by the demand for the product, the number of plants would fall and the share of the market in the hands of a given number of largest plants would rise. This is the simple and familiar case.

A change in the range of plant-sizes brings us to less familiar considerations. If economies of scale were pronounced, as time proceeded it would become clearer to those in the trade where the optimum size lay, and that might be so even if that optimum were changing.[2] Consequently some narrowing in the range of prevailing sizes might be expected over time. (The definition of that 'range' in practice is to a certain extent an arbitrary one and is considered below.) An observed contraction in the range would thus also indicate the likely existence or intensification of scale-economies. The range might contract even if the average size remained constant; this particular combination of circumstances is mentioned here merely as a hypothetical possibility to clarify our ideas, but there are industries which in fact follow this pattern.[3]

Suppose next that the average plant-size remains unchanged, but that the prevailing range of sizes widens. This would happen if the upper limit of the range rose and the lower limit fell correspondingly. Since larger plants have become more important in relation to the remainder, our measure of concentration (based on the share of a given number of the largest plants) would of course rise. But what are we to infer as to the role of economies of scale? The rise in the size of the largest plants might suggest that at that end of the range economies of scale had become more important over time (or, equivalently, that those elements involving diseconomies as size increases – such as the costs of coordination, to take the textbook example – had become less important over time). But, at the other extreme, the fall in the size of the smallest plants would have the reverse implication. It would be easy to conclude that in such an industry there had been on average no change in the importance of economies of scale. But to do so would ignore an important aspect of reality, which is that a greater range of firm-sizes had become practicable; and that seems more consistent with saying that economies of scale have become *less* pronounced over the broad range of sizes.[4]

That there is a practical need to consider the implications of changes in the range or dispersion of sizes, as well as in the average size, will be apparent from the discussion in the previous chapter, and that is why it has been thought worthwhile considering, step by step, a number of hypothetical situations. The conclusion to be drawn from them is that the relation between changes in concentration and changes in what are intuitively termed 'economies of scale' is not as simple as is often implied. Concentration of plant-sizes may rise because:

(i) economies of scale have become *more* important, in the sense that the average size has risen while the market has not expanded proportionally; or

(ii) economies of scale have become *less* important, in the sense that the dispersion of sizes has increased without significant changes in average size.

In reality both the average and the dispersion of sizes may change substantially and one cannot always expect to derive any simple conclusion. If the average and the dispersion move in opposite directions a clear inference may be drawn: thus if the average increases while the dispersion decreases, one would have grounds for pointing to the operation of economies of scale. But if they move in the same direction, both the average and the dispersion increasing for example, one could only say – and it is hardly helpful – that in one respect economies of scale have become more important and in another respect they have apparently become less important.

Only one further case needs to be mentioned at this general level: if the dispersion increases in the same proportion as the average (and this is close to what has happened in practice), we would have the special case of the distribution of sizes having undergone a mere transformation in scale in which the *relative* importance of the various units remains substantially unchanged (rather like the effect of a general inflation on the relative prices of various commodities). In these circumstances the share of any given number of largest plants would remain constant.

The remainder of this chapter examines statistics of changes in plant-sizes that have occurred in this country since 1930, and the contribution of those changes to the rise in manufacturing concentration. In comparing absolute plant-sizes over time, size is measured sometimes by net output but more often by the number of employees; the latter helps to avoid the difficult problems of deflating output valued in the monetary units of different time-periods. Because of the general tendency for labour productivity to increase over time, it will be understood that the rise in absolute plant-sizes would be greater if measured in terms of real output than in terms of employment. A measure in terms of employment nevertheless retains an interest of its own.

As is familiar, the size-distributions published by the Census of Production are on the basis either of establishments (that is plants) or of enterprises (an enterprise consisting of all the establishments which are under its control, whether through direct ownership or through majority shareholdings in subsidiary companies). This distinction helps in forming an impression – one must not put it more strongly – of the sources of economies of scale: of the relative importance of, on the one hand, production economies and, on the other hand, marketing, financial and other economies.[5] To the extent that enterprises have grown in size because their plants have grown, one may suspect that production economies are important; to the extent that enterprises have grown because of an increase in the number of plants owned, one is tempted to look elsewhere, for example to marketing and financial economies. Corresponding considerations apply to changes in the dispersion of plant-sizes and enterprise-sizes.

THE LARGEST FIRMS AND THE LARGEST PLANTS

It may be as well to begin what is inevitably a somewhat heavy statistical exercise by looking first at the principal result, which is relatively simple, and then to examine the more complex factors involved.

Our interest is to discover to what extent the rise in the share of the hundred largest manufacturing firms can be attributed to a rise in plant-sizes. A simple way of approaching this question is to calculate the share of the hundred largest plants in total activity (net output or employment), and to compare this with the share of the hundred largest firms. If these two shares are not very different and have moved together over time, one might well conclude that the rise in plant-sizes is a significant factor in determining the size of the largest firms and, further, that production economies or technological factors have been mainly responsible for the observed rapid rise in the concentration of firms. On the other hand, if all plants expanded at much the same rate, that is at the rate at which total industrial employment was expanding, the share of the hundred largest plants would remain constant, and one could then hardly point to technological factors as having much to do with the rise in the concentration of firms.

The results of our calculations on the shares of the largest plants at various dates are set out in table 3.1, and are compared with the shares of the largest firms in chart 3.1. It will be seen that the share in net output of the hundred largest plants has hardly changed from about 11 per cent throughout the period, although in the same time-span the share of the hundred largest firms has risen from about 23 to 41 per cent. Calculations in terms of the share in employment rather than net output yield very similar results.

It follows that, if firms had changed in size only to the extent that

Table 3.1. *Share of the hundred largest manufacturing establishments[a] in net output and employment, 1930–68*

Percentages

	Share in	
	Net output	Employment
1930	10·8[b]	8·2[b]
1935	11·2	8·4
1948	9·0	9·5
1951	9·4	9·3
1954	10·1	9·6
1958	10·5[c]	9·9
1963	11·1	10·1
1968	10·8	9·2

SOURCES: Censuses of Production, interpolated estimates.

[a] On a ranking by employment in each establishment (distributions ranked by size of net output per establishment are not published in the Census).

[b] Approximate figures. The published size-distribution was based on returns, with an average of 1·17 establishments per return. The largest 85 (= 100/1·17) returns were taken here.

[c] Share in sales (net output not available for this year).

plants changed in size, then the share of the hundred largest firms in net output would have remained virtually unchanged since the 1930s – that is at about 20 per cent. This is an important conclusion. If we wish to understand why the concentration of firms has risen, it is clearly necessary to look to factors other than plant-size, namely to the reasons why the number of plants owned by large firms has risen so rapidly.[6]

Two remarks may be made by way of slight qualification to the above conclusion. First, if our concern is with 'production' economies of scale broadly defined, it might be said that they also manifest themselves to some extent in multi-plant operations. For example, a number of plants in separate locations running in parallel may be served by a common toolroom set up as a separate factory, and all may form part of a single firm. It may be said that certain of the economies that arise in such an organisation fall under the head of 'production' economies, in that a closer integration of production needs is possible than if the plants were all separately owned; to that extent it would not be correct to infer from chart 3.1 that such economies have made no contribution to the rise in the concentration of firms. However, in considering the relative advantages of decentralisation of ownership and control as against their concentration, it is more useful to distinguish between those economies which are internal to the plant and those which are

Chart 3.1. *Shares of the hundred largest enterprises and establishments in manufacturing net output, United Kingdom*

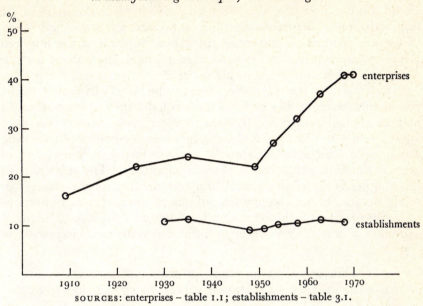

SOURCES: enterprises – table 1.1; establishments – table 3.1.

external; that is, our concern is with what may be called 'plant economies'. And the question is whether it is the greater size of plants that has brought about the rise in concentration, or whether we must look elsewhere; this question seems to be answered clearly enough by the facts summarised in chart 3.1.[7]

The second qualification relates to the statistical material; this is not quite as homogeneous over time as might be wished, since joint returns for two or more establishments have sometimes been accepted by the Census authorities. For 1930 some adjustment has been attempted here, but the estimate shown is probably still slightly too high. For 1924, although the Census published a size-distribution by 'returns', the number of joint returns was so much greater than in 1930 and the classification of sizes so broad that no useful estimate proved possible for present purposes.[8] The apparent slight fall in the share of the hundred largest plants shown in chart 3.1 in the period between the 1930s and 1948 is probably due to fewer joint returns. Equally, however, it appears that the slight rise in the period since 1948 has been influenced by a tendency for larger firms to submit joint returns for an increasing number of their subsidiary plants.[9] Taking into account in a broad way the imperfection resulting from joint returns, it would seem that not too much significance should be attached to the small recorded fluctuations in the share of the hundred largest plants over the period as a whole. However, even if we were prepared to accept that the apparent rise of 2 percentage points between 1948 and 1968 in the share of the hundred largest plants was genuine, one could safely conclude that, of the rise of some 20 percentage points in the share of the hundred largest enterprises in these two decades, no more than about a tenth was attributable to changes in plant-sizes.[10]

In brief, we see that plant-sizes seem to be largely irrelevant to the rise in the concentration of firms, and equally they are not of much help in explaining the acceleration in enterprise-concentration since 1951. From a broader point of view, however, for example in assessing the prospects for smaller firms in manufacturing, a knowledge of general trends in plant-sizes is of some importance. The remainder of this chapter is therefore devoted to a consideration of the changes in recent decades in the absolute sizes of plants; the reader more particularly concerned with the concentration issue, and the role of financial and other factors, may however turn directly to the next chapter.

THE WIDE DISPARITY OF PLANT-SIZES AND THE PROBLEM OF MEASURING THEIR CENTRAL TENDENCY

When considering changes in the average size of plants, one has of course first to agree how to measure that average. This is not a simple matter, nor is it a mere technical or formal matter that can safely be ignored by those wishing to concern themselves only with the 'substance of the issue'; the differences resulting from alternative measures are too great for that. The various ways of measuring the 'average' size of plant used by serious writers on these matters would, if applied to the statistical data on plants in this country in 1963, yield calculated averages varying from under five to as many as 1700 employees per plant. Such a disparity in measuring what is ostensibly the same thing should make one wonder whether that 'thing' really exists; that is, whether there is any sufficiently clear central tendency in the size-distribution of plants which can usefully be summarised in terms of some single number.

In trying to fix our ideas it is helpful to contrast the distribution of plant-sizes with that of human heights.[11] It is known that the arithmetic mean height of males in this country is some 5 feet 7½ inches, and that two-thirds of all men have a height between 5 feet 5 inches and 5 feet 10 inches. The median height (which divides the population so that half are above and half below that height) and the modal height (the height that is most frequently encountered) are not quite the same as the arithmetic mean height, but they are both less than 0·1 inches away from it; it obviously therefore makes a negligible difference which measure of central tendency is used. But for plant-sizes in 1963 the corresponding measures are: arithmetic mean ninety-three employees; median eighteen employees; while the modal plant has under five employees. Such great differences are the consequence of the vast dispersion and skewness of plant-sizes. Using the coefficient of variation (the standard deviation of sizes divided by the mean) to measure relative variability, it can be calculated that for male heights this coefficient is some 4 per cent. For plant-sizes it is over a hundred times greater, being in the region of 500 per cent. Any central tendency in plant-sizes is thus much less distinct (one might say a hundred times less distinct) than in a distribution such as that of human heights, and it is this lack of distinctness that permits different investigators to use measures which are ostensibly of the same 'thing', but which have such diverse numerical values. The relative variability of the sizes of enterprises is of course still greater, being nearer 5000 per cent, that is about ten times greater than for plants and about a thousand times greater than for human heights.

In addition to the three familiar averages already noted, two less familiar measures, which have been used in summarising distributions of plant-sizes and which yield much higher answers than those quoted so far, have now to be explained. They are based on the following approach: suppose we give each employee a ticket on which is written the size of plant in which he works. The employees are then supposed to line up in an order given by the numbers on their tickets, and the figure on the ticket of the employee halfway along the line is taken as a measure of the distribution's average; clearly, half of all employees are to be found in plants greater than this size and half in smaller plants. This measure is called by Florence the 'median' size of plant, but it is important to notice that it differs from the conventional median, in which the *plants* are ordered in size and the middle plant is chosen. Here it is the *employees* in those plants that are ranked and the plant in which the 'central' employee is to be found is taken as the median. This measure comes closer to the notion of the plant in which the 'typical' employee is found, and is also closer to the range of plant-sizes in which the bulk of output is produced; it is much less affected than are the preceding measures by the many very small plants which account for so little of total employment or output. For clarity we shall call this measure the Florence-median, to distinguish it from the conventional median. It will be apparent that in determining the Florence-median more weight is given to larger plants than in the conventional median; the Florence-median is thus always greater than the conventional median. For the distribution of plants in 1963 the Florence-median is 480 employees (as compared with the conventional median of eighteen employees noted above).

Instead of considering the median ticket, as just described, one might take the arithmetic mean of all the tickets; this yields the measure proposed by Niehans,[12] and gives the largest answer of all (it is equivalent to a weighted average of plant-sizes in which each plant is weighted by the number of its employees). For the 1963 distribution of plants it yields an average of 1740 employees.[13]

With such very different candidates all claiming to measure the average size of plants, it will be understood that the 'average' here is a rather elusive matter – more so than in other contexts where the variability of the material is smaller. There is little point in debating the relative virtues of the various measures described above, and it seems better to accept that they are all valid but measure different aspects of the distribution. Yet the magnitude of the differences amongst these measures is such that one must conclude that a single summary figure will often not provide an adequate characterisation of the facts. A more radical approach therefore seems necessary and, again following Florence, we work below not merely in terms of an average expressed in a single figure, but supplement it with a measure of the prevalent range of sizes. It seems convenient to define that range so that it covers the central half of all employees (with a quarter of all employees below and a quarter above that range). Applying this approach to the size-distribution considered above, we find that in 1963 half of all employees in manufacturing were working in plants of between 120 and 1680 employees. It will be noticed that, of the various average measures quoted above, only the Florence-median, at 480 employees lies within that range.[14]

Whilst the central range is a measure that seems to be useful in an analysis of plant-sizes, it must be recognised that, if plant-sizes merely increased in scale over time but otherwise always followed a very regular pattern, all the measures mentioned above would move in sympathy. It would then matter less which measure was used, provided it was regarded only as an indicator of changes over time and provided the wide variability of the distribution was kept in mind. In particular, if the distribution of sizes followed precisely the log-normal form, a simple theoretical relation would hold between the five measures surveyed. They lie in the following ascending order of magnitude: mode, median, arithmetic mean, Florence-median, Niehans-measure; further, each of the last four is the same multiple of its predecessor in the sequence, and the ratio of the first two is the square of that multiple. It may be verified that the figures quoted above approximately satisfy these relations.[15]

CHANGES IN THE MEDIAN AND
RANGE OF PLANT-SIZES

Having sharpened our tools we can now use them to examine the changes that have occurred in the distribution of plant-sizes over time. Table 3.2 shows that plant-sizes have increased steadily since the 1930s, both the Florence-median and the central range having approximately doubled over this period. Before the war half of manufacturing employment was in plants employing between 70 and 750 employees, the Florence-median being at about 250 employees; by 1968 the corresponding range ran from 130 to 1600 employees, with a Florence-median of 480 employees.

Table 3.2. *Plant-sizes in manufacturing,[a] 1930–68*

No. of employees

	Florence-median[b]	Central range[c]	Width of central range	Variability[d]
1930	230[e]	..	..	..
1935	250	70–750	680	1·76
1948	340	100–1220	1120	1·89
1951	360	100–1300	1200	1·88
1954	390	120–1430	1310	1·88
1958	440	120–1650	1530	1·87
1963	480	120–1680	1560	1·84
1968	480	130–1600	1470	1·78

SOURCES: Censuses of Production, size distributions of establishments in all manufacturing industries.

[a] Estimates derived by graphical interpolation (using log-probability graph paper); unsatisfactory returns, when separately shown in the Census, have been treated as falling in the lowest quartile; adjustments for changes in industrial coverage made as indicated in appendix B.1.

[b] Half of all employees in plants below this size, and half above.

[c] The central 50 per cent of employees in plants of sizes between these limits.

[d] Standard deviation of the natural logarithm of size calculated from published group frequencies of the original distribution by the method of quantiles (see appendix C).

[e] Estimated average of 1·17 establishments per return (see note b to table 3.1) applied to the median size of return.

Two sorts of tendencies have therefore been affecting the distribution of plant-sizes. First, there has been the generally recognised tendency for typical plant-sizes to increase, which is adequately conveyed by the approximate doubling of the Florence-median; secondly, there has been an increase in the absolute range of prevailing sizes that account for half of employment in all manufacturing.[16] Some increase in that range is possibly to be expected, since sizes have risen in a general way, but it is perhaps surprising that it has risen in much the same proportion as the median. In absolute terms we have to note that in the economy of today there is wider scope for a variety of plant-sizes than there was a generation ago.

The emergence of larger plants has been accompanied by a reduction in the number of small plants; those employing ten or fewer employees having fallen from about 93,000 plants in 1930 to 35,000 plants in 1968 (as has been seen on pages 10–11 above), but the number of larger plants (those employing more than ten), which of course account for the bulk of total manufacturing employment, has hardly changed over this period, there being close to 50,000 such plants throughout. The continuing important contribution made by relatively small plants is, however, apparent, in that a quarter of all manufacturing employment in 1968 was to be found in some 70,000 plants with less than 130 employees, but the average number of employees in those plants was still only twenty-seven (compared with a corresponding average of thirteen in 1935).

It might be argued that these small plants are little more than the straggling survivors of an earlier age whose end cannot be far off; in certain trades, and to a certain extent, that must be true. But it has to be remembered that the period considered here is longer than a generation, and perhaps nearer two generations if reckoned by the active length of life of the head of a business. Considering manufacturing industry as a whole, the continued survival over such a long period of so many small plants, and the progressive widening of the prevalent range of plant-sizes, suggests rather that technological changes over this long period have probably improved productivity in plants of all sizes in various ways; if small plants have found competition difficult in some trades, other trades have remained or have opened where their relative advantages have proved of greater relevance. The facts that the range of sizes is greater and that it has been growing continually lead to the further conjecture that differences in the costs or economies of operating plants of varying sizes have perhaps narrowed on balance during this period.

Two examples may be quoted of relatively small technological changes which have had quite far-reaching effects on the viability of small plants and which may provide the reader with some intuitive support for this conjecture. Up to the 1930s the application of electric power to a machine in a factory normally involved a vast mechanical link. The advent of electricity had permitted smaller factories to benefit from power-driven machinery by installing their own electric motors; but motors were expensive, and within each factory there was to be found a central transmission shaft driven by that motor. Individual machines were driven by leather belts from that shaft, much as in earlier days when the central shaft was driven by steam or another source of power. A considerable overhead investment was therefore necessary before a plant could take advantage of electric power. Since that time the costs of electric motors have fallen to such an extent that it is normal today for each machine to be equipped with its individual small motor; the central transmission shaft has been abolished, with savings in energy transmission costs and benefits from more flexible plant-layouts. As Siemens had foreseen, in a remarkable passage written a hundred years ago, the development of electric power would 'in the course of time produce a revolution in our conditions of of work in favour of small-scale industry'.[17]

Plastics moulding machinery is another oft-quoted example of the way production can today be organised efficiently in smaller units. It is not merely that a moulding or forming in plastics can be turned out at lower raw-material and labour costs than a metal casting, but a whole gamut of ancillary departments (machining, polishing, finishing, etc.) can be dispensed with. A finished product can be turned out with a much reduced capital stock and a reduced number of specialised workers. The entrepreneur still has to fulfil his traditional role of assessing the potential market demand for the vast variety of special-ised mouldings that are required, and deciding whether he can offer a moulding in plastics which can compete in design or price with something similar, whether made in metal or by someone else already in plastics. Having taken his decision he can be in business, working efficiently and probably employing less resources than would have been required a generation ago. These examples are quoted without wishing to suggest that they epitomise what has been happening throughout industry, but rather to provide the reader with a counterweight to the general overemphasis given to technology's role in promoting large plants. It must be recognised that technological advances have worked to increase the opportunities for small plants as well as for large.[18]

While the range of prevalent sizes has increased in absolute terms, it will have been noticed that the relative variability of the distribution has remained fairly constant; this is shown in the final column of table 3.2, in which the relative variability of the distribution is measured by the standard deviation of the logarithms of size. A value of about 1·8 adequately characterises the whole period. The same result may be observed more simply by comparing the width of the central range with the Florence-median; this yields a ratio close to three throughout. If size were measured in terms of the logarithm of the number of employees we could say, technically, that only the location of the distribution had changed over time, not its dispersion.

The approximate constancy of the share of the hundred largest plants observed over time can be regarded as a consequence of the constant relative variability of the size-distribution; plant-sizes can be thought of as having all increased in much the same proportion, so that the proportionate share of the hundred largest has remained substantially unchanged. Changes in the total number of plants have, of course, also affected that share, but calculations suggest that very little – only a point or two - can be attributed to this source.[19]

VARIATIONS WITHIN AND BETWEEN INDUSTRIES

We have so far considered manufacturing as a whole; the reader may well wonder whether much of the variability that has been observed would disappear if that broad sector were divided into its constituent industry groups, each of which might be expected to be more homogeneous. To provide an indication of what happens on such a division, but without going into the fullest detail, an analysis was carried out based on a division of manufacturing into the fourteen major Industrial Orders distinguished by the Census. The approach of the preceding section was applied to the statistics for one pre-war year, 1935, and one post-war, year, 1963. The results are set out in table 3.3.

It will be seen that the largest plants are to be found in the vehicles group, where half of employment in 1963 was in plants lying in the central range of 1000–8680 employees; the next largest plants were in shipbuilding and in metal manufacture, in both of which they were roughly half that size. At the other end of the spectrum we find timber and leather, in which the central half of employment was in plants varying in size from about 30 to about 200 employees. An eightfold range in the sizes of plants in which the central half of employees in an Industrial Order are to be found can be taken as fairly typical; some Orders such as textiles are somewhat less variable than this, having a central range which is just under fivefold, and others such as shipbuilding have a fifteenfold range (no doubt because its products vary from sailing boats to tankers).

In short, even within individual Industrial Orders, plant-sizes cover an immense span, hardly different from that found on looking at manufacturing as a whole. In fact, in 1935 the relative variability within nearly half the industrial groupings (see the penultimate column in table 3.3) was somewhat greater than in total manufacturing. By 1963 a tendency can be detected for there to be a smaller variability within the separate Industrial Orders than in manufacturing as a whole (see the final column of the table), but that tendency is hardly very strong.

Table 3.3. *Plant-sizes by Industrial Order, 1935 and 1963[a]*

No. of employees

	Florence-median[b]		Central range[b]		Variability[b]	
	1935[c]	1963	1935[c]	1963	1935[c]	1963
Food, drink and tobacco	200	490	50–830	180–1290	2·14	1·44
Chemicals and allied industries	250	720	70–890	240–2130	1·85	1·61
Metal manufacture	560	1260	210–1490	400–3980	1·46	1·71
Engineering and electrical goods	590	800	170–2080	250–2580	1·87	1·74
Shipbuilding and marine engineering	730	1500	230–2310	390–5470	1·70	1·99
Vehicles	1250	2950	270–5700	1000–8680	2·25	1·60
Metal goods n.e.s.	160	250	60–440	80–860	1·55	1·80
Textiles	280	260	140–590	120–580	1·09	1·15
Leather, leather goods and fur	70	80	30–190	40–210	1·46	1·27
Clothing and footwear	160	170	50–450	70–410	1·57	1·27
Bricks, pottery, glass, cement, etc.	160	280	60–420	90–810	1·47	1·60
Timber and furniture	50	90	15–170	30–260	1·85	1·57
Paper, printing, publishing	200	290	60–640	100–850	1·74	1·60
Other manufacturing	300	400	80–1130	130–1320	1·97	1·74
Total manufacturing	250	480	70–750	120–1680	1·76	1·84

SOURCES: Censuses of Production, interpolated estimates using fitted theoretical log-normal distributions.

[a] Only two years compared to avoid an excess of numerical detail. The post-war calculations relate to 1963, having been completed before publication of the final volume of the 1968 Census. Results from the 1968 Census do not differ markedly except for shipbuilding, where large plants have become rather more important.

[b] See table 3.2 for definitions.

[c] Industries in 1935 reclassified for comparability with 1963, see appendix B.2.

Following the discussion in earlier sections we next consider whether prevalent sizes, and their range, have generally increased over time. It appears from table 3.3 that there is no very great uniformity. In textiles, leather and clothing – industries which have a more traditional character – the prevalent sizes of plants have hardly changed. But in food processing (including drink and tobacco), chemicals, metal manufacture, shipbuilding and vehicles – industries in which technology has made stronger advances – prevalent plant-sizes have increased two- or threefold. The lower limit of the central range has risen somewhat more rapidly than the upper limit in three of these industries (food, chemicals, vehicles); in other words it is more particularly in these industries that opportunities for smaller plants have diminished. Nevertheless the range of plant-sizes in absolute terms has increased over time in all Industrial Orders with the exception of the three more traditional industries mentioned (textiles, leather and clothing).

The relative variability of plant-sizes has generally not changed very

Table 3.4. *Estimated shares of eight largest plants in employment,*
by Industrial Order, 1935 and 1963

Percentages

	1935	1963
Food, drink and tobacco	8	7
Chemicals and allied industries	15	9
Metal manufacture	11[a]	14
Engineering and electrical goods	11	6
Shipbuilding and marine engineering	29	32
Vehicles	22[a]	15[a]
Metal goods n.e.s.	4[a]	5
Textiles	3	4
Leather, leather goods and fur	6	7
Clothing and footwear	4	4
Bricks, pottery, glass, cement, etc.	6	8
Timber and furniture	3	4
Paper, printing, publishing	7	6
Other manufacturing	18[a]	13
Average of total manufacturing[b]	10	8

SOURCES: Censuses of Production.

[a] Approximate estimates because of the re-grouping of the Census distributions for 1935 (see appendix B.2); derived from the published frequency distributions by interpolation, and sometimes extrapolation.

[b] Weighted by employment in 1963. .

much (see the last two columns of the table), apart from two Orders – vehicles, and food, drink and tobacco – where a strong decline in relative variability combined with a strong rise in median-size may be taken as an unequivocal indication of the operation of scale-economies.

Concomitant with the rise in aggregate concentration, there has been a general growth in the concentration of individual industries, which we examined on pages 16–21 above on the basis of earlier studies. We may now ask, returning to an earlier theme of this chapter, whether the changes in the distribution of *plant*-sizes within each industry have been responsible for the rise in the concentration of activities within the leading *firms* of each industry. To this end, the share in employment of the eight largest plants has been estimated for each of the fourteen major Industrial Orders in 1935 and 1963.[20] The results set out in table 3.4 show that over these thirty years the shares of the largest plants have hardly altered, and not in any systematic way. The substantial differences in the shares of the largest plants amongst industries that existed in 1935 have more or less remained unchanged. Some industries show small rises in the share of the largest plants, others show small falls; the weighted average share of employment in the hands of the eight largest plants declined from 10 to 8 per cent. It seems clear enough that at this level of aggregation changes in the distribution of plant-sizes had very little to do with the general tendency for the leading firms within each industry to account for a rising proportion of that industry's activity.

It appears from these comparisons that the conclusions reached in the preceding sections based on manufacturing as a whole cannot be taken as applying precisely in all industries. Nevertheless, in broad terms, we have found no reason for altering those conclusions; that is, it still appears that a great variety of plant-sizes is to be found within each industrial group, that prevalent sizes of plants and their absolute size-range have increased in the last generation, that the relative variability has remained fairly constant, and that the shares of the largest plants – in contrast to the shares of the largest firms – have not shown any upward trend. It does not follow that plant-economies of scale are irrelevant in deciding what is the appropriate size of plant to set up in a particular trade, but it seems to be true that changes in such economies have not been particularly relevant in explaining the general rise in concentration.

The division of manufacturing into separate industrial groups can, of course, be taken much further than has been done here. But perhaps there is no need to do so for the reader to accept that, unless the sub-division is pressed to extremes, an immense variety of plant-sizes will be found in almost every trade, and larger plant-sizes have generally made only a limited contribution to the rise in concentration.[21]

This great variety of plant-sizes arises partly from the evolution of small specialist suppliers able efficiently to provide component parts or specialist services to a wide variety of trades, and partly from the great variety of consumers' demands. Some consumers – whether of final or intermediate goods – are often prepared to pay a premium to have a variant of some basic commodity that meets more closely their particular requirements; others are satisfied with a variant that is less durable, and which is made 'cheaply' or even shoddily. Thus, even in trades where there is scope for the mass-production of a commodity in very large plants, generally there are also to be found smaller plants prepared to supply variants of that commodity, whether of higher or lower quality (reflected in higher or lower prices) than is available from the large-scale producers.

If this is taken into consideration it is clear that the idea of a 'technical optimum' size of plant for any industry or product is not clear-cut. Perhaps there is a certain sense in which those large plants producing the standard quality of a commodity may be said to represent the 'technical optimum size' or 'minimum efficient scale', and it is interesting to have estimates of the fraction of the market that can be supplied by such plants. Estimates of this type, based on the views of businessmen or engineers, have been compiled for a number of trades in several recent studies.[22] But simply because such a plant produces, say, a third of an industry's output, it does not follow that the total requirements from that industry could be produced by three plants in a way that is efficient from the point of view of the economy as a whole. A given number of items of standardised qualities could no doubt be produced in this way at least cost to the producing industry, but economic policy requires that other important aspects be taken into account: the market's demand for specialised varieties, the role of distribution costs, and – perhaps most important – the need for an industrial structure that can respond rapidly to changes in demands and in technology. Calculations based on technical optima alone have not much to teach us from that broader point of view.[23]

From that broader point of view it seems better to think in terms of the need for a balanced size-structure for each industry, in which there are simultaneously to be found some plants producing standardised qualities on a large scale and other plants working on a smaller scale to meet specialised demands. This is an unhappily vague prescription. Perhaps a much deeper study might show the optimal range of sizes appropriate to particular stages and circumstances of an economy's development, such that, if the range were smaller the economy would suffer because, for example, individual demands were not being met; and if the range were larger the economy would suffer because of the cost of excessive variety. But that raises much more difficult issues, which appear to be beyond the scope of empirical studies at present, and are certainly beyond the intended scope of this chapter; they will however be touched upon again (in chapter 6 below), when we compare prevalent sizes of enterprises and plants between countries.[24]

THE NEED TO CONSIDER OTHER FACTORS AFFECTING CONCENTRATION

It is time to draw together the various strands that have been developed in this chapter. Our object was to investigate whether changes in plant-sizes resulting from increased economies of scale in production could have made a substantial contribution to the rise in aggregate business concentration. We found that typical plant-sizes measured in terms of the number of employees have doubled in a general way in the past forty years; in the same period the absolute range of prevalent sizes has also doubled. The fact that an ever-greater absolute range of sizes of plant is able to exist suggests that plant-economies of scale are not of crucial significance for our problem. Increased standardisation and specialisation may lead to greater productivity over time with only relatively small changes in plant-sizes. In any closely defined trade a narrow practical range of optimal plant-sizes no doubt prevails; but, considering manufacturing as a whole, or broad industrial groups such as engineering or food production, it is relevant that there is scope today for a wider absolute range of sizes than previously.

Though typical plant-sizes have increased in absolute terms, the relative importance of the largest plants (in relation to the remainder or to the 'average' plant) has not changed over the period examined. In the 1930s the hundred largest *plants* accounted for 11 per cent of manufacturing net output, and in 1968 – surprisingly enough – the proportion was still at that same level. But in the same period, as we have seen, the hundred largest *firms* had increased their share of net output from about 23 to 41 per cent. Closer examination of the post-war period suggests that, of the total rise in the concentration of firms, no more than about a tenth might be attributable to changes in plant-sizes. There is nothing to suggest that the particularly sharp post-war rise in enterprise-concentration is attributable to marked increases in plant-sizes.

In contrast to the popular view, then, we find that modern production technology offers little by way of explanation of increased concentration. We must therefore look to other factors.

CHAPTER 4

THE MULTI-PLANT FIRM AND ITS MARKET

I will rise now and go about the city in its markets, and
in the broad ways I will seek
Song of Solomon 3: 2

THE RISE OF THE MULTI-PLANT FIRM

It has been seen in the preceding chapter that increases in the sizes of
plants have not contributed much towards the great rise in the share
of the hundred largest firms in the economy; it follows, clearly, that it is
the increase in the number of plants owned by those firms that has
formed the means whereby aggregate concentration has risen. The task
of this chapter is to assess the extent of that rise in multi-plant operation
with the help of the available statistics, and to consider what sort of
changes in the economic system might account for it.

In more general terms, we have to consider changes in factors associated with economies of scale that determine the size of the *firm* rather
than the sizes of the *plants* owned by the firm. The topics to be discussed
in this chapter, after a preliminary consideration of the statistical facts
on the rise of large multi-plant manufacturing firms, are, first, whether
the desire for greater market power can be regarded as the dominant
motive explaining that rise; secondly, the part played by reductions
in transport and information costs in facilitating multi-plant operation;
thirdly, the role of advertising. These aspects all relate to the market
in which the individual firm operates and they have therefore been
grouped into a single chapter; financial and managerial aspects are
deferred to the succeeding chapter. It is a large subject to cover, even
if we confine ourselves to those aspects bearing on aggregate concentration, and while at many points it warrants deeper attention
than the resources of the present inquiry permit, it is hoped that the
calculations presented here – limited as they are – may go some way
towards permitting a rough assessment of the relative importance of
the various elements at work.

Statistics on multi-plant ownership are not very extensive, because
only in the Censuses since 1958 has information been collected both on
plants and on the enterprises which own them.[1] The recently organised
Central Register of Businesses may in future provide information more

Notes to this chapter will be found on pp. 243–56.

frequently on this aspect.[2] The main facts relating to large enterprises drawn from a recent analysis of the Register are as follows. In 1972 the hundred largest manufacturing enterprises had an average of 31,000 employees per enterprise spread over an average of seventy-two plants per enterprise; each such plant thus had an average of 430 employees. Only plants engaged in manufacturing and only those situated in this country are covered by these figures (and similarly by the Census); thus, since many giant manufacturing enterprises also have interests outside manufacturing (in retailing, transport, etc.) and also own establishments abroad, their total size will be somewhat greater – perhaps a quarter as great again or, say, an average of nearly 40,000 employees per enterprise.[3] In what follows, however, we shall be relying on Census statistics and thus concerned only with manufacturing plants in this country.

As we go down the size-range and look at enterprises below the hundred largest, the number of plants per enterprise falls off fairly rapidly. Thus, looking at the fuller information available from the Census for 1968, we find the hundred largest enterprises then owned an average of fifty-one plants per enterprise; the thousandth largest enterprise owned only four or five plants; and the smallest 90 per cent of all manufacturing enterprises, those with under a hundred employees, perhaps not surprisingly, owned generally only a single plant each – the average for this group being 1·05 plants per enterprise. However, the median manufacturing enterprise defined as in the preceding chapter is perhaps the best single summary measure of the extent of multi-plant operation in manufacturing as a whole, and that enterprise owned as many as twenty plants in 1968.

The size of the average plant owned by the hundred largest enterprises can be described as being only moderate, with hardly more than some 400 employees. Since there is a certain disparity in plant-sizes, it is clear that many plants owned by giant firms will be rather smaller than this and may employ, say, only a hundred persons; such smallish plants are owned more frequently by the largest enterprises classified in such diverse trades as the manufacture of machine tools and gauges, of women's outerwear, of bricks and of animal feeding stuffs.[4] If we consider the hundred largest manufacturing plants in the whole economy a much larger size is found – an average of nearly 8000 employees in 1968; but that is still very much below the 31,000 persons employed on average by the hundred largest enterprises. One cannot know on the basis of Census statistics to what extent the hundred largest plants were owned by the hundred largest enterprises.

It is apparent from the few figures that have been mentioned that it is far from the truth to typify the giant enterprise of today as consisting

Table 4.1. *The hundred largest enterprises,[a] 1958–72:*
numbers of plants owned and average employment

	Plants per enterprise[b] (averages)	Average employment	
		Per plant	Per enterprise
1958[c]	27	750	20,300
1963	40	620	24,700
1968	52	520	27,200
1972[d]	72	430	31,180

SOURCES: Interpolated from Censuses of Production;
1972 – from Central Production Register.

[a] Ranked by size of employment.

[b] Changes in Census procedures could have led to more separate plants being identified in later years, but there was also a reverse tendency (see note 9 on p. 237) and the net distortion is unlikely to be serious.

[c] This was the first Census which systematically compiled information on enterprises; it is possible therefore that not all subsidiary establishments were identified.

[d] 'Local units' taken as equivalent to 'establishments' in the Censuses prior to 1970 (see also appendix B.3).

of a few giant plants administered from a central office; one should rather think of the typical giant enterprise as owning a host of plants, most of which are only of medium or small size, though in some cases there may be a 'nucleus' of a few very large plants.

Even in the relatively short period since 1958 for which we have satisfactory information, the changes in the extent of multi-plant operation by these giant enterprises have been extraordinarily great. From table 4.1 it is seen that the number of plants owned by the typical giant enterprise has almost tripled in fourteen years and, perhaps more surprisingly, in the same period the average employment per plant has *fallen* by nearly a half. However, allowing for a rise in labour productivity, the net output per plant has probably declined only slightly.[5]

Given the great number of acquisitions during this period, it is likely that the fall in the calculated average employment per plant is mainly to be attributed to the giant firms' acquisitions of other firms which owned smaller plants, rather than to a policy of building new smaller plants to replace existing larger plants. Nevertheless, it is important to note that these acquisitions and mergers have not led to the formation of *plants* that are obviously larger than those owned by the hundred largest enterprises at the beginning of the period.

An alternative way of looking at the growth of the largest multi-plant enterprises in relation to the economy as a whole is set out in table 4.2. This table compares the changing number of firms accounting

Table 4.2. *Enterprises ranked by size accounting for quarters of total net output, and plants they own*

	Enterprises accounting for				
	First quarter	Second quarter	Third quarter	Fourth quarter	Median enterprise
	of net output				
	(Number of enterprises)				
1958	54	369	2,831	..	n.a.
1963	38	198	1,444	63,913	n.a.
1968	26	149	1,100	60,470	n.a.
	(Plants per enterprise)				
1958	33·8	9·4	2·7	..	5·7
1963	56·3	19·2	5·3	1·1	12·4
1968	92·3	32·1	6·6	1·1	20·1
	(Employees per plant)				
1958	850	480	250	32	360
1963	750	446	230	29	320
1968	670	340	240	34	270

SOURCES: For 1958: *Census 1963*, vol. 132, tables 13 and 14. For 1963 and 1968: *Census 1968*, vol. 158, tables 42 and 45.

Note: Values shown are derived by interpolation from the published figures.

for fixed shares of the economy over time, rather than (as hitherto) the changing share of a fixed number of firms. After ranking all enterprises in each year by the size of their net output, they were divided into four groups, each accounting for a quarter of total net output in manufacturing. It will be seen that in 1958 a quarter of all manufacturing net output was produced by the fifty-four largest enterprises and in 1968 by only twenty-six enterprises; in the former year those enterprises owned an average of 33·8 plants each, and in the latter year they owned nearly three times as many – an average of 92·3 plants each. Again we find that the average size of those plants in terms of employment has fallen, from 850 to 670 employees. If we consider the next group of enterprises (those accounting for the second quarter of output) there is a similar pattern: there are now fewer enterprises each owning a greater number of plants and there is a fall in the average size of those plants. It is only when we reach the smallest 'quartile' of enterprises that a mild rise in the sizes of their plants is to be observed. The number of plants owned by the median enterprise has risen from 5·7 to 20·1 in the period 1958–68 – a remarkable change in so short a period.

It is, of course, not to be denied that certain giant enterprises have achieved their stature because of the technical requirements of large plant-sizes, and that other giants have acquired small plants with the intention, one day, of amalgamating their outputs in larger plants. Neverthless, the general impression given by the figures we have been looking at is that the typical giant enterprise has progressively become one that owns an ever-greater multitude of plants and, far from specialising in the ownership of particularly large plants, the average size of its plants has tended to fall. This is consistent with the view advanced in the preceding chapter that purely plant-economies have not been the dominating element in promoting the growth of giant enterprises in recent years.[6] And that seems an important inference when we come to consider the implications for social policy towards 'big business' and towards mergers between large enterprises.

As we have seen, multi-plant operation has advanced at an extraordinarily rapid pace since 1958; this leads naturally to the question whether multi-plant enterprises are very much a recent innovation. Is there perhaps some date before which they were virtually unknown? Though no comprehensive statistics are available for earlier years, some conjectures are possible. It seems clear that already at the end of the last century public flotations of companies often involved the throwing together of many small firms in great mergers. The rapid evolution of the capital market at that stage encouraged a new type of 'company promoter' able to meet the needs of an emerging investing public – a public which was sometimes too credulous and too anxious to participate in ventures which were 'floated off', without the restrictions and safeguards subsequently developed under Companies Acts and Stock Exchange regulations. At that period, also, earlier cartel-like agreements for limiting competition were converted into 'trusts' or 'associations' owning the shares of the constituent members.[7] A survey of the period 1888–1912 lists twenty-nine large mergers, each of which on average involved twenty-one existing firms.[8] Many of these mergers were defensive, and some closures of plants were no doubt intended; one cannot therefore assume that the merged firms continued to operate with quite that many plants. Nevertheless it is apparent that already at the turn of the century the multi-plant firm was an accepted part of the economic scene, but whether the hundred largest enterprises then had an average of twenty plants each or, say, only ten plants each, cannot now be known.

Large mergers in the inter-war period generally involved a smaller number of constituent firms. Utton has listed twenty-seven important mergers and they involved an average of only six firms each. Possibly in this period each constituent firm already owned a number of plants before the merger.

Speaking broadly, then, it would appear that there has been a gradual evolution in multi-plant working since the end of the last century; one cannot point to any particular moment when multi-plant ownership suddenly became a new characteristic of the largest firms. It would obviously also be mistaken to regard multi-plant working as a very recent phenomenon, but it is apparent that there has been a marked acceleration since 1958.

Whether the economies arising from multi-plant operation are of any significance has been questioned by Bain in the course of a much quoted study of barriers to competition in the United States. A preliminary comment seems in order. He suggested that the economies to a 'multi-plant firm over the single-plant firm' where they could be estimated were generally small, probably averaging under 2 per cent of unit costs (Bain, 1956, p. 87). This conclusion was based on posing business 'executives' with questions such as: 'Are there evident reductions of *production* cost attainable by a firm through growing to a size where it operates several plants of efficient size? Of *distribution* cost? If so, how large, in terms of overall output capacity, would the firm need to become to attain maximum efficiency? How much lower costs could it then attain than an efficient single-plant firm?' (ibid. pp. 225-6). But one may wonder whether a business man can give satisfactory answers to questions which arise only rarely in practice in the day-to-day running of his business, and which, when they arise, do so not as issues of general principle, but as urgent problems in which precise cost advantages are not in the forefront. For example, the demand for a firm's products has risen and can no longer be supplied from the existing site. Does it move to a larger site, or is another plant to be acquired elsewhere? A questionnaire addressed to a general cross-section sample of firms must be expected to yield disappointing results. If firms were chosen with recent substantial experience in multi-plant operation and the questions were addressed to a high-level decision-maker, one might hope for more useful results; but even so, one may wonder whether every successful entrepreneur can rationalise and verbalise the reasons for complex decisions, which may involve large elements of judgement as much as systematic calculation. And he may be tempted to give conservative underestimates of the gains, rather than to risk an overstatement. Further, it is sufficient explanation for the growth of multi-plant firms that economies of multi-plant operation exist in particular types of business; high economies over all types of business are not required. Indeed Bain warns the reader in connection with the proportion of firms showing multi-plant economies that 'it would of course be hazardous to project [from his study]' (ibid. p. 87), but this warning has not always been taken sufficiently seriously by those who have quoted his results.[9]

There are undoubtedly many factors contributing to the growth of multi-plant firms and one must be careful not to over-simplify in assessing their relative importance. Thus, we have already seen in chapter 2 how the cumulative growth-patterns of firms can lead to the systematic emergence of a few giant firms, without there being any economies of scale to motivate that growth; the emergence of vast multi-plant firms may form part of that same process. Even if identifiable economies of scale are involved – such as the financial economies treated in the next chapter – one may question whether they always represent net social economies as well as private economies. But it must not be supposed that all the relevant factors leading to multi-plant working are of the kind which do not lead to any real social advantages. The nature of the real advantages gained by a multi-plant business were adumbrated by Robertson fifty years ago in a memorable passage: 'To segregate problems of technique from problems of finance, to deal in large figures with buyers and sellers and transport agencies and banks, to be free to shake one's wings and scan wide horizons and harbour deep designs – these are mighty weapons in the competitive struggle, *even though the actual physical work of production is best carried out in establishments of modester dimensions*. It is the economies of large-scale government rather than of large-scale technique which dictate the size of the modern business unit'.[10] Or, as it was put at about the same time by Gifford, the head of American Telephone and Telegraph, those at the head of modern large businesses must be not 'captains of industry, but statesmen of industry', able to assess new demands, and able to commit large resources to meet them.[11] What are often regarded as very 'modern' tendencies in business and financial organisation have thus been apparent for many decades, and have been recognised as part of the natural evolution of business organisation in a world of ever-widening horizons. Since then these tendencies have moved far ahead, as is clear from the statistics we have examined. Our task in what follows is to elucidate as precisely as we can the nature and contribution of some of the determining factors.

MARKET POWER

The desire to acquire some degree of market power, and perhaps to establish a monopoly position, is certainly the first motive that will spring to the reader's mind in considering reasons for the growth of multi-plant firms. Many of the well known and important mergers in Britain at the turn of the century, such as the Salt Union or that between the Associated and the British Portland Cement Manufacturers, were openly arranged to monopolise particular trades.[12] Periods of falling demand, with consequential excess capacity and 'cut-throat' price competition, provided an obvious stimulus for mergers of this kind. In the United States at that time mergers were similarly motivated but, following the early antitrust legislation, American mergers in the inter-war period seem to have been directed to the achievement more of an oligopolistic than a narrowly defined monopolistic position. In the absence of such legislation in Britain many inter-war mergers continued to be of a monopolising type, though (as noted in the preceding section) the typical large merger no longer involved the massive number of individual firms that it had done at the turn of the century.[13] In the past two decades the rise in diversified or 'conglomerate' mergers has attracted much attention; nevertheless, of the larger British mergers taking place during the period 1954–73, 70–80 per cent of the value of assets transferred related to mergers of the horizontal type, that is to firms engaged in broadly the same industrial group.[14]

Higher concentration, it has often been said, may be more a consequence of a rise in the optimum size of firm, due to operating or other economies, than of a desire for monopoly-like gains. The balance of views on these matters has altered over time, perhaps reflecting the gradual upward drift in the general level of concentration. At the beginning of the century the sizes of the largest firms and the general level of concentration were still moderate; and, despite the number of ostensibly monopolistic amalgamations, the power of actual or potential competition could still be considered to provide an ultimate natural safeguard, perhaps greater in Britain than in other industrial countries. Many examples are to be found in historical studies of particular trades where associations or mergers were organised for the purpose of maintaining prices, only to find that within two or three years outside firms had entered the scene, or foreign competition had increased, so that very little was achieved. The relative absence of protective tariffs in Britain, the small size of the country and its low transport costs were frequently cited as contributing to the difficulty of maintaining a monopolistic advantage for very long.[15]

This was generally the position until the early 1930s; political and business opinion then became less hostile to combinations and cartels following the intense competition – both domestic and international – which was characteristic of those years. The Import Duties Act of 1932 may be regarded as a watershed, and many cartels – again both domestic and international – and 'rationalisation' schemes were formed under its shelter (for example, the cartelisation of the iron and steel industry and its supervision by the official Import Duties Advisory Committee). The predominant motive in these schemes was protective, and followed the collapse of the international free trade economy. Monopolisation increased further during the Second World War and its immediate aftermath, when many came to accept that 'monopoly' was the appropriate form of large-scale industrial organisation to face the economic problems of the post-war world. The 1948 Monopolies and Restrictive Practices Act and the Restrictive Trade Practices Act of 1956, however, represented a change in the direction of official policy. Monopoly was not prohibited, but became subject to control if there was an adverse report by the Monopolies Commission. In the 1956 Act cartels were presumed to be against the public interest and were prohibited unless approved by the Restrictive Practices Court.

It might be expected that one of the consequences of the 1956 Act would be that firms previously bound together by trading agreements (relating to such things as prices, discount rates and other conditions of sale) would be tempted to merge. This would raise the apparent level of concentration, but might make rather less change in economic reality than in its appearance. There is some evidence that this happened. A recent study has drawn attention to the abandonment by 1966 of some 2000 restrictive agreements, forming the overwhelming majority of those registered under the 1956 Act; but it was also shown that the overt degree of concentration (as measured from Census statistics) rose more rapidly in the ensuing decade for those products in which agreements had been terminated than for other products not subject to agreements.[16]

In the light of these developments it might be expected that multi-plant operation and concentration are closely related. But in fact that relation is not at all simple and in some ways contrary to expectation; the relevant statistical evidence may be summarised as follows.

For 1951 – the first year for which multi-plant operation and concentration can be compared in Britain – the earlier study by Evely and Little at the National Institute established that there was a negligible correlation across industries between the level of concentration and the number of plants owned by the three leading firms. The correlation was slightly (but not significantly) negative, at −0·02; in other words, of the sample of industries investigated, those that were more concentrated had, if anything, slightly fewer plants operated by their leading firms than those industries that were less concentrated (Evely and Little, 1960, p. 334). This finding, surprising as it may seem, is consistent with the view that the extent of multi-plant operation – at least at that time – was determined not by monopolistic motivations, but rather by such factors as the availability of industrial sites, and the relative importance of transport costs of raw materials and outputs. Considering a related measure of the extent of multi-plant operation, namely, the average number of plants owned by all firms in the industry (rather than just by the three leading firms as previously),

Evely and Little concluded that one may 'dismiss variations in the number of plants per business unit as a rather unimportant part of any explanation of concentration' (ibid. p. 111).[17]

Despite the great number of mergers since 1951, the Census results for 1968 show much the same pattern. We again found a very similar negligible correlation, this time of −0·01, between the number of plants operated by the five leading firms in an industry and the level of employment-concentration in that industry.[18] It is of interest that Professor Scherer has also reported a small negative correlation, of −0·10, for the United States in 1963.[19] Must we then reject (as Scherer has suggested) the obvious and 'conventional wisdom' that there is a systematic tendency for concentration to be higher where there is more multi-plant operation?[20]

The correct answer would appear to be: not really. For if we examine changes over time in the concentration of a broad sample of industries, we find concentration has risen more rapidly in those industries where multi-plant operation by leading firms has risen more rapidly (we found a correlation of +0·50 for changes in the period 1958–68 in the United Kingdom).[21] The implication is that increased multi-plant operation does indeed tend to increase concentration, but this is a mild effect, superimposed upon stronger factors unrelated to concentration which continue to dominate variations in multi-plant working as amongst industries. It is the changes in such factors that must next be considered.

COSTS OF TRANSPORT AND COMMUNICATION

Amongst the many factors that have altered the geographical dispersion and the centralisation of control of industry, changes in transport and communication costs have a particular relevance in that they determine both the size and the number of plants that can efficiently be controlled from a single centre. The object of this section is to trace the main features of these developments and to assess their importance. At a general level it is obvious that the telephone, the telex machine, the motorway and the aeroplane – to mention the most familiar of modern techniques of communication – have in this generation facilitated and extended the control by a head office of distant plants as much as the railway and the general post did in the last century. The structure of industry inevitably responds with some delay to such technical advances and to the progressive lowering of costs that follows their introduction; consequently it is difficult to trace a precise time-sequence of response to any particular development. Professor Chandler has attached particular importance to the railway system's early needs for new organisational methods to enable an essentially dispersed business to be centrally controlled, and that pattern of organisation 'provided industrialists with useful precedents for organisation building', which eventually led to the modern giant business with its multi-divisional structure.[22] Whether that view is entirely acceptable or not, it is clear that the great and continuing developments in transport and communications, taken as a whole, have had a pervasive influence on the long-term rise of multi-plant firms.

It is a familiar proposition that a lowering in the costs of transporting the products made by a plant leads to an extension of its market. In previous days this would naturally have led to a growth in the output of that plant, which in turn would lead to a fall in production costs and to yet further increases in the size of market supplied from that plant. But where the transport component in total costs remains high, instead of increasing the size of the original plant it is today often easier to reach a distant market by operating a number of dispersed plants in parallel, all sharing to a certain extent a common technology and all directed from a central office. Advantage is taken of lower transport costs from dispersed plants to dispersed markets; workers' travelling time and congestion are reduced; within each plant the span of control is smaller and problems of co-ordination are solved more easily; perhaps not of least importance is that labour relations tend to be better in smaller plants.[23] Managerial orders, managers and technical specialists can rapidly be sent to smaller dispersed plants as and when necessary. These modern dispersive tendencies have, at least to some extent, displaced the earlier tendencies of the industrialisation process, which brought ever-more men and machines under the roof of a single large factory. The growth of international businesses, owning plants in many countries, has of course been encouraged by the same forces.

Improvements in transport and communications, interacting with production economies, thus have complex and continually developing effects on the sizes and geographical dispersion of plants, and on the degree of concentration of their control. The advances in telephones, computers, planes and, more generally, those improvements affecting the transport of managers and the communication of their ideas (the transmission of sales orders, or technical queries to the appropriate department) seem recently to have been of greater consequence than advances that have lowered the costs of transporting goods; such a trend in relative costs would encourage enterprises to grow by increasing the number of their plants, while the sizes of those plants might decline.[24]

It is not, however, easy to quantify the impact of transport costs in some single figure, since it is not merely the freight costs per ton or per cubic foot that are relevant in limiting the size of the market, but also such aspects of the 'quality' of service as the time taken for delivery.[25] Even greater complexities attach to the assessment of the impact of improvements in communication. Much time has to be spent by a manufacturer in reaching agreement on the detailed specification of the item to be produced, the number of items to be made, their price and rate of delivery, as well as in any subsequent alterations in those terms; time has also to be spent in communications on the production side – in securing materials and tools, and in solving the associated problems of quality of supplies and delivery times as they arise with the help of suppliers and others outside the business.

A listing of these detailed, if apparently pedestrian, aspects of the organisation of production is sufficient to make it clear how very great has been the impact of the now-commonplace telephone and other modern communication methods in speeding up business life and in saving costly entrepreneurial time.[26] The full cost of doing things now done by telephone can hardly be compared with the cost of doing them before its advent, but, even if we look only at the changes in the bare out-of-pocket costs of long-distance telephone conversation, it will be appreciated that the brake which distance puts on the expansion of a business has been radically eased. The fact that the greater the distance the greater has been the fall in the cost of a telephone call is also significant. The cost of a telephone call from London to Glasgow, for example, fell by two-thirds (in real terms) in the twenty years to 1950 and by a half again in the following twenty years, that is to under a sixth of its cost forty years previously; that of a transatlantic call from London to New York fell by three-quarters in each of these twenty-year periods, that is to under a fifteenth of its cost forty years previously. To telephone New York from London in the 1970s costs hardly more than it did to telephone Glasgow in the 1930s.[27]

What has happened to the costs of transporting goods in these forty years? For goods sent by rail, summary figures of 'average receipts per ton–mile' of general merchandise suggest a substantial fall in real terms, but this fall, it may be inferred, reflects little more than the transfer to road transport of the more expensive loads, that is those involving shorter distances or smaller loads.[28] An index of rail tariff-rates would be more useful for our purpose, but tariffs cannot easily be compared over time, both because of their immense variety and because of the part played by individual negotiation, which results in considerable departures in practice from published tariffs. No general index number of tariff-rates has so far been compiled. For bulk commodities, such as coal, iron and steel, 'average receipts per ton–mile', may, however, be taken to reflect tariffs more closely, and average receipts for these commodities have moved in the last twenty years in step with the general price level. In real terms, therefore, it seems likely that freight costs by rail have remained fairly stable.

The producer has gained in the transport of his goods in this period by switching his goods from rail to road, and he has done so not because freight-rates per ton–mile are lower by road – they are in fact generally higher – but because of the element of convenience. Goods are moved from door to door, without trans-shipment delays, with less need for packaging safeguards, without the frustration of dealing with a vast railway organisation. While the average size of lorries has remained fairly stable, it is notable that the dispersion of sizes has increased: both small vans (under $1\frac{1}{2}$ tons) and large trucks (over 3 tons unladen, 7 tons payload) are increasing in numbers relative to those of medium size, so providing greater flexibility in meeting the needs of industry.[29] To summarise from the point of view of the manufacturer: the gains arising from developments in the transport of *goods* have been more in time-saving and general convenience than in costs, whereas the gains from developments in communicating *information* have been both in convenience and in costs.[30]

Against the background of these longer-term trends we may now examine, with the help of the Censuses of 1958 and 1968, the extent to which transport costs have recently affected the sizes of plants and the degree of multi-plant working. Over a period of only a decade perhaps not too much of these longer-term trends can be expected to be evident, but we might hope to observe some trace of their working. We consider first how the median-sizes of plants (measured by their employment, as in the preceding chapter) in a broad sample of seventy-six industries are related to the importance of transport costs (taken as a proportion of net output). In each of these years a mild negative association was observed: that is to say, in those industries in which transport costs were higher plant-sizes tended to be smaller. In 1958 the elasticity of plant-sizes with respect to transport costs was estimated at -0.35 (± 0.18).[31] It is again of some interest that in an international comparison of plant-sizes for twelve industries Professor Scherer was able to estimate an elasticity of very similar magnitude (about -0.29 (± 0.07) depending on which other factors are taken into account), though transport costs were measured in rather different ways in his study (Scherer, 1973, p. 142).[32] It may be inferred that in Britain in 1958 transport costs acted as a mild restraining force on the sizes of plants, and that the strength of that force operated in Britain much as elsewhere.

As a result of the reduction over time in the costs of transport and communications, it is to be expected that the restraining force of transport costs on the sizes of plants will become progressively weaker as time proceeds. This is confirmed by the Censuses for the decade 1958–68 that we are able to examine. A positive association was found (for the same sample of industries as examined above) between the changes in median plant-sizes and the importance of transport costs; the elasticity of the relation was estimated at +0·10 (±0·04);[33] that is to say, trades in which plant-sizes had previously been much restrained by heavy transport costs showed the greatest increase in plant-sizes.

The consequence of this offsetting movement was that by the end of the decade, in 1968, the elasticity of plant-sizes with respect to transport costs was only −0·25, having fallen from the value of −0·35 at the beginning of the decade (it is convenient to speak in terms of apparently precise figures, but the reader will have it in mind that these are estimates subject to substantial margins of error).[34] If a trend at that rate were to continue it appears that the elasticity would approach zero by the end of the century; transport costs would at that point become a negligible factor in determining the sizes of plants. Such an extrapolation is hardly justified on the basis of our limited and imprecise calculations; nevertheless, in many trades it is already apparent that transport costs are becoming irrelevant in determining plant-sizes, and it is of interest that there is a certain degree of statistical confirmation for this as a general tendency.

We turn next to examine the changing influence of transport costs on multi-plant working in recent years. Table 4.3 summarises the importance of transport costs for each of the main Industrial Orders and the average number of plants per firm (for firms with over a hundred employees) in 1958 and 1968. All manufacturing plants belonging to a firm are considered, even if some are in industries outside the Order in which the firm is classified (for example, a plant making boxes for a firm predominantly manufacturing food is included in this analysis as a 'food' plant). This is desirable if we are to study the full scale of multi-plant working. The highest degree of multi-plant working in 1968 was in the Industrial Order covering bricks, pottery, glass and cement, where transport costs were by far the heaviest; the second highest degree of multi-plant working was in the Order covering food, drink and tobacco, where transport costs were the second heaviest. Further, it is precisely in these two Orders that the rise in multi-plant working was greatest over the decade. The remaining Orders do not exhibit so close a relation, but, since factors apart from transport obviously affect the degree of multi-plant working, this does not cause surprise – it is only where transport costs are particularly onerous that we may expect their effects to be seen in a simple analysis such as the present one.

The elasticity of the number of plants per enterprise with respect

Table 4.3. *Transport costs and multi-plant working by Industrial Order, 1958–68*

	Transport costs[a]/net output[b] in 1963	Plants per enterprise[c]	
		1958[d]	1968
	(%)		
Food, drink and tobacco	*13·2*	3·2	5·2
Chemicals and allied industries	*6·8*	2·9	4·5
Metal manufacturing	*6·6*	3·3	4·1[e]
Engineering and electrical goods	*2·6*	2·2	3·7
Shipbuilding and marine engineering	*1·2*	2·2	3·4
Vehicles	*2·1*	2·8	4·3
Metal goods n.e.s.	*4·9*	2·0	2·8
Textiles	*3·2*	2·4	3·9
Leather, leather goods and fur	*4·3*	1·7	2·2
Clothing and footwear	*2·3*	1·9	2·6
Bricks, pottery, glass, cement, etc.	*15·2*	3·2	7·4
Timber and furniture	*8·8*	2·0	2·8
Paper, printing, publishing	*5·9*	2·0	3·3
Other manufacturing	*4·4*	2·1	3·1
Total manufacturing	*5·6*	·2·4	3·7

SOURCES: Transport costs: *Census 1963*, vol. 131, table 10; net output: *Census 1963*, vol. 131, table 1; plants per enterprise 1958: *Census 1963*, vol. 132, table 15; plants per enterprise 1968: *Census 1968*, vol. 158, table 46.

[a] Relates only to firms employing twenty-five or more.
[b] Allowance is made for the proportion of persons in small firms.
[c] For private enterprises employing a hundred or more.
[d] Industry groups amalgamated into Industrial Orders.
[e] Excludes nationalised iron and steel.

to transport costs, as estimated from simple regressions of these figures, was 0·20 (±0·09) in 1958 rising to 0·39 (±0·11) in 1968.[35] There is thus a mild positive dependence, increasing over time at a substantial (and statistically significant) rate,[36] and that increasing tendency is of particular relevance to the main theme of this chapter.

It is however worth pausing a moment to make two observations. First, there is an apparently reassuring similarity between the average of our estimated elasticities for 1958 and 1968 and that derived by Professor Scherer in his international comparisons of multi-plant working – his estimate for 1970 is in the region of 0·30 (±0·08) (Scherer, 1974, p. 133).[37]

Secondly, it is of interest to combine the present results relating to the effects of transport costs on multi-plant working with our preceding results relating to the effects of transport costs on plant-size, so deriving the effect of transport costs on firm-size. For a particular year these two sets of results imply that firms in industries with heavier transport costs have smaller plants, but this is offset by their having more plants per firm. The two elasticities concerned (of plant-size and of plants per firm) are of roughly the same order of magnitude but of opposite sign (if we take the average of the results for 1958 and 1968, they are -0.3 and $+0.3$ respectively), with the consequence that the size of firm is virtually independent of transport costs. If we consider changes over time, however, a quite different result emerges: industries with heavier transport costs show a relative increase in plant-size (an increase in elasticity of about $+0.1$ per decade), which reinforces the relative increase in the degree of multi-plant working (an increase in elasticity of about $+0.2$ per decade). The consequence is that the sizes of firms have in this period increased particularly rapidly in those industries with heavy transport costs.

The above paragraphs summarise the broad tendencies to be detected in the Census figures for recent years and they might be thought to provide grounds or justification for the growth of multi-plant firms. However, that justification must be judged to be of a very limited degree for the following reason. The elasticities with respect to transport costs that have emerged from our calculations (and which seem to conform with other international comparisons) are in the region of only a quarter or a third. On the other hand, the increase in multi-plant working by giant firms has been at a very fast rate (an approximate doubling in a decade, as we saw at the beginning of this chapter); with such low elasticities it would need an unduly great change in the significance of transport costs if they were to form an important part of the explanation (if the elasticity was a third, transport costs would have to alter by a factor of eight to bring about a doubling in the effect).

As has been emphasised, improvements in convenience in both communication and transport may well have been more important than reductions in money costs, but the convenience element cannot be brought into the calculations – our ideas of changes in their significance are inevitably impressionistic. Estimates of elasticities based on money costs alone are thus bound to be to some extent imperfect, but they seem unlikely to be sufficiently in error to alter our central conclusions, which may be summarised as follows: that while improvements in transport and communications have indeed played an observable and sigi.ificant part in the recent general growth of multi-plant operation, that part was not a dominant one as far as the growth of giant companies is concerned.[38]

ADVERTISING

One of the long-term accompaniments of the fall in communication costs has been the rise of advertising – that essential tool of modern marketing methods, often regarded as typifying scale-economies in marketing and their consequences. 'That advertising promotes the concentration of economic power cannot reasonably be doubted', asserted Kaldor some thirty years ago;[39] yet, as we shall see, the evidence for that proposition is by no means clear. The subject has interested economists for many decades and has aroused much controversy; the object of this section, whilst avoiding controversial territory as far as possible, is to consider the mechanism through which advertising has promoted the evolution of large firms, and to examine with the help of recent Census statistics whether the sizes of firms and industrial concentration continue to be related to the level of advertising.[40]

By way of background we may begin by restating briefly the positive role of advertising. Through posters and newspapers in the last century (and even earlier), and through television most recently and most powerfully, advertising has acquainted and tempted the mass of consumers with new goods, or new varieties of old goods, before they have been sampled in concrete form. The main features of advertising are that it permits a manufacturer to reach a large and distant market, and to do so rapidly; a modern firm, organised to develop new varieties frequently and equipped to distribute them in large quantities rapidly to distant and dispersed markets, is able to use business methods that were previously not available. The advances in advertising have complemented other advances, in transport (motorways, for example), storage (frozen foods) and communications generally in promoting the growth of the modern mass-marketing enterprise.

The cost of advertising often seems great, unless account is taken of the time of skilled persons that would otherwise be absorbed in the process of selling. The small craftsman spends much of his costly time in agreeing a precise specification and a price with his customer. But the large-scale manufacturer prefers to devote his resources to 'market research', that is to searching for a standardised specification of qualities which, he judges, will appeal with the help of advertising to the greatest number, and which he can then produce at a low cost and sell on a large scale. It is those commodities that are happily consumed in standardised form by the great mass of consumers, such as manufactured foods or tobacco, that gain most from advertisements broadcast indiscriminately into every home; in other words, it is where the costs of an advertisement per consumer reached are low that the size of the representative firm has risen most in consequence of advertising. For commodities not bought by the mass of consumers, and where there is no specialised advertising medium specifically directed to purchasers of those commodities (such as a trade magazine), the structure of the trade will have been little affected by the advent of modern advertising methods.

The source of the advantage that advertising confers on larger firms has generally been attributed to economies of scale that arise in producing the advertisement, and there has been much debate as to whether small firms are in some sense unfairly affected. Advertising costs are like printing costs generally: setting-up costs are high, but running-off costs are low. Tariffs for newspaper advertisements are therefore generally such that total costs are higher for a newspaper with a greater circulation, but the costs per person reached are lower. Advertising (as compared with a situation in which it was prohibited) thus confers an advantage on firms in proportion to the size of market they wish to reach. It has also been said that larger firms enjoy an advantage since they can afford larger advertisements which cost less per column–inch than smaller advertisements, and that a large 'boldly displayed' advertisement attracts proportionately more attention than a small advertisement, to the disadvantage of the small businessman (Marshall, 1923, p. 307). But more recent, if limited, market research tests suggest, on the contrary, that a full-page advertisement has less than double the pulling power of a half-page advertisement.[41] The advantage to the larger firms is thus not quite as compelling as previously thought.

Advertising by means of television has grown immensely, though it still accounts (in 1974) for only about a quarter of all United Kingdom advertising expenditure.[42] It is of interest to consider how manufacturers of various sizes are affected by the very costly advertising charges on television, which may reach thousands of pounds a minute. The rates per minute vary according to the number of persons viewing and are, of course, highest in peak-viewing periods. One naturally asks whether, if reckoned per person viewing, the rates are the same at all times, or perhaps even decline at peak periods (in the same way as suggested above for newspapers of greater circulation). It appears from the limited studies carried out that there have been some notable changes in the structure of tariff-rates. In the early 1950s in the United States the costs reckoned per person viewing were lower in peak-viewing periods. It was consequently argued at that time that, since only large firms could afford to advertise at viewing-peaks, large firms were at an advantage as compared with smaller firms, and they also gained from heavy discounts that were offered for large repeat contracts (these matters were in issue before the American courts in anti-merger proceedings).[43] By the late

1960s, perhaps as a result of increases in demand for advertising at peak periods, it was suggested that costs per person viewing were approximately the same at all hours in the United States. Nevertheless, large firms having the resources to buy time at viewing-peaks could still be at an advantage, since it is more effective to reach persons at peak-viewing times when they are more relaxed.

The situation is an evolving one, partly because viewing habits change (greater ownership of television sets), and perhaps also because viewers' reactions to advertising messages change; partly because the range of commodities that producers think they can usefully advertise changes as the practice of branding commodities spreads. The structure of rates is thus a matter of supply and demand, and there is no sound reason why advertising rates per minute at viewing-peaks when, say, ten million persons are viewing, should not exceed ten times the rate for periods when only a million persons are viewing. The rates for reaching the additional nine million may be higher per person than would be necessary in order to reach only the first million, but may yet be lower than the costs of some other method of reaching them (for example, personal canvassing).

The costs of transmitting an advertisement on commercial television in Britain in the early 1970s were, in fact, such that the tariff-rates per viewer reached were about a third *higher* at viewing-peaks than at off-peak hours; and they were higher (per viewer) for the large and wealthy London region than for a smaller and less wealthy region such as the East of England. The capital costs of producing the advertisement have also to be spread over the number of viewers and offset in part the higher transmission charges per viewer at peaks. A precise calculation of this element is not possible,[44] but it seems likely that it accounts only to a small extent for the higher transmission charges per viewer that apply at peak hours. The main reason for higher peak charges per viewer thus appears to be the demand by large advertisers for the widest possible audience, including those at work during the day who cannot be reached at off-peak times, and the desire to reach them when they are in a relaxed and impressionable mood. Advertisers are prepared to meet the higher tariff-charges demanded in order to achieve these ends. There is thus no prima facie advantage to a large advertiser, as previously thought, in the structure of tariff-rates. A small manufacturer who wishes to advertise on television can do so if he wishes to reach only a small market by advertising at off-peak times and to a smaller regional audience; he pays less in transmission charges per viewer than a large advertiser, and appears not to be at any disadvantage in his transmission costs. But the capital costs of producing an advertisement, at least hitherto, will have been a substantial obstacle. This is changing as a result of the development of video-tape recorders, which have substantially cut production costs, and may lead to an increase in advertising by smaller – if not the very smallest – firms.[45]

The advantage which advertising confers upon big business thus lies not in a tariff-structure differentially favouring a very large, as compared with a moderately large, readership or viewership (on which emphasis was placed in earlier writings), but rather:

(i) in the saving in selling costs by those firms large enough to advertise over those firms selling on too small a scale to warrant any advertising at all;

(ii) in a complementarity between large-scale marketing and large-scale production, that is to say in the entrepreneur's knowledge of marketing and production costs, and his skill in choosing that combination of characteristics which, because he is able to appeal to a large market, yields the greatest total profit (but not necessarily the greatest unit profit margin).

For the smallest producer the costs of advertising may always be too great, but this is not necessarily unfair; he continues to survive in those trades in which the market is small and in which advertising is largely irrelevant.

The optimum scale of firm required by its selling activities is ignored by some writers, who concern themselves only with the resources absorbed by the production process.[46] Yet a certain proportion of the nation's resources must be absorbed in bringing goods from the factory door to the consumer, and in passing through the important selection procedures (wholesalers, agents, retailers) that comprise the distribution and sales system, in which advertising has its part. In some trades the benefits derived from branding and from modern advertising methods have been the prime factor leading to an expansion in firm-size, while changes in production costs considered by themselves (that is apart from selling costs) may not have required any expansion; in such trades plants remain small and heavy advertising is associated with multi-plant operation. In other trades production costs may be so greatly reduced by an increase in the scale of production that it is worth incurring exceptionally heavy advertising expenditure to reach additional purchasers; in such trades heavy advertising is associated with large single-plant firms.

In trades in which advertising raises the size of the representative firm it also tends to raise industrial concentration; this is one reason why advertising and concentration are related. Another reason is the 'feed-back' effect of concentration on advertising, which needs consideration here. In a competitive trade where many firms trade in a staple unbranded commodity, advertising will not be undertaken to any great extent. A local firm may do a little advertising in a local paper, but any large-scale advertising is usually ruled out; no individual producer finds it worth incurring heavy advertising costs where the benefits accrue more to the rest of the trade than to himself. Trade associations and marketing boards are sometimes set up to share the expenses of a joint advertising campaign, but they do not always act very vigorously (compare the advertising for fresh vegetables with that for frozen varieties).[47] As we consider trades with ever-fewer firms and competition becomes less perfect, advertising expenditures may be expected to rise; but in the limit, where there is a complete monopoly, there would seem to be less need to advertise at all. Consequently, it has been argued, advertising may be expected to be most intensive in oligopolistic situations. A study based on pre-war United Kingdom press advertising expenditure on over a hundred consumer goods suggested that when eight firms in a trade accounted for four-fifths of total advertising in that trade (the measure used in that study for the degree of concentration) the ratio of advertising expenditure to sales revenue was at its greatest. As we shall see later there is other support for the proposition that advertising is lower in more competitive trades; however, the view that it is also lower in monopolistic trades does not seem well founded in the statistical studies so far carried out.[48]

In oligopolistic situations some of the advertising is merely combative (to use Marshall's term), is mutually offsetting and involves a greater degree of social waste. 'When I was in business some thirty five years ago competition...was almost entirely as to who could produce the best quality and the best value for money, and considerable experience and practical knowledge of the business were necessary for success. All this is completely changed, and now competition seems to have resolved itself into a question of who could afford to spend the most money on advertising.' This was the view of a British tobacco manufacturer, formed not in consequence of the growth of television advertising, but as long as sixty years ago, before mass-circulation national newspapers had even reached maturity.[49] It was suggested at that period that it was worth forming a monopoly to save some of this wasteful advertising; thus Lever argued in 1906 in favour of his proposed soap monopoly that it would lead to economies in 'the cessation of frenzied advertising, particularly in the curtailment of Press advertising, and the control of the giving of prizes for wrappers'.[50] These quotations illustrate all too clearly how long the problem of avoiding excessive advertising in concentrated industries has been with us.[51]

We now turn to examine the statistics on advertising collected by the

Census of Production for the first time in 1963, and in slightly greater detail in 1968. These figures allow one to form a view of:

    (i) the importance of advertising in various industries,

    (ii) the relation of advertising to concentration,

    (iii) the relation of advertising to the size of firms and multi-plant working.

These new statistics are much more comprehensive than earlier figures and should permit a more reliable view. Earlier studies relied on summaries prepared for the advertising industry and were limited to selected commodities; they were also subject to difficulties of analysis – since the advertising information could not be precisely matched to information on industrial structure derived from the Census, and the samples of commodities investigated in various studies generally related only to particular sectors of the market.

It is, first, interesting to notice again how very high advertising expenditures are in trades producing certain consumer goods. There were nine product-groups (out of the eighty-six groups distinguished in the Census for its analysis of advertising) in which advertising expenditures represented more than a tenth of net output in 1968, all of them producing consumer goods of the frequently purchased, non-durable type. The list is as follows: soaps and detergents, advertising 27 per cent of net output; toilet preparations, 26 per cent; tobacco, 17 per cent; pharmaceutical chemicals and preparations, 14 per cent; miscellaneous foods (including milk, milk products, margarine and starch), 13 per cent; spirit distilling and compounding, 12 per cent; cocoa, chocolate and sugar confectionery, 11 per cent; fruit and vegetable products, 11 per cent; soft drinks (including British wines, cider and perry), 11 per cent.[52] These nine product-groups, representing 8 per cent of net output in manufacturing, accounted for 40 per cent of all advertising expenditure by manufacturing industries. The list of products may not cause the reader much surprise, but the magnitude of the proportions devoted to advertising is perhaps not widely appreciated.[53] It may add perspective to note that for these nine product-groups advertising expenditure exceeded capital expenditure on plant, machinery, etc. by a half (in toilet preparations advertising was four times capital expenditure!). Those selling the hope of eternal youth, or the 'real spiritual comfort' attached to 'a packet of a known and trusted brand of cocoa'[54] must of course spend heavily on messages conveying that hope and comfort.

Over the whole of manufacturing industry advertising expenditures were equal to about 3 per cent of net output, or 1·1 per cent of sales values. If we consider product-groups with very little advertising (those in which advertising expenditures accounted for less than $\frac{1}{2}$ per cent of net output in 1968), we find the following six groups: iron and steel; electrical machinery; insulated wires and cables; shipbuilding; railway carriages and equipment; textile finishing. These are all goods sold primarily to industrial users, where customers are both too few to warrant much advertising, and too expert to be interested in anything other than performance.

A comparison of high- and low-advertising products for the previous Census (of 1963) yielded the slightly different products listed in table 4.4, but having the same characteristics: high advertising is associated with 'mass-consumables' and low advertising with producer goods.

Are these highly advertised, mass-consumable goods sold by industries that are concentrated in a few hands? Table 4.4 suggests this is so. The average degree of sales-concentration for all products distinguished in the Census of 1963 (concentration being measured by the share of sales in the hands of the five enterprises having the largest sales of that product) was about 61 per cent,[55] but for the heavily advertised consumables listed in that table average concentration was distinctly higher, at 85 per cent. For the low-advertised producer goods listed in the table average concentration was marginally below the general average. Comparisons for 1958 and 1968 are also shown in the table and are much the same.

Whilst a degree of association between advertising and concentration is borne out by these figures, many other factors are clearly at work. For example, economies of scale in production (and in 'research and development') lead to relatively few firms in aircraft manufacture and to high concentration in that trade – and low advertising has little relevance. On the other hand, heavy advertising in pharmaceuticals and toilet preparations has contributed to the emergence of certain very large firms, some of which are of international scope, yet firms of moderate size are able to set up and concentration in the group considered as a whole has so far apparently remained relatively low.[56] Again, some items of clothing (for example, swimsuits) are more 'advertisable' than other items (ladies' dresses), and reasons can no doubt be adduced for such variations. The result is that the net relation between advertising and concentration is far from clear in comparisons of different industries at a particular time.[57]

It has been suggested that advertising has a continuing effect on industrial structure, and that even today concentration continues to rise perceptibly in consumer-goods trades where advertising is high, and continues to fall in producer-goods trades where advertising is low.[58] But the real world is not so simple. Between 1958 and 1968 the average concentration of the high-advertising trades listed above did

Table 4.4. *Intensity of advertising, concentration, size of enterprise and multi-plant working*

	Advertising[a] /net output 1963	Concentration[b] 1958	Concentration[b] 1963	Concentration[b] 1968	Average size of enterprise Employees[a] 1963	Average size of enterprise Net output 1963	Plants per enterprise[c] 1963
	(%)	(%)	(%)	(%)		(£m.)	
High-advertising groups[d]							
Soap, oils and fats	24·5	85·1	83·2	82·6	528	1·20	2·4
Pharmaceuticals and toilet preparations	17·9	35·6	34·5	38·3	716	1·36	2·1
Tobacco	17·1	98·5[e]	99·5	99·7	9484	19·26	10·0
Cocoa, chocolate and sugar confectionery	11·3	53·9	65·5	69·5	1448	1·77	2·5
Other food industries	11·0	77·8	83·1	82·4	960	1·39	4·0
Low-advertising groups[f]							
Light metals, copper, brass, etc.	1·0	65·0	65·6	67·3	996	1·45	3·7
Cotton etc. spinning and weaving	1·0	27·8	37·3	49·4	643	0·53	3·3
Textile finishing	0·9	..	..	..	513	0·52	3·2
Coke ovens and mfd. fuels	0·8	61·9	65·3	98·6	472	0·71	1·3
Woollen and worsted	0·7	24·1	28·6	38·0	472	0·48	2·6
Insulated wires and cables	0·7	62·8	75·6	86·5[g]	2542	3·48	4·0
Aircraft mfg. and repairing	0·5	89·8	97·5	99·4	4793	6·12	4·1
Iron and steel	0·4	63·1	63·2	79·5[g]	1968	2·74	4·3
Averages[h]							
High-advertising	14·8	82·3	84·9	84·3	1057	1·65	3·3
Low-advertising	0·6	55·4[i]	58·0[i]	70·9[i]	1311	1·36	3·4
All manufacturing	3·0	54·4[j]	58·8[j]/63·4[k]	67·8[k]	882	1·20	3·2

SOURCES: Censuses of Production.

  [a] For establishments of all sizes.
  [b] Average share of sales of principal products of the group by five enterprises having largest sales of those products; shares of each product weighted by sales to form the average for the group.
  [c] For enterprises with over a hundred employees; based on *Census 1963*, vol. 132, table 15, with interpolated estimates where figures suppressed to avoid infringement of disclosure rules.
  [d] Product-groups for which advertising above 10 per cent of net output.
  [e] Based on Hart, Utton and Walshe, 1973, p. 79.
  [f] Product-groups for which advertising less than 1 per cent of net output.
  [g] Not fully comparable with earlier years.
  [h] Weighted by the denominators of the ratios in the respective columns.
  [i] If insulated wires and cables, and iron and steel, where 1968 ratios not fully comparable, were omitted, these averages would be 45·4 (1958), 49·5 (1963) and 61·8 (1968).
  [j] Relates to 214 product-groups comparable for 1958 and 1963.
  [k] Relates to 295 product-groups comparable for 1963 and 1968.

indeed rise slightly, from a share of 82 per cent of sales in the hands of the five largest firms to a share of 84 per cent; but for the low-advertising trades it also rose, and perhaps even more rapidly, from 55 to 71 per cent.[59] One may infer that the older forms of advertising (in the press, on posters, etc.) had already substantially raised the concentration of high-advertising trades before the advent of television, and that more recent and further effects of advertising – in differentially increasing the concentration of high-advertising trades – are not apparent.

So far we have been concerned with the relation between advertising and concentration, but we must also consider the relation between advertising and firm-size. In those mass-consumer trades in which advertising is important the sizes of firms are no doubt higher than they would be without advertising, but it does not follow that their average size is greater than in trades less subject to advertising; the latter will include trades in 'heavy' industries, in which large plants and large firms are to be found for other reasons. Stigler suggested, on the basis of a sample of American manufacturing industries, that there was no significant relation between advertising and firm-size in the United States in 1950.[60] In Britain the position is more complex: measuring firm-size in terms of employees, table 4.4 does not show a relation between average firm-size and advertising, but if we measure firm-size in terms of net output as is preferable (penultimate column in the table), it appears that the average firm in high-advertising trades tends to be about a fifth larger than in low-advertising trades.[61]

In view of our special interest in giant firms, we should, however, go further than considering only the average sizes of firms; we must also ask whether the very largest firms tend more particularly to be found in high-advertising trades. An answer can be obtained by the following (rather indirect) method from the published information. We can compare the industrial distribution of the hundred largest firms in 1968 (as given in table 1.2) with the distribution of all firms, and calculate the expected total advertising by the hundred largest firms simply as a result of their industrial composition (that is, we reweight the advertising ratios for all firms in each Industrial Order by the industrial composition of the giants); such a calculation leads to the conclusion that the hundred largest firms are in industries that on average are a fifth more 'advertising-intensive' than are manufacturing firms in general.[62]

A shift in the industrial distribution of the largest firms towards advertising-intensive trades can also be detected during the period 1958–68 using a similar method of calculation. The available information relates to those firms with over 5000 employees (approximately

200 firms); characterising each Industrial Order by the proportion of advertising to net output in a particular year (1968), the shift towards more advertising-intensive Industrial Orders can be summarised in terms of a rise of 24 per cent between 1958 and 1968 in the weighted average of the advertising ratios as a result of a shift in weights (the weighted average of the ratios of net advertising to net output rose from 2·5 to 3·1 per cent). The main contributors to this change are those very large and fast-growing concerns in food, drink and tobacco, the the well advertised names of whose products have become household words.

A final aspect of industrial organisation of interest here is the number of plants per enterprise; but, as the final column of table 4.4 shows, there is no indication that firms in high-advertising industries have particularly large numbers of plants.

IN A FEW WORDS

In this chapter we have attempted to examine, using the available Census statistics as far as possible, how marketing factors have contributed to the growth of giant multi-plant enterprises in recent years. In contrast to the previous chapter in which we examined plant-sizes, we have here had to deal with less concrete notions – market power, communication costs and the influence of advertising – and the discussion has at many stages not been as precise nor as conclusive as we should have liked. Nevertheless certain points have been established which can be summarised as follows.

We have seen that the largest firms of today are those that own very many plants, and that those plants are only of medium size (to quote the figures again – the hundred largest firms of 1972 owned an average of seventy-two plants each and those plants on average employed only 430 persons). Multi-plant enterprises have gradually increased in importance since the end of the nineteenth century, and have developed particularly rapidly since the 1950s. Part of that acceleration was probably associated with a change in the law (making restrictive agreements among firms illegal) which led to open amalgamations among firms in place of earlier restrictive agreements. Between 1958 and 1968 concentration rose more rapidly in those trades in which multi-plant working by leading firms increased more rapidly. Nevertheless this was a mild effect, and the position in 1968 was that differences in multi-plant operation amongst industries had little connection with differences in concentration amongst industries.

One of the factors influencing both the extent of multi-plant operation and the size of plants is transport costs. We saw that trades with heavier transport costs tend to have smaller plants, but they have more plants per firm. The constraint on plant-sizes imposed by transport costs has been diminishing with the passage of time and the progress of transport technology; hence it is trades with particularly heavy transport costs that have increased their planr-sizes in recent years. Progress in communications has also made it easier to operate multi-plant concerns, and the rise in multi-plant operation that has occurred over time has tended to be in those trades with particularly heavy transport costs.

Advertising has played a complex part in the development of modern large-scale industry. High advertising and high concentration tend to go together, because advertising increases the size of the representative firm's market and hence (with a given total market) increases concentration; they also go together because in highly con-centrated industries there is scope for heavy 'combative' advertising. Advertising is not an activity equally appropriate to all trades, but is particular to mass-consumable articles, where the heavy costs of an advertisement can be spread over a great many units. The hundred largest firms of today tend to be rather more active in such trades, and in the decade 1958–68 it appears that giant firms have tended to move into such 'advertising-intensive' industries.

Despite the long-term pervasiveness of marketing forces in contribut-ing to larger firm-sizes, our statistical investigations suggest that forces of this type are not powerful enough to explain very much of the dramatic rise observed between 1958 and 1972 in the number of plants owned by giant firms (a rise from twenty-seven to seventy-two plants per firm for the average of the hundred largest firms). This was borne out most clearly in the case of transport costs, where it seemed worth evaluating certain elasticities; in the event these turned out to be low – suggesting that there was a positive contribution from this source, but it was probably small. For the other factors considered the calculations were not carried that far (in view of the difficulties of measuring the forces concerned), but a similar inference is probably also justified.

Marketing forces, in short, have played a detectable role in the rise of aggregate industrial concentration, but it has been a supporting rather than a leading role. In the next chapter we shall consider the even more complex contribution of financial forces.

CHAPTER 5

FINANCIAL FACTORS IN THE GROWTH OF LARGE FIRMS

for the shadow of finance is within the shadow of
wisdom

Ecclesiastes 7: 12

INTRODUCTION: THE OWNERSHIP OF INDUSTRY

This chapter is concerned with finance, that is with the ways in which command over capital resources is made available to industry. We shall see that there have been great changes in the 'financial environment' in which industry operates, and that these changes have had a significant effect in increasing the sizes of business units. Inevitably we shall be dealing with matters that are abstract and somewhat abstruse – with the relations between paper claims, rather than with the physical capital to which those claims relate. It will do no harm, therefore, and it may help to keep our feet on the ground, if we begin by spending a moment looking in the most elementary way at the ownership of industry and its recent transformation, before going on to examine more complex matters, such as the spreading of risks and the rise of diversified enterprises, the lower cost of capital to larger firms, the role of financial gearing and the bias towards larger-sized units imparted to the industrial capital market by the growth of financial intermediary institutions.

Let us begin with the familiar. The variegated industrial resources – machinery, buildings, stocks of materials, knowledge of techniques and so on – that stand at the disposal of a nation are controlled by individual persons or groups of persons, usually today through a chain of claims in the form of shares or debentures with defined rights. Small firms are generally owned, controlled and financed by a single individual; this simple case stands at one extreme of a spectrum. At the other extreme stands the apparently simple notion of resources which are said to be owned by society as a whole, such as the postal and road systems, and the various nationalised corporations, sometimes covering entire industrial sectors (it will be recognised that the concept of 'ownership' is complex, but its naive meaning will suffice here). Between these extremes lie those very large firms the growth of which is our particular

Notes to this chapter will be found on pp. 256–80.

concern. The capital embodied in one of these firms is obviously beyond the means of any single individual, and it would generally be beyond the means of even a group of individuals if that group was small enough to be in working control. As is familiar, the capital of such companies has therefore mainly to be raised from 'the public'. In the nineteenth century, and perhaps even up to 1950, 'the public' consisted of individuals more or less wealthy; but there has been a gradual change, especially in the last two decades, and nowadays 'the public' consists increasingly, if not yet predominantly, of financial intermediary institutions who invest the savings of all sections of society.[1]

The main institutions involved are the pension funds of large concerns, life insurance companies, unit trusts and investment companies. These act as intermediaries in investing the savings placed in their care; their policy is to look for a wide spread of investments so as to offset risks, and they try not to become over-involved in the individual companies in which they invest. The commercial banks in this country do not provide long-term capital directly to industry, but in other countries the lines of demarcation are drawn differently, and the banks there have for some time actively fulfilled the function of suppliers of industrial capital – a role which is now being undertaken here, though as yet somewhat passively, by the financial intermediaries.

Practicality requires that the running of an enterprise, whatever its size, be placed in the hands of a few directors. Where the firm is small, even if it is a public company, the board will often hold a majority of the shares; but for the very largest companies the proportion of shares held by their boards is today generally very small. We examined the shareholdings of the boards of the hundred largest quoted manufacturing companies in 1968 and 1972 (directors' shareholdings have been published in the Annual Reports of companies following the passage of the 1967 Companies Act). Both beneficial interests and interests arising as a trustee were taken into account.[2] In 1972 the median holding by the board was found to be 0·46 per cent, whether we consider the issued ordinary capital or only the voting capital; that is to say, *for half the companies the board held no more than approximately ½ per cent of the ordinary capital.* There was, of course, considerable variation amongst companies: for three-quarters of companies the board's holding was under 2 per cent in 1972, but there were a few companies – in which some individual historical circumstances could usually be pointed out – where the directors retained a more substantial holding (over 10 per cent of the capital was held by the boards of eleven companies) and these raised the unweighted arithmetic mean holding in the total ordinary capital to 4·2 per cent.[3] The proportion of voting capital in the hands of the board declined between 1968 and 1972 for

Table 5.1. *Ordinary share capital owned[a] by directors of the hundred largest[b] manufacturing companies,[c] 1968 and 1972*

No. of companies

	All ordinary shares		Voting shares	
	1968	1972	1968	1972
Directors owned:				
Under $\frac{1}{2}$%	52	56	52	56
$\frac{1}{2}$–1%	8	4	8	4
1–2%	9	13	9	13
2–5%	8	12	8	12
5–10%	11	4	7	1
Over 10%	12	11	16	14

SOURCES: Based on companies' published annual accounts.

[a] Including beneficial ownership, and ownership as trustee when stated.
[b] By size of net assets in 1970.
[c] Excluding foreign-owned companies and those that did not survive. Companies that had merged by 1972 treated as a single company in 1968 also.

two-thirds of companies: the arithmetic mean fell from 7·3 to 5·4 per cent, but the median was unaffected at 0·46 per cent. Further details of the distributions are set out in table 5.1.[4]

It is clear from these few figures that we have long ago passed the stage when a majority of the ordinary voting capital was normally owned by the directors, and the public was typically invited to subscribe only for a minority holding, or to contribute funds by way of debentures, preference shares, or special non-voting ordinary shares ('A-shares' as they are sometimes termed).[5] We have also passed the stage when those who directed the firm retained a substantial minority stake in the company; at the beginning of the century a stake by the board of a third of the ordinary shares was regarded as adequate to control a public company; in the inter-war period it was a fifth.[6] Today a very much smaller holding is considered adequate, at least as long as the remainder of the shareholdings are finely dispersed.

It is important to note that such a situation becomes increasingly unstable, since the smaller the fraction held by the board the easier it is for a larger outside nucleus to be got together to displace the existing board. This risk of instability and diffusion of the 'centre-of-gravity of control' has increased over time, and has far-reaching consequences for motivation and efficiency; it is also undoubtedly one of the factors that has facilitated the rise in the numbers of take-over bids for quoted companies in recent years – a feature considered from other points of view later in this chapter.

The present-day lower fraction of shareholding in the hands of the directors of large companies has been accompanied by relatively larger holdings in such companies by the financial intermediary institutions; this will be considered in detail on pages 113–24 below. But first we must consider a number of related general developments in the economic framework.

DEVELOPMENTS IN THE ECONOMIC FRAMEWORK

The Stock Exchange as a market for industrial capital

In the nineteenth century the Stock Exchange was concerned for the greater part with government securities and those of British and foreign railways; so limited was its concern with industrial and commercial companies that at the beginning of this century no more than 350 such companies had their shares quoted on the Stock Exchange, and their securities were valued (in nominal terms) at under 5 per cent of all quoted securities; twenty years earlier, in the 1880s, there had been barely sixty such companies, accounting for hardly 1 per cent of the value of all quoted securities.[7] The number of quoted industrial and commercial companies rose steadily thereafter, approximately doubling in each decade, to reach a peak of about 3500 companies (excluding subsidiaries) in the early 1950s. At that time the market-value of their securities accounted for about a quarter of all securities traded on the Stock Exchange. In the two most recent decades the number of independent quoted industrial and commercial companies has fallen in consequence of merger activity to about 2100 in 1972; but the market-value of their securities has continued to rise, and since the mid-1960s industrial and commercial companies have accounted for about half the value of all securities quoted on the Stock Exchange (see table 5.2). If we include companies of all types (finance, property, oil, etc.), then in 1972 company securities accounted for four-fifths of the value of all quoted securities.[8] These few figures summarise the transformation of the Stock Exchange within the last half-century into a market for company securities from one previously dealing primarily in government and railway bonds.

The marketability that industrial shares derive as a result of quotation is of great importance to financial institutions, since it enables them to invest in industry in the confidence that the shares they have acquired can be sold without too much trouble and loss when funds are required. The growth of the financial intermediaries' participation in industry has thus, in this country at least, been linked with, and to some extent dependent on, the long-term growth of the Stock Exchange as a market for industrial securities.

Table 5.2. *Quoted industrial and commercial companies, 1950–72*

	All companies[a]	Companies registered in UK[b]	Market valuation[c]	Proportion of value of all SE securities
	(No. of companies)		(£m.)	(%)
1950	..	3,400[d]	4,600	18
1955	4,160	3,400	8,400	25
1960	3,930	3,100	16,400	36
1965	3,640	2,500	39,400	52
1970	3,230	2,300	57,200	48
1972	2,990	2,100	72,800	49

SOURCES: *Stock Exchange Official Year-Books.*

[a] Total number of notices for commercial and industrial, brewing and distilling companies.
[b] Excludes overseas companies, also estimates (based on sample counts in each year) for subsidiaries, unquoted companies and companies in liquidation.
[c] For all companies as in note *a*.
[d] Estimate.

Increased company retentions and reduced personal risk capital

The higher income and profits taxation of this generation has worked to increase the degree of self-financing by companies. Distributed profits are subject to progressive rates of personal taxation, and at various periods have also been subject to distribution charges in the hands of the company ('distributed profits tax'); retained profits have therefore carried a tax advantage as compared with distributed profits. Companies with limited possibilities of expansion in their own field, which might otherwise have distributed surplus funds, have therefore been tempted to employ such funds in other ways, including the acquisition of other companies.

When the time now comes for a medium-sized or even a small firm to be sold to a successor, more often than in previous generations only a large public company has the ready finance, or is able to offer an acceptable share-exchange, to effect a take-over or merger; more rarely than previously is there an individual who can take over the firm and continue it as an independent business. This is the result of a number of factors, such as the higher personal taxation on capital and income, which has reduced the ability and incentive of individuals to engage in risky undertakings; on the other hand, large quoted companies are replete with finance supplied by the market, including the financial intermediaries, and looking for suitable investments.

The role of mergers

Many writers have been content to treat the merger movement as providing in itself a satisfactory explanation of the growth in the share of the largest firms in the economy, without seeking the reasons that bring about those mergers. But it is not sufficient to say that mergers take place because larger firms are expected to be more profitable; we need to know the source of that advantage – whether it lies, for example, in production economies which are socially advantageous, or in monopoly profits which on balance are socially disadvantageous, or in financial economies the social advantages of which may need deeper consideration. A merger, in other words, is a method of growing; it does not explain the motive for that growth.

One of the important features of modern business developments is the emergence of giant enterprises owning plants producing seemingly unrelated products (some numerical estimates of the increase in the number of industrial groups in which the largest firms are involved have been given in chapter 1). Common marketing channels will lead an enterprise to take an interest in something with which it has no obvious connection from the point of view of its production technology, but that does not explain why, for example, shoes and shipbuilding should form part of a single enterprise, nor why car distribution should be combined in a single enterprise with the manufacture of stockings. Financial economies associated with the balancing of risks and the ability of a large firm to raise capital on favourable terms have to be looked to in seeking an understanding of these developments,[9] and the next three sections of this chapter re-examine in general terms the nature of the financial advantages that greater size confers on a firm, with some of the theoretical implications; they are concerned, respectively, with the spreading of risks, the gearing of larger companies and the lower costs of capital to larger companies. This is followed by two historical sections: the first is an account of the rise of financial intermediary institutions and their investments in large firms; the second provides an account of the sources and uses of capital funds of the largest companies over the past twenty years. A summary of the chapter is offered in the final section.[10]

SIZE, RISK AND DIVERSIFICATION

A larger firm derives certain advantages in risk-bearing from its size, quite apart from any advantages that it may derive from production or marketing economies. It is important to clarify the nature of these 'risk-bearing advantages' if we are to understand why large diversified enterprises have arisen and the way in which they affect social welfare. The balancing of risks is an important element in financing and, though a consideration of risk-theory usually soon brings one into a *terra incognita*,[11] much help may be derived from considering certain simple, if not well known, implications of 'the law of large numbers'.

The next few pages attempt to set out these implications as plainly as may be (confining matters of more technical interest to the notes); we shall have to consider at what rate riskiness falls as the size of firm rises, whether there is a limit to the fall in riskiness, and whether that limit may have shifted in recent decades.

Size and variability of returns

The first and familiar implication of the law of large numbers is that a large group is less risky than its constituents; bad fortune in one line of activity tends to be offset by good fortune in another line, so that extreme outcomes for the group as a whole occur less frequently. In particular, as statistical studies have frequently demonstrated, the danger of insolvency is lower for a large firm than for a small one. Even if we combine units all having the same expected rate of return, so that the group's average rate of return is no different from that of its constituents, the lower *variability* of the group's return is sufficient to confer an advantage, which manifests itself in a lower cost of capital. This provides a certain incentive towards the formation of large company groupings.[12]

The precise rate at which the variability in returns may be expected to decline with an increase in size of firm can be derived from the law of large numbers under simplifying assumptions. If we suppose a large firm to be equivalent to a group of independent smaller units, all of equal size and having similar characteristics, we would expect the variability of the rate of return (measured, for example, by the standard deviation of total profits as a fraction of total capital) to fall inversely with the square·root of the number of units in the group; for example, a quadrupling in size may be expected to lead to a halving in variability.

This simple rule holds only if the constituent units are completely independent, but usually there will be a degree of association in the returns of the units belonging to a single enterprise, such that if one member does well in a given period one may expect others to do well also. The association arises partly because the units face the same general economic climate, and partly because they are all subject, at least to some extent, to the managerial influences of their common parent. In consequence the variability of a group does not decline as rapidly as given by the above rule (to put it in intuitive terms, the degree of off-setting of chance fluctuations is not as great when the component units are positively associated as when they are independent). Indeed, if the component units were very similar (being in the same trade, having the same equipment, managed in the same way, and so on), there would in the limit be no reduction at all in variability; the group would be no more than a blown-up version of its components and its variability, in proportionate terms, would be unaffected.

Empirical comparisons of rates of return on net assets for companies of different sizes show that the rate of decline in variability is in reality very much less rapid than the square-root rule. This holds both for comparisons between companies at a given time, and in looking at the variability over time in the profits of companies in various size-groups. As a typical example we can refer to the rates of return of United Kingdom quoted companies in 1954: comparing those with net assets of between £1 million and £5 million with those having net assets between £15 million and £65 million (that is some 13–15 times greater), the fall in the standard deviation of profit-rates was found to be only from 10·7 points to 7·6 points (whereas the square-root rule suggests a fall to about 3 points). Similarly, if we consider the year-to-year variations in the profits of the companies in these two groups, looking at the variability of each company in turn about its trend line over the period 1954–63, we find that the smaller companies displayed a standard deviation of 3·6 percentage points and the larger companies one of 2·8 points (whereas a fall to about 1 point would be expected on the square-root rule). Thus, there is a decline in variability with increasing size, but by no means as rapid as would occur if large firms consisted simply of independent smaller units.[13]

The fact that in practice variability does not decline nearly as rapidly as suggested by the simple square-root rule has puzzled many investigators. Some have suggested that entirely different factors are at work: for example, that small firms engage in riskier classes of business, or that large firms benefit from their monopolistic positions and so are able to enjoy a more stable life. All this may to some extent be true, but it should lead one to expect that variability would decline more rapidly than the square-root rule, and not more slowly as we observe in practice. Thus, the fact that the variability of large firms' returns is not as low as indicated by the square-root rule should lead one to speculate that per unit of resources large firms engage in riskier classes of activity than small firms. But none of this speculation is justified. More careful consideration of the 'law of large numbers', making proper allowance for the association between constituent units, suggests that it adequately explains the available observations. Since that explanation also has an important implication for the limit to the reduction in risk, it is worth setting it out in a little detail.[14]

For simplicity we consider a group consisting of a number (n) of identical and equally correlated constituents. The mathematical relation between the variability of the group and that of its constituents can be developed in terms of the standard deviation of the average of the group (σ_n), the standard deviation of the individual constituents (σ_1) and the correlation (r) between any pair of constituents; the relation[15] is given by

$$\sigma_n = \sigma_1\sqrt{[r+(1-r)/n]} \tag{1}$$

It will be noticed that if the constituents are independent $(r = 0)$, this expression reduces to the simple square-root rule $(\sigma_n = \sigma_1/\sqrt{n})$, and if the constituents move precisely together $(r = 1)$, the group is no different from its constituents $(\sigma_n = \sigma_1)$.[16]

The limit to reduced variability

The two simple cases referred to above are well known. But it is not so well known that the reduction in the variability of the group reaches a positive limit if the constituents are to some extent associated; that limit is given by $\sigma_1\sqrt{r}$ (as may be seen from equation (1) by letting n tend to infinity). However great the number of constituents may be, the variability of the group never falls below that value; in this important respect the more realistic case of correlated constituents differs from the case of theoretically independent constituents (in which, we may recall, the variability of the group tends to zero as the number of constituents grows).

Chart 5.1 illustrates how the variability of the group falls with an increase in the number of its constituents for various degrees of correlation. With a high correlation, say r above 0·75, the formation of a group leads to only a very small fall in variability and, since in practice costs of co-ordination have to be allowed for, it does not pay to enlarge the group very far. If one stopped enlarging a group when the variability was, say, within a tenth of its limiting minimum value, then with a correlation above about 0·83 there would be no point in having more than one unit in a group.[17] As we consider constituents of ever-greater independence of one another, that is as the correlation falls, the number of units worth combining into a group rises; for example, on the same criterion (expanding a group until its variability had fallen to within a tenth of its minimum value) with a correlation of 0·5 we would have five units in the group and with a correlaton of 0·1 forty-three units.

What kind of correlations would one expect to find in practice? A capable individual may be able to choose and group together units that have a low correlation (or even a negative correlation, as discussed

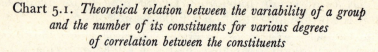

Chart 5.1. *Theoretical relation between the variability of a group and the number of its constituents for various degrees of correlation between the constituents*

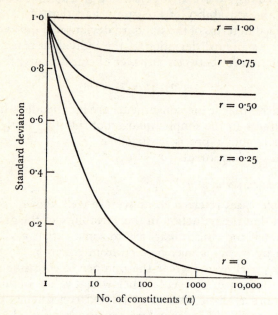

further below) and so gain much by way of lower risk, but one less competent may subject a group to the whims of his personality, so that its constituents have a high correlation, little is gained by way of reduction of risk and something may even be lost. To get an impression of average tendencies, a number of empirical studies of the variability of profit-rates in relation to size have been re-examined in the light of equation (1). The study covering the widest range of firm-sizes relates to the United States and is based on tax-returns of all manufacturing firms for 1955 and 1958;[18] the results are displayed in chart 5.2. A theoretical curve based on equation (1) (with a correlation of 0.72 evaluated at $1 million) has also been drawn in and gives an adequate representation of the curvature observed.[19]

The available British studies relate only to the restricted range in which quoted companies are to be found; the results from the study by Whittington (1971) are shown on the same graph and lie somewhat below the United States observations (probably because the variability of the British data is damped by having been measured over a period of years, whereas the American data relate to a single year, but there

Chart 5.2. *Distribution by firm-size of the standard deviation of firms' rates of return on assets*

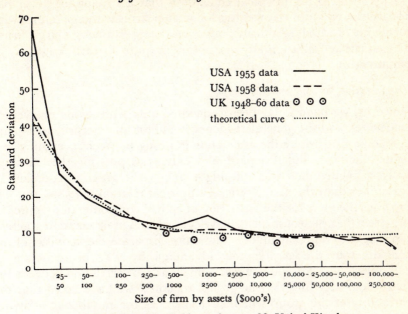

SOURCES: United States – Stekler, 1964, p. 1186; United Kingdom – Whittington, 1971, p. 45; theoretical – see text.

are also other factors leading to a lack of comparability, such as the use of official exchange rates and differences in the definition of assets). The British data support the general relation posited, though by themselves they do not provide much insight into its precise form because of their limited range.

We see from the chart that for firms with gross assets below $1 million – corresponding, say, to firms employing under a hundred persons – there is a very sharp reduction in variability with an increase in size. Our fitted (theoretical) relation suggests that for such small firms a tenfold increase in size, from assets of $100,000 to $1 million (say, from ten to a hundred employees), is accompanied by a fall in the standard deviation of returns from 19 to 10 percentage points. But for larger firms, those with assets over $10 million, say those employing over about a thousand persons, the variability of rates of return does not fall much further: a tenfold increase in size, from assets of $10 million to $100 million (say from 1000 to 10,000 employees), is accompanied by a fall in the standard deviation of returns as calculated from the fitted relation from 8·94 only to 8·79 percentage points. The latter value is very close to the lower limiting value, which the fitted curve puts at 8·78 percentage points.

This leads to the practical conclusion that a striving for lower risk apparently provides an incentive for smaller firms to merge (either with each other or with larger firms), but not for mergers amongst larger firms. The advantage substantially disappears at quite an early stage, say at employment of 1000.

The incentive for conglomerate mergers

However, we have so far been concerned only with *general* or average tendencies, and the general tendency is still for an enterprise to expand in its own field where the association is strong between its existing and its new activity. But if a particular enterprise puts together substantially unrelated activities, it might achieve a greater reduction in variability than the above general empirical relation suggests, and this provides the logic for the formation of 'pure' conglomerates ('pure' in the sense that the constituents have no production or marketing activities that are complementary). The more disparate the activities of the conglomerate the greater the advantage by way of reduction of variability. If an entrepreneur can achieve a zero correlation between the constituent activities that he groups together, we have noted that the variability of the group will tend to zero as the number of activities increases, following the square-root rule. If he is able to go further and attain a negative correlation, by grouping together activities such that if one has a bad year the other may be expected to have a good year (for example, ice-cream and sausages, or beach-wear and raincoats), he would reduce variability more rapidly still. In the limiting case, if he were able to find two activities of equal variability and having a perfect negative correlation, their sum would show no variation at all.[20]

It is the increase in the size of the market for the shares of firms, as embodied in the growth of the Stock Exchange and deriving ultimately, no doubt, from the general improvement in communications, that has permitted entrepreneurs to seek out firms that can suitably be combined into larger, more diversified groups. The limits to the size of such a diversified group have to be sought in managerial diseconomies of scale, which become more apparent over time when management has to adapt itself to changes in technology and in demand; these cause greater problems the greater is the disparity in the nature of the group's activities. What was originally a sensible grouping may, as time passes and circumstances change, turn into a group which – in the now popular phrase – lacks 'industrial logic'; the anticipated low positive (or perhaps even negative) correlations turn into higher positive ones as an over-stretched management attempts to cope with unanticipated conjunctions of events.

The allocation of resources amongst the group's various activities are determined by internal administrative decisions rather than by an external market mechanism, and in periods of changing circumstances the relative efficiency of these two methods of allocation comes into question. We shall examine in some detail on pages 107-13 below the costs of employing the market mechanism in raising new capital for firms of various sizes; at this stage it may be accepted that for the smallest firms, and perhaps for smaller matters generally, the costs of going to the market will be relatively great and administrative decisions will be more economical; but for the largest concerns the social interest may suffer unless the relevant information on profits, prospects, etc. in various lines of activity are put before an open market in which the terms on which capital is to be supplied to each line are determined.[21] These considerations can only be put forward at a general level; it would need a close study of the constituents of a sample of diversified groups over a substantial number of years to come to any more precise conclusions.

Advantages of diversification

It is important to note that the lower variability of the grouped rates of return that follows from grouping small units into large units unaccompanied by any rearrangement of production resources does not yield any obvious saving of resources from the point of view of the economy as a whole. The total social product is unaffected by how those units are grouped for book-keeping purposes; in other words, the inherent risks and uncertainty of the production process are not escaped merely by combining accounting units into ever-larger groups. If there is an advantage from such a grouping, it lies in the restructuring of the ownership claims on industry, so that the prospects associated with the various classes of shares and debt accord more closely with the preferences of their diverse owners; this may confer social advantages which are by no means negligible, but they are of a more subtle type than usually advanced in discussions of this topic.

While, in general, a sceptical attitude seems to be in order towards arguments in favour of the very largest enterprises based purely on economies of risk-spreading, nevertheless some exceptions can be recognised. First, where massive research is important and a great many costly experiments have to be carried out before success is likely, it is possible that inadequate resources would be supplied by the market to a set of independent small firms because of the possibility of failure; whereas a large firm would be able to carry out a sufficiently extensive programme to be fairly sure of eventual success. It is partly the market's aversion to extreme risks that prevents the small firm raising adequate capital in these circumstances – which may only be another way of saying that, when uncertainty is relatively great, investigation and other transaction costs become too high for a small firm in relation to the capital involved.

A second case where a larger group may show social advantages as a result of risk-spreading occurs when it permits increased specialisation within each constituent plant. A small independent firm may not wish to specialise its sales or its machinery on a narrow range of products, despite the opportunity that would provide of greater production economies, because it fears 'to put all its eggs into one basket'; that is, the risk is too great. But, as part of a larger group of similar plants, production may be reallocated so that each plant becomes more specialised; the group therefore produces at lower costs, while facing the same risks as previously.

There are limits to the social benefits from this process, since ultimately (as the firm increases in size) competitive pressures will become less intense and the incentive to produce efficiently will diminish. It is also sometimes found that a change in circumstances causes such a specialised plant to be thrown completely out of work, where a less specialised plant might retain its flexibility and continue in production. But perhaps the main objection to such an argument for larger groups is that each firm has to decide on the limits of its activities and how far to press its degree of specialisation;[22] it would be going too far to suggest that the market mechanism consistently leads to faulty decisions on the degree of specialisation and that this can be put right by means of government fostered mergers. It is commonly observed that in America small firms are more specialised and have longer runs than in Britain, while large merged firms in Britain continue to be castigated for the excessive variety of their production lines.

*   *   *   *   *

The object of the above pages has been to clarify some of the complexities associated with the economies of risk-spreading, and their effects on the optimum size and degree of diversification of an enterprise. We have seen that the desire to reduce riskiness encourages the formation of large combinations of firms, but that in general there appears to be a limit to that reduction, and the gain derived from it may not involve any social economy – that is, it may not bring about any saving in real resources. As we shall see in the following sections there are other financial elements which lead to the same process and to the same qualified conclusion.

THE USE OF LOAN CAPITAL

Larger firms are able to raise a greater proportion of their capital by way of long-term loans than small firms (this proportion is generally known as the firm's 'gearing'), and this has provided larger firms with advantages that have been particularly clear in recent decades of rising general price-levels. We examine in this section the consequent incentive for the formation of larger firms.

Firm-size and gearing

That the proportion of debentures issued tends to increase markedly with firm-size was apparent in an earlier National Institute study of quoted companies, which showed that the ninety-one largest quoted companies – those with over £8 million of net assets – raised half their new external capital in 1949–53 by way of debenture finance, compared with only a quarter for the smallest quoted companies – those with net assets under £¼ million (the proportion for intermediate size-groups rose steadily, as shown in table 5.3).[23]

Since that period quoted manufacturing companies have substantially increased their reliance on debt; if bank borrowings are included, the ratio of borrowings to shareholders' interests for all larger quoted manufacturing companies has risen from 18 per cent in 1955 to over 50 per cent in 1972.[24] The differential between large and small quoted companies in their reliance on borrowed capital has possibly narrowed recently (though the available information is not entirely clear), but undoubtedly it remains important.[25] For small (unquoted) manufacturing companies, the sample inquiry for 1968–9 carried out for the Bolton Committee confirmed that they borrowed much less in relation to their total resources than did quoted companies.[26]

The reason why larger firms are able to raise more finance by debentures and other borrowings is to be sought in the greater 'security' that they can offer, as expressed, for example, in the lower variability of their income-streams (which we considered in the preceding section, but which is apparent also in other ways, such as a lower risk of failure). An increase in the size of a firm may permit a quite disproportionate increase in the proportion financed by debentures; the relevant principles are not entirely simple and are explained most easily with the help of an example. We consider a company with an income-stream expected to average 10 per cent of its assets, with a standard deviation of 5 percentage points. Assuming, again for the sake of simplicity, that the distribution of returns about the average follows the normal probability curve, this would imply that it would make a loss approximately once in forty-four years. The risk that the company may not be able to cover

Table 5.3. *Proportion of debentures in total capital issued*[a]
by quoted industrial and commercial companies, 1949–53

Net assets 1949	No. of companies	Debentures/ total capital
(£000s)		(%)
Under 250	690	20
250–499	610	24
500–999	512	27
1000–1999	379	39
2000–3999	192	38
4000–7999	91	37
8000 and over	105	55

SOURCE: based on Tew and Henderson (eds.), 1959, p. 272, table A.3.

[a] Debenture plus share capital, excluding bonus issues.

its debenture interest is obviously relevant in deciding how much debenture finance such a company can raise and, though one often speaks of debentures as providing a secure return, in reality a certain degree of risk – small as it may be – is always accepted by the investor. Suppose the investor is prepared to accept a 3 per cent chance that the income in any year will be insufficient to cover the interest charge; it may then be calculated that debentures can be issued by this company such that the annual interest charge on them absorbs some 6 per cent of the expected annual income.[27] More debentures could be issued if debenture holders were prepared to accept a higher degree of risk; more could also be issued if the degree of variability of the company's income-stream were lower. It is the balance between the riskiness of the company's income-stream, on the one hand, and the degree of risk-acceptance by debenture holders, on the other, that determines the extent of debenture finance.

We have seen in the preceding section that the result of a merger between two similar firms is that the relative variability of their joint income-stream is generally reduced; thus, if the income-streams of two equal-sized firms were independent and each had the same standard deviation of 5 per cent, we would expect the standard deviation of the group's profit-rate to fall to some $3\frac{1}{2}$ per cent (following the square-root rule: $5/\sqrt{2} = 3.54$). This would permit a considerable increase in the role of debenture finance; if debenture holders accepted the same degree of risk as assumed previously, it can be calculated that the proportion of the income-stream committed to debenture interest could rise from 6 per cent when the firms were separate to 33 per cent. In practice, as we have seen, variability does not decline so rapidly; but, following a merger, a decline by as little as half a point – from a standard deviation of 5 to 4½ percentage points – would be sufficient to permit debenture finance to increase so that debenture interest absorbed 15 instead of 6 per cent of income.[28] Thus, if debenture finance is 'cheap' in some sense, it is to the advantage of firms to combine so that a greater proportion of their capital can be so financed.

Incentives for fixed-interest borrowing

The advantages of debenture finance as compared with financing by issues of shares have become increasingly important in the past generations, so obliging every business to reconsider its balance of financing. First, debenture finance confers a tax advantage, which derives from the accounting convention that debenture interest is a charge before calculating profit; it is therefore not subject to company taxes but only to personal taxes. This convention has been accepted in tax legislation (though its justification is not entirely obvious);[29] thus debenture interest has not been subject to profits tax (and so not to the heavier rates of profits tax that at various periods applied to distributions), nor to Corporation Tax. On the other hand, dividends on shares are paid out of profits that have suffered company taxes and are also subject to personal taxes. Following the 1973 'Reform' of the Corporation Tax, the differential tax advantage in favour of debentures has been narrowed, but it is still significant.

A second, and now very familiar, advantage of debenture finance in periods of inflation is the benefit which accrues to borrowers at the expense of lenders if the rate of inflation is not fully taken into account in fixing the terms of the loan. The nominal rate of interest, gross of income tax, on industrial debentures in the two decades 1951–70 (when inflation was still moderate) averaged some 7 per cent; this rate of interest has to be reduced by tax, from the points of view both of the lender's return and of the borrowing company in considering interest costs in terms of retentions forgone. These tax-rates differ, but for a rough calculation we may consider tax in the region of 40 per cent, giving a net nominal cost of debentures in this period of some 4 per cent. But the general price-level rose on average during this period by about 4 per cent a year, so that the real net cost of debentures to companies and the return to the individual investor paying standard income tax was close to zero. For the wealthier personal investor paying surtax, the return on debentures would have been negative; only for those institutional investors which are exempt from tax ('gross funds') would the net return have been positive. In consequence virtually the whole real return on assets acquired with debenture finance accrued to the

Table 5.4. *Rates of return on industrial debentures, with notional adjustments for income tax and inflation, 1951–74*

Percentages

	Gross yield pre-tax[a]	Income tax rate[b]	Yield net of tax	Rate of inflation[c]	Real rate of return
Averages					
1951–55	4·9	46	2·7	4·4	−1·7
1956–60	6·1	42	3·5	2·0	1·5
1961–65	7·1	39	4·3	3·5	0·8
1966–70	8·9	42	5·2	4·6	0·6
1951–70	6·7	42	3·9	3·6	0·3
Years					
1970	10·5	41	6·2	6·4	−0·2
1971	10·1	39	6·2	9·4	−3·3
1972	9·7	39	5·9	7·1	−1·2
1973	11·4	45	5·9	9·2	−3·3
1974	16·4	48	8·5	16·0	−7·5

SOURCE: Central Statistical Office, *Monthly Digest of Statistics*.

[a] Based on undated stocks up to 1962, and on redemption yields of twenty-year stocks since 1965. Yields for 1963–4 omitted from the averages.
[b] Standard rate for each financial year, including investment income surcharge since 1973.
[c] Annual rise in the retail price index.

benefit of shareholders, and the greater the proportion of total capital financed by debentures the greater was their gain.

Table 5.4 sets out a more detailed calculation for various periods in the past quarter-century. It will be seen that as the expectation of continuing inflation became more widely accepted the gross interest yield on company debentures rose from about 5 to over 16 per cent – but not sufficiently to lead to a substantial real net return to the tax-paying investor. In the 1970s the calculated real net rate became negative, as it had been in the early 1950s.[30]

The situation in the years since the war has been quite different from that before the war: nominal rates on debentures in the inter-war period averaged about 6 per cent gross (somewhat higher in the early 1920s and somewhat lower in the 1930s),[31] equivalent to say 5 per cent net of tax. In that period the general price-level was falling at about 2 per cent a year, so yielding a substantially positive real net interest rate to debenture holders of close on 7 per cent a year.

It may seem surprising that in the post-war period lenders have been prepared to supply finance for virtually a zero return, and that it has taken so long for inflation to become a sufficiently ingrained part of long-term expectations to lead to higher nominal rates. But there are very many slow-moving factors affecting long-term interest rates. The government's policy towards bank rate and 'cheap money' in the early part of the period, its expressed policy of working towards the long-term control of inflation and a general over-optimism with regard to its ability to put that policy into practice have all encouraged low rates. The financial intermediaries have been supplying vast funds to the market (as we shall see in more detail on pages 113–24 below) and have been prepared to accept low interest rates, moving their portfolios only slowly into equities.

We need not go further into these matters at this stage; the main point to be emphasised here is that throughout the post-war period debenture finance has been available to industry at real rates of interest that are very low, and that bear little relation to the yield expected to be earned on capital employed in industry.

The restructuring of a company's capital to benefit from the advantages of cheap debenture finance is subject to substantial 'frictional' delays; this is partly because all capital alterations are expensive matters, to be indulged in only rarely, and partly because of tax legislation. Any change in capital structure that can be construed as being intended to yield a tax advantage (for example, an outright replacement of part of the share capital by a debenture issue) is prohibited, and this inevitably inhibits much refinancing. On the other hand, and this is an important feature from our point of view, an issue of debentures providing finance for the acquisition of the ordinary shares of another company is not subject to such restriction. For example, suppose that there are two companies of equal size and prospects, each originally entirely financed by equity, but which, under present conditions, would prefer a quarter of their capital to be financed by debentures; the first may bid for the second by offering half equity and half debentures. The first company – which is now 'the group' – finishes with an ordinary capital increased by half, with a doubled income and with the desired gearing. The debenture capital, as we have seen, has a negligible real cost attached to it, and its significance as a real capital charge becomes less year by year as the general inflation proceeds. The prospective income per ordinary share rises and so does the market value of the share.

The reader must not suppose that the take-over boom of the past two decades is to be explained entirely in such simple terms; rather, it must be recognised that, when an unrealistic price is set in the industrial capital market for such an important category of capital as debentures, artificial pressures inevitably result, bringing about a restructuring in company organisation. In the present case increasing concentration seems to have been one of the by-products of those pressures.

It is also notable that tax-avoidance legislation provided a curious and roundabout link between the benefits of debenture finance and the merger movement. On the other hand, the de-concentrating operation of company splitting – that is the division of a company into two or more parts by issuing shareholders in the parent company with shares in those hived-off parts – was generally inhibited by tax legislation; the new shares would usually be treated as distributions subject to income tax and surtax.[32]

Social benefits of cheap finance

The above paragraphs have attempted to outline how the technicalities of debenture finance have worked to encourage the formation of large companies; it is next necessary to ask whether the gains made by large companies in using cheaper finance are accompanied by any saving in real resources, or whether these gains result merely in an arbitrary transfer of purchasing power to shareholders in large companies from the rest of the economy. Let us consider the various sources of advantage in turn.

The benefit obtained by a company as a result of the favourable tax treatment of debenture interest is very clearly no more than an arbitrary transfer; equally, the benefit obtained from unrealistically low interest rates in times of inflation falls into that category. But, even if these two advantages were absent, the greater stability of larger companies would enable them to raise a greater proportion of their capital by debenture finance and this aspect raises more difficult issues. While the totality of risks affecting the national product are unchanged by a higher gearing, certain savers gain by being given the opportunity to hold their savings to a greater extent in a less risky form – there is a specialisation in risk-bearing. The large industrial enterprise thus carries out a kind of banking function, modifying the supply of securities of different qualities to meet the needs of savers.[33] It is a function that could, of course, equally be performed by a separate financial institution, such as an investment trust. Taken by itself there is nothing to make us think that it is performed less well by a large, primarily industrial enterprise, but equally, if the need for a more competitive environment made it desirable for society to prevent the formation of giant industrial concentrations, it is difficult to see that anything would be lost by having financial operations carried out by financial organisations that were separate from industrial companies.

THE COST OF RISK CAPITAL

The preceding section considered the advantages that larger companies derive from a greater reliance on debenture finance; we now examine the main features of risk (or 'equity') capital, the possibilities that are open to companies of various sizes in raising new capital, and the extent of the advantages enjoyed by a quoted company when it comes to raising new money by issuing ordinary shares on the Stock Exchange.

Earnings-yields as a measure of cost

It must be said at the outset that the cost to a firm of its risk capital is neither easily defined nor easily measured; there is much academic dispute on such matters as whether retained earnings should be treated as having the same cost as new, externally raised capital; or, to take the investor's point of view, whether the return on his investment is to be measured in terms of the earnings-yield on his shares (earnings being equal to dividends plus retentions), or is better measured in terms of the dividend-yield plus any capital appreciation in the market-value of his shares (the capital appreciation being determined, amongst other factors, by the amount of retained earnings per share). It would take us too far from our central theme to go into these points, which are in the nature of refinements for present purposes; in what follows we are mainly concerned with the *differential* in cost between large and small firms, and for this limited purpose it seems adequate (accepting the approach used in a number of earlier studies) to treat the earnings-yield on a quoted company's shares as a measure of the terms on which the market will supply capital to the firm.[34] When a firm seeks a quotation for its existing shares, the earnings-yields on shares of other quoted firms as near as possible to it in industrial scope, in size and in profit record are generally taken as a guide in settling the terms on which its shares are traded; equally they provide the touchstone when fresh capital is raised.

Issue costs

The earnings-yield represents a running cost year by year, and we shall examine in a moment the results of a number of studies from which may be deduced the rate at which that cost declines with size of firm. It is, however, convenient to consider first a smaller component of costs varying with size, which can be analysed more easily and precisely in relation to quoted companies – namely the initial costs incurred on raising capital or on seeking a quotation (costs of accountants' reports, of the prospectus, advertising, underwriting, and the like). These costs have to be published in the issue-prospectus for quoted companies; the corresponding costs when an unquoted company wishes to raise capital cannot readily be quantified, since they are largely represented by the time spent by the original owners in negotiations. To a large extent these issue costs are in the nature of fixed overheads and, expressed as a proportion of the sum raised, must be expected to decline with the size of that sum.

Various studies of prospectuses of quoted companies have indicated that issue costs fall substantially with size of issue:[35] they range from 10–15 per cent of the sum raised when that sum is at the lower end of what is regarded as practical to raise by means of public issue (say, £¼ million in 1970) to some 3–5 per cent when the sum raised exceeds, say, £1 million.[36] From the point of view of the company, these costs may be capitalised and treated as equivalent to a higher required running yield; then the differences do not appear so very important. For example, if the investor requires a return (in terms of earnings-yield) of 10 per cent a year on his capital and the initial issue costs on a small issue are 12 per cent, the company has to earn £10 a year not on every £100 raised but on the net sum of £88 it receives – that is to say, the running costs are raised to 11·4 per cent; whereas if a large issue is involved, for which initial costs are only a third as high at say 4 per cent, the company has to earn £10 on the £96 it receives - which is a running cost of 10·4 per cent. The apparently very substantial variations in issue costs thus reduce to a difference of only about 1 per cent when expressed in terms of annual running costs.

Stock Exchange quotation

We now turn to the main element in capital costs – the earnings-yield. A great dividing line in the cost and availability of capital is crossed when a company obtains a quotation on the Stock Exchange. As an unquoted company, a medium-sized manufacturing firm having a turnover, say, in the region of £1 million (perhaps with profits after tax of £100,000 and 100–200 employees) and with average prospects of growth might raise capital by finding a buyer for a minority holding in its shares on an earnings-yield basis of some 12 per cent, that is on a capitalisation of eight times its net profit, but the market for such transactions is limited and difficult.[37] However, as soon as the company obtains a quotation, its shares will be traded at something close to the market average of, say, 6 per cent, a capitalisation of some sixteen times its net profit. Because of its newness to the market and its smaller than average size, the share-price may be a little lower than this, but probably not by very much. In other words, as a consequence of quotation the market-value of its shares is approximately doubled. Whereas previously it might contemplate only such projects as yielded returns above 12 per cent on its capital, it can now seriously consider projects well below this level, knowing that very much cheaper finance has become available. Among other things it can, of course, consider acquiring other unquoted firms which do not wish to bother themselves with the formalities entailed in a Stock Exchange quotation.

As has been indicated, the market in shares of unquoted companies is very narrow, the more so the smaller is the company concerned; usually it is a matter for individual negotiation, much dependent on the personal circumstances of seller and buyer. It is only when a company approaches, say, half the minimum size at which it could seek a quotation on its own feet that it becomes easier, and a number of suppliers of capital are prepared to discuss terms; even so, capital is then often available only in special forms, perhaps as a mixture of debentures and shares, perhaps by way of a convertible debenture (so that the lender has the capital security provided by a debenture, which limits his downward risk, but also the option of converting to shares at a later date to benefit from any exceptional success), or perhaps by way of a 'preferred convertible ordinary share' (*sic*; the method recommended by the Estate Duties Investment Trust).[38]

Earnings-yields and size

Once a company has achieved a quotation and its shares are traded regularly on the Stock Exchange, it might be thought that size-differences would become unimportant in determining capital costs. A number of earlier studies have, however, suggested that even amongst quoted companies the smaller stand at a disadvantage in comparison with the larger. If that were a strong disadvantage it would help to explain the rise in mergers amongst quoted companies; it is therefore worth assessing the results of those earlier studies in some detail. In what follows we also present the results of a small and more recent study of the earnings-yields of quoted industrial companies, carried out as part of the present inquiry.

Different approaches have been used in the various studies and it is not easy to compare their results; for our purposes we have summarised the results of each study in an elasticity form, which expresses in a single figure the average percentage decline in earnings-yield associated with a 1 per cent increase in size.

The study by Morgan and Taylor was the first that drew explicit attention to the decline in earnings-yields with size; it was based on an examination of some 500 quoted manufacturing companies in the United Kingdom in 1955.[39] It found that an earnings-yield of 21 per cent applied to the smallest group of quoted companies (those with a capitalised value of shares and debentures of under $£\frac{1}{2}$ million) and only 14 per cent to the largest group (those with a capitalisation of over £16 million). A smooth decline of the yield with increasing size was observed for the intervening size-groups; the rate of decline may be estimated as equivalent to an elasticity of −0·10 (±0·02).[40] A study relating to a period five years later, based on a sample of United Kingdom manufacturing companies in 1960, yielded the very similar elasticity of −0·09 (±0·04).[41]

To test whether this relation has persisted (and to enable us to investigate certain doubts considered below), we examined a small stratified sample of eighty manufacturing companies for 1972. Yields had fallen to much lower levels by then; small companies with average net assets of £½ million were yielding just over 8 per cent, while large companies with average net assets of £250 million were yielding 6½ per cent. The differential in yields between large and small companies had thus apparently narrowed; the elasticity of yield with respect to size was estimated at only −0·032 (±0·004).[42]

We must now consider whether the lower capital costs of larger firms should perhaps be attributed to their lower risk rather than simply to their greater size. A number of refined econometric investigations have been carried out which all point to the independent significance of size, even after allowing for factors such as the variability of a company's earnings-stream, its gearing, industry, etc. A typical example is the study of fifty-nine quoted companies in three British manufacturing industries for the years 1961-3 by Davenport (1971); variations in the cost of capital (defined in that study as the ratio of dividends and interest to the market-value of ordinary shares plus the book-values of preference shares and debt) were attributed to the size of the company (measured by the logarithm of total assets), the variability of earnings (in the preceding seven years after allowing for an exponential trend) and gearing (the ratio of fixed-interest capital to total capital, all at book-values). For each industry and each year regressions were calculated which showed a net decline in earnings-yield with size of company (after allowing for the effects of other factors). The individual results were not well determined because of the small size of the samples; to derive a more precise overall impression we calculated a pooled value and derived an elasticity of the cost of capital with respect to size of −0·06 (±0·015);[43] this is very similar to the values found above on the simple approach in which no allowance was made for other factors.

A number of American studies along analogous econometric lines have yielded surprisingly similar results. For the period 1954–7 an elasticity of −0·09 (±0·02) was derived from a sample of fifty-six companies;[44] for the period 1960–2 a study of 180 companies led – after some manipulation – to an elasticity of −0·07 (±0·04);[45] for 1956–63 a very careful study of fifty manufacturing companies led to an average elasticity of −0·04 (±0·01);[46] and, for the nine years 1958–67, a study of eighty-six companies yielded an average elasticity of −0·07 (±0·01).[47] In all these American studies allowance was made for risk and other factors in addition to the effects of size.

There is thus an exceptional consistency in the results of a number of studies in Britain and the United States, all pointing to a falling cost of equity capital as size of firm increases, with estimated elasticities all in a relatively narrow range of, say, −0·05 to −0·10. Accepting this result for the moment, we have to consider whether such apparently low elasticities could conceivably provide sufficient incentive for a larger company to take over a smaller company. The following illustrative calculation shows the implications of an elasticity at the lower end of the range (−0·05). Suppose that the typical earnings-yield for a company of a given size is 10 per cent. A company ten times that size (measured in terms of average earnings), but similar in other respects, might then be expected to yield just under 9 per cent. If the larger firm were now to take over the smaller firm at its existing market price, a surplus would accrue by way of an increased valuation of the combined firm's equity; that surplus may be calculated as being equivalent to some 18 per cent of the capital value of the smaller firm.[48] If the elasticity were as great as −0·10, the gain on such a transaction would rise to some 39 per cent of the value of the smaller firm. Such gains may not seem overwhelming given the risks and costs involved in an amalgamation of concerns, but they appear sufficient to provide an incentive for mergers where the personalities involved are interested. A progressive increase in concentration must be anticipated so long as such incentives persist.

The financial advantages to a quoted company of taking over an unquoted company are, of course, very much greater, given the greater difference in yields mentioned above. It should also be remembered that the gains considered here are in addition to any that may accrue from a higher gearing of the combined unit, which, as noted in the preceding section, sometimes becomes possible on a take-over.[49]

If we are prepared to accept the results of the various studies mentioned, the capital market's preference for larger units in recent decades would seem to be a well established fact. The preference may not, however, be quite as great as those studies suggest, for the following reason. All the studies mentioned are based on samples of companies that have survived intact over a number of years, or have been profitable over a number of years; companies making losses have been excluded from such studies, no doubt because the calculation of earnings-yields – that is the loss per unit price of share – is not usually regarded as very meaningful in these cases (assets per share are then more often considered relevant when a simple criterion is required to assess a share's market-value).[50] In excluding unsuccessful companies retrospectively a bias is introduced, since smaller companies with their more variable fortunes tend to make losses more frequently than large companies (the average yield of the small companies included in the sample is thus greater than that of all companies of that size). Of course, not many quoted companies make losses, and the greater part of the samples always relate to larger companies where losses are relatively rare; the bias is thus probably not substantial. For our own small study of eighty companies, the results of which were reported above on the usual basis (excluding loss-makers from the calculation), we repeated the calculations including loss-making companies with a view to measuring the likely extent of the bias. Our sample, however, proved too small to yield useful results; the results provided no grounds for questioning the general negative relation, although they suggested that the precision of earlier results had probably been overstated.[51] Our conclusion at present must therefore be that we suspect that, for quoted companies alone, the capital market's preference for larger companies is more moderate than appears from the sample investigations mentioned; yet, if we consider the whole spectrum of sizes, that is the yields relating to unquoted companies together with those for quoted companies, the capital market's preference for larger concerns seems indisputable.

Optimal firm-sizes

To recapitulate: our object in this section has been to assess the implications of a number of complex studies of how the costs of risk capital vary with size of firm. We have seen that the costs of raising capital are greater for a smaller company, partly because of the fixed element in investigation and other issue costs, partly because of the restricted market for the capital of smaller companies. There is a particularly marked preference by the capital market for companies that have reached the size at which their shares can be quoted on a Stock Exchange, in contrast to those that are smaller. Yet from the point of view of the economy as a whole we must recognise that the real resources required for an activity that can function as a small concern are not necessarily reduced simply by making it part of a larger concern, in which it obtains its finance through a head office rather than from the capital market. The higher issue costs that the market would impose on a small concern are avoided, but they are replaced by the administrative costs involved in providing the relevant information to a head office (to justify the need for further capital, to explain why plans for last year had not gone as expected, and so on). One cannot generalise as to which costs are lower; it is the kind of balancing-of-costs problem that one would normally expect the market mechanism to sort out correctly for itself.

Any quick attainment of an optimal balance of firm-sizes is hindered by the constant process of evolution of the capital market. Part at least of that market's present preference for investment in larger units would seem to be attributable to the recent development of vast financial intermediaries, which tend to operate in large sums that can readily be shifted from one investment to another; and there has been a lag – so it has often been suggested – in the development of further institutions which could retail those funds to smaller concerns.[52] We are therefore led to ask whether the development of financial intermediary institutions has been at such a pace, and whether they have now reached such dimensions, that the capital market has in a sense been tilted in favour of large industrial groupings. We turn next to an investigation of this topic.

THE INSTITUTIONAL INVESTOR

To an increasing extent the capital of industrial concerns is owned not directly by persons but indirectly through various financial intermediaries. In this section we attempt to assess the strength of this tendency and consider the implications for the rise of industrial concentration.

The quandary of the financial intermediaries

The reasons for the growth of financial intermediaries are to be sought partly in the increased relative weight of the savings of wage and salary earners (these savings may be regarded as being gathered together and invested on behalf of their owners by insurance companies and pension funds), partly in tax-incentives that have encouraged savings through life insurance policies and pension schemes, and partly in the natural evolution, with the passage of time, of specialist investment companies (and unit and investment trusts), which provide the investor, in return for a charge, with a spread of 'professionally managed' investments, which are changed from time to time in response to changes in circumstances.

The rise of financial intermediary institutions thus forms part of the natural progress of the social economy. Concern has, however, been occasioned by three aspects. First, there is the fear of a concentration of 'financial' power over industry; paradoxical as it may seem, while personal wealth has almost certainly become more evenly distributed in the course of the past century, this has been accompanied by the development of some very large financial intermediaries. The market for industrial capital is thus no longer dominated by that legendary small number of wealthy, nineteenth-century style, individual capitalists, but by a number of infinitely more wealthy institutions.[53] The separation of banking and industry, which has for long distinguished the British financial system from that of Germany and France, is being slowly replaced by an association between the new financial institutions and industry, apparently bringing the British system closer to that of the Continent.

Secondly, despite the size of their holdings in industry, the institutions still look upon them primarily as investments, to be bought or sold according to investment criteria; the financial institutions concerned have their own businesses to run (of providing insurance cover, etc.) and neither wish nor need to be involved in managing the businesses in which they invest. That most owners of shares in large industrial firms do not wish to exercise control is, of course, no new thing; what is perhaps new is that the owners of even the largest stakes in the firm act as investors rather than owners. There is the consequent danger that large firms are left with a weaker directing nucleus to see them through difficult periods. The institutions are faced with a quandary: on the one hand, they do not wish to act as a financial centre of power over industry; on the other hand, as owners very often of the largest single stakes in industrial firms, they are increasingly pressed to take a leading part in ensuring that the direction and management of those firms is sound. Such managerial participation is still very tentative (despite the officially encouraged Institutional Shareholders' Committee) and there is a long way to go in this country before the participation in industry by financial institutions reaches the levels that have long been typical on the Continent.

The third development, noted in earlier sections of this chapter, is the suggestion that institutions prefer to invest in larger companies, and that they have been prepared to supply cheap debenture finance to them; the growth of larger industrial firms is thus favoured at the expense of the smaller ones.

These matters are weighty enough to require closer examination, but the relevant facts are by no means readily available and many of the pages that follow have to be devoted to putting together diverse sources of information before assessing their implications.[54]

Resources in the hands of the institutions

The total funds in the hands of the main financial institutions that are our concern here – insurance companies, pension funds (both public and private), investment companies and unit trusts – amounted to £44,000 million at the end of 1972.[55] To set this sum in perspective we may note that it is equivalent to about two-thirds of the market-value of the securities of *all* United Kingdom registered companies quoted on the Stock Exchange; such a comparison is not entirely apposite since the institutions invest in many other things besides company securities (as we shall consider in a moment), yet it shows in a rough, global way the immense dimensions that the institutions have now reached. If we confined the comparison to the narrower group of United Kingdom commercial and industrial companies (that is excluding financial and property companies, but including breweries, distilleries, etc.), we find that the resources in the hands of the institutions are now in excess of the value of the securities of that group. On the other hand, the value of securities of all sorts quoted on the Stock Exchange, including government and foreign securities (many of which are, of course, quoted also on foreign Stock Exchanges), is about four times that of the present total holdings of financial institutions – but that is perhaps a less relevant comparison.[56]

An attempt to trace the growth since 1938 in the funds at the disposal of these institutions is set out in table 5.5. Inflation makes it difficult to say very precisely what has happened in 'real' terms, especially since the prices of the assets which institutions hold have moved in opposite ways: the prices of government securities have fallen and those of ordinary shares have risen. But if we are only interested in a very rough view of the value of these resources, we may deflate by a general price index of goods and services, as in the final row of that table. On that basis we see that in the years 1938–52 which spanned the war-period there was little real change. The rise in the institutions' resources took place in the twenty years following 1952; this is important in view of our interest in the timing of the rise in industrial concentration. The current rate of increase in institutional resources can be measured in terms of their acquisitions of investments in cash values (on which information is available for recent years); their net acquisitions amounted to an annual average of £2700 million in the period 1970–4, equal to a 6·2 per cent increase on their total resources of £44,000 million in 1972.[57]

Given the demand for improved pension schemes arising from tax-incentives, the need for better protection against inflation and the rapid rise in unit trusts as a popular method of diversified investment, a continued growth of resources in the institutions' hands must be expected, and there seems no reason to think the growth-rate will differ from that experienced recently.

Table 5.5. *Total holdings of financial institutions,[a] 1938–72*

£ millions

	1938[b]	1952	1962	1967	1972
Insurance companies	1,740	4,000	8,180[c]	12,720[c]	22,230[c]
Pension funds[d]	500[e]	1,250	4,180[f]	6,070	12,010
Investment companies	310	580	2,360	4,010	7,520
Unit trusts	80	100	260	790	2,550
Total (current prices)	2,630	5,930	14,900	23,590	43,310
Total (1972 prices)[g]	12,900	12,240	23,970	32,180	43,310

SOURCES: For 1938: Radcliffe Committee's *Report*, 1959, table 20 and para. 313; Central Statistical Office, *Financial Statistics*, October 1965, p. 106.
For 1952: Macrae, 1955, pp. 81–7.
For 1962: Blease, 1964; Roe, 1971; Central Statistical Office, *Financial Statistics*.
For 1967 and 1972: Central Statistical Office, *Financial Statistics*.

[a] At market valuations, based on the adjustments described in note 58 on pp. 270–1 for 1962, 1967 and 1972; see sources quoted for 1938 and 1952.
[b] Approximate figures.
[c] Roe, 1971, p. 85 gives £8796 million for 1962, but the result of the simpler approach in note 58 was retained for consistency with other years.
[d] Includes pension and superannuation funds of the public sector, local authorities and the private sector.
[e] Rough allowance, as no accurate information available.
[f] From Roe, 1971, pp. 87–9. The method described in note 58 gives a similar result.
[g] 1938 and 1952 adjusted by the consumer price index, other years by the price index of total final output.

Institutional investment in equities

About two-thirds of the institutions' assets are today invested in company securities of various sorts, the remaining third being in government ('gilt-edged') securities, mortgages, property, etc. The proportion invested in company securities varies according to the type of institution: unit trusts and investment companies invest almost entirely in ordinary shares (that, indeed, is their *raison d'être*); pension funds have about 60 per cent in ordinary shares and 10 per cent in company debentures and preference shares; insurance companies continue to put the lowest proportion into ordinary shares – only 42 per cent, plus 13 per cent in company debentures and preference shares.

Not only have the total resources of institutions been growing, but the proportion of those resources invested in ordinary shares has also been rising; for all institutions combined, estimates for the last fifteen years suggest that the proportion has nearly doubled, rising from about 33 to 57 per cent (see table 5.6). There have been corresponding falls in the proportions held in both government and company fixed-interest

Table 5.6. *Financial institutions' investments in company ordinary shares,[a] 1957–72*

Percentages

	1957	1962	1967	1972
Insurance companies	23[b]	32	28	42
Pension funds	21[c]	38	43	60
Investment companies	89[d]	89	89	89
Unit trusts	94[e]	94	93	87
Total	33[f]	43	45	57

SOURCES: as table 5.5.

[a] As a proportion of their total resources based on market valuations estimated as explained in note 58 on pp. 270–1; includes ordinary shares in foreign companies.
[b] From Revell, 1967, p. 218.
[c] From Radcliffe Committee's *Report*, 1959, p. 89, table 16.
[d] Ibid. p. 92, para. 265.
[e] Assumed.
[f] Estimates by Roe (1971) would give 30 per cent for this total.

securities, and in loans and mortgages; direct holdings of property have risen, but still account for only 7 per cent of total holdings (see table 5.7), although more realistic property valuations might raise this figure.

For a longer view of trends we have to confine ourselves to insurance companies, which have been the subject of more intensive study and have comprised the greater part of the institutional total throughout. Before the First World War it appears that no more than 3 per cent of insurance companies' assets was invested in ordinary shares, and by the eve of the Second World War that proportion had risen to only 10 per cent. During the war and early post-war years the government's financial policies encouraged the institutions to remain in gilt-edged, so that by 1952 the proportion invested in industrials remained hardly higher than before the war, at 12 per cent.[59] The important switch to investment in ordinary shares occurred in the late 1950s in response to inflation and falling gilt-edged prices. Analysing the investment policies of insurance companies just over a decade ago, an informed comment-ator thought they would be content to maintain the proportion of their resources invested in ordinary shares at just over 30 per cent, which was the proportion then reached.[60] However, while there was a pause in the late 1960s, there has subsequently been the further strong rise to 42 per cent (as already noted).

One is tempted to speculate as to the future trend in this proportion. The collapse of Stock Exchange prices in 1973–4 might be thought sufficient to put a brake on increased institutional investment in

Table 5.7. *Distribution of financial institutions' investments,*
1957–72

Percentages

	1957	1962	1967	1972
Company ordinary shares[a]	33	43	45	57
Company fixed-interest securities[b]	14	13	15	11
Government securities[c]	27	22	19	11
Loans and mortgages[d]		10	9	6
Land, property and ground rents[e]	26	5	6	7
Other[f]		7	6	8

SOURCES: as table 5.5.

[a] See notes to tables 5.5 and 5.6.

[b] Debentures (including convertible debentures) and preference shares of British and foreign companies, as published.

[c] British government and local authority securities; market valuations estimated as explained in note 58 on pp. 270–1.

[d] Includes local authority mortgages; but mostly (about $\frac{6}{7}$ths in 1967) loans by insurance companies.

[e] Mostly at book-values.

[f] Includes short-term assets, overseas government, provincial and municipal loans, and unidentified British and foreign assets.

ordinary shares. It is also possible that much of the rise in the period 1957–62 was of a 'once-for-all' type, reflecting a delayed adjustment to the new inflationary world; those pension funds that previously had deeds which restricted their investment in industrial shares are likely by now to have secured alterations to those deeds, and their investors will have benefited fully from the provisions of the Trustee Investments Act, 1961, which widened the scope of their investments. Nevertheless, the alternatives to investment in ordinary shares have not been any more profitable in the 1973–4 financial collapse, and further increases in the proportion of institutional resources devoted to ordinary shares can hardly be ruled out.

The institutions hold shares not only in British but also in foreign companies: in 1972, for example, of the 57 per cent of their resources held in ordinary shares, it may be estimated that 47 per cent represented investment in domestic and 10 per cent in foreign companies.[61] Further internationalisation of their portfolios seems likely.

The institutions' ownership of industry

How far has this growth in the activities of financial institutions impinged on the ownership of British industrial equities? The answer to

Chart 5.3. *Proportion of all quoted United Kingdom ordinary shares held by financial institutions, 1957–73*

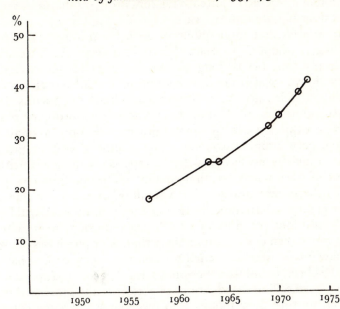

SOURCES: For 1957, 1963 and 1969: Moyle, 1971, p. 18.
For 1964: *Bank of England Quarterly Bulletin*, June 1971, p. 207.
For 1970: Ibid. but excluding investment and unit trusts from the market total as in Moyle's procedure (see note 62 on pp. 271–2).
For 1972: Our calculation based on institutional investments as published in *Financial Statistics* and *Business Monitor. Miscellaneous series M5*, and allowing 7 per cent for foreign investments of private pension funds (information supplied by the Department of Trade and Industry).
For 1973: Diamond Commission, *Report No. 2*, p. 16; Allen *et al.*, 1975, p. 4.

this important question can only be given subject to a number of rather technical reservations,[62] but fairly consistent answers have been arrived at by a number of investigators, some starting from statistics of institutional investment in shares and others from analyses of share-registers of industrial companies. These investigations, which rely partly on special sample inquiries and on various assumptions, lead to the conclusion that in 1957 holdings by institutions (insurance companies, pension funds, investment companies and unit trusts) accounted for about 18 per cent of all quoted ordinary shares of United Kingdom companies, and this proportion has gradually risen to just over 40 per cent in 1973 (see chart 5.3). Apart from the results shown in the chart, there are a number of alternative approaches of which the results vary by a few percentage points,[63] but there can be little doubt as to the main result – that there has been an approximate doubling in the proportion of all quoted United Kingdom ordinary shares in the hands of institutions in only sixteen years.

We have seen that total resources of the institutions have recently been rising at about 6 per cent a year. It is clear, then, that present trends imply that before long the greater part of quoted industrial ordinary shares must come into institutional hands; even with some slackening in their rate of advance we could hardly be surprised if they owned two-thirds of all United Kingdom quoted ordinary shares by 1984. New capital issues by companies provide only a small offset; they have been running at some £200 million a year in the period 1968–72, which is negligible when compared with new institutional resources of over ten times that amount. The quotation of existing unquoted shares may also provide a small offset and so, in due course, may the greater internationalisation of the institutions' portfolios.

The institutions' receipts of new funds requiring investment have for some years been of such dimensions that their purchases of ordinary shares have many times exceeded the volume of new capital issues; the balance has been found from personal sales (Leach, 1971, p. 34). Those who have been selling shares are not necessarily the same as those who have been putting their money into institutions; to some extent it is a matter of the old generation selling shares to meet death duties, while the new generation puts its savings into pension funds and other institutional vehicles. National accounts statistics suggest that individuals ('the personal sector') sold company and overseas securities at a rate of £600 million a year in the period 1964–9, rising to £1400 million a year in 1970–4.[64] On comparing this accelerating volume of sales with total holdings of securities by persons, as estimated by the Inland Revenue on the basis of estate duty returns, Professor Victor Morgan came to the conclusion already in 1967 that 'a continuation of sales at the 1963–5 rate would strip personal portfolios bare by 1982';[65] that conclusion must not be taken too precisely, but in essence it is consistent with the more recent information surveyed above.[66]

One must not strain to be precise in such extrapolations. Whatever the actual assumptions made, we have to recognise that the ownership of industrial shares is undergoing a substantial transformation, and one must expect the consequences for financing, management and concentration to show themselves even more clearly in the coming decade.

Institutions and cheap debenture finance

As we have seen, ordinary shares have interested insurance companies and pension funds in a substantial way only in the past generation.

However, company debentures and preference shares, on account of their lower risk, have absorbed the new investment moneys of these institutions for much longer. It is worth looking at this more closely because of its implications for the merger movement. During much of the 1950s and until the late 1960s insurance companies were putting as much of their new money into company fixed-interest securities as into ordinary shares; not until 1968 did insurance companies invest more in ordinary shares than in company fixed-interest securities. Pension funds had made the move rather earlier. Taking the purchases of securities by insurance companies and pension funds together, it appears that there was a change in policy that may be dated to 1969–70; during the years 1963–8 the sums invested in company fixed-interest securities were equal to about three-quarters of the sums invested in ordinaries, but in the ensuing five years this had fallen to under a fifth![67] The cumulative result of their previous and long-standing policy has been that the institutions owned over half of total United Kingdom company debentures and preference shares by 1970.[68]

Fixed-interest securities are not intended to give controlling powers except in extreme circumstances; thus the fact that institutions already own the majority of company fixed-interest securities is not of such significance as their rapidly growing proportion of ordinary shares, the ownership of which gives a general power of control. But an aspect of their participation in fixed-interest securities that deserves notice is the terms on which they have been supplying fixed-interest finance. As we have seen earlier (table 5.4), companies have been able to obtain debenture finance in the last twenty-five years at a real net rate of interest (after allowing for taxation and inflation) which came out generally at under 1 per cent a year; in certain periods (the early 1950s and 1970–4) the rate was negative, yielding a net subsidy to the borrowing company. For those companies which correctly foresaw the rate of inflation, there was thus an inducement to borrow – and hence an inducement to employ funds for projects that would not have been undertaken had a realistic cost applied.

The spate of take-over activity of the last two decades may perhaps be better understood in the light of the vast financial transfers of ownership of industrial capital that we have seen to characterise this period and which, until about 1970, were accompanied by institutional supplies of cheap debenture finance. We may distinguish four links in the 'take-over chain'. First, companies have had an incentive to switch to debenture finance, because it was cheap and because of the tax advantage (as discussed on pages 103–6 above); secondly, financial institutions have been prepared to supply such finance in substantial amounts;[69] thirdly, the use of such funds by companies to purchase the shares of other companies has provided an opportunity to increase the capital gearing of the group;[70] fourthly, the concentrating effect of this take-over activity is furthered by the tendency of institutions to channel their funds towards larger quoted companies, as we shall discuss later in this section.

This is a complex combination of elements, but we see it provides support for some of the popular scepticism as to the 'real' economic justification of parts of the recent industrial merger movement. The reader who has followed the arguments of previous chapters will not need reminding that financial pressures form only part of an array of forces making for larger enterprises, and that in certain mergers some other force, carrying with it a saving in real resources, may be of greater weight; the contribution of finance, however, deserves emphasis in the present discussion both because of its pervasiveness – companies in all industries are affected – and because of its artificial element. To avoid misunderstanding one must emphasise that certain financial economies undoubtedly represent a saving in real resources (as, for example, when reserves can be economised in a larger firm, or costing specialists are employed), but the pressures resulting from the availability of finance at an unrealistically low interest cost must be recognised as being artificial.[71]

From the institutions' point of view the justification for supplying funds to industry at low rates of interest is to be sought in their long-drawn weaning from government securities, and official pressures to maintain low rates of interest on government securities, which affected fixed-interest securities generally. Buying industrial debentures rather than government stocks was the first step by institutions towards a broader investment policy; it involved only a small additional risk, while yielding an additional $\frac{1}{2}$–$1\frac{1}{2}$ per cent. But to move in a large way into ordinary shares no doubt seemed in the early 1950s to involve too much risk. The prime function of insurance companies, it must be remembered, was simply to provide insurance cover in nominal money terms; by investing in fixed-interest stocks of various maturities they had for long been able to carry out that function satisfactorily, and at that time they had little expertise in industrial investment. The protection of savings against inflation had never been provided directly, but only indirectly through their 'with-profits' policies. Eventually competition to provide better terms on their 'with-profits' policies led to the search for more profitable forms of investment; the move into ordinary shares ensued, which, as we have seen, proved a slow process. The size and rate of increase of the volume of funds that were at that time being attracted to insurance companies and pension funds made a move into ordinary shares seem not a matter of the greatest urgency. An explanation along these lines amounts, perhaps, to saying no more than that there was a lag in the adaptation by the financial institutions to a changed prospect of long-term inflationary conditions.[72] And perhaps the sin of not recognising the persistent nature of the general postwar inflation is one that should be more widely shared. An eventual and full adaptation to these new conditions may lead to an end of cheap lending to industry;[73] however that may be, it must be recognised that the extended transitional period through which we have passed was accompanied by the induced, if unintended, pressures to form larger industrial groups that have been traced out above.

The institutional preference for larger companies

The preceding pages have referred in general terms to the financial institutions' tendency to invest in large rather than small companies (because of better marketability, lower investigation costs and the institutions' desire to take substantial stakes). We now examine the actual strength of this tendency under two heads: first, to what extent institutions invest in quoted rather than unquoted companies; secondly, confining attention to the quoted sector, to what extent they prefer to invest in large quoted rather than small quoted companies.

Estimates for 1961 suggested that institutional holdings of unquoted ordinary shares then amounted to £80 million, equal to a mere $1\frac{1}{2}$ per cent of their total holdings of ordinary shares (Revell, 1967, pp. 394–404 and 457–63).[74] Holdings of unquoted debentures and preference shares were higher at £200 million, equal to a seventh of institutional holdings of these categories; however, most of this relates not to the debentures of small unquoted companies, but to the unquoted debentures of large companies that had their ordinary capital quoted on a Stock Exchange.[75] Later estimates for the period 1967–73 do not suggest that the position has altered.[76] For practical purposes one can therefore say that the vast flows of institutional funds considered above have been directed almost exclusively to the quoted sector, and it is thus quoted companies that have benefited from the new channels through which savings now increasingly tend to flow.

As amongst quoted companies of different sizes, a margin of preference by institutions for larger marketable issues is apparent, though it is now by no means extreme. A limiting factor is that the market in the shares of many of the smaller quoted companies is often so narrow that a large institution finds investment in them difficult. To put approximate figures to it – it is often difficult to deal in £10,000 worth of shares in smaller quoted companies, whereas insurance companies look for investments of at least £25,000–£50,000 (Bolton Committee's *Research Report No. 4*, p. 115).[77]

Investigations have been carried out into shareholders' registers of samples of quoted companies of various sizes in respect of 1955–6 and 1969 (Clayton and Osborn, 1965, p. 171, and Moyle, 1971, p. 13). The earlier inquiry showed that insurance companies' holdings amounted to 3½ per cent of the capital of small quoted companies with net assets of under £1 million, which rose to 6 per cent for large companies with net assets of over £15 million; also, whereas insurance companies had holdings in almost all those large companies, they had holdings only in under half of the quoted companies in the smallest size-group. The later investigation for 1969 showed higher participations; partly because of the increased institutional investment in the intervening period, and partly because this investigation related to holdings by *all* institutions (not merely insurance companies). The variation was from 15 per cent held by institutions in the capital of small companies with a market valuation of under £4 million to 19 per cent for large companies with a market valuation of over £66 million. This seems a very moderate variation, though clearly discernible. Nominee holdings, however, amounted to about 20 per cent of all holdings and prevented an entirely unambiguous inference.[78] It seems possible that among smaller companies nominee holdings tend to represent directors' interests, whereas in larger companies they tend to represent institutional holdings; if that were so, the rise in institutional participation with size of company would be greater than appears from these investigations.[79]

*   *   *   *   *

The main features of the institutional developments surveyed in this section can now be summarised as follows. First, we have seen that the flow of capital funds to industry is being increasingly funnelled through financial intermediary institutions. Secondly, institutions have a preference for investment in quoted companies, so that new capital moves preferentially towards large companies. Thirdly, the institutions are now set on a path (as a result of the savings flows in the economy and the available investment opportunities) which, if pursued, will in a matter of a further decade make them the owners of the greater part of the share capital of all quoted industrial companies. Fourthly, financial pressures brought into being by these vast transfers of capital (working through cheap debenture finance and supported by the subtleties of tax legislation) have provided an incentive for company amalgamations. Fifthly, it is worth noting that the institutions have grown particularly rapidly in the last twenty years, which is the period in which (as we saw in chapter 1) there has been an acceleration in aggregate industrial concentration.[80]

THE LARGEST COMPANIES: FINANCE FOR
THEIR EXPANSION, 1950-73

So far this chapter has described in general terms various financial pressures which have encouraged larger sizes of firms. This section examines the growth of the largest firms as it appears from their annual accounts, and attempts to disentangle the origins of the additional resources that have contributed to their growth. We may distinguish:

(i) internal sources of funds, that is retentions out of profits;

(ii) external sources, that is cash raised by issues of new securities;

(iii) additions to a firm's resources resulting from a merger and involving an exchange of shares or other securities (that is, a paper – rather than a cash – transaction).

It is sometimes suggested that the whole question of the growth of giant enterprises, and of concentration, is simply a matter of the vast retentions of large companies (which permit them to expand free of any 'market discipline'); others have suggested that it is simply due to mergers, and it is often said that the market for new capital issues is irrelevant in modern conditions. If any of these simplifications were supported by the facts it would make analysis and policy prescription much easier; but the relevant facts on the finance of company growth need to be disentangled rather carefully and, as we shall see, the world is too complicated to support these simplifications.

The discussion that follows in this section is based on the experience in the past twenty years of the largest quoted companies. We rely partly on the official compilations of the financial accounts of all quoted companies;[81] partly on some special compilations of the accounts of the hundred largest manufacturing companies, on which we have been able to carry out more detailed calculations. We chose three years for the analysis of the hundred largest companies with intervals of a decade between them – the years being 1950, 1960 and 1970.[82] In 1950 these hundred companies accounted for just under half the pre-tax profits of all quoted manufacturing companies, but such has been their subsequent rate of growth that by 1970 they accounted for just over three-quarters of the profits of the 1200 quoted manufacturing companies then analysed by the Department of Trade and Industry.[83] Consequently there is today little difference between inferences to be drawn from statistics relating to the aggregate of all quoted companies and from those relating only to the hundred largest;[84] for the sake of economy in the discussion that follows only one set of figures is generally referred to.

Company retentions, distributions and taxation

We first consider at what rate companies could have expanded if they had relied solely on internal resources (that is, if they relied solely on retentions out of income and raised no new funds from the market). According to the summarised accounts of all quoted manufacturing companies for the period 1950–73 as a whole, as abstracted in table 5.8, it appears that the expansion of net assets out of their retentions would have averaged 3·0 per cent a year – a little higher in the 1950s at 4 per cent, and a little lower in 1970–3 at 2 per cent. Taking into account that additional assets are required in an expanding economy to provide

Table 5.8. *Summary appropriation account of all quoted manufacturing companies, 1950–73*

	1950–4	1955–9	1960–4	1965–9	1970–3[a]
			(£ millions)		
Total net assets[b]	5,524	8,402	11,950	15,935	18,441
Gross income[c]	1,237	1,685	2,205	2,810	3,957
less: depreciation	180	336	534	801	1,116
less: stock apprecia-tion[d]	118	62	65	225	646
Net income	939	1,287	1,606	1,784	2,195
Appropriations			(Percentages)		
Taxation[e]	*62*	*50*	*47*	*60*	*65*
less: investment grants[f]	—	—	—	*10*	*10*
	62	*50*	*47*	*50*	*55*
Debenture interest, net	*1*	*2*	*3*	*6*	*8*
Preference dividends[g]	*2*	*2*	*2*	*1*	*1*
Ordinary dividends[g]	*14*	*18*	*23*	*23*	*22*
Retentions[h]	*21*	*28*	*25*	*19*	*14*
Retentions/net assets	*3·5*	*4·3*	*3·4*	*2·1*	*1·7*
Retentions/increase in net assets	*57·4*	*56·1*	*48·9*	*27·3*	*29·1*

SOURCES: Central Statistical Office, *Economic Trends*, no. 102, April 1962; Department of Industry, *Business Monitor. Miscellaneous series M3*, 1971 and 1975.

[a] 1973 figures based on preliminary returns adjusted for partial coverage.
[b] Average of opening net assets in the period.
[c] Total income after all charges except those shown (note that debenture interest treated with other appropriations).
[d] Estimates obtained by applying price rises (average of official wholesale price indices for manufacturing inputs and outputs) to opening stocks.
[e] Includes estimated income tax on debenture interest (shown net for comparability with dividends) and prior-year adjustments for tax.
[f] Approximate; not shown explicitly in *Business Monitor*, but grouped with 'Other capital receipts'.
[g] Published figures netted of income tax in 1967–73 to make them comparable with other years.
[h] Net of depreciation and stock appreciation, and including investment grants.

both for the growth of output and for more capital equipment per person employed (the 'widening' and 'deepening' of capital), such a rate seems modest; on the basis of these few figures alone we can already see that retentions cannot account for much of the expansion of large companies.

The calculations presented in this table differ in two important respects from similar calculations by other investigators who have drawn attention to the predominantly 'self-financing' characteristic of large companies. Those investigators have generally compared company retentions gross of depreciation with gross capital expenditure. Since depreciation is such a large item on both sides of the account, the impression is conveyed that internally generated funds form the predominant source of finance for expansion. But, just as we must deduct the cost of materials used from sales receipts before arriving at a firm's profits and its retentions out of those profits, so we must deduct the cost of capital equipment consumed; equally, we must deduct capital consumption in arriving at a measure of the firm's net expansion. The estimate of capital consumption, or depreciation, may not be easy to arrive at, but that does not permit us to ignore it. The first difference, then, is that we are here concerned with retentions net of depreciation; the second difference is that we have here made an allowance for stock appreciation (the element in accounting profits as conventionally measured which is attributable to the rise in prices of stocks). At earlier lower rates of inflation the amount of stock appreciation was not large and could often be ignored; but the need to make such an allowance became more widely recognised with the persistently higher rates of inflation experienced at the beginning of the 1970s, and at the time of writing the questions that remain to be settled seem matters of detail.[85]

One must bear in mind the possibility that the generally conservative principles governing accounting procedures may have led to the creation of hidden reserves in respect of certain items (for example, depreciation may be over-provided, improvements to capital may be written-off as maintenance, patents and research may be written-off in the current year rather than capitalised). True retentions may therefore be somewhat higher than appears in accounts; but the true value of a company is also probably higher than the book-values of its net assets (influenced by historical costs) suggest. In calculating a proportionate growth-rate (retentions in relation to net assets) these biases act in opposite directions; the net bias may therefore not be very great.

If we look at the allocations out of profits in the period 1950–73 as a whole, it will be seen that there have been important changes (table 5.8). Debenture interest was negligible in 1950, but by 1970–3 it was absorbing 8 per cent of pre-tax income (reckoning debenture interest net of income tax for comparability with dividends). This rise reflects the switch to debenture financing (as noted on page 101 *et seq.* above). Net dividend distributions on shares (taking ordinary and preference shares together) rose from 16 per cent of company income in 1950–4 to 23 per cent in 1970–3; some of this rise (just over 1 point) is the result of the fall in the standard rate of income tax, but most of it may be regarded as a slow reaction to the war and post-war policy of restraint and freeze on dividends. Taking dividends and debenture interest together for present purposes, net distributions have risen from 17 to 31 per cent of total pre-tax income over these twenty years; most of the rise occurred in the first half of the period.[86]

Preference shares have declined in importance and have been more than replaced by debentures; as we shall see below (table 5.12) quoted manufacturing companies showed a net balance of redemptions of preference issues from 1965 onwards. The transposition of debentures and preference shares in this period is apparent from the fact that in 1950–4 preference dividends absorbed twice as much as debenture interest, but in 1970–3 debenture interest took about ten times as much as preference dividends.

In considering changes in distributions and in retentions, a word on company taxation policy is in order. Corporation Tax was introduced in 1965 and discriminated more heavily against dividends than did the previous system of taxes. It might have been expected to encourage retentions, but one must not expect large and immediate changes in distribution patterns.[87] In any event, after extended discussion, company taxation was 'Reformed' and shunted back on to its previous track in April 1973, when the discrimination against dividends was once again reduced; the situation now is similar for most purposes to that before the introduction of Corporation Tax in 1965.[88] This 'Reform', it was said at the time, was intended to encourage the distribution of profits, so that greater use might be made of the capital market mechanism in the allocation of resources.[89]

The rates of Corporation Tax set were such that they absorbed rather more than the previous system of taxation; if company retentions have not fallen more in the 1970s, it is because of the introduction of investment grants, which should perhaps properly be considered as part of the whole system of company taxation. This is not the place to attempt to trace a rational thread through the ever-changing maze of technicalities governing the tax allowances permitted in lieu of the depreciation of fixed assets, but it is worth noting that investment grants have been very substantial and equivalent to over half of net retentions by companies in recent years.[90]

Capital issues as a source of finance

External finance, that is issues of shares and debentures for cash, provided new resources at the rate of 2·2 per cent a year of the net assets of quoted industrial and commercial companies in the period 1949–73, with relatively little variation if we take periods of three to five years at a time (see table 5.9). Compared with net retentions, which, as we have just seen, contributed some 3·0 per cent a year to the growth of the net assets, new cash issues must be reckoned as having been significant, accounting for 40 per cent of new net resources. For fast-growing companies new cash issues will have played an even more important role than appears here, since the figures relate to all companies, whatever their rate of growth.[91] Figures for the hundred largest companies are set out in table 5.10 and yield similar orders of magnitude.

For 1970 (a not untypical recent year for new issues) we found that as many as half of the hundred largest companies issued new capital for cash, and many of the remainder were involved in some adjustment to their capital structure, such as redemption of a debenture or a preference issue (often associated with a capital issue in another year). Comparing this result with a study relating to 1949–53, one may infer that the proportion of giant companies going to the new issue market each year has perhaps about doubled in the intervening period.[92]

Table 5.9. *Issues of capital by quoted industrial and commercial companies, 1949–73*

	Issue values			Proportions of net assets		
	For cash	For acquisitions	Total	For cash	For acquisitions	Total
	(£ millions)			(Percentages)		
1949–53	128	14	142	2·1	0·2	2·3
1954–58	227	54	281	2·5	0·6	3·1
1959–61	280	198	478	2·2	1·6	3·8
1962–65	331	217	548	2·1	1·4	3·5
1966–68	474	747	1221	2·4	3·8	6·2
1969–73	427	719	1146	1·8	3·1	4·9

SOURCES: For 1949–53: Central Statistical Office, *Economic Trends*, no. 102, April 1962, p.54; Henderson, 1959, p. 73.
For 1954–63: Central Statistical Office, *Economic Trends*, no. 102, April 1962, p. 45, and November 1965, no. 145, p. xxiv; Department of Industry, *Business Monitor. Miscellaneous series M3* (2nd issue).
For 1964–73: Department of Industry, *Business Monitor. Miscellaneous series M3.*
Notes:
   (i) Compiled from a number of sources; coverage has varied slightly from time to time, as shown in the original sources.
   (ii) Composition of issues for cash not available separately for the period 1949–53, but assumed to be the same as that of total issues (issues for acquisition formed a very small proportion of the total).

Table 5.10. *Issues of shares^a and debentures by the hundred largest manufacturing companies, 1950, 1960 and 1970*

	Issue values			Proportions of net assets		
	For cash	For acquisitions	Total	For cash	For acquisitions	Total
	(£ millions)			(Percentages)		
1950	80	5^b	85	*3·2*	*0·2^b*	*3·4*
1960	106	80	186	*2·1*	*1·6*	*3·7*
1970	182	323	505	*1·3*	*2·3*	*3·6*

SOURCES: For 1950: based on figures in NIESR, 1956, p. 66, reduced by 9 per cent to allow for non-manufacturing companies (see relevant net assets, ibid. p. 71).
For 1960 and 1970: from standardised summaries of accounts at Companies House for hundred largest companies by net assets as shown in *The Times 1000* lists and Board of Trade lists.

^{a} Excludes bonus issues.
^{b} Approximate: revised from the original estimates by NIESR, 1956, p. 23, in Central Statistical Office, *Economic Trends*, no. 102, April 1962, p. 48.

Take-over financing

The rise of capital issues made in exchange for acquisitions is one of the remarkable features of the last twenty years. Such issues represented only a tenth of all issues in the period 1949–53, but by 1969–73 they accounted for nearly two-thirds of all issues (see tables 5.9 and 5.10). Taking issues for cash and for acquisitions together, it appears that in the most recent period total capital issues contributed, say, twice as much as retentions to the growth of large companies. The rise of issues in exchange for acquisitions is obviously, first, the result of the rise in acquisition activity – by 1970 over half of the expansion of net assets of the hundred largest companies consisted of acquisitions (see table 5.11); secondly, it is the result of an increasing tendency by the owners of acquired companies to accept paper-consideration in exchange for the shares in their companies – only a quarter of the cost of acquisitions by giant companies in 1970 was paid for in cash.

Whether cash or paper is accepted in exchange for the acquisition of another company varies according to the type of company acquired; it is influenced also by tax considerations. When unquoted companies are taken over the bulk of the payment tends to be in cash, but when a quoted company is taken over the bulk of the consideration tends to be in paper.[93] The reason, no doubt, is simply that the owner of a small unquoted company will more often have a suspicion of strange paper and prefers an offer in cash, but the holder of shares in a quoted company is often indifferent to what paper he holds. Further, when a

Table 5.11. *Expenditure on acquisitions by the hundred largest manufacturing companies, 1950, 1960 and 1970*

	Expenditure			Proportion of increase in net assets
	In cash	In securities[a]	Total	
	(£ millions)			(%)
1950[b]	5	5	10	5
1960	54	80	134	28
1970	93	323	416	53

SOURCES : as table 5.10.

[a] Shares and debentures.

[b] Approximate; see note b to table 5.10.

quoted company is taken over the bidder will generally be a larger company, the paper of which is more marketable and therefore more acceptable, but unquoted companies are more frequently acquired by smaller quoted companies, the shares of which do not carry such a degree of marketability or liquidity.[94] Following the introduction of Capital Gains Tax in 1965 the incentive to accept paper has been increased, since no tax is levied on a 'paper exchange'.

In considering the financing of acquisitions more generally, the distinction between issues for cash and issues in exchange for an acquisition is sometimes drawn too sharply. It may happen, for example, that the resources provided by a prior 'cash issue' are used almost immediately to effect an acquisition; and even if there has been no capital issue it does not follow that retentions are necessarily the ultimate source of finance – for example, an acquisition may initially be financed by a bank loan, which is subsequently repaid from the proceeds of a cash issue (and which may include a debenture secured on the property of the company taken over). Whether an acquisition is to be paid for in cash or by a capital issue in exchange depends on a fine weighing of the costs of alternative ultimate sources of financing, and often on the nature of the existing shareholders. An issue in exchange to existing shareholders involves lower issue costs than an issue for cash to the market generally, but sometimes better terms can be settled if the bidder is able to offer cash.

Though in reality an immense variety of financial arrangements are adopted in a take-over situation, there are great differences in the average composition of those capital issues that are for cash and those that are in respect of acquisitions (see table 5.12). Cash issues consisted predominantly (three-quarters) of debentures in the 1960s, and even in the 1950s nearly half of cash issues took the form of debentures. The

Table 5.12. *Composition of capital issues for cash and for acquisition by quoted industrial and commercial companies, 1949–73*

Percentages

	1949–53	1954–8	1959–61	1962–5	1966–8	1969–73
Issues for cash						
Ordinary shares	47	49	74	27	25	26
Preference shares	11	6	3	2	−12	−1
Debentures	42	45	23	71	87	75
Issues for acquisition						
Ordinary shares	..	87	93	79	75	69
Preference shares	..	11	6	7	1	1
Debentures	..	2	1	14	24	30

SOURCES: as table 5.9.

high gearing of these cash issues contrasts with that of the total out-standing capital of industrial and commercial companies, of which only 16 per cent at market-values consisted of fixed-interest securities in both 1966 and 1970 (see table 5.13). Of course, the total outstanding capital can adjust only slowly by means of new issues to any change in the desired level of gearing; it is therefore not altogether surprising that there should be such a large difference between the gearing of the 'stock' and of the 'flow'. In addition we have to remember that prices of fixed-interest securities have been falling in this period, while those of ordinary shares have been rising, so offsetting the tendency for the gearing of the outstanding capital stock to rise as a result of new issues of debentures. Indeed, this trend in relative prices of securities has con-tinually provided fresh opportunities for debenture issues (a company that issues debentures to bring itself up to its desired degree of gearing finds next year that its gearing is not as high as it had thought it was).

Issues in exchange for acquisitions, being replacements for existing shares, are not as highly geared as issues for cash; those who hold equity in an acquired company prefer to exchange it for equity in the acquiring company, and will generally only accept a small part of the price in the form of debentures. Since 1966 issues in exchange have been somewhat more highly geared than the outstanding stock of capital of all companies (over a quarter of issues for acquisitions since then have consisted of fixed-interest securities, compared with 16 per cent of the outstanding capital of all companies). However, the effect of acquisitions in raising gearing is greater than suggested by this comparison, since the issues shown in table 5.12 as being 'for acquisition' relate only to the issues made in exchange for the ordinary and preference shares of the acquired company (thus, in 1969–73, 30 per

Table 5.13. *Estimated market-values and gearing of quoted industrial and commercial companies,[a] 1966 and 1970*

	Nominal capital[b]	Multiplier[c]	Market-value	
	(£m.)		(£m.)	(%)
1966				
Ordinary shares	6,180	2·91	17,950	*84*
Preference shares	930	0·77	730	*3*
Debentures	3,160	0·86	2,730	*13*
Total			21,410	*100*
1970				
Ordinary shares	6,190	3·45	21,320	*84*
Preference shares	530	0·58	310	*1*
Debentures	4,770	0·79	3,740	*15*
Total			25,380	*100*

SOURCES: Nominal capital from summarised accounts in Department of Industry, *Business Monitor*; multipliers from *Stock Exchange Official Year-Books*, 'general information' section.

[a] Includes brewing and distilling companies, also some securities of overseas companies denominated in sterling. Excludes companies not registered and managed in the United Kingdom.
[b] Valued at par.
[c] Ratios of market to nominal values. Similar figures not available for earlier years.

cent of the acquired share capital in value terms was replaced by debentures). The original debentures of the acquired company either continue unchanged as a charge on what has become a subsidiary or, if they are replaced by an equivalent charge on the new parent (and there is no reason why they should be), they are not treated in these statistics as part of the issue in exchange for the acquisition.[95]

Finance and the variability of growth-rates

This is not the place to pursue in further detail the technical complexities of the financing of large companies. The features described above make it clear that important parts in the growth of the largest concerns are played by all three constituents – retentions, new capital issues for cash, and capital issues in exchange for acquisition of other companies. From the average figures quoted one might conclude that each of these three components has contributed roughly equally to the growth-rates of the largest companies, taking the twenty-year period as a whole. In considering the rise in concentration, a calculation based on averages is not, however, strictly sufficient, since, as we have seen in chapter 2, the rise in concentration is much influenced by the variability of growth-rates. It is very often the case that the contribution of various constituents to the variability of a phenomenon stand in the same relative importance as their contribution to its average value, but it is unwise to take this for granted. A special analysis of the variability of the growth-rates of the hundred largest companies was therefore undertaken for 1970. For each company the growth in net assets in that year was expressed as a percentage of net assets at the end of the year. The component sources financing that growth – retentions, capital issues for cash and capital issues in exchange for acquisitions – were similarly expressed as a proportion of net assets; the components so calculated thus summed to the total proportionate increase in net assets.[96]

The variability amongst these companies in their percentage total growth-rates was measured in terms of the standard deviation, which was calculated at 7·2 percentage points; it was found that the three components contributed almost precisely equal shares to the total (their standard deviations were: retentions, 4·3 per cent; cash issues, 4·3 per cent; exchange issues, 4·5 per cent).[97] While the calculation relates only to a single year, it seems to support our earlier conclusion that none of the three components can be neglected when considering the growth of concentration.

It may be worth putting this conclusion in another way. If a barrier were placed in the way of one of these constituents, for example if mergers were to be prohibited, it is not to be denied that this would reduce the rate of increase in concentration. But the additional resources accruing to large companies by way of mergers amounts to, say, only a third of the total additional resources that accrue to them; the remaining two-thirds of their growth, arising from retentions and new cash issues, would continue to provide resources for their expansion.

It may finally be said that, while mergers and take-overs have undoubtedly become more important over time, and have increased concentration in particular markets and in the economy as a whole, one cannot deduce from that fact alone the nature of the motives for mergers – whether, say, financial rather than technological factors have been predominant. If a small firm has resources enabling it to grow, an extension to its plant is the natural next step; but when a large firm has the resources to grow, it naturally considers an entirely new plant, and perhaps a new line of activity, in which the take-over of an existing firm may well appear as the efficient way of proceeding. We have therefore to be concerned not with particular methods of growth, but rather with the totality of factors leading to the growth of large firms, and the possible ultimate constraints on that growth.[98]

FINANCIAL FACTORS AND CONCENTRATION:
A SUMMARY

This chapter has considered a number of aspects of the financial environment which bear on the size-distribution of industrial firms. No doubt much of what has been said will have been familiar to the reader in general terms, but in the course of our investigations it has become clear that many important features of the financial world have been changing more rapidly than is often thought, and some have virtually been transformed in the course of only one or two generations.

If we are to summarise our findings in order of importance, perhaps first place should be given to the rise of the financial intermediaries and their effects on the industrial capital market. To quote again an indicator of the change that has taken place: the proportion of the ordinary shares of United Kingdom quoted industrial companies held by financial intermediaries rose from 18 to 41 per cent in the sixteen years 1957–73. Though interrupted by the financial crisis of 1974–5, that rise may be expected to continue and, on the basis of past trends, it seems plausible that within a further decade the institutions will become owners of the predominant share of the capital of quoted industrial companies. The vast funds placed at the disposal of these institutional intermediaries, by being invested preferentially in large quoted companies, have contributed to financial pressures which have encouraged the formation of large industrial groups.

Secondly, the desired gearing-ratio of companies (that is the proportion of their capital financed by long-term loans rather than by share capital) has risen in the past generation, and through a complex chain (described on pages 121–2 above) this rise has played its part in encouraging mergers. Two artificial elements in that chain are the exemption of debenture interest from company taxation and the restrictions on refinancing imposed by tax legislation; the low real interest rates (after allowing for inflation) that have applied to industrial debentures in the past generation have also contributed a largely artificial stimulus.

Thirdly, we have seen that a diversified group benefits from risk-spreading and this provides some incentive for a merging of disparate activities; but we have also seen that this stimulus usually becomes insignificant once a group has reached a medium size (say, 1000 employees) and thus has little to do with the growth of giant firms.

Fourthly, we have noted that the largest industrial firms have increasingly become 'management-controlled' – the median holding by the board of directors of the hundred largest manufacturing companies is today only $\frac{1}{2}$ per cent of the ordinary voting capital. The precariousness of control that is a feature of the present system makes it more vulnerable to take-over operations initiated by factors of the kind mentioned above. The process has therefore to some extent become cumulatively reinforcing (a greater size of company leads to lower boardroom ownership, which leads to precarious control, which leads to take-overs, which lead to even larger companies, ...) and that is partly why merger activity has accelerated in the last two decades.

Finally, perhaps it should be said that it does not seem easy to point to relevant ultimate factors determining the general financial organisation of society and of industry in particular. In the presence of profound changes in the distribution of wealth and in the patterns of wealth-holding, we have seen that there are inevitably changes in the sizes of industrial firms and in their financial grouping and control; but those changes do not necessarily improve the productive efficiency and progressiveness of the economy.

CHAPTER 6

INDUSTRIAL CONCENTRATION IN
OTHER COUNTRIES

Their line is gone out through all the earth, and their
words to the end of the world.

Psalms 19: 4

THE LIMITED OBJECTS OF THIS CHAPTER

It hardly needs saying that the forces contributing to the emergence of
large-scale enterprises in this country have also been at work elsewhere. As communication costs fall over time, so the effective distance
between countries diminishes, and one must expect an increasing similarity in their industrial structures, as well as in a host of other features.
Knowledge of new methods of production spreads; new advertising
techniques have a similar influence; similar legislation is enacted, permitting as a mere formality the incorporation of companies with limited
liability; centralised capital markets evolve. And so the processes
governing the growth and decline in the sizes of businesses increasingly
resemble one another.

But there have also been differences amongst countries in such important matters as precisely when the 'industrial revolution' began
making an impact, the subsequent role of government-sponsored enterprises and the strength of public policy inhibiting monopolistic practices
– to mention only a few. As a result, notwithstanding the general
tendency towards similarity, one must still expect to find differences
amongst countries in the importance of large enterprises and in the
degree of economic concentration. The differing natural resources of
each country will, of course, continue to exert an influence on industrial
structure – though perhaps not so strongly as in earlier times before
knowledge of manufacturing techniques had become widespread. It is
thus instructive to study differences in industrial size-distributions; to
ask, for example, whether Britain has a significantly higher degree of
concentration than other countries, or a greater proportion of its work-
force engaged in large plants, and to consider, however tentatively,
how those differences may be related to differences in national productivity. That, in general intent, is the object of this chapter.

It is as well to notice at the outset the serious difficulties which stand

Notes to this chapter will be found on pp. 280–95.

in the way of any precise international comparisons of industrial structure. Whilst Censuses of manufacturing are now held as a matter of routine in most countries and seek to follow the guiding principles laid down for them by international statistical agencies, yet only in the English-speaking countries are Census results shown according to size of enterprise, where each enterprise is understood to include subsidiary companies in which a majority of the shares is owned by the parent. In other countries results are generally available by size of plant, and sometimes by size of company, but each subsidiary may then be treated as a separate entity and not grouped with its parent, so that the full extent of the resources under the control of the largest enterprises is not shown, and the degree of industrial concentration and changes in it cannot be ascertained.[1] In earlier times subsidiary companies were rarer and these distinctions were of less importance; but, as we have seen in chapter 4, the modern large enterprise tends to be a multi-plant concern and those plants are often owned through a chain of subsidiary companies. It has, therefore, become increasingly important to treat subsidiary companies together with their parent as a single entity; regrettably most foreign Censuses are deficient in this respect. It is equally to be regretted that the precise treatment of subsidiaries is usually not made adequately clear in foreign Census publications and, to add to the reader's confusion, the term 'enterprise' is often used to refer to each single company (or unincorporated firm) excluding its subsidiaries, while in English usage the term 'enterprise' is understood to include subsidiaries.

The lack of information on subsidiaries in most foreign countries is not confined to their Censuses of production, but affects also the published annual accounts of companies, even if their shares are quoted on a Stock Exchange; company accounts cannot therefore take the student of concentration as far as might be thought. The requirement (and perhaps even the idea) that a 'true and fair view' of a company's affairs should be conveyed in its annual accounts, and that those accounts should consolidate the affairs of subsidiary companies, has until very recently been confined to the English-speaking world; and, whilst some of the largest international enterprises have begun to adopt these standards (often with an eye to their shares being quoted on the Stock Exchanges of London or New York), international comparisons of sizes of enterprises based on published company accounts remain subject to serious limitations.[2]

When it comes to the narrower issue of the sizes of plants, we should be on safer ground in basing international comparisons on Censuses of manufacturing. Even so, if similar products are produced in geographically adjacent buildings under common ownership, they may appear on a single return according to the Census rules of one country, but on separate returns according to the rules of another. Which procedure is adopted may depend on whether detailed accounts are kept in respect of each building. The initial unit of enumeration may also affect the ultimate treatment: thus in Britain the establishment is the basic Census unit and totals for the enterprise are built up from the constituent establishments; whereas in other countries the basic unit is the legal entity and its total is apportioned to the constituent establishments as far as possible. One may suspect that in a large company, owning a number of plants of varying sizes, the British approach will tend to distinguish more plants than the foreign procedure. Despite the efforts of international agencies to standardise procedures, only limited progress has been made; to some extent therefore reservations are attached also to comparisons of plant-sizes, and unless the differences are large no confident conclusion can be drawn.[3]

In the statistical comparisons that follow much the most attention has been given to the United States, partly because of its obvious interest, but mainly because the American statistics and the many research studies carried out there appear satisfactorily comparable with those for the United Kingdom (or at least the residual incomparabilities can be surmounted). In the ensuing section we compare the trends in the United States and the United Kingdom of the estimated shares of the hundred largest manufacturing enterprises; this is followed by a comparison of the average sizes of manufacturing enterprises and their dispersion, and similarly plants; finally, the variability of the rates of growth of enterprises in America and Britain is compared for its bearing on the development of concentration.

We then turn to comparisons with the main European countries, but these have been severely restricted to ensure that we are on moderately reliable ground. We compare only the numbers of the very largest enterprises, based on their Annual Reports, and the numbers of very smallest firms, based on the Censuses.[4]

AGGREGATE CONCENTRATION IN THE UNITED STATES

The United States has for long been the natural home of 'big business' – also the country where it has aroused the most public concern, and where it has received the most intensive public scrutiny and academic examination. The main implications of a great many detailed studies of the growth of industrial concentration are brought together here in chart 6.1, in terms of the estimated share in manufacturing net output accounted for by the hundred largest manufacturing enterprises in the United States. The series displayed in this graph is intended to be

Chart 6.1. *Shares of the hundred largest enterprises in manufacturing net output, United Kingdom and United States*

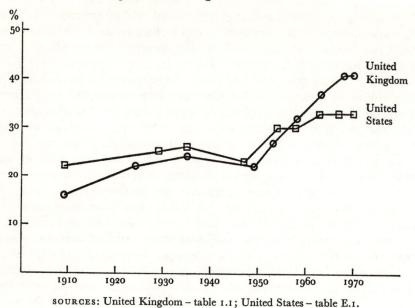

SOURCES: United Kingdom – table 1.1; United States – table E.1.

comparable in concept with that for the United Kingdom considered in chapter 1 above (which is also shown). The underlying sources and the methods and approximations used to derive the summary series for the United States are described in appendix E.1. We need only note here, by way of summary, that the figures for 1947 and later years are more reliable in that they are derived from Censuses of Manufactures, that earlier figures are based on relative movements of asset totals compiled from company accounts, and that particular reservations are attached to the very earliest period, 1909–29, in respect of which other writers have formed a view implying that the starting point in 1909 should be somewhat lower than shown here and its initial rate of rise somewhat sharper (see appendix E.1).

If we are prepared for the moment to accept that it is valid, or at least of interest, to compare the share of the same number of enterprises between countries of different sizes, we may put the main lessons of this chart as follows. Up to the mid-1950s the hundred largest manufacturing enterprises were responsible for a greater share of net output in the United States than were the hundred largest in the United Kingdom, and that may well be an important reason why 'big business' aroused more concern there than here. Since the 1950s the position has been reversed; the much more rapid rise of the British giants has now given them a substantially greater share here. There is a remarkable contrast since 1963 between the virtual constancy of the share of the hundred largest enterprises in America and the rise of their share in the United Kingdom. In the United States the share of the hundred largest, if reckoned to the nearest percentage point,[5] has remained at 33 per cent throughout the seven years 1963–70, while in the United Kingdom there has been a rise of 4 percentage points.[6]

Looking back, the dip in concentration during the period covering the Second World War will be noticed. That the movement is so similar in the two countries provides some incidental support for both sets of figures, which might otherwise warrant greater reserve, both being based on sources that are less than ideal. The substantive reason for the similarity is, of course, that both countries were subject to the same sequence of grave economic and political upheavals – the Great Depression, and then the war and the mobilisation of resources by the government. The rise in concentration at the beginning of the 1930s has been attributed in the United States to the greater vulnerability of smaller firms to the economic crisis of those years; the subsequent decline has been attributed to New Deal policies which inhibited mergers, and to the opportunities subsequently provided for small firms by reflation and, later, by the post-war sellers' market.[7] That decline, as we now see, was in the nature of a temporary aberration. With the facts now before us it seems clear that the long-term trend in the United States over the past sixty years may be described as mildly rising; accordingly those early commentators who could see, or foresee, that this was the direction of events were right (Berle and Means, 1932). But, given the size of the wartime dip in concentration and the margin of error attached to certain of the figures, we can also understand why there has previously been scope for dispute. The direction of the underlying trend was not entirely clear until the Census figure for 1954 appeared. And again today, given the constancy in the share of the hundred largest since 1963, it can be argued that the trend has changed – that the powerful series of restrictions imposed by American law on mergers and on transactions which reduce potential competition are now apparently sufficient to restrain any further general rise in concentration.[8]

SIZES OF ENTERPRISES IN THE UNITED STATES AND BRITAIN

There is thus a substantial contrast between the United States and Britain in the historical development of industrial concentration and in the levels of concentration now reached. If we were to assume that broadly similar factors determined the sizes of enterprises in both countries, one must expect that in Britain, being the smaller country, a given number of large enterprises would account for a greater share of total activity; yet the fact is that only in the last twenty years has this been so.

Before drawing any practical conclusions as to whether concentration and the sizes of enterprises are in some sense too high in Britain, it is necessary to attempt some direct comparisons of the largest concerns in both countries.[9] This is not a straightforward task, because 'size' is very different if measured in terms of output or in terms of employment (since output per person is so very much higher in America). The number and types of comparison that can validly be made are somewhat restricted by differences in statistical procedures in the two countries;[10] the following are some of the more important facts to be deduced from the American Census of 1967 and the British Census of 1968, and bear on various facets of the question.

First, it is clear that the largest American enterprises have a far greater absolute production than the largest enterprises in this country, even though (as we have seen) the largest enterprises in America account for a smaller share of total activity than the largest here. The net output of the hundred largest manufacturing enterprises in the United States is six times that of the hundred largest here (this comparison is at official exchange rates; an adjustment to allow for differences in purchasing power might lower that multiple to perhaps four or five). Indeed, it appears that the net output of the thirty largest American manufacturing enterprises exceeds that of the whole of United Kingdom manufacturing![11] Any policy based on the belief that it was necessary for British firms to merge to match the largest American concerns in terms of output would thus have to go unrealistically far along the road towards concentration, and virtually eliminate any possibility of domestic competition.[12]

Secondly, if we take employment as our measure of size rather than output (and avoid the problems of comparing outputs valued in different currencies), the apparent differences are reduced: the hundred largest manufacturing enterprises in the United States each employ 50,000 persons on average, compared with 27,000 for the average of the hundred largest in the United Kingdom.[13] This comparison and the preceding one are influenced by the sizes of the two countries: the United States, being larger in all senses, will have more large enterprises, and if the same *number* of largest enterprises is taken in both countries one should not be surprised if those of the larger country are 'higher up the scale'.

As a third comparison relating to the very largest enterprises, we therefore consider the proportion of employees in each country to be found in enterprises above a certain absolute threshold; here it is convenient, having regard to the available data, to take employment of 20,000 persons as that threshold. Intuitively it may seem that the smaller country would have less relative scope for such large enterprises and therefore a lower proportion of its employment above such a threshold; but specialisation often permits a small country to produce a few items on a large scale, and it is therefore not obvious that there is a bias in this criterion. Surprising as it may seem our calculations suggest that in both the United States and the United Kingdom a very similar proportion of employees, namely about 27 per cent, are engaged in manufacturing enterprises with over 20,000 employees.[14] Thus there is no indication that in manufacturing in Britain too low a proportion of the labour force is to be found in the very largest enterprises, provided we define them in terms of the number of employees.

Proceeding further down the size-distribution, it is interesting to compare, as between the two countries, the size of enterprise above which half the labour force is absorbed (this is the 'Florence-median' defined in chapter 3). It turns out that in 1963 half the manufacturing labour force in Britain was employed in enterprises having over 3000 employees, but in America this point was substantially lower at 1500 employees. The 'typical' American manufacturing firm is thus only half the size of the 'typical' British firm.[15]

The greater importance of small enterprises in America has also to be noted. Enterprises with under a hundred employees accounted for 15 per cent of all manufacturing employment in the United Kingdom in 1968,[16] and for 19 per cent in the United States in 1967.[17]

To summarise: the largest American enterprises have a much greater output than is conceivable here. However, in terms of employment there is less difference between the relative frequencies of firms of various sizes, and the median manufacturing enterprise has only half the employment of that in this country. If we are looking for reasons why output per person is so very much higher there, it is thus not because the typical American enterprise today employs more persons. The real difference between the two countries is in the spread or dispersion of sizes: America has relatively more large and more small enterprises, but fewer middle-sized enterprises than Britain. Paradoxical as it may seem, though America is thought of as the home of 'big business', it is also in a sense the home of 'small business'. From the statistics examined so far we cannot rule out that perhaps plant-sizes are greater there – that is, that the typical American enterprise may have fewer but larger plants; this is to be examined in the next section. Finally, to return to concentration, the lower share of the hundred largest enterprises in America today can be regarded as a consequence mainly of the greater size of that economy, the same proportion of total employment being engaged in both countries in the very largest enterprises, those with over 20,000 employees.

SIZES OF PLANTS IN THE UNITED STATES AND BRITAIN

In view of the wide interest in production economies of scale, and in whether the size of plant dictated by modern technology entails a high degree of enterprise-concentration, it is worth comparing rather carefully the typical sizes of manufacturing plants in the United States and Britain, and their changes over the past generation or so. The Censuses of the two countries provide much information on this topic (very much more than is available on enterprises), and this section attempts to set out the main features in terms of a few summary measures. Size is again considered in terms of employment; this is partly a matter of doing what is statistically more feasible, but partly also that it enables one to ask whether higher American productivity may be the consequence of a larger employment per plant (permitting a greater division of labour), or whether it must be considered the consequence of other factors such as higher capital per person, greater standardisation, longer runs and the like.

Considering manufacturing industry as a whole (table 6.1), the statistics indicate that half of United States manufacturing employment is in plants employing over 420 persons, whereas in Britain the corresponding size is 14 per cent greater at 480 persons (these comparisons, as in the preceding section, relate to the United States in 1967 and the United Kingdom in 1968). The slightly greater employment in the median plant in Britain today takes on more significance when contrasted with the pre-war situation: the median plant in Britain in 1929–30 was then considerably smaller than that in America, at 230 as against 330 employees. In other words, median plant-sizes in the past forty years have increased much less in America than in Britain. Before the war one might have pointed to the typically greater employment in American plants and considered whether that was related in some way to higher productivity there;[18] but that is no

Table 6.1. *Plant-sizes in British and American manufacturing,*
1930–68

	Florence-median[a]		Central range[a]		Proportion of employment in:			
					Small plants[b]		Large plants[c]	
	UK	US	UK	US	UK	US	UK	US
	(No. of employees)				(Percentages)			
1930 (29)[de]	230	330	..	90–1150	19[f]	18	10[f]	13
1935 (39)[de]	250	320	70–750	90–1100	19	17	9	13
1948 (47)[d]	340	400	100–1220	90–1550	16	16	15	18
1954	390	390	120–1430	90–1550	14	16	16	18
1958	440	350	120–1650	90–1450	14	17	18	17
1963	480	360	120–1680	90–1450	12	16	18	18
1968 (67)[d]	480	420	130–1600	110–1600	12	14	17	20

SOURCES: United Kingdom: table 3.2 above; United States: Department of Commerce, *Census of Manufactures* (various years).

[a] See notes *a–c* of table 3.2.
[b] Under 50 employees.
[c] 2500 employees and over.
[d] Dates of United States Censuses shown in brackets where they differ from the corresponding United Kingdom Censuses.
[e] Published United States data relate to wage-earners only; figures here adjusted for salaried staff on the basis of the distribution in *Census of Manufactures 1954*, vol. I, p. 203. 1929 figures also affected by inclusion of some employees in distribution and construction, and by inclusion of two or more plants in one return.
[f] Based on the published size-distribution relating to returns (see note *b* to table 3.1). Consequently the true proportion in small plants is somewhat higher than shown, and the true proportion in large plants is somewhat lower.

longer relevant today, when output per person is lower in Britain despite a greater employment per plant (whether this is to some extent *because* of 'over-manning' would obviously need more investigation than can be given here).

Though the median American plant has lower employment, output per head is so much greater that the median American plant's net output is just over double that of the median British plant.[19]

Looking merely at average sizes, however, gives too simple an impression; we must look also at the dispersion of plant-sizes. This was measured in chapter 3 above in terms of the central range of plant-sizes in Britain – half of the labour force being engaged in plants with between 130 and 1600 employees (with a quarter of the labour force in plants below the lower figure and a quarter above the upper figure); in the

United States the corresponding range is slightly wider – running from 110 to 1600 employees. There is thus a greater dispersion of plant-sizes in America.

This may usefully be considered further. If we take the percentage of employees to be found in small plants, for example those with fewer than fifty employees, that proportion is somewhat greater in America – at 14 per cent compared with 12 per cent in Britain. In large plants, those employing over 2500, there is also a somewhat greater proportion of employees to be found in America than in Britain – 20 per cent compared with 17 per cent. Just as in our comparisons of enterprise-sizes in the preceding section, we find that in the United States today there is a greater proportion of employment in both small plants and large plants – that is there are relatively fewer persons engaged in plants of medium size; this somewhat greater dispersion of sizes in America as compared with Britain deserves notice as much as the lower median-size there.

The changes over the preceding thirty years in the industrial size-distributions of the two countries may be assessed from the earlier Censuses as summarised in table 6.1 (but some of the minor changes between adjacent Censuses are better ignored as being due to the imperfections of our measuring instruments).[20] The American size-structure seems to have been particularly stable at the lower end, with a quarter of the labour force employed throughout in plants of below about ninety employees (though there has been some decline in the proportion engaged in plants of below fifty employees). In Britain smaller plants have declined more rapidly; to find the 'lower quarter' of the labour force (that is, the quarter employed in the smallest plants) we have to look to ever-larger plants as time proceeds (from plants with seventy employees in 1935 to plants with 130 employees in 1968). The size of the median-plant in America, as already noted, remained relatively stable over the period 1929–63, compared with a sharp rise in Britain. But there has been a clearer increase in both countries in the size of plants employing the 'top quarter' of the labour force, with the rise being faster in Britain. In short, while in Britain plants are today larger in terms of employment whichever point of the size-distribution we consider, in America the increase has been more apparent at the top end of the distribution and is barely discernible at the lower end.

The comparison of enterprises (set out in the preceding section) and the comparison of plants (in this section) both yield an interestingly similar general inference with regard to the present position: the dispersion of sizes is greater in America, but the median-size is lower there. And this similarity holds even though enterprises are so very much larger than plants – the median enterprise in each country being eight to ten times the size of the median plant.

This similarity in the distribution of plants and enterprises is obviously connected with the degree of multi-plant working which, for the largest enterprises, appears to be fairly similar in the two countries; however we cannot be very precise, since only a single comparison can properly be made from the available information. In 1963 the 200 largest United States manufacturing enterprises (ranked by value added) controlled an average of forty-five plants each,[21] and they accounted for 41 per cent of value added in all manufacturing. If we consider the largest enterprises in the United Kingdom accounting for the same share of manufacturing net output in that year, we would arrive at about 125 enterprises, which controlled an average of about thirty-three plants each. This is somewhat lower than the United States average, but the degree of multi-plant working in Britain is rising very rapidly (as we saw in chapter 4), thus it seems prudent to note only the broad similarity between the United States and the United Kingdom in this respect and to refrain from speculating on any finer difference.

The tendency noted above for employment in the median plant to be lower in America than in Britain applies also to the plants owned by these very largest enterprises; in America an average of 580 persons per plant were employed in the forty-five plants controlled by the 200 largest enterprises, whereas in Britain the average employment was 640 persons per plant owned by the comparable enterprises.

In our comparisons of British plant-sizes over time we saw that the hundred largest plants have accounted for a virtually constant 10 per cent of manufacturing employment in the last forty years (table 3.1 above), in contrast to the rising share of the hundred largest enterprises. A computation for America suggests that the hundred largest plants there have, very similarly, accounted for a fairly stable 9 per cent of employment over that period (a 1 point rise over those forty years is perhaps to be detected, but the calculation is approximate).[22] In neither country, therefore, can plant-sizes account for much of the rise in enterprise-concentration. If we went back to the beginning of the century, when the share of the hundred largest enterprises was closer to that of the hundred largest plants, it seems quite possible that some of the largest plants formed the nucleus around which other plants, by one means or another, increasingly clustered with the passage of time; deeper historical research would be needed to establish to what extent this was true, and Census statistics alone cannot provide any information.

We must now examine whether our general finding on plant-sizes (namely that median plant-sizes are somewhat greater in Britain, while the dispersion is somewhat greater in America) applies equally to all

Table 6.2. *Plant-sizes by industry,[a] United Kingdom (1968)
and United States (1967)*

			Proportion of employment in:			
	Florence-median[b]		Small plants[c]		Large plants[d]	
	UK	US	UK	US	UK	US
	(No. of employees)		(Percentages)			
Food, drink and tobacco	510	210	9	19	12	4
Chemicals and allied industries	740	540	8	12	19	20
Metal manufacture	1180	1480	6	5	34	40
Engineering and electrical goods	710	750	10	11	16	24
Shipbuilding and marine engineering	2600	1380	6	8	51	46
Vehicles	3000	6000[e]	3	2	55	68
Metal goods n.e.s.	220	230	23	19	2	8
Textiles	280	450	10	9	4	9
Leather, leather goods and fur	120[e]	140	35	26	—	3
Clothing and footwear	180	200	21	17	1[e]	1
Bricks, pottery, glass, cement, etc.	300	180	18	26	4	3
Timber and furniture	90	120	37	30	—	1
Paper, printing, publishing	290	240	19	20	7	6
Other manufacturing	370	280	15	16	14	6[e]
Total manufacturing	480	420	12	14	17	20

SOURCES: United Kingdom: Censuses of Production; United States: Censuses of Manufactures.

[a] United States industries reclassified for comparability with the United Kingdom (see appendix E.2).
[b] Half of all employees in plants below that size, and half above.
[c] Under 50 employees (and including all unsatisfactory returns for the United Kingdom).
[d] 2500 employees and over.
[e] Approximate.

industrial groups. Table 6.2 sets out our calculations based on reclassifying the American Census to correspond with the British industrial classification; the table shows the median plant-size for each of the fourteen Industrial Orders and gives for each Order the proportion of all employees to be found in plants with up to fifty employees and over 2500 employees.[23]

The influence of a common technology in both countries is obvious in the broad correspondence in the size-patterns of each industry. Thus, production of vehicles, shipbuilding, metal manufacture and engineering tend to be carried out in both countries in large plants, while leather goods, timber and furniture tend to be produced in smaller plants. Nevertheless there are some important differences. Median plant-sizes are very much larger in America for vehicles and textiles, and there are three groups in which British median plant-sizes are clearly greater – food (including drink and tobacco), chemicals, and bricks, etc. – it is these last three which may be regarded as reponsible for the calculated median plant in manufacturing as a whole being greater in Britain. For the remaining nine industrial groups the differences in median-sizes do not warrant attention.

The industrial differences between the countries are thus not of a uniform sort. They stand out a little more clearly on considering the extremes of the size-ranges. If we consider the proportion of employment in plants with over 2500 employees, we find that in half the industrial groups that proportion is greater in America – an apparently trivial finding suggesting no systematic difference between the countries in this respect. Nevertheless, it is of interest that those industrial groups where American employment tends to be proportionately greater in large plants are at the 'heavy' end – namely in the metal-producing and metal-working trades, and also in textiles. At the other end of the size-range, plants with fewer than fifty employees, Britain has a greater proportion of employment in small plants in the 'lighter' trades – leather, furniture and small metal goods. The story cannot however be reduced to a mere contrast between 'light' and 'heavy' industry in the two countries, since, even in the 'heavy' industries, in which, as has just been said, there is a greater proportion of employment in large plants in America, the Americans also have a greater proportion in small plants (this is true of chemicals and engineering). The greater dispersion of plant-sizes in America is thus characteristic also of industrial groups where, it might perhaps be thought, modern technology would impose uniformity and large size.[24]

More careful study would enable one to point to a host of individual factors contributing to these variations, but our concern here is less with these than with any general conclusions that may be drawn.[25] At that level it seems sufficient (and not unimportant) to note that, while there are variations amongst industries, there is no case for thinking that plants in Britain today are generally smaller in terms of their employment than those in America; further, in Britain one can detect a tendency for fewer plants to be found at both extremes of the size-distribution.

The difference with regard to the number of the very smallest plants is particularly vivid. In Britain (as we saw in chapter 1) the number of plants with up to ten employees has declined from almost 100,000 before the war to some 30,000 today, but in America their number has risen, from some 120,000 in the 1930s to 160,000 today. In relation to the number of inhabitants of each country, before the war there were more small plants in Britain than in America; today there are fewer in Britain (six as against eight plants per 10,000 inhabitants).

The above series of comparisons has been reported at what may seem undue length in relation to the simplicity of the conclusions, but it appeared to be worth doing so because of the widespread notion that plants are in some sense too small in this country, so that mergers and greater industrial concentration are essential to promote higher productivity.[26] That notion is probably based on out-of-date facts; as we have seen, before the war the median British plant did indeed employ fewer persons than the median American plant, but that is no longer so today in any general way. On the other hand, as there are now relatively fewer small plants and small enterprises in this country than in America, and their number has declined sharply in the past generation, one should perhaps ask whether the causes of lower productivity ought not rather to be sought in a lower rate of formation of new firms in Britain, and the reasons for it; however, this is a field in which statistical comparisons cannot be made with reliability.

DIFFERENCES IN AGGREGATE CONCENTRATION BETWEEN THE UNITED STATES AND BRITAIN

The contrast between the rapid rise in the share of the hundred largest manufacturing enterprises in Britain and its recent stability in America is both of practical and of theoretical interest. On the practical side, as already said, the American experience suggests that, even in a modern economy, whether because of constraints imposed by public policy on the largest firms or because of the thriving growth of smaller firms, it is possible to inhibit the largest firms absorbing an ever-greater share of the economy. On the theoretical side, one is tempted to analyse the reasons for that stability in terms of what is known of the growth-patterns of the largest firms. By comparing the corresponding American and British studies of growth-patterns of firms, one might hope to have a clearer view as to the sources of the different evolution of the industrial size-structure in the two economies.

The present section, in addition to comparing previous studies of company growth in the two countries, reports on a study of the growth of the hundred largest manufacturing companies in both countries during the recent five-year period 1967–72 carried out for the purposes of this inquiry (the methods used in this analysis of the two countries are much more on the same footing than in the earlier studies – carried out by different investigators – where there are serious problems in adjusting for differences in methods).[27]

The frequency of large mergers

Of the various contrasts between the two countries that emerged from our study for 1967–72, the clearest related to the frequency of large mergers. Of the hundred largest industrial enterprises in the United States in 1967, ranked by capital, only three were taken over in the following five years,[28] but in Britain fourteen of the hundred largest companies – nearly five times as many – were taken over or merged with other firms in that period. Further, none of the American firms taken over were among the top twenty-five in the 1967-list, but three of the British companies taken over had been in the top twenty-five.[29]

We may first assess the effects of this difference, considered in isolation from other factors, on our crude measure of aggregate concentration, namely the share of the hundred largest in each country. That measure rises in consequence of take-overs within the hundred largest by an amount depending on the sizes of the companies at the bottom of the hierarchy introduced to make up the fixed number of a hundred companies. In America, where three companies disappeared due to take-over, an additional three companies have to be introduced to replace them, and they increased the total capital of the hundred largest by 0·97 per cent (on the basis of their 1967-capital values).[30] From the Census we know that the hundred largest accounted for 33 per cent of manufacturing net output in that period; approximately, therefore, the direct effect of these three take-overs was to raise that share by about 0·32 percentage points (0·97 per cent of 33). That rise relates to a five-year period; the rise per annum in the share of the hundred largest in manufacturing output due to take-overs within the hundred largest alone can thus be put at 0·06 points, or just over half a point per decade.

In Britain the calculation for this period leads to a quite different magnitude. The fourteen additional companies introduced at the bottom of the list to make up our fixed total of a hundred companies increased the capital of the hundred largest by 3.5 per cent. The share of the hundred largest in manufacturing net output in 1968 was 41 per cent, and the rise in that share due to these take-overs may therefore be put at approximately 1·4 percentage points over five years (3·5 per cent of 41). The rise in the share of the hundred largest due to take-overs within the hundred largest alone may therefore be put at about 3 points a decade. Both in their number, and in their effect on the share of the hundred largest, take-overs within the hundred largest were thus about five times greater in Britain than in America in this period.[31] This is an important difference; we must now assess it in relation to changes in the share of the hundred largest due to other causes.

In America, as we noted at the outset, the share of the hundred largest remained constant in the period 1963–70; take-overs within the hundred largest might have been expected to raise that share in those seven years (on the basis of the above calculation and assuming that the rate calculated for 1967–72 can be applied to 1963–70) by about seven times 0·06, that is 0·42 points. It follows that other factors that affect concentration either were sufficient to offset that rise, or were too small in their aggregate effect to lead to a full one point change in the published share of the hundred largest.[32] In this respect too there is a contrast with Britain. In the period 1958–68 the share of the hundred largest in Britain rose by 9 percentage points; on the basis of the above calculations we might thus expect take-overs within the hundred largest to account for only some 3 points, and factors apart from take-overs within the hundred largest to account for something like 6 points. Thus both large mergers and other factors contributed to the fact that concentration rose faster in Britain than in America, and the greater frequency of large mergers in Britain was responsible for only about a third of the excess.

The variability of growth-rates

In attempting to understand the factors other than large mergers we have to make use of the analytical framework set out in chapter 2. It will be remembered from that chapter that, under certain simple and apparently realistic conditions, an increase in the concentration of surviving firms is generally to be expected because not all firms grow at the same rate (there is a certain dispersion of growth-rates, or 'size-mobility'), leading over time to the emergence of ever-larger giant enterprises. Nevertheless, concentration can be stabilised if, despite the variability of growth-rates, smaller firms grow on average somewhat more rapidly than larger firms (that is, if there is a 'Regression towards the mean' or, in more familiar terms, an optimum range of firm-sizes to which firms tend as time proceeds, and if 'by chance' they exceed it their further growth tends to be inhibited).

In contrasting the American and British development of concentration we are therefore led to ask in which of these two aspects American firms differ from British firms. First, are firms in America today much more uniform in their growth-rates than in Britain, so that changes in the size-hierarchy arise relatively rarely (that is, is size-mobility there much lower than here)? Or, secondly, is there perhaps a stronger tendency in America for smaller firms to grow on average more rapidly than large firms? Of course, some combination of these two aspects is conceivable.

When the questions are posed in this way it is seen that a full answer ideally requires careful, comparable studies of the growth-rates of enterprises over a broad range of sizes, relating in both countries to an extensive period of time, but the available studies – though there are quite a number of them – fall short of that ideal. The published studies of the growth-patterns of large firms in America are limited to the hundred (sometimes 200) largest firms, and do not extend even to the larger population of all quoted industrial firms as do the British studies.[33] It must also be said that there are a number of serious methodological problems in interpreting the American studies.[34] Nevertheless, with careful sifting, some conclusions can be drawn.

To begin with the question of the variability of growth-rates: our comparison of the growth-rates of the hundred largest in both countries in the period 1967–72 indicates that there was a negligible difference – the standard deviation of the growth-rates of capital employed was 5·7 percentage points in both countries.[35]

Values of similar magnitude for the dispersion of growth-rates in Britain have been derived for earlier periods. A calculation for the hundred largest companies in the years 1948–53 yielded a standard deviation of growth-rates of 6·1 percentage points (Prais, 1957, p. 260), and fairly similar, if slightly higher, figures are to be inferred from studies relating to all quoted manufacturing companies in Britain for periods between 1951 and 1965.[36]

Earlier studies of the hundred largest American companies, on the other hand, showed a declining variability of growth-rates since the beginning of the century, falling to about 3 percentage points in the post-war period (up to 1964);[37] one might conclude that the lower variability of growth-rates in America may have made a contribution at earlier stages to the slower rise in concentration there. However, the American studies suffer from a suspected bias and that conclusion need not be accepted.[38] But, whether it is accepted or not (and the many incomparabilities introduced by different investigators into these studies make it difficult to speak with certainty), it seems clear that recently there has been little difference in the variability of growth-rates. Reasons for the recent stability of concentration in America must therefore be sought elsewhere, that is in the degree of Regression towards the mean in the sizes of firms.

The Regression of firm-sizes

Studies for Britain (as will be remembered from chapter 2) indicate that at certain times during the post-war period larger companies have been showing rates of growth that on average exceeded those of smaller companies; that is to say, during those times there were dispersive forces at work making for a faster rise in concentration, rather than the Regressive tendencies which stabilised concentration during the war and moderated its rise in the pre-war period.

It is possible to calculate the theoretical degree of Regression that would be adequate to stabilise concentration at its present level; following the approach of chapter 2, equation (7), this depends on the variability of growth-rates and on the existing degree of concentration. Inserting recent values into the mathematical formula suggests that a Regression of about $c = -0.05$ would be adequate to stabilise the degree of concentration.[39] Such a low degree of Regression is adequate today because the hypothetical question we are considering is that of keeping concentration stable at the very high level it has already reached; to see concentration fall to a lower level and be maintained would require a greater degree of Regression. In considering the reasons for the stability of American concentration, we are thus led to ask whether it is possible that a degree of Regression of about -0.05 has operated in the United States.

Our analysis for the hundred largest enterprises in America and Britain for 1967–72 pointed in that direction, but the sampling errors were regrettably too great to permit one to speak with sufficient precision on the degree of Regression;[40] a rather larger sample is necessary on grounds of precision alone, but this was beyond our resources.

The results of the earlier American study by Mermelstein (1969) also point in this direction, but are not conclusive because of the sampling bias already mentioned.[41] His analysis for the period 1909–64 of the hundred largest surviving companies suggested that until 1948 the largest of those companies grew less rapidly than those below them, so providing some offset to factors making for higher concentration; but, as in Britain, this was reversed in the period 1948–58, when the largest companies grew more rapidly.[42] However, in the most recent period 1958–64 that ceased, and there is a mild suggestion that smaller concerns have a slight advantage.

The direct evidence on the degree of Regression in America is thus weak (perhaps mainly because of the small size of the samples that have been investigated). The evidence is also subject to the important reservation that it relates only to differential movements within the hundred largest companies, whereas we should be more interested in how the hundred largest have fared in relation to the rest.

*　*　*　*　*

Putting together the various pieces of evidence at our disposal, we arrive at the following conclusions. The variability of growth-rates is much the same in the two countries, but large mergers account for relatively more of that variability in Britain. Aggregate concentration has risen faster in Britain and, since this is not attributable to a greater variability of growth-rates, we might infer that it is due to a difference in Regressive tendencies – the growth of the very largest firms being more inhibited, while the growth of smaller firms is stronger, in America than in Britain. That would seem an obvious way of reconciling the difference in trends; a full investigation to provide direct evidence on this, based on large samples covering a wide range of firm-sizes, is much to be desired.

LARGE AND SMALL ENTERPRISES IN EUROPE AND AMERICA

The difficulties of statistical comparisons relating to the sizes of enterprises in Europe have been noted in the opening paragraphs of this chapter, and the reader will have it in mind that all numerical estimates in this section must be treated with some reserve. If nevertheless we are prepared to take a broad view, some instructive comparisons emerge regarding the sizes and relative importance of the very largest enterprises in each country, and the numbers of the very smallest enterprises (it is on enterprises of intermediate size that the information is too weak to be worth reporting, and this gap prevents any comprehensive view of the size-distribution).

The number of giant enterprises

Table 6.3 sets out the number of the largest manufacturing enterprises and their total employment in the main European countries in 1972, with comparable figures for Britain and the United States, the largest enterprises being defined here as those having over 40,000 employees. This group includes nearly a hundred American enterprises and smaller numbers of European enterprises, varying approximately according to the size of the country concerned, from some thirty for Britain to three for Switzerland. The enterprises are listed by name in appendix F.2, which draws attention to the many difficulties in compiling such a list.[43]

Much of the production activities and employment of these giant concerns lies outside their host country. Indeed, if the host country is small the majority of their employment will be abroad: for example, over 80 per cent of the world employment of the 'four giants of Dutch industry' (Royal Dutch–Shell, Unilever, Philips and Akzo) lies outside the Netherlands.[44] In the present comparisons we are interested in the total size of these large enterprises, so their world (rather than domestic) employment is shown in the table. It would also be of interest

Table 6.3. *Manufacturing enterprises*[a] *employing over 40,000,*
United Kingdom compared with other countries, 1972

	Size of country		Large enterprises		Importance of large enterprises relative to:[c]	
	Population	Manu- facturing employment	Number	Employ- ment[b]	Population	Manu- facturing employment
	(Millions)			(Millions)	(Indices, UK = *100*)	
UK	55·8	7·78	30	2·67	*100*	*100*
US	208·8	18·93	89	8·05	*81*	*124*
France	51·7	5·93	12	1·15	*46*	*56*
Germany	61·7	10·53	12	1·59	*54*	*44*
Italy	54·4	5·83	6	0·64	*24*	*32*
Benelux	23·4	2·47	5	0·80	*72*	*95*
EEC – 6	191·1	24·75	32[d]	4·17	*46*	*49*
Sweden	8·1	1·05	3	0·18	*46*	*50*
Switzerland	6·3	0·85	3	0·28	*93*	*96*

SOURCES: large enterprises – see appendix F.2; population – United Nations Statistical Office, *Monthly Bulletin of Statistics*; employment – International Labour Office, *Yearbook of Labour Statistics*.

[a] Excluding iron and steel.

[b] World employment by parent and subsidiary companies (also used to determine which enterprises employ over 40,000).

[c] Ratios of employment in large enterprises to national population and to manufacturing employment converted to indices.

[d] Allowing for double counting of multinationals (see appendix F.2).

to compare the share in manufacturing activities of domestic employment by these giants (as we were able to do for Britain and the United States on page 143 on the basis of Census returns relating to manufacturing establishments in the home country only), but the relevant figures are not available for most European countries.

In relation to the sizes of the countries concerned, whether measured by their population or their employment in manufacturing, the calculations in table 6.3 suggest that in France and Germany large enterprises occur only about half as frequently as in Britain or the United States.[45] Italy's industrialisation is more recent, and large enterprises have their homes there only a third or a quarter as frequently as in Britain. Of the smaller countries, Sweden is similar to France and Germany, while in Switzerland and the Benelux countries large enterprises are to be found almost as frequently as in Britain.[46] The Netherlands considered alone has the greatest density of giant enterprises in relation to its small domestic employment in manufacturing.[47] In the original six EEC countries together, in relation to their total size large enterprises occur only about half as frequently as in Britain or America.

While there are differences amongst the various countries, it is equally important to notice that they lie within limits that are not so far apart – that is to say giant concerns are not outstandingly the prerogative of a particular country. It appears, rather, as if the development of large enterprises in all economically advanced countries has followed a more or less similar evolutionary process and, if some countries lag behind others, the time-lag cannot be said to be enormous. To put it more specifically: the largest concern in the world is indeed American (General Motors, with an employment of $\frac{3}{4}$ million), but the next half dozen largest enterprises in the United States take one down quite rapidly to 170,000 employees, and eight enterprises are to be found in Europe having an employment exceeding that figure (Philips, Unilever, General Electric, Volkswagen, ICI, British Leyland, Fiat and Royal Dutch–Shell). A slightly different picture would emerge if we considered other size-levels, or if size was measured in terms of output rather than employment;[48] nevertheless, given the differences in the sizes and natural resources of the various countries, it is remarkable that the frequencies of giant concerns are as close together as they are.

It will be seen from table 6.3 that it makes little difference whether we take the total population of a country or its manufacturing employment as the standard against which to measure the relative importance of the largest companies. The only exception is the United States – partly because of its very high labour productivity in manufacturing, a relatively lower proportion of the labour force there is engaged in manufacturing. The more appropriate standard of that country's size for the present comparison is probably its total manufacturing employment, and on that basis giant enterprises are rather more important in the United States than elsewhere.[49]

The informed reader will not have been surprised by the results of these calculations; the importance of the United States as the breeding-ground of giant industrial concerns operating on a world scale is legendary. Britain's empire may today be a matter of memory, but not such a distant memory that the giant enterprises which flourished under its hegemony have lost their previous worldwide scope.[50] The commercial flair of the Dutch and the acumen of the Swiss are bywords not only in Amsterdam and Zurich. Germany, the country most similar to Britain in the size of its population and its total manufacturing employment, appears with many fewer giant industrial concerns: only twelve enterprises have more than 40,000 employees (with total employment of 1·6 million), compared with thirty such enterprises in Britain (employing a total of 2·7 million); perhaps this is the mark left by Germany's loss of two world wars.

Giant enterprises in Britain and Germany

The suggestion that aggregate concentration is substantially lower in Germany than in Britain is of some importance and deserves closer examination. The figures on Germany presented above rely ultimately on what is published by companies in their annual accounts, and on what can be discovered by journalists and research workers concerning inter-company connections.[51] It will be understood that it is only too possible that not all those connections have been elucidated, and that the number and sizes of the largest companies and the degree of concentration in Germany may therefore be understated. However, these lists represent all that is available and form the basis of other statements that have been made regarding the state of concentration in Germany as compared with other countries. There should not therefore be any discrepancies between the inferences drawn from them; but different inferences have been reached by other commentators, who have suggested that aggregate concentration in Germany is as high as in Britain. Thus, Professor H. Arndt has pointed out that the sales of the hundred largest industrial companies in Germany in 1966, as listed in the *Frankfurter Allgemeine Zeitung*, amounted to 46 per cent of the sales of 'total industry' (the latter concept will be examined further in a moment);[52] more recently, an EEC report has suggested that the 'hundred largest industrial undertakings' accounted for 50 per cent of 'total industrial turnover' in both Britain and Germany in 1969–70.[53]

Closer examination shows that the comparison made by the EEC exaggerates the level of German concentration in relation to that of Britain. The German proportion is based on company accounts, whereas the British proportion is based on the Census of Production. The following seem to be important sources of bias:

(*a*) The sales of 'total industry' used in the calculation for Germany excluded those craft establishments coming under what is known in Germany as 'Handwerk', which add some 15 per cent to total sales reported under the heading of 'Industrie'.[54]

(*b*) Total sales of the largest firms as shown in their accounts include those of any non-industrial establishments that they own, and occasionally of establishments operating abroad; they are therefore greater than would be recorded in a Census of domestic industrial establishments. By comparing a total for the hundred largest based on their annual accounts with a grand total based on a Census of domestic manufacturing production inevitably an unduly high fraction emerges for Germany as compared with Britain.

If we wish to compare the share of the hundred largest enterprises in Britain and in Germany on the basis of the limited information that is available, we must use identical tools in both countries; that is, we must start from company accounts in both countries. A possible calculation would then run as follows. If we allow for 'Handwerk', the estimate of 50 per cent quoted above for the share in sales of the hundred largest industrial enterprises in Germany in 1969 would fall to about 43 per cent. Next, a comparable British proportion might be constructed for 1968 by comparing the sales of the hundred largest industrial companies as recorded in *The Times 1000* list (£29·7 million from the list of 1969–70, which relates mainly to 1968) with the total of sales for all industries (£48·2 million shown as 'gross output' in the 1968 Census); this yields an estimate of 62 per cent of industrial sales in Britain accounted for by the hundred largest. Aggregate concentration (on the basis of the share of the hundred largest industrial enterprises) is thus apparently two-thirds as high in Germany as in Britain, which is more consistent with the impression yielded by table 6.3 (based on enterprises with over 40,000 employees).[55]

That seems to be as far as we can go on the basis of what is known of the largest German enterprises. Differences in aggregate concentration are not necessarily a reliable guide to differences in concentration in particular markets, and it would be of the greatest interest to compare explicitly the shares of (for example) the four largest firms in comparably defined industries in Britain and Germany. Other investigators, who have been prepared to ignore the limitations of the definition of 'enterprise' in the official German industrial Census (namely, that subsidiary concerns are not consolidated with their parent) have published statistics indicating that on average German industries are significantly less concentrated than those in Britain.[56] Such a conclusion would be reassuringly consistent with that derived above on the difference in aggregate concentration, but its validity cannot be wholeheartedly accepted until some further investigation has demonstrated that subsidiary companies can in practice be ignored in assessments of concentration in Germany.

The number of small firms

We turn next to consider differences amongst countries in the number of small manufacturing firms as recorded in their Censuses. In what follows we take an employment of under ten persons as our criterion for a small firm; in the EEC industrial Census of 1963, 87 per cent of the number of all manufacturing establishments ('local units') and 88 per cent of the number of all 'enterprises' fell into this category, and accounted for about 15 per cent of manufacturing employment.[57] It

Table 6.4. *Manufacturing establishments^a employing under ten persons,
United Kingdom compared with other countries, 1963*

| | Small establishments^b | | Proportion of total manu-facturing employment |
	Number	Per 1000 manufacturing employees	
	(000s)		(%)
UK	27	4	*2·1*
US	121	6	*2·4*
France	186	31	*10·8*
Germany	157	15	*6·2*
Italy	245	42	*18·5*
Benelux	57	23	*8·7*

SOURCES: United Kingdom: *Census of Production 1963;* United States:
Census of Manufactures 1963; EEC – *Industriezensus 1963.*

^{a} Excludes certain branches of manufacturing bordering on service trades (see note 58
on p. 294).
^{b} Defined for the United Kingdom as one with 1–10 employees, for elsewhere as one with
1–9 employees. British figures therefore slightly overstated in comparison.

should be noted that certain small manufacturing trades bordering on
services and distribution (such as bakers and tailors) have been omitted
from the present comparisons with a view to improving the comparability of the figures for Continental Europe with those of Britain and
America (though in practice this reduces the differences amongst countries only slightly).[58]

Table 6.4 sets out the results of our calculations. We see that Britain
has the lowest number of small manufacturing establishments in
relation to the size of its manufacturing sector. Small firms are progressively more numerous in the different countries in the following
order: United States, Germany, Benelux, France, Italy. In Germany
small firms are three to four times as frequent as in Britain; in Italy
they are about ten times as frequent.

These differences amongst countries in the relative number of small
firms seem much greater than those observed above in relation to the
importance of large enterprises. It might once have been argued that
a lag in industrialisation between countries is shown by a greater survival of small entrepreneurs, but the fact that Britain has recently
lagged in its industrial progress now makes one wonder, on the contrary, whether the elimination of small firms has not gone too far here,
and whether the rigidity of the economy and its undistinguished progress
is not, at least partly, attributable to the lack of small entrepreneurs.

The industrial involvement of the banks

The few statistics that have been considered above seem consistent in suggesting that the British economy is more 'concentrated' than that of other major countries – giant firms appear to be of greater importance here and small firms are found less frequently. But that is too simple a view, given the long-established differences in other environmental matters such as the role of banking. In Germany the industrial involvement of the banks is such that there must be, in actuality, a greater centralisation of control than appears from the figures presented above. The same is true of Belgium and, to a smaller extent, of the other Continental countries (except perhaps the Netherlands, where the banking system is closer to that of Britain).

It would not be sensible within the limits of the present chapter to attempt a historical account of differences amongst countries in the principal factors affecting the growth of large enterprises; nevertheless, with a view to qualifying the summary view that emerges from the bare statistics considered here, we have set out in appendix F.1 a brief survey of three aspects of the economic framework bearing particularly on the growth of large enterprises. These are:

(i) the date of legislation governing the formation of limited liability companies;

(ii) the role of banks as industrial financiers;

(iii) the role of the government or state as entrepreneur.[59]

The very wide variety amongst countries in the circumstances described there can, however, only lead the observer to wonder why differences in the ultimate importance of giant enterprises are not greater than they are. Perhaps the growth of giant enterprises in all countries is ultimately subject to rather similar factors and constraints, such as the rate of profit, and the rate at which new capital can successfully be incorporated into an existing firm without encountering severe dynamic diseconomies of scale. Whether the banks, or some apparatus of state, or groups of individuals take the major initiative in promoting large concerns seems to have had less effect than might have been expected on the relative importance of giant concerns in the leading industrial countries today.[60]

A SUMMARY OF OUR INTERNATIONAL COMPARISONS

Our attempts to compare the levels and paths of industrial concentration between Britain and other countries have not gone as far as might have been hoped; neverthless some progress has been made and it may be useful to summarise the more important of the comparisons set out in this chapter. We have seen that before the war median plant-sizes in British manufacturing used to be lower than those in American manufacturing, but now they are larger in terms of employment – the median British manufacturing enterprise employs about double the number employed by the median American manufacturing enterprise.

The hundred largest enterprises in both these countries controlled an average of about fifty plants each in 1963, and it is this high degree of multi-plant ownership – rather than the sizes of plants – that accounts for the great share of these giant enterprises in total economic activity in both countries. The share in net output of the hundred largest manufacturing enterprises is today rather lower in America than in Britain (in 1970, 33 per cent in America, 41 per cent in Britain); the larger total size of the American economy may be regarded as the most important source of this difference, since the same proportion of the work-force in both countries is employed in enterprises with over 20,000 employees.

During this century the share of the hundred largest enterprises has on the whole risen more slowly in America than in Britain. The American share stabilised in the period 1963–70, when the British share was rising rapidly. Antitrust legislation has been stricter in America and we have seen that there has been a great difference between the two countries in the number of the largest enterprises that lost their independence through mergers (in 1967–72 five times as many of the hundred largest in Britain as in America). It also seems very possible that smaller companies in America have better prospects of growth in relation to large companies than is the case in Britain, but it would need a much larger sample study than those surveyed here to establish explicitly to what extent this was so, and to assess the likely contribution of this element to the differing paths of concentration.

Our comparisons with several European countries suggested that Britain has relatively more large enterprises. No simple conclusion can be drawn because of the very differing roles of the banks and the state in the various countries. At the very least, however, it can be said that, if we are looking for reasons for Britain's slower industrial progress, the idea that it is because enterprises are smaller here than elsewhere is not supported by the facts. And it may finally be noted that the lack of small firms in Britain has appeared consistently in all the figures examined in this chapter.

CHAPTER 7

REFLECTIONS

> There was an Arch of Reckoning outside Jerusalem,
> and anyone who wished to draw up his accounts went
> there. In this way his distress (on finding his reckoning
> not in accord with his expectations) would not disturb
> the city which, in the words of the Psalmist, was 'the
> joy of the whole earth'.
>
> Midrash Rabbah 52

The task of establishing and putting together a great variety of facts
bearing on general tendencies in the sizes of industrial enterprises and
in the organisation of our industrial structure has not proved easy.
The results of many disparate investigations have had to be assessed;
sometimes the discussion proved less than conclusive and often the need
for further extensive inquiry was all too apparent. Nevertheless a number of conclusions have been reached and, at the close of this study, it
may be helpful to put down the essence of those which bear centrally
on the general development of the economy, and to reflect on their
implications.

'General tendencies are not always beneficial' was the warning that
Marshall put in the caption to his discussion half a century ago of the
'broad tendencies towards the dominance of the joint-stock form of
administration and towards combinations of semi-monopolistic scope'.
He well understood the Marxian view 'that history showed a steadily
hastening growth of large businesses and of mechanical administration
by vast joint-stock companies', from which its exponents 'deduced the
fatalistic conclusion that this tendency is irresistible; and must fulfil
its destiny by making the whole state into one large joint-stock holding company, in which everyone would be a shareholder' (1923,
pp. 176–7). Marshall was much concerned by that prospect, and he
warned repeatedly of the loss in industrial efficiency and progress that
must be expected to ensue from the falling numbers of independent
competing producers.

Perhaps the most important result of the present study has been to
put some measure on the strength of that historical tendency towards
the concentration of economic activity, and to show that it has been
far stronger than generally thought. The estimates presented in

Notes to this chapter will be found on pp. 295–6.

chapter 1 suggest that the share in net output of the hundred largest manufacturing enterprises has risen from about 16 per cent in 1909 to about 41 per cent in 1970. The extent of the transformation of the industrial structure is perhaps more directly appreciated if we consider the drastic reduction in the number of largest firms that produce half the nation's manufacturing output: whereas before the First World War about 2000 of the largest enterprises accounted for half manufacturing output, today the figure is under 150.

These aggregate figures for all manufacturing activities summarise the great declines that have taken place in the numbers of alternative and competing suppliers for individual products. What has happened to the 'competitive climate' – to use an admittedly imprecise notion – is however more a matter of judgement. The growth of both domestic and foreign trade in manufactured goods has mitigated the effect of falls in the numbers of local producers, and in some products no doubt has offset it entirely; but on the whole the vast decline in the number of independent large producers must be regarded as supporting in a more urgent way those worries about the future of the competitive system that were in Marshall's mind.

The rise of giant businesses is, of course, not peculiar to Britain; it is a worldwide phenomenon characteristic of an advanced economy – yet it seems now to have gone further here than in other important countries. In the United States 'big business' developed earlier – the share of the hundred largest manufacturing firms having been greater in America than in Britain until the middle 1950s; since 1954, however, the share in net output of the hundred largest in the United States has virtually stabilised and remained within the range 30–33 per cent, while in this country the estimated share of the hundred largest has risen between 1954 and 1970 from about 28 to 41 per cent. The contrast in these summary figures reflects the very different histories and sizes of the two economies; the recent stability in the share of the largest American firms perhaps also reflects a greater public awareness of the threat posed by excessive concentration to the competitive system, and a stronger public policy designed to maintain competition. A further contrast between Britain and other countries that gives cause for thought concerns the number of small firms: the statistical comparisons on this are not as reliable as we should like, but in France and Germany, which are much the same size as this country and where output per head has now risen to exceed that in this country, it appears that the number of small manufacturing firms (those with fewer than ten employees) is about five times greater than here; other European countries show the same effect when allowance is made for their smaller size. Again we cannot say just how this mass of small

entrepreneurs may have contributed to faster economic growth –
whether it is the sharper stimulus to inventiveness provided by the more
competitive climate they engender, or whether it is the more extensive
seedbed which the smaller firms provide for the training of those who
subsequently take positions of responsibility in larger enterprises.[1]
But one is again led to ask whether the decline of the small firm in this
country, and the rise of the giant firm, has not gone further than
industrial efficiency requires.

We turn next to attempt a view of the relative importance of the
varied factors examined in this study for their contribution to increased
concentration. It is perhaps easiest to begin with a factor which,
contrary to the popular view, appears to have contributed very little.
The popular view is that technological developments have increased
the optimum sizes of manufacturing plants and that this is the main
reason why the sizes of firms have risen. Taking manufacturing as a
whole, however, we have seen (in chapter 3) that the hundred largest
plants accounted for 11 per cent of manufacturing net output in 1930
and exactly that same proportion in 1968; during that same period, it
will be recalled, the share of the hundred largest manufacturing enterprises rose from 23 to just over 40 per cent. It is thus not so much the
rise in plant-sizes but the rise in the number of plants owned by the
typical giant enterprise that has led to the rise in aggregate business
concentration. Of course, it is not to be doubted that larger optimum
plant-sizes have been responsible for increased concentration in
particular sectors of industry, but this simple comparison suggests that
on the whole one cannot ascribe to technological factors (more strictly,
those factors that determine plant-size rather than firm-size) any great
part in the process we are examining. More refined investigation, perhaps using other measures of size or other measures of concentration,
may well show that changes in plant-sizes had a certain effect on
the rise in aggregate concentration; all that we should conclude from
our comparison here (of shares of largest plants and largest enterprises) is that it would be surprising if the role of plant-sizes proved
to be other than minor.

On considering the very rapid expansion in multi-plant operation
by giant firms in recent years (the hundred largest manufacturing
firms – as will be remembered from chapter 4 – owned an average
of seventy-two manufacturing plants each in 1972 compared with only
twenty-seven in 1958), it might be thought that a striving for market
power would be a clearly dominating element. A comparison of the
changes in concentration between 1958 and 1968 in a sample of
individual trades based on a broad cross-section of manufacturing does
indeed show that concentration rose more rapidly in those trades in

which multi-plant operation rose more rapidly; yet the extent of the rise in concentration in particular trades attributable to increased multi-plant operation (by leading firms in those trades) was small – it was only a mild effect. At the end of the period (in 1968) there was a negligible correlation between the levels of concentration of different trades and their degree of multi-plant working. The extent of multi-plant working in particular trades (and the optimum size, number and geographical dispersion of production units owned by a typical firm in a trade) is significantly influenced by other factors, such as the transport costs of the raw materials and the products of the trade, and communication costs. Some of the observed rise in multi-plant working has been in response to lower transport and communication costs, but again the amount that is attributable to this factor is not sufficient to account for much of the very rapid increase in multi-plant working by giant firms.

Our study, thus, has not been able to ascribe any very substantial role to two apparently obvious factors – the technical requirement of greater plant-sizes and the desire for greater market power – in the total process governing the evolution of giant firms. On the other hand, our study assigns a major role to a hitherto elusive element, namely the way in which the growth-rates of firms must be expected to cumulate over time. This somewhat complex process was explained in chapter 2; its main features, in brief, are that we do not have to suppose, in order to explain increasing concentration, that large firms on average have net advantages over small firms on average. It is sufficient:

(i) that there is a degree of variability in the growth-rates of firms;

(ii) that average growth-rates are not related to firm-size – that is both large and small firms are subject to the same probabilities of success or failure and of growth or decline.

It follows from these circumstances alone that as time proceeds one must expect the emergence of a certain proportion of firms of ever-greater size. Only if there were some limiting factor, such as a life-cycle for firms in which they eventually matured and died (like trees in a forest), or strong long-run private diseconomies of scale – so that condition (ii) did not hold – would there be a possibility of avoiding increasing concentration.

This aspect of the long-term dynamic instability of the distribution of firm-sizes has not received much attention previously; its importance depends on the degree of variability in growth-rates and on the stage reached in the evolution of the economic system. The calculations reported in chapter 2 suggest that the observed variability amongst firms in their growth-rates is, by itself, sufficient to explain much of the development in the first half of this century of the share of giant firms. The theoretical trend in concentration to be expected from this process is a slow one, manifesting itself over a number of decades and following a 'sigmoid' path – slow at first, then accelerating, then slowing down again. Our calculations put the initial slow phase in the nineteenth century and the phase of greatest acceleration in the middle of the present century. Yet this trend explains only about half of the rather sharper rise in concentration observed in this country since 1950.

Even leaving aside this recent sharper rise (the possible causes of which will be considered in a moment), it appears that an important long-term tendency towards increasing concentration is inherent in our economic system as a result merely of the cumulative operation over time of the simple conditions labelled (i) and (ii) above. So long as the level of concentration in the economy was low this aspect of the system could be ignored, but at the present level of concentration some form of public intervention would seem necessary to halt, and perhaps reverse, the current trend.

Our discussion of financial factors in chapter 5 pointed to the importance of evolutionary changes in the ownership of capital: the rise of financial intermediary institutions, particularly since 1950, which together now own (or must shortly be expected to own) the greater part of the equity of the largest enterprises; the preferential channelling of new capital funds by those financial intermediaries towards larger concerns; the decline in owner-control of the largest enterprises and the concomitant rise in management-control; the instability of the managerial nucleus of the largest firms which, together with certain biases in the capital market, has encouraged take-over bids and so hastened the cumulative concentration of economic resources. These elements would account for the rather sharper rise in concentration observed since 1950. However, and without going into detail here, it appears that many of the financial advantages were in the nature of private rather than social economies, so that the social product would not be diminished if they were not reaped.

These two very different types of factors – the inherent diffusionary tendencies in the growth of firms, and the changes in the ownership pattern of capital and associated financial development – seem to deserve great weight in explaining the rise of aggregate concentration in the past half century.[2] To these may be added a third factor (though its importance is difficult to assess), namely the long-term fall in communication costs. As discussed in chapter 4, those developments which have made the world 'a smaller place' have permitted firms both to market commodities on a massive scale with the help of modern advertising methods and successfully to control production in many distant plants. Finally, one must remember government policy (for example via the Industrial Reorganisation Corporation and special schemes relating to the aircraft, shipbuilding and textile industries) encouraging with varying degrees of enthusiasm the formation of larger firms.[3]

The main concern of this book has been with providing an understanding of the historical trends in our economy, rather than with methods of altering those trends. It would not be right to conclude, however, without a word on policy. It will be understood that any proposal requires consideration from a much wider spectrum of views than is feasible here; what follows is therefore little more than a hint on possible lines of action.

Public policy has alternated between, on the one hand, encouraging the formation of large firms in the hope (and often little more than that hope) of reaping economies of scale and, on the other hand, discouraging or controlling large firms so as to avoid the evils of monopoly. The latter has expressed itself in two ways. First, where a monopoly is difficult to avoid (for example, in electricity distribution), nationalisation has seemed the obvious answer – better a public than a private monopoly, it is said. Questions have been raised as to the operational efficiency of large public monopolies and whether there might be advantages in separating those parts that can be run as independent competing units from those that cannot, but so far there have been no experiments in that direction.[4] Secondly, the Monopolies Commission has undertaken inquiries with a view to protecting the consumer's interests, and with the result that particular mergers have been disallowed, or profits and prices have been supervised; difficult as such inquiries are, no one can doubt their need.[5] And in the light of the present study, with its suggestion that large firms must be expected to emerge in growing numbers, one is drawn to the conclusion that the provision for such special inquiries must also be continuously increased.

One is, however, also led to ask whether a more general approach is required to put into reverse the present trend in the size-distribution of firms and which, if implemented, could eventually reduce the necessity for those more specific and difficult remedies. We have seen that there are general pressures, unconnected with efficiency, leading to the emergence of ever-larger firms: additional resources accrue to firms year by year, but, short of insolvency, there is at present no obvious way in which the largest firms can divide themselves into smaller parts. The natural question is thus whether we can devise some counteracting pressure to encourage the eventual division of the largest enterprises, so that the previous constituent units are operated independently and on the smallest scale that can be economically justified.

Once the need for such a counteracting pressure is accepted, it is not too difficult to conceive of practical measures that would promote the desired end. An obligatory independent 'social audit' of the hundred largest firms, for example at quinquennial intervals, could report on which parts might be hived-off into independent concerns without loss in productive efficiency. If that course seems too beset with administrative delays and arguments (and American experience of divestiture cases suggests it might be), a progressive Corporation Tax could be contemplated (say, a reduction of 10 per cent on the 'standard rate' when net assets are below £1 million, balanced by a surcharge of 10 per cent when assets exceed £30 million);[6] this would provide larger firms with an incentive to decide for themselves which parts could operate on a smaller scale. There would, of course, have to be safeguards to avoid interlocking directorships, and the degree of progressiveness of the tax could be adjusted pragmatically so that it had the desired effects.

This method allows each firm to make its own calculation of the best interest of its shareholders. Where, for example, production economies of scale are substantial and outweigh the progressiveness of the tax system, the firm would resist any temptation to split itself up;[7] but where the advantages of size are not obvious, the firm's present large size being the result of the accidents of history, a division would provide shareholders with the same type of tax advantage that hitherto has accrued from certain other types of financial reconstruction.

Measures of this kind may seem in some sense artificial, but it must be remembered that the problem we are considering stems ultimately from something which is no less artificial, namely the right of existence and privileges granted by society to the limited liability company. In the century or so that has elapsed since incorporation with limited liability became generally available, the development of companies has reached the stage where it is necessary to search for bounds to the growth of those that have attained gigantic dimensions; and to impose those bounds in such a way as will interfere as little as possible with the growth of the economy, and indeed promote its growth as a whole. It could be argued in favour of the proposed measure that, by raising the private cost of capital to larger firms and lowering it to smaller firms, it would offset the capital market's present bias in favour of larger firms (as discussed in chapter 5); also, by bringing private costs into line with social costs, it would lead to a more efficient allocation of the nation's capital resources. Such an argument implies a closer knowledge of social costs than is perhaps warranted and, in setting the progressiveness of the tax, it seems better to proceed pragmatically as suggested above. But it is perhaps worth noting that the raising of the costs of

capital to the larger firms may in itself lead to a rechannelling of investment flows towards more productive uses.

The approach suggested here attempts to meet the problem at a very
general level and would have its effects on the whole size-distribution
of firms. From our discussion of finance in chapter 5 it would also seem
desirable – at least from the point of view of our problem – to re-examine
some specific matters connected with taxation. First, attention was
drawn there to the great flows of savings into life insurance and pension
funds, which ultimately provide resources for the expansion of the
largest firms; without wishing to reduce the tax advantages attached to
personal savings, the question may be raised whether our tax system
must necessarily encourage the direction of those funds to large financial
intermediary institutions. Should it perhaps be made easier for the
owner of a small firm to reinvest pension provisions in certain of the
assets of his own firm (for example, secured by a mortgage on a given
fraction of the firm's properties), while gaining the same tax advantages
as apply to pension contributions? Secondly, the tax advantages
attached to debentures – as compared with shares – warrant re-examination, so that they cease to provide an incentive for refinancing associated with a merger.[8] Similarly, attention seems to be required to those
tax provisions which encourage a United Kingdom company operating
overseas to acquire a company with domestic income merely to permit
tax-saving.

The provision of additional capital funds to small firms also merits
reconsideration.[9] A specialised government-sponsored investment bank
for small firms is not necessarily the right method; an alteration in the
tax treatment of interest on loans may be better and easier to administer.
For example, it may be better to disallow interest on bank loans as a
charge in computing profits for Corporation Tax purposes for large firms
(in the same way as preference dividends are not a permissible deduction, and similarly as proposed above for debenture interest), whilst
continuing to allow bank interest to be deducted by smaller firms (as is
normal practice under present legislation).

It may finally be asked whether stricter controls on giant mergers
might be sufficient to solve our problem; can the stability of aggregate
concentration in the United States be accepted as showing that further
concentration can be inhibited merely by stronger anti-monopoly
measures and by stricter controls on giant mergers?[10] Stricter merger
controls on giants must obviously help, but mergers account for only
the smaller part (about a third, according to the calculations in
chapter 5) of the growth of giant enterprises;[11] it is thus by no means
clear that a radical change in the evolution of the size-distribution can
be expected from such a measure in isolation. The growth of the very

largest concerns would be inhibited; but there would continue to be
an expansion in the numbers just below them in size, and the share
of smaller firms would continue to decline.

One must not look too narrowly at the problem. The growing share
of the hundred largest enterprises is no more than one indicator of
deeper and more widespread changes in the economic system. Anyone
concerned at the loss of competitiveness and inadequate progress in
British industry must search for a more comprehensive policy than
merely fettering the giants. The author's view (put forward at the risk
of closing on a controversial note) is that the encouragement of a progressive and competitive economy now requires a systematic series of
policy measures aimed at tilting the balance throughout the range of
firm-sizes; measures are required to offset the private financial advantages enjoyed by the largest firms, to encourage individual plants to
be run as independent businesses rather than as subsidiaries of a distant
head office, and to foster an increase in the number of smaller independent firms to the levels found in other economically advanced
countries.

ESTIMATING THE SHARE OF THE
HUNDRED LARGEST
BRITISH MANUFACTURING FIRMS

One of the main objects of this inquiry was to estimate the share of the hundred largest manufacturing enterprises in national economic activity in Britain over as long a period as possible in this century. This appendix describes how our estimates were derived, together with a number of associated technical investigations which may be of more interest to research workers in this field than to the general reader. We consider the characteristics of the Census as a source of information on this subject in comparison with published company accounts, the different possible measures of a firm's size, the need for care in comparing concentration at different dates when different measures are used, and the methods and assumptions that were employed in combining the results of a great many earlier studies to yield the single series of estimates which were our target.

Characteristics of the Census data

Earlier studies of aggregate concentration, both in the United States and in this country,[1] were based on compilations of the financial accounts of a given number of large companies compared with a corresponding national total. More recently, information on the size-distributions of enterprises has become available from the Census of Production, and this source has important advantages over company financial accounts in comparisons of this type. The differences between the Census and financial accounts can be considered under five heads:

(*a*) Before the 1948 Companies Act consolidated accounts were not obligatory, and so it was never clear whether the whole ambit of an enterprise's activities was fully reflected in a firm's accounts. Census material is now available for the United Kingdom on a consolidated enterprise basis (that is, with all subsidiaries grouped with their parent into a single unit) for 1968, 1963, 1958 and 1935 (the last thanks to the work of Leak and Maizels, 1945), so that reliable comparisons can be made showing developments in recent years and the position in relation to that before the war.

(*b*) As far as the measure of size is concerned, the Census enables

Notes to this appendix will be found on pp. 296–8.

comparisons to be made using either employment or net output, whereas until 1967 profits as given in financial accounts were the only readily usable measure. Some investigators have relied on assets taken from accounts, although there is no estimate available of a corresponding national total of assets with which the assets of the hundred largest can be compared (they therefore used a total of assets restricted to quoted public companies, which imposed a certain limitation on the results). Following the 1967 Companies Act published accounts became more useful, because employment and turnover now have to be disclosed, but certain difficulties still remain (for example, the treatment of part-time and overseas employees is often obscure).

(c) In comparing a Census total for the hundred largest firms with the Census total for all firms, both figures are comparable in their coverage: that is to say, subsidiary establishments trading abroad are omitted in both numerator and denominator and, similarly, subsidiaries outside the industrial scope of the Census (for example, non-manufacturing establishments belonging to a predominantly manufacturing enterprise); subsidiaries of foreign companies operating here are included insofar as they have manufacturing establishments here. If a similar calculation is attempted on the basis of published company accounts, allowance for these factors affecting coverage can only be made in a very rough-and-ready way (generally by excluding entirely from the calculation companies that trade mainly abroad, and including in their entirety those that trade mainly at home); these factors are of substantial magnitude in practice.

(d) In comparing the profits of the hundred largest companies with a series for national profits, it has to be remembered that the latter is affected in various ways by the long-term trend towards corporate status and the decline in unincorporated firms. These problems do not arise with Census data, since both companies and unincorporated firms are included.

(e) There are serious problems in comparing the profits of the hundred largest companies based on financial accounts with the profit-series prepared for the national accounts, due to differences in the accounting treatment of depreciation, income from abroad, etc.

It is apparent that wherever possible it is better to rely on Census information rather than financial accounts; nevertheless, financial accounts have been relied on in this study for two purposes. First, comparisons with the situation in the 1920s and before the First World War were thought worthwhile, however approximate; we therefore relied upon a study relating to the profits of the fifty largest companies in 1909 and 1924 (Hart, 1960), and linked the results of that study to our calculations based on the Census (further details are given below).

Secondly, financial accounts have been used to interpolate for some intermediate years between Censuses. In all these cases it should be understood that financial accounts have been used only to provide indices of change from the nearest available Census benchmark.

Alternative measures of enterprise-size

The importance of a firm can be measured in various ways: for example, by its net output, employment, profits or sales.[2] In the present study net output (a measure of work done, as defined for the Census of Production) has been chosen as the preferred measure of the importance of the hundred largest enterprises. Net output is a better measure than profits, though that measure was used in our earlier study (Prais, 1957); at that time, however, there was no practical alternative. Profits reflect mainly the amount of capital employed, rather than 'work done'; this is particularly apparent if profits are taken before depreciation, since depreciation is conventionally calculated as a certain fraction of assets employed. Profits have the further disadvantages that they are more volatile over time than are the other measures mentioned, one may suspect they are influenced by monopoly elements, and their measurement for unincorporated firms (which is necessary if we are to make comparisons with profits in the whole economy and not merely with the corporate sector) is beset with difficulties.

Employment has much in its favour as a measure of size: it is a simple and relatively unambiguous concept, and it answers the obvious question of what proportion of the labour force is employed by the hundred largest enterprises. This latter issue is of interest quite apart from the associated issue of the concentration of output. However, it does not reflect the full extent of the dominance of the largest firms.

Different measures of size will yield measures of concentration that are related to one another in a more or less systematic way. The share of the largest firms in employment is generally observed to be lower than their share in output. The reasons are that large firms tend to have more capital equipment per employee, less female (and probably less part-time) labour, and a higher skill-mix on average.[3] Further, the share of the largest firms in gross profits is generally higher than their share in output, again because of the higher capital intensity of large firms. To put it another way, regarding output as resulting from labour and capital inputs it is to be expected that the share of large firms in output would be a weighted average of their shares in labour and capital (the share in capital can be approximated by the share in gross profits) and, since capital per person is higher in larger firms, we would expect the share of the largest firms to be highest if measured in terms of profits or net assets, lowest if measured in terms of employment and somewhere in-between if measured in terms of output.

These points have been set out at some length because they have occasionally been ignored by other writers, even though they are of considerable practical significance. Different measures of firm-size yield concentration ratios that differ by amounts that can significantly affect comparisons over time or between countries. The following figures for manufacturing (*Census 1963*, vol. 132, tables 13 and 14) illustrate the size of the differences involved: the hundred largest enterprises ranked in terms of their employment accounted for 32·6 per cent of all employment and 36·2 per cent of net output; if the enterprises were ranked in order of their net output, the share of the hundred largest in net output rose further to 38·1 per cent. There is therefore a gap of some 5½ percentage points between a measure based on employment and one based on output.

The difference between the shares of large companies in profits and in net output is perhaps of the same order of magnitude, but it is not possible to examine it with precision. An earlier National Institute study of quoted companies, which made use of a special tabulation prepared by the Census office, noted that quoted companies accounted for some 50–52 per cent of net output in manufacturing, but for as much as 71 per cent of corporate profits. However, this exaggerates the difference, because the comparison was with corporate profits and not total national profits (NIESR, 1956, pp. 7–8). The Census does not give information on profits, but a rough indication may be obtained by deducting wages and salaries from net output. Even this is not easy, since wages and salaries are not tabulated by size of firm in recent Censuses – all that is available are the numbers employed by size-group, together with an average wage based on all size-groups combined. On multiplying numbers employed by the average wage (that is, neglecting for the moment that wages per employee rise with size of firm), it is found that the share of the hundred largest enterprises in 'profits' so defined is 40·3 per cent, compared with the share of 36·2 per cent in net output noted above. If it is assumed that wages per employee in the hundred largest enterprises are 7 per cent higher than average,[4] the calculated share of the hundred largest in profits is 37·7 per cent, that is, 1½ percentage points above the share in net output. It should be remembered that these figures are based on a common ranking by employment-size; if the enterprises were ranked by capital or by profits the differential would be very much larger. Thus, the difference between the highest and lowest measures (profits and employment respectively) of the share of the hundred largest enterprises could amount to something like 10 percentage points. Great care is obviously necessary in any comparisons between studies using different measures of size.

It is sometimes argued that a measure in terms of capital or assets is particularly relevant in tracing the changing nature of the capitalist system – the change from the system of small-scale owner-control of society's capital resources to the present day large corporations, the managers of which have a negligible equity in the gigantic resources under their control. This is the view put forward in particular by Berle and Means in their classic study (1932, p. 345). The argument is not, however, overwhelming. In practice net output has the important advantage that it can be measured with the help of Census material with very much greater precision than can capital (or profits). In view of the serious disputes that have taken place in the literature as to the long-term trend in concentration in the United States,[5] considerable importance attaches to precision; in our view measures of concentration based on net output are therefore to be preferred. The meaning of the net output share is as clear and as relevant for policy considerations as is the capital measure. And, as mentioned above, it can also be regarded as a convenient compromise measure, in that it can be expected to lie beween a measure in terms of employment and one in terms of capital.

Derivation of the estimates

The paragraphs that follow explain how the present estimates were derived from the published sources, together with an account of various subsidiary problems of interpretation that arose. The exposition has been condensed with a view to meeting the needs of most readers who will be interested in following only the general principles of the calculation; at the same time it is hoped that sufficient information has been given (by way of references to the underlying source material) to enable anyone who so wishes to repeat the calculations. The estimates for the most recent years are described first.

For the years 1958–70 the Census provides size-distributions of private-sector enterprises ranked by employment and by net output. The estimates were derived from the published tables ranked by net output, interpolating as necessary. 'Unsatisfactory returns' when shown for all enterprises together (as, for example, in table 42 of the 1968 Census) were allocated to manufacturing and non-manufacturing totals in proportion to the numbers shown in the tables for Industrial Orders (table 42A). Steel companies were treated as separate companies by the Census in 1958 and 1963, and included in the published size-distributions for those years. From 1968 they were, however, excluded following their renationalisation. A rough calculation suggests that, if steel companies had been excluded from the published size-distribution for 1963, the share of the hundred largest calculated for that year would have been 0·7 points lower.

The 1970 Census is thought to have a fuller coverage of small firms than the 1968 Census; this follows rearrangements connected with the new Central Production Register. The Censuses show a rise of 2·6 per cent in manufacturing employment between 1968 and 1970, whereas the index of employment in manufacturing rose only by 1·1 per cent. If an allowance is made for this element there is virtually no change in the share of the hundred largest between 1968 and 1970.

A somewhat fine qualification must be added, both for the sake of precision and for the sake of providing a proper link with any further calculations that might be made of the share of the hundred largest. The recent estimates based directly on the Census size-distributions relate to enterprises that are predominantly engaged in manufacturing. These figures are subject to two partially offsetting disturbances. First, they include the activities of any non-manufacturing establishments which such enterprises may own and which come within the scope of the Census (for example, an establishment engaged in construction would be included if owned by a predominantly manufacturing enterprise, but a retailing establishment so owned would, of course, be excluded). Secondly, any manufacturing establishments owned by enterprises predominantly engaged in those non-manufacturing activities covered by the Census are excluded (for example, an establishment making bricks would be excluded if owned by an enterprise predominantly engaged in construction, but, if owned by an enterprise predominantly engaged in retailing, it would be treated as a separate manufacturing enterprise). These matters are probably of small consequence today, but with the growing diversification of enterprises over time, some adjustment – or change in Census definitions or procedures – may eventually be necessary to take account of these elements.[6]

In the post-war period up to 1958 a number of Censuses of Production were taken, but no size-distributions were prepared according to size of enterprise. To assess the trend in concentration during this period, the shares of the hundred largest in profits were calculated on the basis of company accounts for the years 1949, 1953 and 1957 (the 1949 accounts were the first to be governed by the more comprehensive requirements of the 1948 company legislation). The calculations for 1949 and 1953 are broadly on the same lines as in an earlier article (Prais, 1957, p. 257). For present purposes however, we excluded non-manufacturing companies (with the help of the list in NIESR, 1956, p. 71) and, by way of a small refinement, an allowance was made for profits of the self-employed in preparing a total of national profits in manufacturing. The calculation for 1957 was carried out in the same

way and was based on the list published by the Board of Trade for that
year.[7] The results were linked to the Census benchmark for 1958
(making allowance for the year's gap getween 1957 and 1958), and led
to estimates of the shares in net output of the hundred largest manufacturing enterprises of 22 and 27 per cent for 1949 and 1953 respectively. This procedure assumes, in accordance with the results for 1935,
1958 and 1963 noted below (table A.1 and pages 182–4), that profit-
shares in that period were an adequately reliable indicator of output-
shares; on the limited evidence that is available that seems a reasonable
assumption.

In 1935 the size-distribution of enterprises, then termed 'business
units', given by Leak and Maizels in their important paper on the
structure of industry and based on Census returns, relates to all industry
(1945, p. 145); the share in net output of the hundred largest business
units (ranked by size of employment) was calculated from their table
as 20·3 per cent. These hundred enterprises each employed over about
6600 persons. The industrial coverage of these enterprises differs,
however, from that in the post-war Censuses (mainly because of the
inclusion of non-factory trades) and a number of complex adjustments
were therefore made which are described in the paragraphs that
follow; these adjustments have the effect of slightly raising the proportion just given.

We may note here that one of the reasons for restricting our analysis
to manufacturing (that is to 'factory trades' as they were termed in
1935) rather than to the broader field of all industry covered by the
Census (which includes mining, building and public utilities amongst
'non-factory trades') is that nationalisation has affected comparisons
spanning the war-period. By 1958 large sections of industry, accounting
for 15 per cent of total industrial employment, had passed into the
public sector.[8] Within the somewhat narrower field of manufacturing,
nationalisation only affected the steel industry, and this was treated as
noted above in relation to the estimates for 1968. In relation to the
pre-war size-distribution, the investigator is faced with the difficulty
that in 1935 size-distributions of enterprises were not published for
factory and non-factory trades separately; all that is available is the
combined size-distribution for factory and non-factory trades together,
and some limited information on the largest enterprises in 'certain
trades' given by way of supplementary information by Leak and
Maizels (1945, p. 166, table XV).[9] The latter information was utilised
to estimate the approximate output of the largest non-factory enterprises; this was deducted from the total output of an appropriate number of the largest industrial (factory plus non-factory) enterprises so as
to arrive at a net total of a hundred enterprises in factory trades.

We started by examining the industrial enterprises employing more than 5000. There were 135 such enterprises with a total net output of £413 million (Leak and Maizels, 1945, p. 145). We then made deductions as follows:

(*a*) For coal mines, in which the major adjustment was required. There were forty-eight enterprises with over 5000 employees each, and their total employment was 0·6 million (out of a total employment in the trade of 0·8 million). Multiplying by the value of net output per head and allowing for double counting (to be explained below), the net output that has to be deducted in respect of these large enterprises was estimated at about £60 million. The main uncertainty in this calculation is the allowance for double counting; in the Leak and Maizels table each enterprise appears as many times as there are industrial groups in which it operates; we assumed that the proportion of total employment outside the trade, as shown in that table, could be used as a measure of the extent of double counting and reduced the number of units accordingly.

(*b*) For public utilities, where the Census shows fourteen undertakings (of which seven were railway companies) with employment over 5000, having a total employment of 304,000 and a net output of £70 million. (Leak and Maizels' table XV could not be used here since it gives information only on 'local authorities', with a much smaller industrial coverage than this Census group.)

(*c*) For non-metalliferous mines and quarries, where there were nineteen enterprises with over 5000 employees in these trades, but there was very considerable duplication and most of their employment was outside these trades.

(*d*) For building and contracting, where there were eight enterprises employing over 5000 persons, and again most of the employment was outside the trade. Because so much of their activity is outside the trade, it is difficult to arrive at a precise estimate for the net output of the large enterprises in this and the preceding group (*c*), but £10 million seems to be the order of magnitude involved for the two groups together.

(*e*) For government departments, which, it should be noted, were included in the Census tabulations of non-factory firms;[10] they were omitted from the Leak and Maizels table and have been excluded here.

On the above basis, out of the original 135 enterprises with over 5000 employees in factory plus non-factory trades, it appeared that there was a substantial proportion in non-factory trades. Allowing for duplication as noted above, their number was estimated at about forty-five, with a net output of about £140 million. If these enterprises are omitted, we are left with ninety enterprises in factory trades and a further ten enterprises must be included to bring the number of large enterprises back to a hundred. The employment of the latter ten would be just under 5000 employees each, and inspection of the size-distribution suggests an average of about 4850 (Leak and Maizels, 1945, p. 145). Multiplying by a net output of £223 per person, we arrive at a net output of £11 million for these ten enterprises. For the hundred largest manufacturing enterprises in 1935 we therefore finally arrived at an estimated total net output of about £285 million.

It will be clear that it is difficult to be precise as to the correct number of enterprises excluded above because of the double counting problem (ibid. pp. 167 et seq.); however, it is reassuring that, at this final stage, the addition of even an extra ten firms would alter the calculated concentration ratio by only half a percentage point. Alternative assumptions that we tried also led to very similar results.

In relation to a total net output in manufacturing of £1290 million in 1935,[11] it appears that the hundred largest enterprises accounted for about 22 per cent. This is based on a ranking of enterprises by employment; on a ranking by net output we would expect the proportion to be raised slightly.[12] Further, to bring the results on to a comparable coverage with the 1958 Census, when certain trades with small units were excluded, it was necessary to increase this ratio by 5 per cent (Inter-departmental Committee, Guides to Official Sources: no 6, p. 24). This brought our final estimate to 24·2 per cent.

The size-distributions published in the Censuses before 1935 are based, as already indicated, not on size of enterprise, but on the size of their establishments or size of return (a return may relate to more than one establishment under common ownership), or on the size of firm (a firm is a group of establishments trading under the same name – it is wider than a return but narrower than an enterprise). We examined a number of these published size-distributions but concluded that they were not helpful for the present inquiry. This is evident from the size-distributions for three measures – establishment, firm and enterprise – for which statistics were published for 1935 (in other years all three of these distributions are not available). In that year the hundred largest manufacturing establishments accounted for only 11 per cent of net output, the hundred largest manufacturing firms accounted for 15 per cent of net output, and the hundred largest manufacturing enterprises (as derived in the preceding paragraphs) accounted for 24 per cent of net output. These differences are too great to allow inferences with regard to the trend in enterprise-concentration to be drawn from trends in the Census statistics relating to establishments, returns or firms.

We came to the conclusion that to ascertain the trend in enterprise-concentration in these earlier years it was better to rely on a previous study (1960) of the profits of the largest companies by Professor Hart, which related to four years 1909, 1924, 1938 and 1950. We made use of his results for the first two of those years by linking them to our Census estimate for 1935.[13] The data available in Professor Hart's paper are the total gross profits of the fifty largest profit-earning companies in manufacturing (as published in the *Economist* newspaper) expressed as a ratio of all profits in manufacturing assessed for schedule D tax. Using his results as an index of change linked to our result for 1935, we estimated the share of the hundred largest firms in net output at some 22 per cent in 1924 and some 16 per cent in 1909.[14]

Aside from the general limitations attached to financial accounts already mentioned, two further qualifications have to be considered: first, the information used here related to the fifty and not the hundred largest companies; secondly, the comparison is with total assessed profits only, and so generally excludes firms making losses and those below the exemption limit. Given the regularity in the observed size-distributions of firms, the former qualification is probably not a serious matter. Firms ranking between 51 and 100 have resources which in total form a fairly stable and fairly small fraction of those of the first fifty firms (employment or profits of those ranked 51–100 generally total between a quarter and a third of those ranked 1–50). A slight fall in this fraction over time is perhaps to be expected, consistent with an increasing dispersion of firm-sizes, but it is difficult to see (on the basis of trial calculations we carried out) that this could involve the addition of more than 1 percentage point to the estimate for the earliest year – that is, the true share in 1909 might have been 17 rather than 16 per cent.

The smaller tax net in relation to assessed profits in earlier years works in the opposite direction, but again its effect was probably not great. It would have made the share of the largest companies appear artificially high in earlier years, but the amount of this excess would have declined as the tax net widened over time. The number of schedule D assessments in manufacturing increased substantially, from 63,000 to 106,000 between 1909 and 1927, and then fell somewhat to 90,000 in 1938. No doubt this reflects to some extent a true growth initially in the size of the manufacturing sector, then a subsequent period of amalgamations (see Worswick and Tipping, 1967, pp. 37 and 45). Tax exemption limits also changed over the period, but such changes affect the total amount of income assessed very much less than the number of assessments; the only pre-war size-distribution that we have seen relates to 1927, and it is indicative of the very small effect that changes in the exemption limits have on total assessments that the lowest 49 per cent of schedule D assessments in that year accounted for as little as 3 per cent of gross income assessments. This problem too was therefore probably not of any significance for present purposes.

Financial accounts as a basis for measuring concentration

We next report some calculations designed to elucidate to what extent measures of concentration based on financial accounts might differ in those earlier years from measures of concentration of output. A reconciliation was attempted between the share of the largest firms in profits, based on Hart's study (1960) of financial accounts for 1938, and their share in net output as measured from the 1935 Census; these are the earliest years for which such a comparison can be attempted. Explicit allowance was made for the following four sources of difference:

(i) the difference in dates (by interpolating between 1924 and 1938 from the profits-data);

(ii) the difference in the number of companies involved (fifty as against a hundred – the adjustment was made on the basis of the observed regularities in the distribution of firm-sizes for other years);

(iii) the difference to be expected between the shares in net output and in profits;

(iv) differences caused by the different criterion used for ranking (on the basis of some experimental calculations for recent years).

Without burdening the reader with the details of the calculation, we merely report the ultimate result, which was that on the basis of Hart's published estimate of 27 per cent of schedule D profits earned by the fifty largest firms in 1938, we would have guessed that the hundred largest firms would account for some 30 per cent of net output in 1935. But our Census estimate for that year came to only 24 per cent. This substantial discrepancy is probably due to two factors for which no explicit allowance can be made, namely the greater role in large companies of income from abroad and from activities other than manufacturing. Census information, it should be remembered, relates strictly to the share of large firms based on those of their establishments that are situated in this country and are concerned with manufacturing activities, but the information based on accounts includes also the results of their foreign and non-manufacturing activities.

We must therefore conclude that, for the purpose of estimating the importance of large manufacturing companies in the net output of this country at a given point of time, information based on financial accounts gives too large an answer. If, nevertheless, we wish to rely on financial accounts to provide estimates of trends over time which can be linked to Census benchmarks, we have to consider whether there is likely to have been any substantial trend in that discrepancy over time. It is known that income from abroad declined somewhat in relative importance between 1909 and 1938,[15] and on that basis the estimate we have derived for 1909 based on a profits-link should perhaps be lowered.

Table A.1. *Shares of the hundred largest enterprises based on financial accounts and Census data, 1935, 1958 and 1963*

Percentages

	1935	1958	1963
Gross profits from accounts	30·8	44·8	51·9
Net output from Census	24·2	31·9	37·3
Ratio	*1·27*	*1·40*	*1·39*

On the other hand, the degree of horizontal integration between manufacturing and distribution, etc. was probably smaller at the beginning of the century; the growing importance of non-manufacturing interests over time would to some extent offset the diminishing relative importance of foreign activities. It is not possible to come to a view on where the balance lay, but it seems unlikely (in view of the low orders of magnitude involved) that these factors could move our estimate for the beginning of this century by more than about a percentage point.

Reconciliations between the accounts-method and the Census-method were also attempted for 1958 and 1963, and showed similar excesses to that found for 1935.[16] The near-constancy of this excess (at about a third, as shown in table A.1) perhaps provides some reassurance that the estimates derived above for the years before 1935 are of the correct order of magnitude. However, for the most recently available Census year, 1968, the excess between the share in profits (based on accounts) and the share in net output (based on the Census) rose substantially, to 67 per cent; this presumably is partly the consequence of the great merger wave of the 1960s, which brought many distribution firms under the same roof as manufacturing firms. There is inevitably a delay of some years in the publication of Census results; thus, there does not seem to be any reliable way for the most recent years of obtaining provisional up-to-date estimates of aggregate industrial concentration using company accounts. However, in view of this increase in the divergency and by way of setting a margin of error to our estimates for 1949 and 1953, it seems worth asking how much would those estimates be altered if there had been a *small* increasing divergency in the earlier period. We therefore carried out a hypothetical calculation assuming that there was a divergency in the period 1949–58 which increased at a rate equal to a quarter of that in the period 1963–8; the results were that the estimates for 1949 and 1953 would be raised by just over 1 percentage point (to 23 and 28 per cent respectively). As already indicated, the assumptions leading to the estimates given originally for 1949 and 1953 seem to us more reasonable, but equally it seems reasonable to keep in mind a possible margin of error of about 1 percentage point.

ADJUSTMENTS TO UNITED KINGDOM CENSUS DATA

B.I SMALL ESTABLISHMENTS

This section outlines the main adjustments made to the published Census figures for numbers of establishments with ten or fewer employees to allow for changes in scope and coverage. The object was to bring the earlier data on to the same basis as that adopted in the 1958 and subsequent Censuses.[1]

Trades removed from the Census

The main changes over time have been the removal from the Census of Production of trades that are on the borders of retailing and repairing. Under retailing are bakers ('bakehouses attached to retail shops') and tailors ('retail bespoke tailoring and dressmaking and workrooms operated by retail shops'); under repairing are repairers of motor cars and cycles, and of boots and shoes. These four trades account for 95 per cent of the adjustments made to the 1930 figures (roughly similar proportions apply to later years). The remaining 5 per cent of the adjustments made here are in respect of the following trades or parts of trades that have been removed from the scope of the Census: wholesale bottling, except for manufacturers' bottling of their own products; scrap metal processing by dealers; the processing of cotton rags and cotton and rayon waste; the production and processing of cinematograph films; fish-curing by wholesalers or retailers; laundries and dry cleaning; tea and coffee blending. In addition, establishments specialising in repairs of the following goods were removed from the Census at various dates: jewellery and plate, watches and clocks, sports goods. In considering repairers a distinction has also to be drawn between those working directly for the public and those working for the trade – for some trades both types were withdrawn in the same year, but in other trades the former were withdrawn from the Census in 1948 and the latter in 1958. For certain other trades that were removed from the Census no adjustments were made here – for flax processing, textile converting and wholesale slaughtering, since no small firms were reported; for milk processing and bottling, and for musical instruments, since no

Notes to this appendix will be found on p. 298.

adjustment was possible on the basis of the available data – but these trades are of negligible importance in relation to the total number of small firms. We now consider these matters in more detail.

In 1958 bakehouses attached to retail shops were removed from the Census and only unattached bakehouses were retained; in consequence, the recorded number of small bakers fell from 11,100 to 800 between the Censuses of 1954 and 1958. There is no distinction in the earlier Censuses between these two types of baker; consequently it is not possible to say precisely how many were omitted, but an approximate estimate can be derived as follows. In the earlier period 1951–4 the number of bakers fell from 13,200 to 11,100, that is by 16 per cent; in the period before that, 1948–51, there had been a fall from 15,100 to 13,200, that is by 13 per cent. On that basis one might have expected the number of bakers on the old definition to have been some 13–16 per cent below the 1954 figure in 1958, that is in the region of 9300–9700. The Census for 1958 returned only 800; it follows that about 8500–8900, or 91–92 per cent, had been withdrawn from Census coverage. That proportion was accordingly removed from all earlier Census totals; in 1930, for example, when there were many more bakers, this implied the removal of 21,400 firms from the published Census total. It is possible that the proportion of pure bakehouses (those without retail shops) was smaller in 1930 than in 1958 and that an even larger proportion should properly have been removed; we have not found any basis for making a further adjustment to allow for such a trend, but we doubt whether it could substantially affect our conclusions.

A similar method was adopted for tailoring, leading to the removal in 1930 of 16,500 out of the 27,900 firms in the published total.

The 'motor cars and cycles (manufacturing and repairing)' trade is more complex, in that in earlier Censuses it comprised three sections – manufacturers, repairers for the trade and repairers for the general public. From 1958 only the first of these categories is included; for 1948–54 the second category is included but published as a separate total and can be eliminated without difficulty. The third and largest category was included for Censuses before 1948 but not published as a separate total; its magnitude was estimated following the method outlined above for bakers, leading to the retention of only some 5 per cent of the published Census total.

The procedures adopted for footwear were similar to those in the preceding paragraphs. Only some 10 per cent of the published Census total of small firms was retained in 1930 as being manufacturers.

The remaining trades presented less of a problem. Eight could be eliminated precisely, as they were explicitly distinguished in earlier

Censuses. They are fish-curing, wholesale bottling, cinematograph films, scrap metal, laundries and dry cleaning, tea and coffee blending, and the flock and rag trade. Three were estimated by the approximate method outlined above, but the numbers involved were not very large (1300 firms were removed from the 1930 figures for watches and clocks, jewellery and precious metals, and toys and sports goods).

Other adjustments

The number of unsatisfactory returns shown separately in the Censuses for 1958, 1963 and 1968 was allocated proportionately to each size-group. For earlier years it appears that the published totals incorporated such allowances.

To allow for Northern Ireland (not included in the Census for 1948) an addition of 2 per cent was made.

It is very difficult to form a satisfactory idea of the number of small establishments in 1924. The *Census 1930, Report*, vol. v, p. 9, hazards a guess, but this is very rough and includes non-manufacturing; we have preferred not to rely on it in this study.

Adjusted and original figures compared

The total number of small establishments as originally published in the Census is compared in table B.1 with our revised figures, which are intended to relate to a consistent industrial coverage throughout. The adjustments for the earlier years are substantial and amount in 1930 and 1935 to a reduction of the published total by 42 per cent. The decline in numbers over the period 1930–68 as a whole is now estimated to be from 93,400 establishments to 34,800, that is by 63 per cent, as compared with a decline from 160,000 to 31,600, that is by 80 per cent, in the original Census publications.

Table B.1. *Effects of adjustments to published Census data on establishments with ten employees or less, 1930–68*

	Establishments		Employees (000s)	
	Published	Adjusted	Published	Adjusted
1930	160,000	93,400	569	380
1935	132,300	76,900	537	350
1948	75,440	51,900	350	270
1951	63,890	45,300	317	250
1954	61,319	44,000	299	240
1958	32,640	34,700		
1963	30,831	32,900		
1968	31,627	34,800		

The effects on the estimated number of employees in these small establishments for the years 1930–54 are also set out in table B.1 (these estimates are required for chapter 3, table 3.2). They are not quite of such great relative importance, but warrant taking into account.

B.2   TRADE CLASSIFICATIONS, 1935 AND 1958

Comparisons are made in chapter 3 and elsewhere in this volume of the size-distributions of the main trade groups in 1935 and in various post-war years. The pre-war Census differed substantially in its industrial classification from that followed by the Censuses since 1958, the differences being particularly marked in the engineering and metal-using trades. We have attempted to bring the 1935 results on to the same

Table B.2. *Reconciliation of trade classifications, Censuses 1935 and 1958*

1958 Industrial Orders	1935 groups as adjusted
Food, drink and tobacco	Food, drink and tobacco *less* fish-curing; wholesale bottling
Chemicals and allied industries	Chemicals and allied trades *less* matches; ink, gum and typewriter requisites; *plus* coke and by-products; manufactured fuel
Engineering and electrical goods	Mechanical engineering; electrical engineering; small arms; watches and clocks; scientific instruments and apparatus
Metal manufacture	Iron and steel trade (blast furnaces; smelting and rolling; foundries); wrought iron and steel tubes; copper and brass; aluminium, lead and tin
Shipbuilding	Shipbuilding
Vehicles	Motor and cycle (manufacturing); aircraft; railway carriage and wagon building; carriages, carts and wagons
Metal goods n.e.s.	Hardware and hollow-ware; chains, nails and screws; wire; tools and implements; cutlery, needles, pins and metal smallwares; gold and silver refining; finished brass; plate and jewellery
Textiles	Textiles *less* roofing felts; packing; flock and rag
Leather, leather goods, fur	Leather group *plus* fur
Clothing and footwear	Clothing group *less* fur
Bricks, pottery, glass cement, etc.	Clay and building materials *plus* roofing felts; manufactured abrasives
Timber and furniture	Timber
Paper, printing, publishing	Paper, printing and stationery group *less* pens, pencils and artists' materials
Other manufacturing	Rubber; linoleum and oilcloth; brushes; games and toys; sports requisites; ink, gum and typewriter requisites; pens, pencils and artists' materials; plastic materials, buttons; musical instruments; matches

industrial grouping as that used since 1958. A precise reclassification is not possible, but we believe that the regroupings listed in table B.2 yield fairly valid comparisons; apart from those adjustments, small traders on the border of retailing and services (bakers, tailors, etc.) have been omitted from the 1935 totals as explained on pages 185–7 above.[2]

B.3 CHANGES IN THE DEFINITION OF 'ESTABLISHMENT'

There have been some minor, but not entirely negligible, changes since the 1958–63 Censuses in the definition of an establishment; the following notes have been included in the hope that they will clarify the degree of arbitrariness that the changes have introduced in certain of the tables, and be of help to other students.[3]

In the 1968 Census a greater degree of multi-unit reporting was accepted than previously (see *Census 1968, Report No. 1*, para. 17); that is to say, certain plants previously counted as separate establishments were then treated as a single establishment. The extent to which this took place is not known; the impression conveyed in official publications is that it may be ignored for most purposes. However, for our purposes we have to note that this may have led to a slight downward bias (as compared with earlier practice) in the recorded number of plants owned by the hundred largest enterprises in 1968.

The comparison of the quinquennial Census results for 1968 with figures derived from subsequent annual Censuses (1970 onwards) and from the Register of Businesses is affected by new definitions of 'local units' and 'establishments' (local units were introduced in the 1970 Census and the definition of an establishment was then altered slightly). A local unit may be a manufacturing local unit or a non-manufacturing local unit (for example, providing transport services). An establishment on the new definition is defined as the smallest unit providing the information required on employment, sales, costs, capital expenditure, etc. It may consist of a set of local units (including any non-manufacturing local units) which are closely integrated and in close proximity to one another; they now submit a combined return, with employment and capital expenditure the only items of information requested for each local unit separately. Where the addresses were not in close proximity, until 1968 the Census office treated the individual addresses as separate establishments in preparing counts and size-distributions of establishments, but from 1970 onwards they have been combined and treated as a single establishment (except that local units in different countries – treating England, Scotland, Wales and Northern Ireland as separate – are combined only within each country), and separate analyses are provided of the numbers and sizes of local units. At the top end of the size-distribution (that is to say, when considering the largest plants and enterprises as in this book), it appears that a manufacturing local unit can be regarded as substantially equivalent to an establishment on the old (1968) definition. An establishment on the new definition consists of a number of old-style establishments and is closer to what in pre-war Censuses was called a 'return'. For the hundred largest enterprises it appears from a special analysis carried out by the Central Statistical Office that in 1972 each new-style establishment consisted on average of approximately 1·5 manufacturing local units.

The changes between 1968 and 1970 affected only those local units that were *not* in close proximity; those that were situated in close proximity were treated as a single establishment both in 1968 and 1970. It seems likely that where a small establishment consists of a number of local units they will tend to be located in close proximity; it is larger establishments that will tend to control local units not in close proximity. Hence the changes in definition between 1968 and 1970 particularly affect the top of the size-distribution (as noted in the preceding paragraph), but at the bottom end an establishment on the 1968-definition tends to be similar to an establishment on the 1970-definition.

The new definitions represent an advance, in that they are easier to interpret. The local unit represents an address or a workplace, but separate accounts are not necessarily drawn up for it, since it forms part of a larger establishment. An establishment can be regarded as an economic or accounting entity, at least to the extent that the minimal figures on sales and the cost of sales are compiled.

There is a final pitfall to be noted, the effect of which is to reduce slightly the apparent sizes of plants in recent statistics based on the current Register of Businesses as compared with the quinquennial Censuses of 1968 and previously (but this does not affect their number). In the 1968 Census any non-manufacturing local unit included in a combined return (for example, a transport department) was disregarded in the count of establishments, but its employment was added to that of the manufacturing unit. The effect of this spreading of non-manufacturing employment between manufacturing units was to increase the apparent average employment of the latter compared with the average employment recorded against manufacturing units on the current Register of Businesses. There is thus a slight exaggeration in the recorded fall after 1968 in the size of the plants owned by the hundred largest enterprises (as shown in table 4.1). But the bias is unlikely to be great, since the problem arises only in combined returns, and where the largest enterprises own units of this type (garages, etc.) one may expect them often to be large enough to warrant a separate return.

THE PRINCIPAL PROPERTIES OF THE LOG-NORMAL DISTRIBUTION

This appendix provides an introductory account of those properties of the log-normal distribution that are useful in the statistical analysis of industrial concentration, illustrated with empirical data from the Census of Production and with some specimen calculations relevant to the exposition in the main text. The aim is to provide a 'cookbook recipe' for the reader who wishes to carry out similar calculations himself; for a thorough treatment the reader should refer to the monograph by Aitchison and Brown (1957).

The first-moment distribution

An elementary point that sometimes causes trouble even to the trained statistician may first be explained. Published frequency distributions of the sizes of enterprises are usually in a form showing that within a certain size-range there are a certain number of enterprises and they account for a certain quantity of total activity; for example, according to the Census for 1963, in the size-range 10,000–20,000 employees there were fifty-seven manufacturing enterprises with a total employment of 790,000.[1] We are thus concerned with two frequency distributions: the number of enterprises, which may be called the original distribution, and the number of employees (or total net output, if the classification into size-groups is in terms of the size of net output, etc.), which may be called the first-moment distribution.[2] The technical statistician usually works with the former (for example, in calculating averages or standard deviations), but the economist turns more naturally to the latter (asking, for example, what fraction of total manufacturing employment is in enterprises with more than 10,000 employees), and he is also concerned with the relation between the two distributions (what fraction of total employment is accounted for by the largest 1 per cent of enterprises, or by the hundred largest enterprises).

If we consider a familiar theoretical distribution (such as the normal curve), it will be found that the mathematical relation between the original and the first-moment distributions generally presents difficulties. But it happens in the particular case of the log-normal distribution

Notes to this appendix will be found on pp. 298–9.

that this relation is fortunately very simple, and it is this which makes it possible to examine relatively easily various possible time-paths of concentration, as will be seen below.[3]

Goodness of fit

The log-normal distribution attempts to provide a representation of a real frequency distribution in terms of two parameters: the mean of the logarithms of size and the standard deviation of the logarithms of size (there are also three- and four-parameter versions, but these may be ignored here). We must next ask how well this theoretical distribution fits in practice and how we should estimate its parameters. In many respects what has to be said under these heads follows naturally from what will be known to the reader of the familiar normal distribution since, essentially, the log-normal distribution is one in which the logarithm of the variable is distributed normally.

On goodness of fit, perhaps the first point worth emphasising is that it would be wrong to expect the theoretical log-normal curve to fit precisely an empirical distribution of firm-sizes, just as one does not expect the normal curve to fit precisely an empirical distribution of human heights or other natural phenomena. If the sample of observations is large enough it will (almost) always be found that there are some deviations from any theoretical distribution, and those deviations may be judged to be significant in terms of some statistical test criterion. Such a finding may be taken to indicate that a further refinement of the theoretical formulation, perhaps by the introduction of a third parameter, is likely to yield a significantly better graduation of the data. It should not, however, be taken to mean that the approximation given by the simpler curve is necessarily inadequate for the purpose of a particular analysis. This point has been the source of much difficulty in the literature: some investigators on finding deviations that are not statistically significant write as if their empirical data prove in some sense the validity of a particular theoretical distribution (or other hypothesis), when it might be better to say that, given the limited size of their sample, there is no point in pursuing further refinements; other investigators on finding statistically significant deviations will often say that they 'reject the hypothesis', when it would be better to say that the size of the sample is so great that even relatively small divergences from the hypothesis can be detected. In the kind of application considered here the number of observations, that is the number of firms covered by the Census, is generally large by the standards of statistical sampling theory and, in terms of 'statistical significance', the deviations from any theoretical distribution will generally be found to be significant. Nevertheless, the simple hypothesis may often be

Table C.1. *Distribution of manufacturing enterprises, United Kingdom 1963, and corresponding theoretical log-normal curves*

Percentages

	Enterprises		Employees	
	Actual	Fitted	Actual	Fitted
Enterprises employing:				
50,000+	0·01	0·01	10	13
20,000–49,999	0·04	0·04	12	10
10,000–19,999	0·09	0·09	10	9
5,000–9,999	0·20	0·20	10	10
2,000–4,999	0·50	0·60	12	14
1,000–1,999	0·70	1·00	8	11
500–999	1·30	1·70	8	9
200–499	3·50	4·00	10	10
100–199	5·10	4·80	6	5
25–99	17·60	14·90	8	6
Under 25	71·10	72·70	6	3

SOURCES: actual distributions – *Census 1968*, vol. 158, p. 10;
fitted distributions – see text.

acceptable as a useful approximation in further scientific work; its 'validity' – if one wishes to use that concept – depends as much on its help in that further work as on the substantial adequacy of fit to the original data.

The reader must judge the goodness of fit of the log-normal distributions in table C.1 with the above general considerations in mind; that table shows the actual distributions of the number of enterprises (the original distribution) and of the number of their employees (the first-moment distribution) classified by size of enterprise measured in terms of employment, together with the corresponding fitted log-normal distributions. The range of sizes stretches from those with under twenty-five employees, accounting for 71 per cent of the number of enterprises but only 6 per cent of total employment, to those with over 50,000 employees, accounting for 0·01 per cent of the number of enterprises and 10 per cent of employment. Given the very great range covered (a coefficient of variation of about twenty), perhaps the reader will agree that it is remarkable that fitted curves based on only two parameters should be as close as they are to reality; it is the more remarkable since the same pair of parameters were used for both the original and the first-moment distributions (as will be explained below). There are certain discrepancies, but the log-normal distribution seems to capture the broad essentials of the matter; bearing in mind also that the original data are not free of errors of measurement, what discrepancies remain may well be thought not worth pursuing unless some further definite and practical purpose is to be attained.

There are various methods of fitting a theoretical log-normal curve to an empirical frequency distribution, and the method adopted has some bearing on the goodness of fit at various parts of the distribution. We next turn to describe some of these methods.[4]

Fitting by the method of quantiles

It might be thought that the most straightforward and best way of fitting would be to take the logarithms of the size-variable for each of the observations in the samples, and then find their mean and standard deviation. That is indeed a possible way. But an alternative method, known as the method of quantiles, is computationally simpler and is generally to be preferred. It will be familiar that in a normal distribution approximately 95 per cent of the observations lie within two standard deviations on each side of the mean; merely by inspecting the cumulative distribution we can find the sizes of firms which span the central 95 per cent of observations, and the difference between the logarithms of the end-points of that span would obviously correspond to four standard deviations. This is the essence of the method of quantiles. We can, of course, take any other two points and carry out an equivalent computation, provided we are prepared to look up in a normal probability table the corresponding number of standard deviations spanned; it is, in fact, more efficient to choose points covering the central 86 per cent of observations if we are particularly interested in estimating the standard deviation, and the central 46 per cent if we are particularly interested in estimating the mean. In practice the published class-intervals often impose a severe constraint and the intervals just quoted serve only as a general guide.

An example may be helpful at this stage. From the first column of table C.1 we see that the smallest 71 per cent of enterprises are those with fewer than twenty-five employees (no finer breakdown is available of this group), and the largest 6 per cent of enterprises are those employing over 200. From normal probability tables it will be seen that the former corresponds to the cumulative proportion up to $+0.56$ standard deviates to the right of the mean and the latter to $+1.54$ standard deviates. Hence 0.98 standard deviates span the range 25–200 employees, and the required standard deviation is estimated as $(\log 200 - \log 25)/0.98 = 0.92$ in terms of common logarithms. The mean can be calculated in an analogous way: the upper point considered is 1.54 standard deviates to the right of the mean; the mean may therefore be estimated as $\log 200 - 1.54 \times 0.92 = 0.88$. The anti-log of this number, namely 7·6, provides an estimate of the fitted median-size of enterprise in terms of the number of employees (equal to the fitted geometric mean).

Next let us consider the first-moment distribution in the third column of the same table. Here we can come closer to the recommended quantiles by considering the 14 per cent of employees in enterprises having under a hundred employees and the 10 per cent of employees in enterprises with over 50,000 employees. Proceeding as before we would estimate the standard deviation as (log 50,000 − log 100)/(1·302 + 1·083) = 1·13. The mean of the distribution can analogously be estimated as log 50,000 − 1·302 × 1·13 = 3·23. The anti-log of this number, namely 1700, corresponds to the median (and also the geometric mean) of the distribution of the number of employees by size of enterprise, that is half of all employees are in enterprises with over 1700 employees and half in enterprises with fewer than that number.

Some important properties

If the observations had followed the log-normal distribution precisely, the two standard deviations quoted above – those of the original and the first-moment distributions – would have been exactly the same, apart from sampling fluctuations; this is one of the important and practically useful properties of the log-normal distribution. It sometimes happens that the original frequency distribution as published does not give a very fine breakdown, making the estimation of parameters difficult (as in the above example where 71 per cent of enterprises were in a single size-group); a more efficient estimate can then be obtained from the first-moment distribution.

A second important property is that the mean of the first-moment distribution exceeds the mean of the original distribution by an amount equal to the variance (that is the square of the standard deviation). This property holds in the simple form stated provided these quantities are all expressed in terms of natural (not common) logarithms. To illustrate from the above example: the difference between the two means is 3·23 − 0·88 = 2·35 in common logarithms; in terms of natural logarithms (that is on multiplying by 2·303) this corresponds to 5·41. Its square-root, namely 2·33, provides an estimate of the standard deviation in natural logarithms, corresponding to 1·01 in common logarithms; this is seen to lie between the two estimates obtained above directly from the original and the first-moment distributions, namely 0·92 and 1·13.[5]

The above two properties are covered by the general proposition that, if the original distribution is log-normal and has a mean and variance of μ and σ^2 respectively, then the first-moment distribution is also log-normal and has a mean of $\mu + \sigma^2$ and a variance of σ^2. That is (to speak in terms of our example) the frequency distribution of the number of enterprises according to their size is the same as the frequency distribution of the number of employees according to size of enterprise, except for a shift to the right in the latter by an amount equal to the variance. To illustrate the practical value of this proposition it is necessary to refer to tables of the normal probability function. It will be remembered that these are usually in the form that a proportion $p = \phi(x)$ of the observations are smaller than x, where x is a standardised deviate having zero mean and unit variance; conversely, the same tables may be used to find the value of the standardised deviate x (or, more familiarly, the number of standard deviations) corresponding to a given cumulative proportion p of the observations, which, in formal terms, can be represented by $x = \phi^{-1}(p)$. (The reader perplexed by this notation will find his difficulties disappear if he works through the numerical example in the next paragraph.) If we now suppose that a proportion p of the largest firms employ a proportion q of all employees, then the following very useful relation follows:

$$\phi^{-1}(1 - q) = \phi^{-1}(1 - p) - \sigma. \tag{1}$$

Once we know σ, we can, with the help of standard probability tables, use this equation to plot the full relation between p and q, a procedure which corresponds to drawing a Lorenz curve of concentration. The value of the Gini coefficient corresponding to that curve is also determined by the value of σ, and can conveniently be found from the table prepared by Aitchison and Brown (1957, p. 155).

Estimating the standard deviation on the basis of shares

The equation just quoted can also be used to provide an estimate of the standard deviation, and it is this method that has been mainly used in this study. As an example we may consider again the data summarised in table C.1; referring back to the original Census table for greater accuracy, it is seen that the largest ninety-three enterprises (those employing over 10,000) form a proportion $p = 93/65{,}593 = 0{\cdot}00142$ of all enterprises and account for a proportion $q = 2{,}431{,}000/7{,}543{,}000 = 0{\cdot}322$ of all employees. From (1) we can estimate the standard deviation as:

$$\begin{aligned}
\sigma &= \phi^{-1}(1 - p) - \phi^{-1}(1 - q) \\
&= \phi^{-1}(0{\cdot}9986) - \phi^{-1}(0{\cdot}678) \\
&= 2{\cdot}99 - 0{\cdot}47 \\
&= 2{\cdot}52 \text{ in natural logarithms, corresponding}
\end{aligned}$$

to $1{\cdot}093$ in common logarithms. Accepting this value, the mean of the original distribution can be estimated as $\log 10{,}000 - 2{\cdot}99 \times 1{\cdot}093 = 0{\cdot}74$, and the mean of the first-moment distribution as log $10,000 - 0.47 \times 1.093 = 3.49$.

The results of the various methods of estimation that have been set out indicate a certain – but by no means excessive – margin of arbitrariness in the estimates. As already suggested, this reflects the fact that empirical distributions do not follow precisely the theoretical log-normal curve; each method gives different weights to various sections of the distribution. It is because we are particularly interested in the upper tail of the distribution and its development over time that we have adopted the method just explained for the estimates in the main text. It is also the method that was used in calculating the fitted values in table C.1, and it will now be understood in what sense both the original and the first-moment distributions are based on a single pair of estimated parameters (it is only necessary to have an estimate of the variance and of one of the means in order to calculate both fitted curves). Indeed it may now seem even more remarkable that, simply from what may be regarded as a single observation at one tail of the distribution (the knowledge that the largest 0.14 per cent of enterprises all have over 10,000 employees and account for 32.2 per cent of all employment), it has been possible to estimate with such precision all the fitted values in that table on the basis of the log-normal hypothesis.

Examples

For the sake of clarity some further examples, the results of which are used in the main text, are worked through here.

1. *The distribution of net output.* Our main estimates relate to the share of the very largest enterprises in net output (rather than in employment, which it has been convenient to use in the exposition in this appendix). The standard deviation of this distribution in 1963 has been calculated from the published information (*Census 1968*, vol. 158, p. 166, table 45); the nearest published class-interval to the hundred largest is obtained by considering the sixty-six largest enterprises with net output over £20 million, which form a fraction $p = 0.001006$ of all enterprises and account for a fraction $q = 0.3321$ of total manufacturing net output (the absolute figures for all enterprises are from p.10, table 42 of that volume). Proceeding as previously, we derive an estimate of $\sigma = 2.65$ for the logarithmic dispersion of the sizes of enterprises in terms of their net output. This slightly exceeds the value 2.52 found above on measuring enterprise-size in terms of employment, reflecting the fact that output is more concentrated than employment (because of the higher capital intensity of large firms).

2. *The share of the largest firms at various dates.* Assuming (as appears from appendix D) that the standard deviation of growth-rates per

decade may be taken as $s = 0.82$ and, starting from a standard deviation of sizes in 1963 at $\sigma = 2.65$ as just derived, we may next calculate the expected share of the hundred largest enterprises at some future date, say 2073, on the assumptions made in chapter 2, equation (3). The variance of the size-distribution after the passage of eleven decades would be $\sigma^2 = 2.65^2 + 11 \times 0.82^2 = 14.42 = 3.80^2$, so that $\sigma = 3.80$.

We assume that the total number of enterprises remains unchanged at 65,593; we are therefore interested in the proportion $p = 100/65,593 = 0.00152$, and wish to find the share of net output q that they produce as σ rises from 2.65 to 3.80.

Applying equation (1) first to 1963 as a check, we have
$$\phi^{-1}(1-q) = \phi^{-1}(1-0.00152) - 2.65$$
$$= 2.96 - 2.65 = 0.31,$$
and $1 - q = \phi(0.31) = 0.62.$

Hence $q = 38$ per cent, as may be confirmed by interpolating from the published Census table.

For 2073 the above calculation is modified only slightly:
$$1 - q = \phi(2.96 - 3.80) = \phi(-0.84) = 1 - 0.80,$$
so that $q = 80$ per cent.

The share of the single largest firm in 2073 is found by setting $p = 0.0000152$ and repeating the calculation. We find from tables that $\phi^{-1}(1-p) = 4.17$, and hence $1 - q = \phi(4.17 - 3.80) = \phi(0.37) = 0.64$, so that $q = 36$ per cent.

3. *The number of firms accounting for half net output.* We may also calculate, under the same assumptions, the number of largest enterprises accounting for half net output at the beginning of the century, say in 1903. We first calculate the variance at that date as

$$\sigma^2 = 2.65^2 - 6 \times 0.82^2 = 2.99 = 1.73^2.$$

Then, from equation (1) we have

$$\phi^{-1}(1-p) = \phi^{-1}(1-0.5) + \sigma = \sigma \qquad \text{(since } \phi(0.5) = 0\text{)};$$

from which the simple result follows that $1 - p = \phi(\sigma)$

and $$p_{0.5} = 1 - \phi(\sigma), \qquad (2)$$

where $p_{0.5}$ represents the proportion of enterprises accounting for half of output.

In this case $p = 1 - \phi(1.73) = 1 - 0.958 = 0.042$ and, taking the total number of firms as before at $N = 66,000$, it is found that the number accounting for half of output is $Np \simeq 2800$. A similar calculation for 1913, a decade later, leads to an estimate of 1800 firms.

4. *The logarithmic standard deviation*. Equation (2) incidentally provides the basis for a very simple method of estimating the logarithmic standard deviation of a log-normal distribution virtually 'by inspection'. The steps are as follows. Find how many enterprises account for half of total employment (or of net output, etc.); then find what proportion these form of the total number of enterprises and look up in a normal probability table the corresponding number of standard deviates. This is equal to the required value. For example, if half of employment is in the largest $2\frac{1}{2}$ per cent of firms, the required logarithmic standard deviation is about 2; if half were in the hands of the largest $\frac{1}{2}$ per cent of firms, the required logarithmic standard deviation is about 2·5; if half were in the hands of the largest 0·1 per cent of firms, the required value would be about 3. The practising statistician will be familiar with these tail-points of the normal distribution as used in conventional tests of statistical significance.

SIZE-TRANSITION MATRICES IN THE STATISTICAL ANALYSIS OF THE GROWTH OF FIRMS

It is shown in chapter 2 how concentration develops over time on the basis of a simple stochastic model of the growth of the firm:

$$x_t = bx_{t-1} + \epsilon_t \tag{1}$$

or, equivalently,

$$x_t - x_{t-1} = cx_{t-1} + \epsilon_t, \tag{2}$$

where x is the logarithm of the size of a firm measured from its mean, and ϵ is a random variable having a variance s^2. The values of b (as of $c = b - 1$) and of s adopted in the exposition in that chapter were based on a number of earlier studies of quoted firms, together with a new analysis using for the first time returns made to the Census of Production relating to a much broader sample of all manufacturing enterprises. The object of this appendix is to explain the method used in these various studies, and to compare and assesss their results. Some methodological comments are also offered on alternative mathematical approaches.

Growth of firms 1951–8

First, however, we consider the new information on the growth of firms provided by the Censuses of 1951 and 1958 which is set out in table D.1. This table provides a convenient starting point for the reader not familiar with this type of analysis; it will be seen that it provides a frequency distribution of enterprises cross-classified by size of employment in 1951 and 1958. For example, the third column shows that there was a total of forty-five enterprises in 1958 that had between 10,000 and 20,000 employees; seven years earlier in 1951, twenty of those forty-five enterprises had been in the same size-group, two had declined during that period from the higher size-group of 20,000–50,000 employees, seventeen had risen from the lower size-group of 5000–10,000 employees and six had risen from the even lower size-group of 2000–5000 employees. The table summarises in this way the growth-pattern of some 20,000 enterprises.[1]

Not all the information in this table can however be used in the

Notes to this appendix will be found on p. 299.

Table D.1. *Changes in the sizes of enterprises, 1951–8*

No. of enterprises[a]

	Employment in 1958										Sur-vivors, 1951
	Over 50,000	20,000–49,999	10,000–19,999	5,000–9,999	2,000–4,999	1,000–1,999	500–999	200–499	100–199	25–99	
Employment in 1951:											
Over 50,000	3										3
20,000–49,999	4	18	2								24
10,000–19,999		8	20	6							34
5,000–9,999		1	17	57	10						85
2,000–4,999			6	42	181	9	3				241
1,000–1,999					83	324	48				455
500–999					12	135	600	220	20		987
200–499					2	6	231	1,710	500	50	2,499
100–199						6	12	630	2,446	1,020	4,114
25–99						3	12	140	800	9,923	10,878
Under 25									20	1,150	1,170
Survivors, 1958	7	27	45	105	288	483	906	2,700	3,786	12,143	20,490
Births	—	—	—	4	2	6	12	80	120	1,500	1,724
Total, 1958	7	27	45	109	290	489	918	2,780	3,906	13,643	22,214

SOURCE: Business Statistics Office, special tabulation based on *Census 1951* and *Census 1958*.

[a] Those that in 1951 were in the size-group indicated by the row heading and had moved by 1958 into the size-group indicated by the column heading.

present analysis. The reason is that it was compiled starting from the end of the period examined, that is from the 1958 Census, and includes only those enterprises that employed more than twenty-five persons in that year. Enterprises that had employed more than twenty-five persons in 1951 but by 1958 had declined below that level were thus excluded, together with all others that had fewer than twenty-five employees in both years. For this reason there is no column for those with under twenty-five employees in 1958, and the three rows for those employing under 200 in 1951 have a distinct J-shaped distribution, indicating omission of frequencies further to the right. In other words, the table gives the history of those firms that survived during the period 1951–8, provided that at the end of it they had at least twenty-five employees; by excluding firms that declined to less than twenty-five employees, it gives – speaking broadly – too optimistic a picture. This bias is, however, of serious proportions only at the lower end of the distribution, near the boundary line of twenty-five employees. Inspection of the table suggests that for firms with over 200 employees in 1951 the bias can be ignored; the frequency distributions for each of the eight size-groups above that level are unimodal and seem to tail off satisfactorily to zero in both directions. In the analysis that follows information relating to enterprises with fewer than 200 employees has therefore been omitted. This is regrettable, but there seems no satisfactory way of using the partial information relating to the smaller enterprises.[2]

Nevertheless, the amount of information retained in the analysis – relating to 4300 surviving enterprises – is twice as great as used in any previous analysis of this type; in addition, the information is of better quality in its coverage, since it comes from Census sources, and also perhaps in its use of employment as the measure of size.

Deriving estimates of Regression and growth-variability

The standard correlation technique was applied to the data, using the mid-points of the natural logarithms of the class-intervals as the values applicable to each frequency; this yielded a value for the Regression of the final-year size on the opening-year size of $b = 1 \cdot 079$, with a standard error of $\pm 0 \cdot 009$. The standard deviation of the residuals, which measures the variability of the growth-rates after allowing for Regression, was found to be $s = 0 \cdot 50$.

The greater the interval of time the greater will be the changes in the sizes of firms; consequently, the coefficients evaluated from any set of observations depend on the time-interval, which in this example was seven years. For purposes of comparison with studies carried out over different lengths of time, it is clearly necessary to standardise the coefficients on to some common basis, which might conveniently be taken as a decade (the procedure is equivalent to converting 30 mph to 44 feet per second – but the mathematics is a little more complex!) When this is done as explained in the next section, the resulting standardised values in relation to a decade are $\bar{b} = 1 \cdot 12 \pm 0 \cdot 01$ and $\bar{s} = 0 \cdot 60$.

Standardising on to a constant time-interval

The method of standardisation supposes that the basic growth process

$$x_1 = bx_0 + \epsilon_1 \tag{3}$$

applies to the real world in terms of some arbitrary unit of time. This time-unit may be thought of as a year; the only theoretical requirement is that the unit be long enough for the correlation between the growth terms (ϵ) in successive time-units to be negligible. The observations on which the Regression estimates are based we may suppose to have been taken at an interval of n such time-units, and it is required to standardise the results to correspond to $t = rn$ time-units. For example, if the equation has been fitted to observations covering a seventeen-year period and it is required to standardise to a ten-year period, then $r = 10/17$.

By applying the relation (3) to successive units of time and substituting recursively it is found that

$$x_2 = bx_1 + \epsilon_2$$
$$= b^2 x_0 + b\epsilon_1 + \epsilon_2$$

and, in general,

$$x_n = b^n x_0 + b^{n-1}\epsilon_1 + b^{n-2}\epsilon_2 + \ldots + \epsilon_n \tag{4}$$

Consequently, a Regression estimated over a period of observation of n time-units, yields an estimate of b^n; whereas the standardised value required, say $\bar{b}_t$, should correspond to an estimate of b^t.

It is clear therefore that we may standardise by taking

$$\bar{b}_t = b_n{}^{t/n} = b_n{}^r$$

A convenient approximation may be found by substituting $b = 1 + c$, so that $1 + \bar{c}_t = (1 + c_n)^r$ and, since c is small, we find on taking a Taylor expansion,

$$\bar{c}_t = rc_n + r(r-1)c_n^2/2 + \ldots \tag{5}$$

It follows that for a first approximation it is adequate to adjust c in direct proportion to the time-periods covered; a closer approximation is obtained by adding the term in c^2, but this is usually very small.

The standardisation of the residual variance proceeds as follows. The residual growth over n time periods from (4) is

$$b^{n-1}\epsilon_1 + b^{n-2}\epsilon_2 + \ldots + \epsilon_n$$

and, if the variance of ϵ is denoted by s^2, the variance of this expression is given by $s_n^2 = s^2(1 - b^{2n})/(1 - b^2)$.

A similar expression holds in terms of t, and it follows that $\bar{s}_t^2$ may be estimated from $\bar{s}_t^2 = s_n^2 (1 - b_n^{2r})/(1 - b_n^2)$. By substituting and expanding as before the following approximation may be derived which is adequate for most purposes:
$$\bar{s}_t^2 = rs_n^2 [1 + c_n(r-1)] \tag{6}$$

As before, the adjustment to the variance is in proportion to the length of the time-periods, but there is a correction factor which depends on the value of c_n.

Some interesting theorems are to be derived on assuming a non-zero correlation between the values of ϵ for a given firm in adjacent periods; these are mainly of help in explaining findings by various writers on the persistence of growth.[3] The standardisation formulae given above would also be affected, but in practice it appears that the adjustment required is generally small. The algebra is somewhat laborious, and an exploration of these matters must be deferred to another occasion.

Results of earlier studies

Table D.2 summarises the results of a number of earlier studies after standardisation.[4] The original studies for the period up to 1955 were based on the Stock Exchange valuation of the company's shares and debentures as the best measure of size then available; subsequent studies have used the book-value of net assets or, for the Census matrix, employment. The impression given by this table is that the variability of growth-rates is greater when measured in terms of market valuation of capital; this is not surprising since share-prices are subject to an additional source of volatility of their own due to speculative factors. It does not follow, however, that share-prices provide a seriously exaggerated measure of the variability of 'true' growth-rates of firms when growth is measured over a period as long as a decade or so, although for shorter periods the speculative factors will be more of a hindrance. On the other hand, there are reasons for regarding the alternative measures of growth that have been used as understating the variability in the 'true' rate of growth: for example, measuring size in terms of employment leaves out the variability in capital per head; measuring size in terms of net assets yields a sluggish measure of changes, since it is based on book-values which are only sporadically revalued. And neither employment nor net assets take into account the changing prospects of a firm as techniques and markets change; such developments may reduce, and even wipe out, the capital values of some firms, while the values of others are increased. It is by no means a disadvantage to have such changes in a firm's viability taken into account, and the market valuation of its capital thus yields a superior measure of size to a certain extent.

Taken all in all it is reassuring that the differences between the various measures of the variability of growth-rates over such diverse periods is not greater than shown in the table: the range is only twofold, from 0·6 to 1·2 The two highest values may, in any case, be treated with some reserve. The highest is for the short five-year period 1950–5, where the measurement may be less reliable because of the greater importance of speculative factors in the short run. The standardisation process may also be less accurate for shorter periods; this is because the element of persistence of growth is more important in the short run, but is not taken into account by the present process of standardisation. The next highest value relates to the years 1885–96; it deserves less weight in considering the period as a whole, since it is based on relatively few observations (only forty-five companies survived during that period out of sixty industrial companies with a Stock Exchange quotation in 1885). The realistic range to be considered for $\bar{s}$ is thus

Table D.2. *Standardised Regression and residual growth-variability of the concentration process, 1885–1969*

	Measure of size	Regression $(\bar{c})^a$	Growth-variability$(\bar{s})^b$
1885–96		$-0\cdot05(\pm0\cdot15)$	$1\cdot02$
1896–1907		$-0\cdot09(\pm0\cdot05)$	$0\cdot78$
1907–24	Market	$+0\cdot05(\pm0\cdot02)$	$0\cdot71$
1924–39	valuation	$-0\cdot05(\pm0\cdot02)$	$0\cdot98$
1939–50		$-0\cdot23(\pm0\cdot02)$	$0\cdot77$
1950–55		$-0\cdot01(\pm0\cdot03)$	$1\cdot21$
1951–58	Employment	$+0\cdot12(\pm0\cdot01)$	$0\cdot60$
1951–60		$+0\cdot12(\pm0\cdot02)$	$0\cdot69$
1954–65	Net assets	$+0\cdot08(\pm0\cdot02)$	$0\cdot58$
1960–69		$-0\cdot04(\pm0\cdot03)$	$0\cdot76$

SOURCES: 1885–1955: Hart and Prais, 1956, pp. 173 and 190.
1951–58: table D.1.
1951–60: Samuels, 1965 (amended, see text).
1954–65: Utton, 1971 (amended, see text).
1960–69: Samuels and Chesher, 1972, p. 46 (first weighted equation in table 3) and p. 52 (line 15 from foot of page).

[a] Standardised to a common period of a decade; standard errors of estimates shown in brackets.
[b] Standard deviation of the residual logarithmic growth-rate, i.e. of $x_t-(1+c)x_{t-1}$; natural logarithms used throughout, and standardised to a common period of a decade.

between about 0·6, when measured in terms of employment or the book-value of net assets, and about 0·9, when measured in terms of the market-value of the company's capital.

The central calculations reported in chapter 2 are based on the share of the hundred largest in net ouput rather than in employment, so that a compromise value of $\bar{s}$ giving somewhat more weight to capital at market-values seemed to be appropriate, and a value of 0·82 was chosen.[5] That value is the standard deviation of the residual growth-rate adjusted to a ten-year period; it would correspond to a notional value standardised in relation to a single year of approximately $0\cdot82/\sqrt{10} = 0\cdot26$.

Though $\bar{s}$ is measured in terms of logarithms it has a simple intuitive meaning: it is equal, approximately, to the standard deviation of the proportional growth-rates of the firms. This may be shown as follows. Assume, without loss of generality, that the firms in the population at both dates have the same mean logarithmic size, log M, and let X denote the absolute size of the firm, so that $x = \log X - \log M$, and let $c = 0$, as is approximately true. Then, from (2), $\epsilon = \log X_t - \log X_{t-1} = \log (X_t/X_{t-1}) = \log (1+g)$, when g is the proportional rate of growth of the firm. The familiar Taylor expansion for the natural logarithm yields $\epsilon = g - g^2/2 + \ldots$ To a first approximation, therefore, the residual logarithmic rate of growth is equal to the proportional rate of growth; consequently the standard deviations of these quantities are approximately the same. The equivalence holds only for natural logarithms, which is the reason they have been employed in presenting the standardised results in table D.2 and elsewhere in this exposition. In terms of the above example, the standard deviation of the annual rates of growth would therefore be about 26 percentage points.

For the post-war period it will be noted from table D.2 that the well determined Regressions are all positive and in the region of $\bar{c} \simeq$ 0·10; a pooled value for all the five post-war Regressions (weighting each in proportion to its precision) can be calculated as 0·10 ($\pm$0·01). For the pre-war periods the Regressions are generally less precisely determined; taking together the results spanning the years 1896–1939 yields a pooled negative value of $\bar{c} = -0·02(\pm 0·02)$; if the subsequent period 1939–50 with its substantial negative value is included, the pooled value becomes $\bar{c} = -0·06(\pm 0·01)$. (The value for the earliest period 1885–96 has a very large standard error; its inclusion in a pooled estimate would not change the central value of these results, but would slightly increase the margin of uncertainty.) For the period up to 1939 one can therefore not speak with precision as to whether c was zero or slightly negative, or whether in truth it was sometimes slightly positive and sometimes slightly negative.

Nevertheless, it is clear that c was not sufficiently negative for the period as a whole before 1939 to avoid an increase in concentration; for concentration to have remained unchanged we should require, according to what we have called the Galton criterion – equation (7) of chapter 2 – values of c_g as follows: 1903, −0·12; 1913, −0·09; 1923, −0·08; 1933, −0·07. These critical values are significantly lower than the pooled average of $-0·02(\pm 0·02)$ noted above for the period 1896–1939.

It remains to note two small technical matters in relation to two of the post-war analyses quoted in table D.2. The equation presented by Utton (1971) in his paper for 1954–65 has been recalculated here omitting the lowest size-group, which is open-ended and includes all sizes under £½ million. It was thought that the inclusion of an open-ended group might bias downwards the estimate of the growth-variability (many firms are recorded as apparently not changing their size in this group, yet large changes may have taken place which are not explicitly shown because the group is open-ended). This accounts for some slight differences between the earlier published results and those quoted here.[6]

The data published by Samuels (1965) have also been recomputed for the purposes of the present study, using natural logarithms through-out and allowing for certain misprints in the original paper.

Alternative approaches

This may be a convenient point to comment on alternative mathe-matical approaches to the analysis of size-transition matrices by means of Markov processes. The Markov approach treats each size-class as a discrete category and considers the long-term implications of the (assumed constant) probabilities of movement from one class to another. Such processes have been extensively studied by mathematicians and have been applied in a limited way in the social sciences to problems such as social mobility.[7] Their relevance to the analysis of business con-centration was naturally considered at the time of our original paper, but was not thought helpful (Hart and Prais, 1956, p. 165n.). Notwith-standing Professor Irma Adelman's subsequent application of that method to statistics of the United States steel industry,[8] it may still be regarded as being 'of limited use' in this kind of problem for the follow-ing reason. The fundamental theorem of a Markov process with a finite number of classes is that the distribution necessarily approaches a stable state as time proceeds; in other words, it is inherent in the mathematical assumptions of the method that the level of concentration reaches some limiting value. The possibility of a limitless growth in concentration is ruled out *ab initio*. In this it differs from the Regression model, in which stable, increasing, or decreasing concentration are possible in the long run, depending on the values of the parameters. The difference in the asymptotic behaviour of the two approaches stems from the Regression model being based conceptually on a continuous size-measure extending to infinity, rather than on a finite set of discrete size-groups. A Markov model with an infinite number of size-groups can be constructed which would not be subject to this fundamental restriction, but so far no practical attempt has been made in this con-text. It may be thought that the interest of either approach lies not in its predictions for the ultimate state of the system but in its predictions for the more immediate future, and of course the differences between them would then be smaller. Even so it seems a disadvantage that the Markov method (with a finite number of states) embodies an inbuilt convergence to stability which, in the present context, is not clearly justified by the facts and which may therefore hinder a proper under-standing of long-term trends.

On the other hand, it is of interest, as Professor Adelman has shown, that constant probabilities of births and deaths can be incorporated into the Markov approach. It might indeed be asked whether it is sensible to deal with the growth of firms ignoring their births and deaths, as has been done here and throughout chapter 2, other writers having taken the view that some form of combined treatment is in some sense essential. Three answers may be offered in excuse of our more limited aims here. The first is that, as we have seen, the growth-process of surviving firms has interesting and important consequences for concentration, and deserves examination in its own right in as much depth as possible. The second is that the empirical information on the births and deaths of firms is particularly deficient; any analytical treatment is thus bound to involve introducing assumptions not well supported by facts, so that a combined treatment of growth and of births and deaths tends to take on the flavour of an exercise in speculative reasoning. Thirdly, some earlier analyses that we carried out on statistics of quoted companies suggested that births and deaths were of much smaller importance in accounting for changes in concentration over time than were the growth-rates of surviving firms (Hart and Prais, 1956, pp. 165–8).

The reader who nevertheless wishes to explore the formal complexities of combining birth and death processes with probabilities of growth may refer to the works of Steindl and Champernowne,[9] and the survey by Cramer.[10] Cramer conveniently summarises the properties of the various sophisticated models recently proposed and their concern with providing an explanation for the Pareto distribution which fits the upper tail of many observed economic cumulative size-distributions. However, since only one tail of the distribution is involved, since a cumulative distribution is necessarily monotonic and since all that is involved in the Pareto distribution is a type of log-linear approximation, the need for a rationalisation of this kind is perhaps not so very great. Further, the alternative combined models that have been proposed have no obvious implications for the increase of concentration over time, which is our main interest in the present study These, in brief, are the reasons for not pursuing here some of the fascinating speculations to be found in the academic literature surveyed by Cramer.

With the increase in the last decade or so of 'death by take-over', there is, however, scope for further empirical work on the deaths of firms and their effect on concentration, and this may one day lead to a fuller understanding of the concentration process.

UNITED STATES STATISTICS ON LARGE ENTERPRISES

E.I ESTIMATING THE SHARE OF THE HUNDRED LARGEST UNITED STATES MANUFACTURING FIRMS

This section describes the statistical sources and methods used in preparing the estimates (referred to in chapter 6) of the share in net output of the hundred largest manufacturing enterprises in the United States for the period 1909–70. As in the corresponding exercise for the United Kingdom (described in appendix A), the object has been to bring together and put on to a comparable basis the results of a great many earlier studies relating to the importance of the largest firms. Not all those studies were based on the same number of firms (for example, some relate to 200 firms), nor did they all use the same concepts (for example, some relate to the assets owned by the companies rather than their output); but it seemed worth putting together the results of the various studies to see what they say about the long-term trend in aggregate concentration, and to permit some simple comparisons with the corresponding figures derived for the United Kingdom.

Characteristics of the Census data

The more recent information is, of course, more reliable. Since 1947 information on the share in manufacturing net output of the 200 largest (including a sub-total for the hundred largest) enterprises in the United States is available from the Censuses of Manufactures. This is comparable in its concepts to the corresponding information for Britain, in that all manufacturing plants owned by an enterprise, whether directly or through subsidiaries, are grouped together with their parent, and any non-manufacturing plants are omitted.[1] The industrial coverage of the British and United States Censuses is also satisfactorily comparable for present purposes (the exceptions are noted in section E.2 of this appendix and are too small to warrant specific adjustment in this context).

For the period before 1947 no information from the Census is available on this topic (in this respect we are more fortunate in the United Kingdom, since we have a pre-war estimate based on the Census for

Notes to this appendix will be found on p. 300.

1935 from the work of Leak and Maizels). The pre-war estimates that we have used for the United States are therefore based on movements of asset totals compiled from company balance sheets for various years, with adjustments for the proportion of value added in unincorporated businesses.[2] The figures have been linked to the post-war Census series in order to obtain a consistent series going back to 1909.

Changes in asset totals taken from balance sheets at book-values do not provide a guide which is altogether consistent with changes in output as they would be recorded in a Census, partly because asset totals from balance sheets are affected by non-manufacturing assets and by operations abroad, and partly because inflation may not affect equally the asset values of small and large companies (there are, of course, other factors, but these two seem the most important). For the post-war period comparisons are possible of the direct Census results with indirect estimates using asset-links, and two experimental calculations may be quoted to illustrate the order of magnitude of the difference. If we started with the Census estimate of some 31 per cent of manufacturing net output controlled by the hundred largest in 1960 (derived by interpolating between the 1958 and 1963 Censuses) and attempted an estimate for 1948 on the basis of changes in asset totals from balance sheets between 1948 and 1960,[3] we would derive an estimate of 26 per cent for 1948; a Census result is available for 1947 (only one year earlier) and shows 23 per cent. This suggests that the indirect method relying on asset-links understates the rise in concentration in that period.

A comparison for the period 1950–62 is also possible. If we started with a Census estimate for 1962 obtained as above and attempted an estimate for 1950 from the movements in asset totals, we would arrive at 28 per cent,[4] while the Census suggests 26–27 per cent. Again, the indirect estimate suggests a slightly slower rise than the Census.

The periods covered in these two comparisons are largely overlapping and the comparisons are not quite independent. Further, one must not conclude that the indirect method always necessarily understates the rise in concentration for earlier periods since, to mention only one factor, certain pre-war periods were marked by sharp deflations; but inflation has been the long-term order of things and the suggestion conveyed by the above comparisons is perhaps worth bearing in mind. The implication would thus be that the true rate of increase in aggregate concentration in the United States before the war was somewhat faster than indicated here (the reader may wish to be reminded that the level and changes shown for the post-war period are based entirely on Census returns and are not affected by these considerations).

Derivation of the pre-war estimates

For 1929 and 1935 the most suitable of the various series available is that recently published by the Federal Trade Commission relating to the share in corporate assets of the hundred largest manufacturing corporations during the period 1925–68.[5] This series has been linked to the observed Census share in net output to provide our estimates for the years 1929 and 1935. Allowance was made for the proportion of value added in unincorporated businesses (the Federal Trade Commission publication provides an estimate which allows for their share of assets, but for present purposes it seems better to use the estimates that are available relating to their share in value added).

Slightly different results are arrived at according to which Census year is chosen as the link; we eventually decided to take an average of the results of linking to each of the first three Census years (1947, 1954 and 1958) for which those concentration ratios were calculated. More than a single year's link seemed desirable, partly to reduce rounding errors (the Census series is only published correct to the nearest percentage point), and partly because we did not wish to rely entirely on 1947 as a link-year, since that was the first time the Census had prepared an estimate of the share of the largest companies and one may suspect that the coverage of subsidiaries was not as full as subsequently.

The results of this calculation were that we estimated the share in net output of the hundred largest manufacturing companies in 1929 and 1935 at 25 and 26 per cent respectively.

It is worth looking briefly at an earlier study which enables an alternative estimate to be made for 1929. A comparison of the consolidated accounts of the hundred largest manufacturing companies had previously been prepared for 1929 and 1962 (Means, 1968, pp. 352–3). This suggested that the share of the hundred largest companies in gross (that is undepreciated) corporate assets rose from 40 to 49 per cent over this period; the rise in their share of net assets was from 44 to 58 per cent. There is no very clear reason for preferring one of these measures to the other and we have taken an average in our workings.[6] We must also allow for the reduction from 8 to 4 per cent during that period in the share of unincorporated businesses in manufacturing net output. Combining these figures and linking them to the Census estimate interpolated for 1962 yields an estimate for 1929 of 24 per cent, which is virtually identical to the estimate derived above for that year.[7]

Changes in concentration before 1929 are difficult to measure with any precision and have been the subject of heated controversy in the American literature (see the account given by Means, 1968, p. 344). Kaplan's warning must be kept in mind that: 'Approximations are especially rough for the year 1909, which antedates regular income tax returns and modern standards for publicly issued financial statements.' (1964, p. 119).

There are three studies on the role of the largest companies in the period 1909–29 to which we must refer. All three are based on movements in the assets of the largest corporations in relation to the assets of all corporations. The original study by Berle and Means (1932, p. 36) relied on the gross assets of the 200 largest non-financial corporations, which increased by a factor of 3·1 in this period. Kaplan's later study (1964, p. 120) of the total assets of the hundred largest industrials showed a rise by a factor of 3·3, and a revision of that series by Collins and Preston (1961, p. 989) showed a rise by a factor of 3·5. These differences would not have much effect on our estimate for 1909. The important differences relate to the movements in the total for all corporations: Berle and Means show a rise by a factor of only 2·1, Kaplan by 3·4 and Collins and Preston by 2·4. In Kaplan's study there is therefore little change in the relative *share* of the largest corporations between 1909 and 1929, but the other two studies show a substantial rise; if allowance is further made for the substantial decrease in the role of unincorporated businesses (22 per cent in 1909, 8 per cent in 1929) Kaplan's figures when linked to ours for 1929 imply an estimated share of the hundred largest in 1909 of 23 per cent, while the other two studies lead to estimates of 14 per cent. There are remarks in the paper by Collins and Preston (1961, p. 989, table 1, footnotes *a* and *b*) which indicate that they were aware that their figure for all industrial corporations differed crucially from that used by Kaplan, but no reasons are given why their figure should be preferred.

It appears that none of these studies had access to the more recent and very careful National Bureau study, which shows that capital in manufacturing at book-values rose in the period 1909–29 by a factor of 3·5;[8] this thus supports Kaplan's estimates. We thought it as well to retain Kaplan's figures here, since they are based on Internal Revenue sources throughout and are thus more comparable with the sources relating to the largest companies, whereas the figures by Creamer *et al.* rely partly on the Census of Manufactures (for 1909) and partly on the Internal Revenue (for 1929). As already noted we have adjusted Kaplan's figures to allow for unincorporated businesses. The result is that we adopt 22 per cent as our best estimate of the share of the hundred largest in 1909. The above discussion of the alternatives will, however, have made it clear that there is a fair margin of possible error.

Other sources

An attempt to derive a consistent series for the period 1924–67 has previously been made by Scherer (1970, p. 43), but it differs from ours in the sources used and also in concepts; his series relates to the corporate manufacturing sector rather than to all firms in manufacturing, and to assets rather than output. Over that period he shows a rise in the share of the hundred largest from 36 to 50 per cent of corporate manufacturing assets, compared with our rise from 23 to 33 per cent of all manufacturing net output; the decline during the war-period is similar in both series (but, as Scherer elliptically indicates in his graph, he has some reservations about the figures for this period).

Blair's valuable discussion of the various sources (1972, pp. 62–70) should also be mentioned; regrettably he does not refer to Kaplan's study (and he does not attempt to derive a single compromise estimate).

*   *   *   *   *

Table E.1. *Share of the hundred largest enterprises in manufacturing net output, United States, 1909–70*

	1909	1929	1935	1947	1954	1958	1963	1967	1970
Share (%)	22	25	26	23	30	30	33	33[a]	33[a]

SOURCES: see text.

[a] Reduced to 32 per cent approximately if steel companies are excluded.

The view of the development of aggregate manufacturing concentration yielded by the above combination of a multiplicity of studies can thus be summarised as in table E.1. For comparison with British statistics we should take into account the fact that steel is now (from 1968) excluded from the calculated share of the hundred largest. An adjustment based on the size-distribution of steel firms (eight enterprises with over 25,000 employees)[9] leads to the conclusion that the share of the hundred largest American enterprises would fall by about 0·7 points if steel companies were excluded (the same fall as estimated for Britain, see appendix A). Compared with the share of the British hundred largest in 1968 of 41 per cent, the American share in 1967 should thus probably be put at 32 per cent (rather than 33 per cent as shown in the table).

Table E.2. *Reconciliation of United States industries with
United Kingdom Industrial Orders*

UK Industrial Orders[a]	US '4-digit' industries
Food, drink and tobacco	Food and tobacco *less* 2011, 2015, 2026, 2087
Coal and petroleum products	Petroleum refining and related industries *less* 2951–2
Chemical and allied industries	Chemicals and allied products *less* 2823–4; *plus* 1929, 2087
Metal manufacture	Primary metal industries *less* 3315, 3357; *plus* 3431, 3496–8
Mechanical engineering	Machinery except electrical *less* 3573; *plus* 1911, 1931, 1951, 1961, 1999, 2655, 3441, 3443, 3451, 3494, 3623, 3636
Instrument engineering	Professional, scientific and controlling instruments *plus* 1941, 3611, 3622
Electrical engineering	Electrical machinery, equipment and supplies *less* 3611, 3622–4, 3636; *plus* 3573
Shipbuilding and marine engineering	Ship and boat building and repairing
Vehicles	Transportation equipment *less* 3731–2; *plus* 1925
Metal goods n.e.s.	Fabricated metal products *less* 3431, 3441, 3443, 3451, 3494, 3496–8; *plus* 2514, 2515 (part) 2522, 2542, 3315, 3357, 3911–14, 3963–4
Textiles	Textile mill products *less* 2295; *plus* 2393–7, 2399, 2823–4, 3292–3
Leather, leather goods and fur	Leather and leather products *less* 3131, 3141–2, 3151; *plus* 2371, 2387 (part)
Clothing and footwear	Apparel and other finished products *less* 2371, 2387 (part), 2391–7, 2399; *plus* 3021 (part), 3131, 3141–2, 3151
Bricks, pottery, glass, cement, etc.	Stone, clay, glass and concrete products *less* 3292–3; *plus* 2951–2, 3624
Timber and furniture	Lumber and wood products *and* Furniture and fixtures *less* 2411, 2514, 2515 (part), 2522, 2542; *plus* 2391–2, 3993–4
Paper, printing, publishing	Paper and allied products *and* Printing, publishing and allied industries *less* 2655
Other manufacturing	Rubber and miscellaneous plastic products *less* 3021 (part); *plus* 2295, 3931, 3941–3, 3949, 3951–3, 3955, 3961–2, 3991

SOURCES: United Kingdom: Central Statistical Office, *Standard Industrial Classification 1958
and 1968*; United States: Executive Office of the President, Office of Management and
Budgets, *Standard Industrial Classification Manual, 1967*.

[a] As in the 1968 Standard Industrial Classification; but in table 6.2 and elsewhere in this
study some Orders are combined as in the 1958 Standard Industrial Classification.

E.2 RECONCILIATION OF CLASSIFICATION IN THE UNITED STATES CENSUS OF MANUFACTURES (1967) AND THE UNITED KINGDOM CENSUS OF PRODUCTION (1968)

In order to compare sizes of plants by main industry groups in the United States and the United Kingdom (in chapter 6), the United States Census groups (the 420 '4-digit' industries) were reclassified as far as possible to agree with the equivalent British classification by Industrial Orders, as shown in table E.2. The total coverage of the Censuses is very similar in both countries; the only exceptions appear to be the inclusion in the United States of meat and poultry packing and fluid milk in the food industry, and of logging camps and contractors in the lumber industry; these groups are not covered in the British Census and were excluded here. The reconciliation cannot be carried out precisely (occasionally an American 4-digit industry covers trades that are in two British Orders, in which case we have crudely halved the figures), but this should not be misleading at the level of aggregation considered here.

INTERNATIONAL COMPARISONS OF GIANT ENTERPRISES

F.I SOME FACTORS AFFECTING THE GROWTH OF LARGE FIRMS

The paragraphs that follow relate to three aspects of the economic framework which particularly bear on the differences among countries in the sizes of large enterprises (as distinct from plants, which are governed more strongly by technological factors); these aspects are legislation governing the formation of limited liability companies, the banks as industrial financiers and the government or state as entrepreneur.[1]

Limited liability legislation

It is clear that the giant enterprises of today could not exist without the social artifice of the limited liability company; we may begin therefore by considering the dating of the relevant legislation. The general availability of limited liability, as opposed to its exceptional availability on the basis of special charters or individual legislation, may be dated for all the countries considered here in various parts of the nineteenth century. In England the legislation of 1856 is usually regarded as marking the important change,[2] legislation in earlier decades having broadened the path towards general availability step by step. In the United States legislation was passed separately in each state, its timing lying on the whole within a few years of that in England. It appears, however, that Belgium was the first country in which the joint stock company (*société anonyme*) was adopted for industrial purposes and not confined to public utilities, and in 1850 she already had a total of 120 such companies including many important mining and metallurgical concerns. The largest Belgian combine of the present day, the Société Générale (of which more will be said below), was founded as early as 1822 (under the patronage of King William I) as a joint stock 'industrial bank'; during the 1830s it was particularly active as a promoter of industrial companies. In France official authorisation was required for the setting up of each individual *société anonyme* until the laws of 1867–8, and by 1870 there were only some 220 in existence. Individual authorisation was also required in Germany (except for

Notes to this appendix will be found on pp. 300–1.

certain limited areas such as the Hanse Towns) until general rules for joint stock companies were laid down in 1870–2. These were supplemented during the following twenty years and by the end of the century Germany had a very comprehensive body of company law. Even at that time, however, the joint stock form of business organisation was much less used in France or Germany than in Britain. Clapham estimates that by 1909 the total number of such companies in Germany numbered approximately 22,000 and in France possibly only 12,000, whereas in Britain in that year there were 46,000 limited companies under the various Companies Acts, apart from railways and chartered companies for imperial development (Clapham, 1945, pp. 231–2 and 395–400).

Holland, by virtue of its early establishment as an important commercial centre, had an elaborate Stock Exchange early in the eighteenth century and had adopted the French type of *société anonyme* early in the nineteenth century. Its industrialisation took place only gradually and mostly after 1870, but thereafter, helped by its trading background, it soon became the home of a number of giant enterprises of international stature.

In Sweden there was no general company legislation until as late as 1895; since that date this form of organisation has proved unusually popular. Heckscher (1954, p. 247) suggests that a great many more small firms have been incorporated in this way than is usual in other countries.

But is company legislation of ultimate importance? Professor Landes has pointed out that the industrial revolution in Britain took place without recourse to the joint stock company and businessmen 'have always found ways of evading or transcending legislative limitations in this sphere when the rewards were sufficient'. The form of the enterprise, he has suggested, is the 'symptom rather than the determinant of the means and ends of the economic process' (1960, pp. 109 and 122). There was little or no need for a limited company in the early stages of industrialisation when the economic unit was still relatively small, but as soon as the railways arrived with their urgent need for large capital sums the new business form thrived. And, having become established as a tool of the business world, with its help the giant enterprises that we know today eventually evolved. It is always difficult to talk of 'ultimate causes' in social affairs, but if we are satisfied with the more modest aim of listing the prerequisites of the giant enterprise system of today – as distinct from the prerequisites of the early industrial revolution – then company legislation must rank high on such a list.

We have noticed that Belgium was the first country in which industry based itself in a substantial way on the limited liability company, and that factor must have contributed to the early attainment there of that high level of financial control over industry which (as Professor de Jong has recently described) now lies in the hands of a mere half dozen major groups.[3]

The role of the banks

The difference between the 'English' and the 'European' attitudes to the banking system's relations with industry is well known. In England, America and the Netherlands the over-riding view has always been that a secure and 'sound' banking and monetary system requires that the banks do not involve themselves in industrial risks. The banks in other European countries, following the lead of the Belgian Société Générale, began acting at an early stage as financiers and promoters of industrial concerns, and with the passage of time that involvement has become ever-closer. As we have seen Germany was relatively late with its general company legislation, but the industrial involvement of the few large banks was so great that high concentration became an early feature of its industrial scene. The power of the main German banks was proverbial even before the First World War.[4] As in Belgium, the present ramifications of these banking connections and the full extent of industrial concentration cannot be ascertained from the usual published information; the special government inquiry into concentration in Germany in the early 1960s indicated that the five main commercial banks there had maintained their long-characteristic participation in industry. We are told, for example, that, as a consequence of both direct stockholdings and acting as nominees for other companies or individual investors, bank representatives were chairmen of the supervisory boards of 150 large companies outside banking; and at the general meetings of ninety companies the banks controlled more than half the votes (Deutscher Bundestag, 1964, pp. 38 and 40–1). However we are not told to what extent these were the leading concerns in the country (there is no satisfactory analysis by size), nor to what extent inter-company shareholdings and common control effectively reduced the number of independent large enterprises; that, it appears, will require further investigation.[5]

The often-noted 'absence of powerful investment banks' in Britain has led to a different industrial structure.[6] From the point of view of the present discussion we might say that in Britain the control of many large groups of industrial firms is centralised in a non-banking parent company (an industrial holding company or a conglomerate, but of which all the subsidiaries are disclosed); the head office of each such group can to some extent be regarded as carrying out banking or financial functions in relation to its subsidiaries which are analogous to those carried out by industrial bankers in Continental Euɩope. Of course, that is an over-simplification, but one that is worth noting in making comparisons with other countries, as an indication of the universality of the pressures making for financial interdependence of industrial concerns. As noted in chapter 6, the bare statistics indicate that today giant enterprises are of greater relative consequence in Britain than in Germany; but if the full financial connections were known, and could be taken into account in some simple way, one cannot be certain that the balance might not be found to lie the other way. That, however, must remain a matter of speculation until official Census information is one day gathered in other European countries on the full ambit of each enterprise and the subsidiaries it controls.

State intervention

Finally, we must notice that state intervention has varied immensely amongst countries, both in the type of intervention and in its extent: from the early royal sponsorship of the Belgian Société Générale, to the heavy nationalisation programme of post-war Britain and, at the other extreme, to the opposition to state intervention in post-war Germany, which led to the sale to private investors (presumably, in practice, to the banks) of the state-owned car concern (Volkswagen). In most countries at some periods there was official encouragement of mergers; at other and more recent periods there has been a certain amount of discouragement of monopolistic tendencies. It is difficult usefully to summarise this varied experience beyond saying that, in terms of total industrial employment in the 1960s, about a fifth was accounted for by nationalised industry in those countries in which nationalisation was important, that is in Britain, France and Italy.[7] Large enterprises inevitably ensued in those branches of industry in which the state was involved.

Italy may serve as an extreme example of state intervention in industry arising on a very broad front and as a result of a combination of individual circumstances.[8] Until the economic crisis of 1929 the banks provided industrial finance in Italy in much the same way as in Germany, but in previous decades the state had taken a rather more active role in industrial affairs (including such small matters as a state monopoly in cigarette lighters in 1922). The 1929 financial collapse led to a strengthening of the state's role. The banks were saved only by the state taking over their industrial interests, which were merged (in 1933) into a state holding company (IRI), having important interests in steel, shipping, shipbuilding, telephones, electricity, etc. These events substantially coloured further developments. A state petroleum company was subsequently established (ENI) and electricity supply became a separate nationalised corporation (ENEL). Public ownership of the main national banks in Italy (which became subsidiaries of IRI) also gave the state indirect influence in many privately owned firms.

At the same time as the Fascist system of the 1930s brought about strong state intervention and exclusive government control in the supply of certain goods, it pursued a policy whereby cartels were not only encouraged by favourable legislation, but in certain instances the government set up compulsory consortia to meet its requirements. By the end of the Second World War, therefore, many industries were very highly concentrated. Bernini suggested that by then 'a few groups or individual enterprises controlled more than 50 per cent of the total output in steel, aluminium, machinery, textiles, chemicals, sugar and cement'.[9] Fiscal benefits now apply in Italy in the case of any mergers of enterprises which operate at the same level. By legislation enacted in 1968 these are to be revoked 'if amelioration and rationalisation of the plant structure and equipment does not take place within five years'.[10]

* * * * *

The above paragraphs provide an indication of the extraordinary range of environments in which the modern giant enterprise has developed; an observer of the present scene can only express surprise that the differences amongst countries in the importance of those giant enterprises are not greater than can be discerned through the statistical haze.

F.2   MANUFACTURING ENTERPRISES WITH OVER 40,000 EMPLOYEES

In chapter 6 an attempt is made to compare the importance of large manufacturing enterprises in other major countries with their importance in Britain. The comparisons are based on the companies listed in table F.1, which are those having over 40,000 employees and appearing in the lists of large companies published by *Fortune*, *The Times*, *Forbes*, *Les Dossiers de l'Entreprise*, etc.; the figures are taken from company accounts ending mainly in 1972. Since steel is nationalised in Britain, for the sake of comparability any companies in other countries primarily engaged in steel production have been excluded here, as also have been public utilities and mining companies. Subsidiaries of foreign companies have been excluded from national lists (for example, Ford in Germany is treated as if it were an American company and excluded from the German list).

A number of difficulties are associated with this table. First, some companies have interests both in distribution and in industry: the

Table F.1. *Manufacturing enterprises with over*
40,000 employees,[a] 1972

	Main products	Employment (000s)
BELGIUM		
Solvay	Chemicals, etc.	45
FRANCE		
Renault	Cars	157
Saint Gobain-Pont à Mousson	Construction materials	129
Cie Générale d'Electricité	Electrical equipment	125
Rhône-Poulenc	Chemicals, synthetic fibres	118
Citroën	Cars	104
Péchiney-Ugine Kuhlmann	Non-ferrous metals, chemicals	95
Peugeot	Cars	90
Michelin	Tyres	89
Thomson-Brandt	Electrical equipment	85
Boussois-Souchon-Neuvesel[b]	Glass, food products	70
Aerospatiale	Aircraft	43
Creusot-Loire	Steel, machinery	42
GERMANY		
Siemens	Electrical equipment	301
Volkswagenwerk	Cars	192
AEG-Telefunken	Electrical equipment	166
Daimler-Benz	Cars	150
Farbwerke Hoechst	Chemicals, pharmaceuticals	146
Bayer	Chemicals	137
Robert Bosch	Electrical equipment	108
BASF	Chemicals	104
Gutehoffnungshütte	Machinery, engineering	93
Mannesmann	Tubes, machinery, chemicals	85
Flick Group	Heavy industry, chemicals, paper	67
KHD	Engines, trucks, buses	41
ITALY		
Fiat	Cars	189
Montedison	Chemicals	168
Pirelli	Tyres	85[c]
ENI	Petroleum products	79
Olivetti	Office equipment	72
Alfa Romeo	Cars	42
NETHERLANDS		
Philips	Electrical equipment, etc.	371
Unilever	Food, detergents	181[d]
Royal Dutch–Shell	Petroleum products, chemicals	104[e]
Akzo	Synthetic fibres	101
SWEDEN		
Ericsson Telephone	Telecommunications	71
SKF	Bearings	65
Volvo	Cars	45

Table F.1. *cont.*

	Main products	Employment (000s)
SWITZERLAND		
Nestlé	Food products	116
Brown, Boveri	Machinery	92
Ciba-Geigy	Pharmaceuticals	71
UNITED KINGDOM[f]		
General Electric	Electrical equipment	211
Imperial Chemical Industries	Chemicals	199
British Leyland	Cars	191
Unilever	Food, detergents	156[d]
Courtaulds	Synthetic fibres, textiles	150
British-American Tobacco	Tobacco, paper products	110
Guest, Keen & Nettlefolds	Engineering	109
Imperial (Tobacco) Group[g]	Tobacco, beer, food	108
Associated British Foods	Food products	108
Dunlop	Tyres	85[c]
Lucas	Vehicle equipment	83
Thorn	Electrical equipment	82
Hawker Siddeley	Aircraft, engineering	81
Reed International	Paper products	80
Plessey	Telecommunications, electronics	79
Coats, Patons	Threads and cloth	76
Royal Dutch–Shell	Petroleum products	70[e]
British Petroleum	Petroleum products	70
Rolls Royce	Aircraft engines	64
Rank-Hovis-McDougall	Milling, baking, foods	63
Bass Charrington	Beer	58
Cavenham	Foods	56
Metal Box	Packaging, machinery	55
British Insulated Callenders Cables	Cables, engineering	54
Tube Investments	Engineering	53
Allied Breweries	Beer	53
Cadbury-Schweppes	Confectionery, soft drinks	45
British Oxygen	Industrial gases	41
EMI	Gramophone records	40
Thomas Tilling	Building materials, etc.	40
UNITED STATES[h]		
General Motors	Cars	760
Ford	Cars	443
International Telephone & Telegraph	Telecommunication, controls, food, etc.	428
General Electric	Electrical equipment	369
International Business Machines	Office/electronic equipment	262
Chrysler	Cars	245
Westinghouse Electric	Electrical equipment	176
Goodyear	Tyres	145
Exxon	Petroleum products	141
RCA	Electronics etc.	122

Table F.1. *cont.*

	Main products	Employment (000s)
UNITED STATES[h] *cont.*		
Singer	Diversified manufacturing	117
Eastman Kodak	Photographics, etc.	115
Litton Industries	Electronic controls, etc.	114
Du Pont	Fibres, chemicals	111
Firestone Tire & Rubber	Tyres	109
International Harvester	Farm machinery	100
Union Carbide	Chemicals, gases, alloys	98
Honeywell	Electronics	97
National Cash Register	Office equipment	90

[a] Excluding companies engaged primarily in steel production (for comparability with United Kingdom, where steel is nationalised), public utilities and mining companies.

[b] Including Gervais-Danone.

[c] World employment by the Dunlop–Pirelli Union is 170,000; half each has here been allocated to the United Kingdom and to Italy.

[d] World employment by the Dutch and British Unilever companies is 337,000; in accordance with the 'equalisation agreement' between the companies, 54 per cent has here been allocated to the Dutch company and 46 per cent to the British company.

[e] World employment by Royal Dutch–Shell is 174,000, of which 60 per cent has been allocated to the Dutch company and 40 per cent to the British.

[f] It is not clear whether Sears (employment 62,000) and Tate and Lyle (employment 40,000) have more or less than a half of their activities in manufacturing; they have been excluded here in order to avoid biasing the comparisons in favour of our conclusion.

[g] Including Courage.

[h] Twenty largest companies only, see text.

principle adopted, both in the original publications and here, is to include them if the greater part of their activities is industrial, but the available information is limited and the decision is sometimes somewhat arbitrary (for Britain, for example, we have excluded Brooke Bond as wholesalers and this differs from the treatment in *Fortune*). Secondly, the number of employees shown here is intended to be the world employment by the parent company and its subsidiaries (occasionally where a parent owns less than half the shares of an associated company, that proportion of the associated company's employment has been included); world employment is more easily and more consistently obtainable from the majority of company accounts than is the alternative concept of domestic employment (which was adopted in the earlier sections of chapter 6 in the comparisons for Britain and America based on their Censuses) – nevertheless European company accounts are often such that one cannot be sure that all subsidiaries have been included. Thirdly, a few concerns are multi-national in their original constitution. For purposes of the present comparisons they have been apportioned to each country according to their interests; for example, the Unilever concern is jointly owned by two legally distinct companies, one British and one Dutch linked by an 'equalisation agreement', which has been used as the basis for division. Any division of such concerns is inevitably unsatisfactory, but no better solution has been found for making comparisons between countries; in considering Europe as a whole such a division is, of course, not necessary.

The table relates to the main European countries including Britain; the twenty largest companies in the United States have also been included. A further sixty-nine industrial companies in the United States are listed by *Fortune* with over 40,000 employees, but there is little point in reproducing their names here. The employment of those sixty-nine companies totalled 4,003,000, an average of 58,000 per company. Together with the twenty companies listed in the table, the employment in all United States industrial companies with over 40,000 employees is 8,045,000 (excluding steel companies, also Western Electric, where we have followed Moody's in treating it as a public utility, though *Fortune* lists it as an industrial company). This should enable the reader to check the results arrived at in chapter 6 but, as pointed out, the figures are not as precise as may be wished and incorporate a degree of judgement.

NOTES TO THE TEXT

Notes to chapter 1 (pages 1–24)

1 The period 1935–51 was examined by R. Evely and I. M. D. Little in *Concentration in British Industry*, Cambridge University Press, 1960; the period 1958–63 by P. E. Hart, M. A. Utton and G. Walshe in *Mergers and Concentration in British Industry*, Cambridge University Press, 1973, and by G. Walshe in *Recent Trends in Monopoly in Great Britain*, Cambridge University Press, 1974. A study for the period 1958–68 is in preparation at the National Institute by P. E. Hart and R. Clarke (*Concentration in Manufacturing Industries in the United Kingdom, 1958–68*, Cambridge University Press, forthcoming).

2 For a fuller account see Interdepartmental Committee on Social and Economic Research, *Guides to Official Sources: no. 6, Census of Production Reports*, London, HMSO, 1961, p. 15.

3 A. A. Berle and G. Means, *The Modern Corporation and Private Property*, New York, Macmillan, 1932 (rev. edn 1968).

4 S. J. Prais, 'The financial experience of giant companies', *Economic Journal*, vol. 67, June 1957; P. E. Hart, 'Business concentration in the United Kingdom', *Journal of the Royal Statistical Society* (series A), vol. 123, part 1, 1960; G. Bannock, *The Juggernauts*, London, Weidenfeld and Nicholson, 1971.

5 The *ex cathedra* condemnation of studies of aggregate concentration by Stigler, and his uncharitable remarks on the study by Kaplan of the hundred largest industrial enterprises in the United States, seem surprising to the modern reader who is familiar with more recent trends (see G. J. Stigler, 'The statistics of monopoly and merger', *Journal of Political Economy*, vol. 64, February 1956, p. 37; A. D. H. Kaplan, *Big Enterprise in a Competitive System*, Washington (DC), Brookings Institution, 1954 (2nd edn, 1964)).

6 M. A. Utton, 'Aggregate versus market concentration', *Economic Journal*, vol. 84, March 1974.

7 Provisional versions of these estimates have formed the basis of lectures I have given while this work was in progress (S. J. Prais, 'A new look at the growth of industrial concentration', *Oxford Economic Papers*, vol. 26, July 1974) and have been incorporated in other studies (L. Hannah, *The Corporate Economy* (forthcoming); S. Aaronovitch and M. C. Sawyer, 'The concentration of British manufacturing', *Lloyds Bank Review*, no. 114, October 1974). Those provisional figures showed broadly the same development over the period as a whole, but the present estimates for the latest years based on the Census are somewhat lower than had provisionally been inferred from the rise in the ratio of the profits of the hundred largest to total profits. The reason for the greater rise in 'profit concentration' lies in the expansion of the largest

companies into non-manufacturing and activities abroad (which are not covered in Census totals relating to manufacturing only).

8 P. E. Hart and S. J. Prais, 'The analysis of business concentration: a statistical approach', *Journal of the Royal Statistical Society* (series A), vol. 119, part 2, 1956, where changes in the dispersion of sizes of quoted industrial companies during five sub-periods between 1885 and 1950 gave an impression of the trends in aggregate concentration which was generally similar to that conveyed by table 1.1. Being confined to quoted companies it was not clear whether those earlier results could properly be regarded as representing what had been happening in industry generally including the non-quoted sector. It appears now that we need not have been so hesitant in generalising from those results.

9 The pre-war estimates are derived in a somewhat complex way which the reader may find easier to follow after he has read chapter 2. The assumption made is that enterprise-sizes are distributed log-normally, and that the variance of the distribution has increased over time in such a way as to lead to the observed changes in the share of the hundred largest enterprises. The corresponding 50 per cent values are calculated from those theoretical distributions (see appendix C, example 3). We also take as a working assumption that the total number of independent enterprises has been 66,000 throughout (equal to the figure for the 1960s); it is possible that this total number was greater in earlier years, but the answer is not sensitive to this assumption (it makes a negligible difference if we assume there were 100,000 firms in 1909). The tables of H. Leak and A. Maizels in 'The structure of British industry', *Journal of the Royal Statistical Society* (series A), vol. 108, parts 1–2, 1942, pp. 144–5, relating to 1935, seem consistent with an estimate of 800 enterprises accounting for half the total net output in manufacturing, but in examining them it should be remembered that they include certain non-factory trades (as described further in appendix A).

10 Estimates were derived as follows:

For 1968: from special tabulations relating to the hundred largest enterprises by employment and by net output. These two sets of enterprises are not quite identical; the differences between the last two columns of the table are due partly to this, and partly to the different measure of size.

For 1963: selected by interpolation as enterprises employing over 9400 from the size-distribution of enterprises by Industrial Order in the 1968 Census. A further 12 per cent of employment by the hundred largest needs to be included to allow for establishments outside the main Industrial Order of each enterprise. This was estimated by carrying out a similar calculation for 1968, and linking with the results for that year from the special tabulation referred to above.

For 1958: from the 1963 Census by similar methods to those used for 1963, but since the size-distributions for 1958 were published on the basis of fifty-three 'industrial groups', not by Industrial Orders, the groups with over 5000 employees were first combined to yield Industrial Orders. Figures suppressed to avoid disclosure of individual returns were estimated by us having regard to the published marginal totals. Employment by the hundred largest enterprises was then estimated, with the help of a Pareto curve, as that in enterprises employing over 7800; this was compared with total employment for each industry (including establishments employing under a hundred) and the results for 1958 were linked to the estimate for 1963.

11 In 1973 the Spearman rank correlation between the shares of the hundred largest firms for the various industries and the gross capital expenditure per head in those industries was 0.71; this is significant at the 1 per cent level.

12 Throughout this section statistics are quoted in terms of establishments (or plants) rather than enterprises; statistics on enterprises are not available and in this size-range no great error should arise from assuming that enterprises are identical with establishments. It is not possible to go back earlier than 1930 because of limitations in the Census coverage of small firms.

13 The wide range of the observations makes a ratio-scale more appropriate here; on the other hand, in chart 1.1 an absolute scale was adopted, partly because the range is narrower and partly because a ratio-scale would introduce a curvature into the recent observations which might be thought artificial. The number of unsatisfactory returns to the Census authorities is particularly great amongst small firms and makes it difficult to draw any very definite conclusion as to the recent trend. For example, in 1968 in all manufacturing industries together there were unsatisfactory returns relating to 8000 establishments, having an estimated average employment of seventeen persons per establishment; many of these establishments will have had less than ten persons. It is clearly difficult to be sure of the true movements in the number of small establishments when the recorded movements are small in relation to the number of unsatisfactory returns.

14 In 1969 the government appointed a committee (chairman J. F. Bolton) which issued a lengthy report (Department of Trade and Industry, *Report of the Committee of Inquiry on Small Firms*, Cmnd 4811, London, HMSO, 1971), together with an accompanying series of eighteen research reports, covering firms employing under 200 persons. We have here preferred the lower criterion of ten employees because:

(*a*) In looking at the lower tail of the distribution – which is our interest here – it does not seem sensible to go higher than the lower half of the number of enterprises.

(*b*) It brings the statistical definition closer to the kind of small firm that one or two persons may set up out of their own accumulated resources, rather than the kind of firm founded by a previous generation of owners.

In terms of numbers, small manufacturing firms as here defined accounted in 1963 for just over half those that would be covered on the Bolton Committee's definition.

15 Ideally table 1.4 should have been compiled in terms of enterprises rather

than establishments; the student of Census curiosities will however know that no figures are published for the number of enterprises in each Industrial Order. For present purposes it did not seem worth straining to produce approximate estimates, since the industrial pattern would hardly change. For all manufacturing industry together an average of 1·3 establishments per enterprise was recorded for 1968; if this factor is applied to the first column of table 1.4, it would raise the apparent relative importance of the *number* of small firms (the estimates in the final column, relating to the share of employment, would of course not be affected).

16 These remarks are based on fuller studies of certain trades in which small firms have been particularly important – clothing, baking, furniture and plastics fabrication. Their ambit, however, lay too far outside the central theme of this inquiry to warrant inclusion in this book.

17 A more detailed re-examination of the trade concentration ratios from 1935 onwards is at present being carried out at the Institute by my colleagues Peter Hart and Roger Clarke, the results of whose work will appear in a forthcoming Institute study. The dependence of weighted average trade concentration ratios on the precise sample of trades chosen, on the precise measures of size and on weighting patterns is fully explored there.

18 The following hypothetical and extreme sample may make this point clearer. Suppose that the economy consists of twenty trades all of equal size in terms of output and that each trade consists of a hundred firms having the same size-distribution, with the five largest firms in each trade producing 30 per cent of that trade's output. If there was no overlap amongst the largest firms, each working only in its own trade, the hundred largest firms in the economy as a whole would be identical with the five largest in each of the twenty trades; the hundred largest firms would therefore also account for 30 per cent of national output. In other words, the aggregate concentration ratio relating to the hundred largest firms in the whole economy would be the same as the average concentration ratio for the five firms in each of the twenty trades. Now suppose there is a series of amalgamations across all trades by size-ranking, such that the top firm in each trade merges with the top firms in all other trades; similarly, the second largest firms in all trades merge to become one firm, the third largest firms in each trade merge, and so on right down to the last firm in each trade. We would end with a hundred enterprises controlling the whole economy, and with an aggregate concentration ratio that would have risen from its initial 30 per cent to a final 100 per cent. Yet a Census tabulation relating to each trade would show an unchanged picture: there would still be a hundred enterprises active in each trade, and in each trade the five largest would account for an unchanged 30 per cent of output! The latter of course remains a relevant aspect of the truth in this hypothetical situation, but it is obviously not the only aspect. In the general case of unrelated size-distributions for each trade, the relation between the average of individual trade concen-

tration ratios and the aggregate concentration ratio is complex; I have not succeeded in deriving any empirically useful and simple relations.

19 In the original publication it will be found that what we have here called 'trades' are, on the strict Census definitions, sometimes more properly termed 'sub-trades'. The weighted averages, which were not given by Evely and Little, relate partly to 'trades' and partly to 'sub-trades'. In calculating them we have used employment in 1935 as the weights (taken from Evely and Little, 1960, pp. 52–9 and 340); where a range of possible values was given for the concentration ratio in a particular trade we have taken the mid-point for the present calculations. On using 1951 weights the calculated rise would be slightly greater, from 28 to 34 per cent; a larger rise on an *un*weighted calculation (from 42 to 52 per cent) is shown by P. E. Hart in 'Concentration in the United Kingdom' in H. Arndt (ed.), *Die Konzentration in der Wirtschaft*, Berlin, Duncker and Humblot, 1971, but in our view the weighted average is more relevant in the present comparisons.

Using a simple test of statistical significance (comparing the weighted average change with its standard error), one would draw the conclusion that, if the population had a zero mean change, a change as great as that shown by the 1935-weighted average would occur by chance in 5 per cent of samples, and one as great as the 1951-weighted average would occur in less than 1 per cent of samples.

20 A. Armstrong and A. Silberston, 'Size of plant, size of enterprise and concentration in British manufacturing industry, 1935–58', *Journal of the Royal Statistical Society* (series A), vol. 128, part 3, 1965, p. 418. No general average was calculated in the original paper. We have here taken mid-points where a range of possible values was given for individual trades, and the weights taken were employment in 1958. Hart (1960) gives an unweighted average for a sub-sample of thirty-five trades (omitting those where there is a range), which shows a very similar proportionate rise.

21 W. G. Shepherd, 'Changes in British industrial concentration, 1951–1958', *Oxford Economic Papers*, vol. 18, March 1966, especially p. 128. K. D. George in 'Changes in British industrial concentration, 1951–1958', *Journal of Industrial Economics*, vol. 15, July 1967, p. 205, has certain reservations on Shepherd's study, but they are probably not substantial enough to affect the averages quoted here.

22 The frequency distributions for these sales concentration ratios were first published by Hart (1971, p. 249), and then in the study by Hart, Utton and Walshe (1973, p. 25). The weighted averages quoted here are taken from the calculations subsequently revised by Clarke.

23 M. C. Sawyer, 'Concentration in British manufacturing industry', *Oxford Economic Papers*, vol. 23, November 1971.

24 The unweighted average was given in an article introducing the final volume of the 1968 Census in *Trade and Industry*, 1 August 1974, p. 240. The weighted average has been calculated by Clarke and relates to 288 products.

25 Employment was used as the weights in calculating the average number

of industrial groups in which these enterprises were active (see *Census 1963*, vol. 132, table 19). It is conceptually possible that a change in the balance of activities within an establishment (for example, a hitherto minor activity becoming a major activity) could lead to a rise in the number of industrial groups in which an enterprise is recorded as being engaged by the Census, but the rise in the number of establishments owned by the average giant firm has been so rapid in this period (as we shall consider further in chapter 4) that this must be regarded as no more than a conceptual possibility which can probably be ignored in practice.

26 Regrettably, statistical information of this type for other years is not on a comparable basis, so that the changes over time cannot be assessed. Leak and Maizels, 1945, pp. 145 *et seq.*, attempted to measure diversification in their study of the 1935 Census, but the information given there is on a finer industrial classification (about five times as many trades), and relates only to all enterprises employing over 500. The 1968 Census presents an analysis in terms of seventeen Orders instead of the fifty-one groups used in 1963, and there appears to be no way of joining the two sets of results. A study of the period 1968–72 being undertaken by M. A. Utton of this Institute in conjunction with the Census authorities promises to cast much new light on the pattern of diversification.

27 From 'Some aspects of competition', Alfred Marshall's Presidential Address to the Economic Science and Statistics Section of the British Association, Leeds, 1890, quoted by A. C. Pigou in *Memorials of Alfred Marshall*, London, Macmillan, 1925, pp. 279–80.

28 Monopolies and Mergers Commission, *Boots Company Limited and the House of Fraser Limited. Report on the proposed merger*, London, HMSO, 1974.

Notes to chapter 2 (pages 25–40)

1 Two statistical studies carried out over half a century ago – T. S. Ashton and S. J. Chapman, 'The size of businesses, mainly in the textile industries', *Journal of the Royal Statistical Society*, vol. 77, April 1914, and T. S. Ashton, 'The growth of textile businesses in the Oldham district, 1884–1924, *Journal of the Royal Statistical Society*, vol. 89, May 1926 – appear to have been inspired by similar motives to those of the present chapter, and remain of interest. Size-distributions of firms were given there for a number of years, and an attempt was made to explain their evolution; however, no cross-tabulations of sizes at different dates were prepared and that, perhaps, hindered the development of the kind of analysis suggested in this chapter. In the formal terms that are in fashion today, it may be said that they were concerned with comparative statics, whereas we are here concerned with dynamics.

2 For some empirical evidence see the chart in our earlier paper (Hart and Prais, 1956, p. 170) which compares the distributions during a sixteen-year period of rates of growth of three groups of firms differing in size at the beginning of the period. The group of large firms were on average about a thousand times as great as the group of small firms,

yet the frequency distributions of the proportionate growth-rates of the groups can hardly be distinguished.

3 The fact that in *logarithmic* terms the distribution retains its symmetry is no more than a mathematical abstraction and should not distract the reader from the underlying economic reality. The process described above is familiar to physicists as the theory of Brownian motion, with the difference that the disturbances here act multiplicatively rather than additively; P. A. Samuelson, in a study of share prices – 'Rational theory of warrant pricing' in P. H. Cootner (ed.), *The Random Character of Stock Market Prices*, Cambridge (Mass.), MIT Press, 1964 – terms it a 'geometric Brownian motion'. A distribution governed by a 'law of absolute growth' would also lose its symmetry if negative sizes were disallowed; see next note.

4 There is no need here to enter into a discussion of the mathematical properties of the log-normal distribution and its many applications; a full account is given in the monograph by J. Aitchison and J. A. C. Brown, *The Lognormal Distribution*, Cambridge University Press, 1957, and in the earlier fundamental work by R. Gibrat, *Les Inégalités Economiques*, Paris, Sirey, 1931. The principal properties of the distribution that have been found useful in analysing concentration are briefly set out in appendix C, together with some numerical applications. By way of a technical footnote, three more general points may be made here.

The first is that the dispersion of the distribution increases irrespective of whether growth is multiplicative or additive; accordingly, M. Kalecki's criticism in 'On the Gibrat distribution', *Econometrica*, vol. 13, April 1945, is not quite to the point (and, as we shall see in note 13 below, his argument on the need for a negative correlation between growth and size is merely a rephrasing of the classical problem treated long ago by Galton).

Secondly, the reader may have noticed that, on our initial model of absolute changes in size, after a certain period (ten years in the example above) some firms have a chance of reaching the barrier of a zero size. At that stage the assumptions about the probabilities of growth have necessarily to be varied, otherwise unacceptable negative sizes emerge in the subsequent year. Various ways of proceeding can be developed mathematically (such as that firms die on reaching the zero-state, or that a certain fraction are born or reborn each year out of that state and reach a positive size), but the theorems that have been derived from such a conceptual framework do not seem of much help in studying the trend in concentration. The model of absolute growth and its implications for increasing concentration are thus of limited value; it can be used for short-term analyses and it is convenient heuristically. On the other hand, with the multiplicative law of growth and decline a zero absolute size is never reached – by whatever factor size falls the size still remains positive (although the logarithm of size eventually becomes negative, it will be remembered that the anti-log of a negative number is still positive); consequently the process can be treated as continuing for an indefinitely long period of time without reaching a barrier which necessitates a modification in its logic. The long-term properties of the multiplicative model can thus readily be worked out; whereas the long-term properties of a law of absolute growth cannot, and they depend very much on the assumptions made with regard to births and deaths. On the neglect of births and deaths on the approach here, see appendix D, pp. 207–8, which also gives references to the rather different approaches adopted by other authors.

The final point requiring notice here is that on the multiplicative growth model there is a small upward drift in the arithmetic mean size of the distribution; this arises because equal positive and negative changes in the logarithm of a number are not offsetting in absolute terms. In the above example of symmetric changes of 10 per cent, the firms falling in size are to be understood as finishing at a fraction of their original size ($10/11 = 90.9$ per cent), whereas those that rise in size finish at 110 per cent of the original size; there is thus a small rise in the average size of all firms, which works out at about $\frac{1}{4}$ per cent a year. This upward drift arises if the sole modification to the distribution over time is due to increasing dispersion; the mean can, however, easily be stabilised by superimposing an offsetting change in the scale of the distribution. This modification is only of formal interest and can be ignored in what follows.

5 If the empirical distribution were strictly log-normal, the various possible methods of estimating its logarithmic standard deviation (see Aitchison and Brown, 1957, chap. 5) would all yield the same value apart from sampling fluctuations. In practice there are always deviations from any simple theoretical distribution, and the method of estimation has to be chosen with a little care. In the present application we are particularly interested in that point of the distribution which relates to the hundred largest firms and the value of σ was estimated so that the theoretical curve went precisely through it; these matters are explained further in appendix C.

6 This follows from the familiar property of the log-normal distribution that about a sixth of the observations lie beyond one standard deviation from the mean and a twentieth beyond two standard deviations. Further, all these changes in size are to be understood as additional to any change in the mean size of all firms – for example, if firms on average grew by 10 per cent, a rise of a quarter in relation to the mean size would correspond to a total increase in size of 37.5 per cent, since $1.25 \times 1.1 = 1.375$.

7 There was a rise of 4.8 percentage points in the 'theoretical' share of the hundred largest in the decade 1953–63, compared with a theoretical rise of 3.4 points a decade at the beginning of the century and of 3.9 points a decade in sixty years' time.

8 This quotation will be found in Alfred Marshall's *Principles of Economics* (9th *variorum* edn, ed. C. W. Guillebaud), Macmillan, London, 1961, p. 315.

9 Alfred Marshall, *Industry and Trade*, London, Macmillan, 1919, pp. 315–16.

10 For other comments on the role of limited liability see Ashton, 1926, p. 574. R. Marris in 'Why economics needs a theory of the firm', *Economic Journal*, vol. 82, March 1972 (supplement), p. 329n., has also recently drawn attention to Marshall's treatment of this topic.

11 Galton's use of this term is to be distinguished from modern usage, where it is often taken to be no more than a curve fitted by the method of least squares. To ensure that the original meaning is kept in mind, a capital R is here used for Regression.

12 F. Galton, *Hereditary Genius*, London, Macmillan, 1869 (reprinted 1925).

13 The need for a negative correlation between growth and size in order to stabilise the variance was noted by Kalecki (1945), but he did not recognise the relation of his remarks to Galton's solution of the problem.

14 The proof is as follows. If the variance is constant over time and equal to σ^2, it follows from equation (5) that $\sigma^2(1 - b^2) = s^2$, or that $(1 - b)(1 + b) = s^2/\sigma^2$. On substituting $1 + c$ for b, this reduces to $-c(2 + c) = s^2/\sigma^2$; and, on ignoring the term in c^2 as being small, equation (7) results. In earlier writings we used the critical condition $b = r$ (where r is the correlation coefficient), which is mathematically equivalent to the exact form of this condition (concentration increases or decreases depending on whether $b \gtrless r$). I now, however, think equation (7) more useful, both in drawing explicit attention to the role of random variations in determining the required degree of Regression and, from the point of view of estimation, drawing attention to the need for unbiased estimates of both s and σ. If a truncated sample is used in empirical work (for example, of quoted companies rather than of all companies) the estimate of σ must be expected to be too low (considered in relation to the whole population) since the full size-range is not encompassed by the observations. Consequently the estimate of r based on such a sample is not an unbiased estimate of its value in the population. In the present application, on the other hand, we have been able to rely on Census material for the estimate of σ, as explained above. The estimate of s is, however, based mainly on quoted companies and presents certain problems. As considered at length in chapter 5, large companies have less variable profits and growth-rates than smaller companies, but in comparing quoted companies as a whole with all companies the differences are not too great. This appears from the studies surveyed in appendix D (table D.2), where an estimate of s based on Census sources for the period 1951–8 is seen to be of much the same order of magnitude as estimates based on quoted companies (in fact, it is somewhat lower, but this is partly because the Census measure of size is in terms of employment). By considering in this way the separate estimates of s and σ a more reliable view can be obtained of the critical value of the Regression required to stabilise the level of concentration.

At a theoretical level of discussion a distinction has to be drawn between the ultimate and the immediate behaviour of a statistical distribution. In theoretical treatises on stochastic processes emphasis is placed on whether c is positive or negative (or $b \gtrless 1$), rather than on whether c differs from c_g as here. If c is positive the variance of the process increases without limit; if it is negative the variance converges asymptotically to a limiting value which is equal to $s^2/(1-b^2) \simeq -s^2/2c$. If c lies in the negative zone between c_g and zero it might appear that there was a conflict between the implications of our criterion (7), which would warn that concentration was increasing, and the implications of the criterion in the theoretical treatises, which would calmly indicate that, though concentration was increasing, it was clearly anticipated that it would reach some finite limit. That limit may, however, be very distant from the current situation and not relevant to practical issues. For example, taking the pre-war average values of $c = -0.02$ and $s = 0.82$, which on the theoretical criterion indicate convergence, a limiting value can be calculated of $\sigma = 4.1$, corresponding to a share for the hundred largest firms of as much as 88 per cent of the economy! The usual criterion of the theoretical texts does not therefore seem a useful guide to policy, since it is concerned only with the ultimate behaviour of the system (after an infinite time has elapsed, or as near as makes no difference), whereas our criterion relates to the behaviour of the system in the immediate future, which, of course, is more relevant to practical issues.

Another technical matter that may be mentioned here is that in the presence of Regression the above process does not converge precisely to a log-normal distribution unless the random effects are themselves log-normal; it may be that this has some bearing on the slight lepto-kurtosis that has been observed (Hart and Prais, 1956, p. 159). I am grateful to Mr E. Rowthorn (Cambridge) for showing me his unpublished theoretical paper on this aspect.

15 Further details of the studies referred to in this and the next two paragraphs will be found in appendix D. The sampling errors are such that one cannot speak with too much precision about the pre-war period; it is hoped that the above simplified summary of the various studies will not mislead.

16 J. M. Samuels, 'Size and growth of firms', *Review of Economic Studies*, vol. 32, April 1965.

17 M. A. Utton, 'The effect of mergers on concentration: UK manufacturing industry, 1954-65', *Journal of Industrial Economics*, vol. 20, November 1971.

18 These studies of the post-war period are not entirely independent, since they cover partially overlapping periods and the samples also partially overlap; they are however reassuringly consistent, and taken together span the period 1951-65. The sampling standard errors of these three values of c are in the region 0.01 to 0.02. An earlier study covering the short period 1950-5, based on market valuations of quoted companies, had not detected the change to a positive value (Hart and Prais, 1956, p. 190, found $c = -0.02 \pm 0.03$); possibly the change did

not take place till, say, 1952 or 1953, but, taking into account the size of the sampling error, little weight can be attached to this apparently different finding. The most recent study quoted in appendix D relates to the period 1960–9 and, while it suggests a return to a negative value of c, the sampling error is too great to warrant any significant inference.

19 If we took a slightly lower value of $c = +0.05$ (which would, however, only be consistent with a somewhat lower increase than that recorded by the Censuses between 1958 and 1968), the prediction for the year 2000 would be that half of total manufacturing output would be produced by the ten (rather than seven) largest enterprises.

20 To avoid confusing the central theme of this chapter, only passing reference has been made to those three old boxes – bearing the labels 'constant', 'decreasing' and 'increasing' returns – which are part of the professional economist's essential baggage. At this stage it may, however, be helpful to repeat what has in part already been said, and to set out more explicitly how those boxes broadly relate to the statistical ideas put forward here (though it must be recognised that there is no precise correspondence).

(a) Where firms of various sizes co-exist and there is no tendency for any particular size of firm to grow or decline at a different rate from any other size, it may be said that there is no apparent optimum size within the observed range; this is consistent with constant returns to scale within that range, and with a zero Regression. The consequence of random forces superimposed on such a situation, following the theory put forward in this chapter, is a tendency towards increased concentration (it does not matter whether those random factors act additively or multiplicatively).

(b) In an industry in which there is an optimum size of firm, but some firms are below or above that size, one may expect a tendency over time for those below it to grow in size towards that optimum and those above it to decline; such an industry has decreasing returns to scale and would exhibit normal (negative) Regression. The consequence of *strong* random forces superimposed on such a situation may again be a tendency towards increased concentration, as in the preceding case; but if the optimum size is clear enough, that is if the Regressive forces are strong enough in relation to the random factors, concentration may be stabilised and may even fall.

(c) Where an industry is subject to increasing returns, that is to a long-run decreasing supply price, there is a lack of equilibrium in the size-distribution similar to that implied by a positive Regression; superimposed random factors then merely accelerate the underlying tendency towards increased concentration.

The above sentences have been concerned with an industry's supply or cost conditions. Demand factors have been ignored because we are concerned here with aggregate concentration – if a firm growing in a particular market finds itself faced with a limited demand, it is supposed that it diversifies into some other sector. This does not seem an unrealistic way of looking at the modern world, in which larger firms are typically also more diversified. If our concern was with the size-distribution of suppliers to a particular market, more attention to demand factors might be necessary.

21 It would be of interest to examine to what extent there was a comparable process of concentration in the ownership of land before the industrial revolution, but it would carry us far beyond the limits of our present investigation. It may, however, be recalled that, in order to prevent the accumulation of massive entailed estates, a 'law against perpetuities' had to be instituted.

Notes to chapter 3 (pages 41–59)

1 The idea that the forces of standardisation and specialisation affect the size-distribution of firms to a certain extent in opposing ways is not new, though it seems often to be forgotten. The effect of the differential growth in productivity on the size-distribution was noted by Marshall: 'For instance, if machinery takes over what used to be regarded as three-fourths of a process of manufacture, and after a time performs it at a tenth of the original cost; then, though the real importance of that part remains as great as ever to the consumer, its importance in the statistics of both industry and trade will fall to less than a third of that which used to be *three times* as important as it.' (1919, p. 248n.) For the words in italics (italics not in the original) it seems better to substitute 'a third'.

2 With rapid technical progress in a trade, an initial increase in dispersion seems likely as part of the process of finding a new equilibrium distribution. These matters have not been extensively studied; cf. the remarks by G. D. N. Worswick on the dispersion of profit-rates in relation to restrictive practices in the manufacture of black bolts and nuts in 'On the benefits of being denied the opportunity to "go shopping" ', *Bulletin of the Oxford University Institute of Statistics*, vol. 23, August 1961, p. 275.

3 See the statistics for clothing and footwear in table 3.3.

4 This is consonant with the approach of G. J. Stigler who writes: '... argument and casual observation suggest that economies of scale are unimportant over a wide range of sizes in most American industries, for we commonly find both small and large firms persisting' ('Monopoly and oligopoly by merger', *American Economic Association Papers and Proceedings*, vol. 40, May 1950, p. 26). He does not, however, go on to consider whether that range has been increasing or decreasing.

5 This distinction was already drawn by Marshall in his consideration of the early United States Censuses (1923, p. 830).

6 Ideally we should like to know rather more before drawing this conclusion (for example, we would like to compare the size-distributions of plants owned by the hundred largest firms in 1930 and today), but with the available information, the long-term comparison made seems to be the most relevant that is possible. The next chapter presents comparisons on

average multi-plant working by the largest firms for the period 1958–72.

7 Our conclusion therefore agrees with that of J. Jewkes, who wrote: 'The familiar features of industrial concentration are not, in the main, attributable to some inescapable technical law of universal growth' ('The size of the factory', *Economic Journal*, vol. 62, June 1952, p. 251). He based his conclusion on a summary of the statistical evidence ('there have been no very spectacular changes in size in either direction', ibid. p. 245), which however now seems faulty, as appears on pp. 51–2, and Florence was correct in disputing it (P. Sargant Florence, 'The size of the factory: a reply', *Economic Journal*, vol. 64, September 1954). Jewkes was probably guided correctly on his central conclusion as much by his intuitive appreciation of the role of the *variability* of sizes – cf. his emphasis on the great 'variety in the size of factories' (p. 251) – as by the statistics he quotes.

8 What is known of the size-distribution for 1924 is best examined in its revised version as published in the *Census 1930*, part v, p. 27. However, the published size-distribution relates to returns for all trades (factory plus non-factory) and the 1930 *Census Report* notes that 'no further information relating to the size of firms in 1924 is available'.

9 Cf. the recent remarks by Fessey and Browning on the Census authorities having to accept returns relating to several physically separated units which are part of large multi-establishment enterprises (Central Statistical Office, 'The statistical unit in business inquiries' by M. C. Fessey and H. E. Browning, *Statistical News*, no. 13, May 1971, p. 2).

10 A technical qualification warrants noting: the hundred largest plants referred to here are those that are largest in terms of employment, no tables based on a ranking by net output being available. One can only conjecture that, if ranked by net output, the share of the hundred largest as shown in table 3.1 might be raised by an extra point or so in recent years, but the substance of the conclusion would hardly be affected.

11 The remarks in this section have been influenced by the lectures and writings of Professor P. Sargant Florence, as set out, for example, in *The Logic of British and American Industry* (3rd edn), London, Routledge and Kegan Paul, 1972, pp. 24 *et seq*. The analogy with human heights is also taken up by J. Pen in *Income Distribution*, London, Allen Lane, 1971, p. 48.

12 J. Niehans, 'An index of the size of industrial establishments', *International Economic Papers*, no. 8, 1959, p. 122.

13 The reader familiar with the notion of a first-moment distribution (see appendix C) will recognise the last two measures as the median and mean of the first-moment distribution. Minor variants of the above measures which have been used by other investigators involve omitting the lower portion of the distribution, for example establishments with under five or under ten employees. When these are not covered by the Census this is regrettable but inevitable. A recent study by F. L. Pryor ('Size of establishments in manufacturing', *Economic Journal*, vol. 82, June 1972) goes further, however, in deliberately omitting establishments with less than twenty employees in order to sidestep international in-

comparabilities 'in the treatment of very small establishments'. Since these often comprise half of all establishments, it is difficult to know what to make of such computed 'averages'; such a truncation leads to an uncomfortable arbitrariness in the results.

14 Our definition of the central range, though inspired by Professor Florence's approach, differs somewhat. Florence works with Census size-intervals as published and characterises industries in a qualitative way governed by the Census size-groupings; for example, he labels plant-sizes as 'medium' if the central half of the employment is in the range 100–499, as 'largish' if half the employment is in units of 500 or over, etc. To trace changes over time from one Census to another a more precise measure is, however, desirable, leading to the approach adopted here. If the size-distribution follows a log-normal pattern, the upper and lower limits of the central size-range so defined also form the shortest *relative* range that includes half the employees; the Florence-median is equal to the geometric mean of the upper and lower limits.

The study of changes in the characteristic range of sizes of plants or firms has become known in America as Stigler's 'survivor technique'; while there are certain differences, it would seem to involve the same basic notions as those expounded here.

15 The multiple is $k = $ anti-log $\sigma^2/2$, where σ is the standard deviation of the (natural) logarithms of size. For example, if $\sigma = 1\cdot8$ as in the present case (see p. 53), $k = 5\cdot05$, and the arithmetic mean would thus be expected to be about five times the median, etc. The actual multiples for the last four measures in the above example (beginning with the largest) are $3\cdot6$, $5\cdot2$ and $5\cdot2$, which seem close enough to the theoretical value. The modal plant cannot be determined very precisely from the empirical distribution; it lies in the range of one to five employees, while the theoretical modal value (as determined from the above method of multiples) would be one employee. On the same assumption the central size-range can be derived from the first-moment distribution by the following formula: its limits lie symmetrically (in relative terms) on either side of the Florence-median, and are found by multiplying and dividing the latter by anti-log$_e$ $0\cdot6745\sigma = $ anti-log$_{10}$ $0\cdot293$ σ.

16 For the last quinquennium, 1963–8, a slight narrowing in the central range is to be observed, running against the previous trend. This arises from a fall in the number of very large plants: twenty-three plants with over 10,000 employees were recorded in 1963 but only fourteen in 1968. The industries accounting for this difference cannot be traced from the Censuses because of some curious changes in the published class-intervals (disclosure rules cannot be blamed on this occasion since we find, for example, that results for single establishments have been published for 1968 in industry no. 385). Some change in Census procedures with regard to joint returns by a few of the very largest establishments is not to be ruled out. It may be a mistake to place any substantive reliance on this final observation in the series at this stage.

17 See F. Klemm, *A History of Western Technology* (transl. D. W. Singer),

London, George Allen & Unwin, 1959, p. 354. The advantages of 'unit drive' electric motors were already appreciated in the United States in the 1890s (see R. B. Du Boff, 'The introduction of electric power in American manufacturing', *Economic History Review* (second series), vol. 20, December 1967, p. 511, and the references to various technical publications from that period).

18 The argument that today technology favours smaller plants, and that in this there has been a reversal from the trend that held until the early part of this century, was pursued in an early paper by J. M. Blair, ('Technology and size', *American Economic Association Papers and Proceedings*, vol. 38, May 1948). This includes many interesting illustrations, but the difficulty of providing any comprehensive or representative survey is recognised. Dr Blair has subsequently developed this theme before the United States Senate's Committee on the Judiciary, Subcommittee on Antitrust and Monopoly in *Hearings: Economic Concentration*, Washington (DC), US Government Printing Office, 1964-8, Part 4, pp. 1539-56, and Part 5, p. 2960; it also appears in his recent book, *Economic Concentration: structure, behavior and public policy*, New York, Harcourt, Brace & World, 1972, pp. 114-51.

The judgement of Mr Ray Macdonald, president of the American Burroughs Corporation, though perhaps over-influenced by his experience in the computing industry, nevertheless carries weight. Speaking on the general theme of the changing pattern of industry and employment, he noted that 'the old pattern of plants of up to 1 million square feet employing 5000 people has changed to a much greater number of smaller plants typically covering 100,000 square feet and employing 500 people' (*Financial Times*, 20 October 1972). He also noted the modern trend away from high labour intensity to high 'design intensity', involving a high ratio of qualified engineers and technicians to unqualified shop personnel: a sermon that needs to be preached more often in this country.

19 The following is one of many possible hypothetical calculations that illustrate this point. If the total number of plants in 1968 had been as great as in 1930 (say 140,000 plants instead of the actual 90,000 plants), but the distribution had maintained a log-normal form with a constant logarithmic variance of 1·82, the effect would be to reduce the share of the hundred largest plants in 1968 from a calculated value of 11 to one of 9 per cent.

20 The eight largest have been chosen, rather than some other number, following the exercise carried out by Blair for the United States in the period 1947-58 (United States Senate, *Hearings: Economic Concentration*, Part 4, p. 1550), which showed that the share of the eight largest plants declined in more trades than it rose (out of 125 trades, it fell in sixty-seven, showed no change in ten and rose in forty-eight).

21 A subdivision into the approximately 150 industries distinguished by the Census (the minimum list headings of the Standard Industrial Classification) enables a more precise comparison to be made between changes in

enterprise-concentration (y) and proportionate changes in median plant-sizes (x), as is shown by my colleague R. Clarke in a forthcoming paper. On the basis of a sample of seventy-six such industries for which comparable information is available for 1958 and 1968, he estimates a relation of the form $y = -3 \cdot 01 + 10 \cdot 16$ ($\pm 2 \cdot 81$) x, with $r = 0 \cdot 38$; by introducing other explanatory factors he is able to improve the correlation, but the particular relation in which we are interested here remains substantially as stated. For his sample the average increase in plant-size in the period 1958–68 was 17 per cent (that is $x = 1 \cdot 17$), and so accounts for a rise of $1 \cdot 7$ out of the total rise of $8 \cdot 9$ points in the average five-firm concentration ratio – that is, it explains a fifth of the rise in average concentration. The sample analysed happens to be over-weighted with industries showing rather large increases in plant-sizes; if we substitute into that equation something corresponding more closely to the average increase in plant-sizes in the population, such as the increase of 9 per cent in median plant-sizes for all manufacturing (from table 3.2), we would conclude that the change in median plant-sizes accounts for a rise of only $0 \cdot 9$ out of $8 \cdot 9$ points, that is for about a tenth of the rise in concentration in this period. This is very similar to the conclusion derived on p. 48 on the basis of the movements in the shares of the hundred largest firms and the hundred largest plants.

22 See, for example, for the United States, J. S. Bain, *Barriers to New Competition*, Cambridge (Mass.), Harvard University Press, 1956, and J. Haldi and D. Whitcomb, 'Economics of scale in industrial plants', *Journal of Political Economy*, vol. 75, August 1967; for Britain, see C. F. Pratten, *Economies of Scale in Manufacturing Industry*, Cambridge University Press, 1971. A careful reading of such studies will reveal that a 'minimum cost point' has usually not been evaluated, but the investigators have contented themselves with estimating a size beyond which a further increase, by say a half, will lead to a fall in costs of less than, say a tenth. This substantial element of arbitrariness does not invalidate the method, but the results of such investigations require careful qualification.

23 Pratten (1971) is impressed by the importance of economies of scale as a result of his studies, but his final views are somewhat equivocal. If 'the benefits of competition were ignored... there should be a very high degree of concentration of production of many products' (p. 313). But presumably the benefits of competition are *not* to be ignored. He goes on to express the view 'that a high degree of concentration is compatible with efficient operation, and that the importance of economies of scale should be emphasised'; but then he says, 'This view is difficult to support with data.'

The conclusion reached by A. Silberston, who was associated with Pratten's researches, is more cautious. At the end of his survey of 'Economies of scale in theory and practice', *Economic Journal*, vol. 82, March 1972 (supplement), he writes: 'In practice, therefore, conclusions about the comparative efficiency of existing firms of different scale, or even of plants of different scale, cannot be drawn simply from what we know about the economies of scale that are theoretically possible under ideal conditions.' (The term 'ideal' is perhaps to be understood here not as being desirable, but as relating to the realm of 'ideas' in contrast to the realm of 'practical reality'.)

24 The reader may feel that something relevant to economies of scale, and hence to the main theme of this chapter, may be learnt from comparisons of profitability, or of output per head, between firms of different sizes, and a word on these matters may be added. Despite the large amount of statistics that has been accumulated in recent decades and the many analyses that have been carried out, it has to be said regrettably that no satisfactory conclusion has emerged from comparisons of this kind. The difficulties no doubt ultimately stem from the relevant material having been compiled originally for different purposes. The financial accounts of a firm, on which comparisons of profitability are based, are drawn up partly for tax assessment and partly to indicate the trend of the firm's affairs to its owners and creditors; they are not drawn up with a view to making efficiency comparisons with other firms of different sizes, so that there are serious problems of comparability between firms. The other main source of data, the Census of Production, is of course also not intended to provide efficiency comparisons, but to provide national totals of output, employment and the like.

The financial accounts of small firms generally show a higher rate of return on capital than those of large quoted companies (18 per cent in firms employing under 200 persons, as against 14 per cent in quoted companies, to quote the recent comparisons for British firms in 1968 made by M. Tamari in the Bolton Committee's *Research Report No. 16: A Postal Questionnaire Survey of Small Firms. An analysis of financial data*, London, HMSO, 1972, p. 29). But it is impossible to know to what extent this result has been brought about by two artificial elements: first, the generally more up-to-date valuations of the assets of large companies, which would lower their measured rate of return; secondly, the arbitrariness in small firms of the amounts shown as directors' remuneration rather than as dividend or profit, depending on tax considerations. The former element also probably disturbs comparisons between quoted companies of different sizes in times of substantial changes in price-levels.

A greater net output per person employed in larger plants is almost invariably shown by the Census of Production, but the Census also clearly indicates that the capital equipment available per person is greater in larger plants. The main difficulty is thus to know to what extent greater labour productivity is attributable to size by itself, and to what extent to capital. But there are also other disturbing factors, which are today often overlooked (though they were well appreciated by that very expert commentator Flux in his writings in 1913 and 1924 on the early Censuses). If large plants employ fewer women and fewer part-timers, but all are counted equally in numbers employed, that would contribute to an apparently higher output per person in large plants.

It may therefore be better to compare output per 'man-equivalent' reckoned in terms of wage-units, rather than simply output per person (this suggestion was already put forward by Flux); similarly, the information available in the Census on capital expenditure in the Census year (the only comprehensive indicator on capital intensity available in the Census) is better considered in relation to the number of wage-units.

In an attempt to separate the contributions to output of variations in capital intensity from those in size, a comparison was made between the 119 trades (minimum list headings) distinguished in the 1963 Census. The net output per wage-unit in each trade (x_0) was correlated with both capital expenditure per wage-unit in each trade (x_1) and average size of plant in each trade (x_2), also measured in wage-units; the wage-unit was taken as the average wage paid per person in all manufacturing. The correlation attributed all the rise in net output to the capital factor and, perhaps even more interesting, suggested that *at equal capital intensities larger plants have a lower net output than smaller plants*. It thus reverses the usual impression gained from the simple Census tabulation of output by size. The calculated regression was:

$$\log x_0 = \text{constant} + 0 \cdot 281 (\pm 0 \cdot 026) \ \log x_1 - 0 \cdot 037 (\pm 0 \cdot 016) \ \log x_2;$$
$$R = 0 \cdot 70.$$

To translate these coefficients into more practical terms, it may be noted that the equation suggests that a doubling in size of plant would lead to a fall of about 3 per cent in net output per wage-unit (or a ten-fold increase in size to a fall of 7 per cent in net output per wage-unit).

This result is presented here more in order to show how much caution is necessary in examining productivity comparisons than for its intrinsic validity. Net output as defined for Census purposes has not been netted of expenditure on services such as advertising which rise with size, nor can one eliminate the element of monopoly profit, which may also be presumed to rise with size. Both of these artificially raise the apparent net output of large firms. At $0 \cdot 28$ the elasticity of output with respect to capital expenditure is high because capital expenditure is recorded gross of depreciation; similarly 'net' output (as defined for the Census) is gross of depreciation. It should also not be forgotten that industries that are profitable attract high investment – and that too affects the results of this correlation. There is clearly scope for a fuller investigation, ideally based on special Census tabulations of net output by industry, size of plant and capital expenditure.

The reader interested in pursuing this line of inquiry may refer to the recent writings of Z. Griliches and V. Ringstad, (*Economies of Scale and the Form of the Production Function*, Amsterdam, North-Holland, 1971) and Pratten (1971, pp. 334–52); also to the Bolton Committee's comparisons in their *Report*, 1971, pp. 40–7.

Notes to chapter 4 (pp. 60–86)

1 The analysis by Leak and Maizels (1945) of the 1935 Census, though providing information for the first time on large enterprises (then termed 'business units'), did not provide information on the numbers of plants they owned. For the 1951 Census a special tabulation was provided for the analysis by Evely and Little (1960) relating to the (generally three) largest enterprises in each trade, giving the plants owned by those enterprises in *that* trade; but no information was provided on the total number of plants in *all* trades owned by the largest enterprises. (Since the reader may wish to refer to the original Census statistics, it has been thought less confusing to use the technical Census term 'enterprise' in much of this section, though elsewhere the shorter term 'firm' has been preferred.)

2 See Central Statistical Office, 'The development of a central register of businesses' by D. R. Lewis, *Statistical News*, no. 31, November 1975, p. 7.

3 This may be inferred indirectly, and not very precisely, by comparing the total employment of the hundred largest manufacturing companies operating mainly in the United Kingdom, as published in *The Times 1000* list (but subject to qualifications relating to overseas employment), with the comparable Census total, which is restricted to domestic manufacturing establishments. Similarly, in the United States it appears that the hundred largest manufacturing enterprises had a total employment in manufacturing and non-manufacturing establishments (as reported in United States Department of Commerce, Bureau of the Census, *Enterprise Statistics 1967*, Part I: *General Report on Industrial Organization*, Washington (DC), US Government Printing Office, 1972) about a quarter greater than the employment of the hundred largest enterprises in manufacturing establishments alone (as reported in the United States Department of Commerce, Bureau of the Census, *Census of Manufactures*). The latter comparison is also not exact, since not precisely the same set of enterprises are compared, but it may be taken as indicating the order of magnitude of the overlap between manufacturing and other activities.

4 This may be inferred from a Census table relating to the 210 largest enterprises in 1963 (*Census 1963*, vol. 132. p. 10) and from special tabulations relating to the 200 largest enterprises in 1968 prepared for the National Institute by the Business Statistics Office (detailed tables relating to the industrial distribution of the plants owned by the hundred largest enterprises are not available).

5 The average real net output per plant owned by the hundred largest enterprises in the 1968 Census was lower by about 5 per cent than in the 1958 Census (calculated by deflating Census net output per plant by the index of wholesale prices of manufactured products). For the sake of clarity it may again be emphasised that the comparison is not between the same set of plants in both years – the latter year's plants might well have consisted of most of those in the former year plus the smaller plants subsequently acquired. Though the calculation reported in this section

would perhaps have been better if carried out in terms of median enterprises and median plants, the available statistics necessitated a reliance
on arithmetic averages.

6 On p. 100 we consider the possible gains arising from a greater specialisation of activities amongst plants when a number of independent plants
are controlled as a single group. Plant-sizes may remain much the same,
and employment may even fall, but longer production runs of a narrower
range of items may permit increased output.

7 A full account is given by Hermann Levy in *Monopoly and Competition,
a study of English industrial organisation*, London, Macmillan, 1911. The
account given by P. L. Payne in 'The emergence of the large-scale
company in Great Britain 1870–1914', *Economic History Review* (second
series), vol. 20, December 1967, draws attention to large amalgamations
at that time in textiles, brewing, iron and steel, cement, wallpaper and
tobacco.

8 M. A. Utton, 'Some features of the early merger movements in British
manufacturing industry', *Business History*, vol. 14, January 1972, based
on the studies by H. W. Macrosty (*The Trust Movement in British Industries*,
London, Longmans, 1907) and P. Fitzgerald (*Industrial Combination in
England* (2nd edn), London, Pitman, 1927).

9 At the time of writing preliminary results are available of a substantial
empirical study under the direction of F. M. Scherer of the economies of
multi-plant operation ('The determinants of industrial plant sizes in
six nations', *Review of Economics and Statistics*, vol. 55, May 1973, and 'The
determinants of multi-plant operation in six nations and twelve industries',
Kyklos, vol. 27, fasc. 1, 1974); the final report is due shortly. The study
based on twelve selected industries in six countries is concerned – as we
are in this chapter – with the nature of the real advantages accruing to
multi-plant concerns. Comparisons with Scherer's study referred to in
the course of the present chapter are based on the preliminary articles
mentioned.

10 D. H. Robertson, *The Control of Industry*, London, Nisbet, and Cambridge
University Press, 1923, p. 25 (unchanged in the new edition with Dennison, 1960, p. 20); our italics.

11 Quoted from H. A. Marquand's study, *The Dynamics of Industrial Combination*, London, Longmans, Green, 1931, p. 170.

12 Other examples of such mergers were Calico Printers, Bradford Dyers,
Imperial Tobacco and Wall Paper Manufacturers (see Utton, 1971,
p. 53).

13 These matters are examined in the paper by Utton (1972), on the basis
of an earlier suggestion by Stigler (1950). Among the more important
inter-war mergers leading to highly concentrated trades were Distillers
(1925), British Match (1927), Tate & Lyle (1927), Renold and Coventry
Chain (1930) and Unilever (1930); ICI was formed in 1926, but its
components at that stage covered a number of – to some extent –
separate industries.

14 The period 1954–65 has been analysed by Utton (1971) and the period

1965–73 by J. D. Gribbin in 'The conglomerate merger', *Applied Economics*, vol. 8, March 1976; the industrial classifications used were not quite the same, but no substantial increase in the proportion of conglomerate mergers can be detected between the two decades. A similar analysis for 1957–69 is given by D. Kuehn in *Takeovers and the Theory of the Firm*, London, Macmillan, 1974, p. 24, using a finer industrial classification. There is no need here to do more than remind the reader of a few of the series of gigantic mergers that took place: in vehicles – Austin, Morris, Fisher and Ludlow, Pressed Steel, Aveling Barford, Rover, Standard-Triumph, Jaguar, ACV, Leyland, etc., all of which eventually became British Leyland; in electrical engineering – AEI, (British) Siemens, English Electric, Elliott-Automation, GEC; in brewing – a series of mergers reducing the trade to the few well known giant groups; in textiles – Courtaulds taking over a vast number of concerns, including British Celanese, Lancashire Cotton Corporation and Fine Spinners; in milling – a series of amalgamations, involving also bakers, leading to the eventual domination of the trade by three firms. The gigantic mergers in vehicles and electrical engineering were mid-wifed by the government-sponsored Industrial Reorganisation Corporation; the latter's activities in concentrating aircraft production, shipbuilding and the computer industry will also be remembered (see the chapter on industrial policy by P. Mottershead in the Institute's forthcoming study of British economic policy since 1960).

15 Marshall, *Industry and Trade* (4th edn), 1923, p. 577n., in referring to Macrosty's study of the trust movement (1907) remarks that 'most of the businesses described in it however have had no considerable monopolistic tendencies; and belong to the class which are described in the present work merely as "giant businesses"'. The suggestion, as I understand it, is that the growth of giant businesses is not to be understood simply in terms of a desire for greater market power, but more in terms of the economies of large-scale marketing and finance (see also Levy, 1911, p. 219). Similarly, the Monopolies Commission in their *Report on the Supply of Cigarettes and Tobacco, and of Cigarette and Tobacco Machinery*, London, HMSO, 1961, p. 184, remarked with respect to the dominant position of the Imperial Tobacco Company: 'There is no evidence that those responsible for the formation of Imperial in 1901 set out to monopolise the United Kingdom market, but it was clearly their view that only a much larger unit than any of the businesses which contributed to the amalgamation could hope to offer successful resistance to the competition from American interests which was being experienced at that time.' To quote another example, it was said of Pilkington's in the 1920s that, though it was the sole United Kingdom producer of plate glass and machine-made sheet glass, it faced intense competition from Belgian producers (T. C. Barker, *Pilkington Brothers and the Glass Industry*, London, George Allen & Unwin, 1960, p. 207); today it still has a domestic monopoly in production and perhaps finds a certain amount of Belgian imports not unwelcome as indicating a limit (of sorts) to its market power.

16 For ninety products in which agreements had been terminated the average share in sales of the five largest firms rose from 56·3 to 66·3 per cent in the period 1958–68, whereas for sixty-four products not subject to agreements the rise was from 56·8 to 63·5 per cent (the difference is statistically significant on the usual criterion) – see table 2 of the forthcoming paper by D. Elliott and J. D. Gribbin of the Office of Fair Trading, 'The abolition of cartels and structural change in the United Kingdom'. A recently published survey of restrictive practices legislation (D. Swann, D. P. O'Brien, W. P. Maunder and W. S. Howe, *Competition in British Industry*, London, George Allen & Unwin, 1974, pp. 172–7 and 195–7) also draws attention to the counteracting role of certain mergers in this period.

17 Their conclusion, though correct in relation to variations amongst industries, does not follow quite so simply from the correlations they quote. It makes a crucial difference whether the extent of multi-plant operation is measured in respect of all firms, or in respect of the leading few firms in an industry, and a certain degree of confusion is to be found in the literature because this distinction is not carefully drawn. The reason for the difference may be put briefly as follows. Multi-plant operation is a prerogative of large enterprises. Those industries that are very much in the hands of a few large enterprises, such as tobacco or artificial fibres, tend to have a high average number of plants when reckoned over the comparatively few firms in their industry, whereas those industries which are partly in the hands of a few large firms and partly in the hands of many small firms tend to have a low average number of plants when reckoned over all firms (since that average is overwhelmingly influenced by the mass of small single-plant firms). The former type of industry tends to be more concentrated than the latter, and there is consequently a substantial positive correlation between concentration and such an *average* measure of multi-plant working. Nevertheless, the leading firms in the former type of concentrated industry (for example, artificial fibres) tend to have fewer plants per firm than leading firms in unconcentrated industries (for example, men's clothing), and the result is no correlation – or even a negative correlation – between concentration and multi-plant operation by *leading* firms.

As noted in the text, Evely and Little's analysis for 1951 led them to dismiss variations in multi-plant operation by the average firms as unimportant in explaining variations in concentration, but by saying (1960, p. 111) that 'the same does not of course necessarily follow if we look at variations in the number of plants per (business) unit among the top three units in each trade', they might mislead the quick reader into thinking that the latter correlation was greater than the former. In fact, the reverse is the case: the correlation between concentration and the number of plants operated by the average firms was 0·39 (not explicitly given by the authors, but may be derived from the information on variables and other correlations on pp. 110 and 334), whereas the correlation between concentration and the number of plants operated by the three leading firms was −0·02 (as noted in the text). A very similar contrast has persisted for later years; in 1968, for example, the corresponding correlations are +0·51 and −0·01. Sawyer (1971, p. 370) in his study of concentration patterns in 1963 noted a strong positive correlation between concentration and plants per firm; it is to be inferred that the latter variable was defined in relation to all firms in the industry.

Our main interest is in the evolution of giant enterprises and their nature; the main text is therefore concerned with the degree of multi-plant operation by the largest firms. A fuller analysis of industrial structure would need to consider also what has happened to the median firm and its degree of multi-plant operation, rather than the arithmetic average number of plants for all firms in the trade which, as we saw in the preceding chapter, may not be a helpful measure when the distribution has a large variance.

18 The calculation was based on the sample of seventy-six industries (minimum list headings) selected by Hart and Clarke for their forthcoming study. These industries were selected after an examination of their Census definitions so as to permit the calculation of comparable concentration ratios for 1958 and 1968 (however, we omitted two trades, nos 469(2) and 472, where we suspected a change in definitional scope which affected our variables).

The regressions quoted in this section are unweighted by size of industry, to permit comparison with earlier work; a limited number of weighted regressions were calculated for 1963 (using employment in each industry as the weights), but the results are not substantially different.

19 Scherer, 1974, p. 136; the calculation was based on 153 of the 'largest' United States 4-digit manufacturing industries. While none of the individual correlations reported is statistically significant, when they are all taken together it appears that a mild degree of confidence can be placed at least in the absence of any positive association.

Scherer's main study, though based on only twelve industries in six countries, shows a stronger negative correlation between these variables (−0·37), no doubt reflecting the characteristics of the particular industries in his sample (his claim that his co-author deserves credit for 'first discovering' this lack of, or negative, association between concentration and multi-plant working would, however, appear to be unjustified, in that it overlooks the results of Evely and Little). R. L. Nelson's study for the United States in 1954 (*Concentration in Manufacturing Industries of the United States: a midcentury report*, New Haven and London, Yale University Press, 1963, pp. 67 *et seq.*) is also of interest in this connection.

20 As suggested by Scherer (1974).

21 Based on the seventy-four industries referred to in note 18 above. For the period 1935–51 Evely and Little (1960, p. 349; see also p. 166) found a correlation of only 0·09 between changes in concentration and changes in the degree of multi-plant working, but the latter variable was calculated as an average for the whole industry. Regrettably no information was

available on changes in multi-plant working by the leading firms over that period; we cannot therefore compare 1935–51 with 1958–68 in this respect. It is worth noting that in the period 1958–68, for which we have information on multi-plant working both for leading firms and for all firms, the correlation with changes in concentration is higher for changes in multi-plant working for leading firms (at 0·50, see text) than for all firms (where it is virtually zero). There is thus a double paradoxical contrast between these correlations according to whether they are considered:

(i) in relation to changes over time or to levels at a particular date;

(ii) in relation to leading firms or to all firms.

The following table summarises these paradoxes:

Correlations between concentration and
multi-plant working

	Changes 1958–68	Levels in 1968
Leading firms	0·5	0
All firms	0	0·5

22 A. D. Chandler (Jr), *Strategy and Structure: chapters in the history of the industrial enterprise*, Cambridge (Mass.), MIT Press, 1962, especially p.23.

23 Fewer industrial disputes and strikes, and lower labour turnover, are mentioned in the Bolton Committee's *Report* (1971, p. 21) as accompanying the greater informality and flexibility of the smaller firm.

24 The balance of production costs and transport costs is considered in treatises dealing with location theory, in which the theoretically optimum number of plants in the economy and their location are derived under simplifying assumptions. An increase in the market area served by a firm is regarded as leading to lower production costs but higher transport costs; at the point of least *total* cost production costs are still declining, and the rate of decline is such that it is just offset by the additional transport costs that have to be incurred in order to extend the market. Production costs considered alone (that is, apart from transport costs) are thus not a minimum at the optimal point; this is an important and realistic extension of the simpler theories taught in elementary texts. As time proceeds technological developments may be expected to reduce both production and transport costs, and thus to change the optimum size of plants – but either a rise or a decline is conceivable depending on the importance and elasticities of the two cost elements and the changes in them. Similar considerations apply to the optimum number of plants that should be combined into a single firm: the advantages of being able to afford more specialists at head office have to be balanced against the increased costs of communication (and co-ordination

generally) as an additional plant is brought into the firm; as costs of communication fall over time so the optimum number of plants rises. These may seem essential and important considerations, but not much is in fact to be learnt from a merely theoretical treatment.

25 An example of the long-term changes in the market of even a very simple trade such as chair-making may be helpful in conveying these complexities (the details are taken from J. L. Oliver's study, *The Development and Structure of the Furniture Industry*, Oxford, Pergamon, 1966). This is a trade of some antiquity, changed to some extent by new materials, but more so by market developments. In England, High Wycombe has for long been a specialist production centre for chairs, its origin being connected with the neighbouring beech forests. In the eighteenth century the market for chairs made there would normally have been limited by the distance a man could travel by horse and cart and return the same day, which was roughly set by the boundaries of Buckinghamshire. Some chairs would be sent for sale to London, though the journey in each direction took two days by horse and carriage, with an overnight stop in Uxbridge (compared with under two hours by road today). The development of paved roads and then railways in the nineteenth century, and of motorways in the twentieth century, has enabled production in High Wycombe to grow progressively and to displace smaller producers in other parts of the country, while the techniques of production have remained very simple. Chairs have today also entered into international trade, and chairs made in Scandinavia, Italy and the United States now compete with those made in High Wycombe and other parts of England.

26 The telephone 'enables, for instance, the chief chemist to be largely responsible for the chemical side of the [scattered branches of a manufacturing business]: this promotes order and economy in the first instance'. So wrote Marshall fifty years ago (1923, p. 363, n. 2). But, with his concern for long-term managerial problems, he added: this 'may weaken the character of his assistants'.

27 J. H. H. Merriman, 'Engineering innovation in a service industry: Post Office telecommunications', *Proceedings of the Institution of Electrical Engineers*, vol. 122, January 1975, figs. 4 and 5. Local telephone calls are now doubling in number every seven to nine years, inland trunk calls every five to seven years and international calls perhaps every four years. With postage rates in excess of the costs of local and even some international telephone calls, more rapid growth-rates may be anticipated. See also L. Hannah, 'Managerial innovation and the rise of the large-scale company', *Economic History Review* (second series), vol. 27, May 1974, p. 257.

28 Putting together figures from the Annual Reports of the British Transport Commission and from Gilbert Walker's valuable study, *Road and Rail*, London, George Allen & Unwin, 1942, and converting to 1970 prices, average railway receipts per ton–mile on general merchandise appear as follows: 1930, 3·5p; 1950, 2·6p; 1970, 1·3p. In addition to the qualifications mentioned in the text, it is to be noted that these figures are

affected by the inclusion of minerals with general merchandise in the later years.

29 See K. F. Glover, 'Statistics of the transport of goods by road', *Journal of the Royal Statistical Society* (series A), vol. 123, part 2, 1960, and the discussion on his paper. The liberalisation of the earlier licensing restrictions on transport vehicles which took place under the 1953 and 1968 Acts should be noticed here; see the Bolton Committee's *Research Report No. 1: The Small Firm in the Road Haulage Industry* by B. T. Bayliss, London, HMSO, 1971, pp. 36–41.

30 Difficult as it is to form a time-series summarising costs and convenience yet, in relation to a particular trade at a particular time, such estimates are possible for the transmission both of goods and of information. A manufacturer deciding how to locate his various plants to serve a dispersed market so as to economise his total costs will have some notion of their magnitude in mind, on the basis of which a decision is made. Costs of communication and their consequences for the optimal location of plants have been analysed in some detail for Sweden in a series of studies directed by G. Tornquist (see his *Contact Requirements and Travel Facilities*, Department of Geography, Lund University, 1973, and G. Tornquist, S. Nordbeck, B. Rystedt and P. Gould, *Multiple Location Analysis*, Department of Geography, Lund University, 1971).

31 The calculation was based on the seventy-six industries referred to in note 18. The correlation was weak, at $r = 0.21$, reflecting the over-riding importance of other (technological, etc.) factors in determining plant-sizes; on the usual statistical criterion the correlation is significant, but its credibility depends also on the associated calculations reported in the text. The correlations were calculated after taking logarithms of the variables, so that the regression coefficients represent elasticities. Transport costs were taken as 'total costs' as defined in the Census (see *Census 1968*, vol. 156, table 8); adjustments were made for small establishments (ibid. table 1). It was thought best to use the same transport variable both for the regressions of sizes of plants at the two dates and for the change in sizes between those dates, as this facilitates the analysis of changes in the elasticities; the transport variable was therefore based throughout on 1963, the mid-year of the period examined. Similar calculations were carried out based on a broader aggregation of industry groups (that is, using Industrial Orders) and arithmetic mean sizes of plants instead of medians; while they sometimes yielded slightly higher correlations, the elasticities and other inferences to be drawn were much the same.

32 Scherer used American transport tariffs for bulk lots of representative commodities for fixed distances, whereas we used transport expenditures, which are more readily available in the Census but which, it may be presumed, show a smaller variability amongst industries; in principle his method should be superior and it is gratifying that the final results are so similar.

33 Estimated from a regression of the difference between 1968 and 1958 in

the logarithms of median-sizes on transport costs in 1963 for the seventy-six industries referred to. An alternative calculation based on 108 industry groups (using slightly laxer criteria of definitional comparability over time in the Censuses) and arithmetic mean plant-sizes yielded a slightly higher correlation of 0·40 and a similar but slightly more precisely determined elasticity of 0·13(±0·03). The 'elasticity' referred to in this context should strictly be described as the *change in the elasticity* of size with respect to transport costs (rather than the *elasticity of the change* – a concept that is ill-defined if the average change is near zero).

34 The correlation coefficient in 1968 fell to 0·16 (from 0·21 in 1958), which may also be regarded as indicating the progressive weakening of the role of transport costs. The standard error of the elasticity in 1968 remained at ±0·18; taken by itself the analysis for this year would be inconclusive, but it falls into place when considered in conjunction with the statistically significant results for 1958 and for the period 1958–68. That there is scope for further verification of the above relations will be apparent.

35 The regressions were based directly on the data in table 4.3, but shipbuilding was excluded since transport costs for the final product are usually not applicable. A fuller analysis would have to take into account that industries vary in their conventions on transport costs: in some the producer meets the costs of sending his goods from the factory to the customer or to local distribution points, but in others the customer pays for transport from the factory and such costs enter into the customer's rather than the producer's accounts.

The correlation coefficients for the two regressions quoted are 0·58 and 0·72 respectively. The corresponding correlations in logarithmic form were somewhat lower (at 0·46 and 0·51), because they gave relatively less weight to the two Industrial Orders that are so very much away from the mean. This suggests caution, but there is no obvious reason for preferring the latter regressions to the former.

36 The regression of the arithmetic change in multi-plant working over the period 1958–68 on transport costs was 0·16(±0·05).

37 For transport costs (see note 32 above) Scherer uses tariff-rates whereas we use expenditures; for multi-plant working his variable relates to the three largest firms (rather than to all firms or all large firms), and to those plants within the main industry considered. As will be seen from the next note the differences in the latter variable are of some importance.

38 Thus, while table 4.3, relating to all firms with over a hundred employees, exhibits a significant association between transport costs and multi-plant working, a similar table drawn up for the five largest firms in each Order exhibited only a barely significant association. This is consistent with the view that, while changes in transport and communication costs provide an impetus for an initial increase in multi-plant operation, the causes of the subsequent immense growth of multi-plant working by leading firms have to be sought elsewhere. At least that may be so in Britain, where there have been the very important developments in the financial sector to be surveyed in chapter 5. The fact that Professor Scherer was able to

detect a significant relation on the basis of *leading* firms in only a dozen industries (as mentioned on p. 74; it will remembered that the elasticity he derived was indistinguishable from ours relating to all larger firms) may be due to two elements. First, his comparison related to six countries combined, where financial developments may have been of less significance in total. Secondly, his definitions of variables and more refined analysis may have been more successful in extracting significant results. Only further research can show whether his results for a dozen industries would be confirmed in a broader sample.

39   N. Kaldor, 'The economic aspects of advertising', *Review of Economic Studies*, vol. 18, no. 1, 1949–51, p. 15. This theoretical analysis was written in 1943 in connection with the National Institute's study of advertising, but published in 1950.

40   Only a brief account can be given here of a subject around which a vast literature has developed, much of it controversial and requiring a critical eye. A full and practical account of the subject is given in N. H. Borden's impressive treatise, *The Economic Effects of Advertising*, Chicago, Irwin, 1942. The articles by L. G. Telser in the *Journal of Political Economy* ('Advertising and competition', vol. 72, December 1964, and 'On the regulation of industry: a note', vol. 77, December 1969) contain valuable critical assessments of more recent studies. A useful survey of the literature is provided by P. Doyle in 'Economic aspects of advertising: a survey', *Economic Journal*, vol. 78, September 1968.

41   J. L. Simon in *Issues in the Economics of Advertising*, Urbana, University of Illinois Press, 1970, p. 15, quotes three studies of press advertising which suggest that a half-page advertisement is about two-thirds as effective as a full-page advertisement in terms of inquiry coupons returned, or of recollection by readers.

42   From the statistical summaries published by the Advertising Association in its *Advertising Quarterly*; more detailed figures are given by R. A. Critchley in *UK Advertising Statistics*, London, Advertising Association, 1972. Radio advertising is still negligible in Britain, at under 1 per cent of all advertising expenditure. In the United States television and radio advertising is relatively more important, but even there newspapers and magazines remain the predominant media.

43   The interpretation of published tariffs is complicated by a host of special factors, such as booking in advance and the buying up of left-over bargains at the last minute (that is, time reserved for advertising which has not been sold to anyone before the programme is due to be transmitted), in which individual negotiation plays a substantial part. The alleged advantages gained by large-scale advertisers in the United States have been the source of prolonged resentment and controversy there. The merger of a leading manufacturer of household bleach (Clorox) with one of the detergent giants (Proctor & Gamble) was disallowed on the Federal Trade Commission's argument that competition in the bleach industry would be unfairly reduced as a result of the improved advertising terms Clorox would receive from bulk-buying of advertising time

by the merged group. D. M. Blank in 'Television advertising; the great discount illusion or Tonypandy revisited', *Journal of Business*, vol. 41, January 1968, pp. 11 and 23, has since suggested that discounts for large-scale advertising began to lose their importance in the 1950s, and were completely abolished by 1966. His article, and the subsequent comments on it (W. N. Leonard, 'Network television pricing: a comment', and D. M. Blank, 'Tonypandy once again', *Journal of Business*, vol. 42, January 1969) provide much interesting background material. Cf. also J. L. Peterman, 'The Clorox case and the television rate structures', *Journal of Law and Economics*, vol. 11, October 1968, and R. Schmalensee, *The Economics of Advertising*, Amsterdam, North-Holland, 1972, pp. 322–3.

44 Film production costs vary immensely, and so does the number of times a particular advertisement is displayed; no statistical summaries are available on these matters.

45 Some specimen costs may be of interest. Transmission charges in September 1972 for a half-minute advertisement varied from some £2000 in the London region at peak hours to £50 in the Eastern region at off-peak hours (still lower rates applied to Ireland and the Channel Islands). Film production costs of £5000 are not untypical, the range being from half to ten times that figure; with video-tape machines costs may be brought down to some £500 (see, for example, 'Costing the television commercial' in the *British Bureau of Television Advertising Bulletin*, no. 18, January 1973). Vast and frequent statistical compilations of numbers of viewers and costs of advertising per 1000 homes reached are prepared for the advertising industry by the Joint Industry Committee for Television Advertising Research. The comparisons in the text of costs per viewer at peak and off-peak times are based on published tariffs and the proportions viewing at various times of day as given by B. P. Emmett in 'The television and radio audience in Britain' in D. McQuail (ed.), *Sociology of Mass Communications. Selected readings*, Harmondsworth, Penguin, 1972, p. 201. Volume discounts are probably greater in relation to peak-hour transmissions, and might reduce the excess cost per viewer from a third to perhaps a fifth.

46 For example, the otherwise valuable Report by a Commission of Inquiry into Advertising under the chairmanship of Lord Reith prepared for the Labour Party (mimeographed, 1966) seems deficient in this respect (on pp. 39–41).

47 There are exceptions: for example, the American orange growers mounted a spectacularly successful campaign in the 1930s (see Borden, 1942, pp. 337 *et seq.*), and the wool industry in recent years has attempted to popularise its 'Woolmark' on an international scale. The British Milk Marketing Board's 'pinta' campaign is often regarded as highly successful, but appears less so when contrasted with that of the national brewers (milk consumption per person declined slightly in the decade 1964–74, while beer consumption more than doubled).

48 See N. Kaldor and R. Silverman, *A Statistical Analysis of Advertising Expenditure and of the Revenue of the Press*, Cambridge University Press,

1948, p. 34, for the original study of press advertising. A re-examination of the statistics used in that study by M. Schnabel in 'A note on advertising and industrial concentration', *Journal of Political Economy*, vol. 78, September/October 1970, suggested that the peak was somewhat less obvious than originally suggested. More recently the statistics in that study were re-examined at the National Institute by Alice Knight and, on applying standard statistical tests of significance, it emerged that the significance of the rising portion of the curve was doubtful, but the decline in the right-hand portion of the curve (between oligopolistic and competitive trades) was just significant. A sophisticated study by J. Cable, 'Market structure, advertising policy and inter-market differences in advertising intensity' in K. Cowling (ed.), *Market Structure and Corporate Behaviour*, London, Gray-Mills, 1972, apparently finds support for an inverted U-curve, but since the sample of twenty-six products analysed was subject to a selection procedure – the 'sample was chosen so as to minimise intermarket differences in the more troublesome variables' (p. 118) – the wider significance of the result is not quite clear.

49 Quoted from Levy, 1911, p. 268.

50 Quoted by R. Cohen in P. L. Cook and R. Cohen (eds.), *Effects of Mergers*, London, George Allen & Unwin, 1958, p. 223, from the brief in the libel action brought by Lever against the *Daily Mail*, which had attacked him following the cancellation of advertising contracts. Marshall in his *Principles* (8th edn, 1920, p. 484) also draws attention to the potential savings in advertising costs on forming a monopoly; cf. also F. M Scherer, *Industrial Market Structure and Economic Performance*, Chicago, Rand McNally, 1970, p. 336.

51 It is often said that advertising forms an 'entry barrier' which inhibits competition, but the concept needs clarification. In trades in which large machinery or a large capital is needed the small and inexperienced man inevitably faces difficulties in starting up: when Bloggins asks his bank manager for £100 million to carry out research and development, and then to manufacture an artificial fibre with marvellous properties, he will find an 'entry barrier' in his way. Society rightly protects its capital from the inexperienced and possibly over-adventurous dreamer. In trades in which large-scale advertising forms an integral part of the whole process it may equally be said that the heavy advertising outlays form an 'entry barrier', but it is not obvious that this differs in principle from any other capital requirement or requires separate consideration.

52 The figures are taken from the *Census 1968*, vol. 156, tables 1 and 4. Net output as defined for the Census of Production includes expenditure on advertising. Expressed as a proportion of sales values, advertising would appear about a third as important; it would account, for example, for 10 per cent of sales of soap and detergents, as compared with 27 per cent of net output as shown in the text. For tobacco, advertising represents 2 per cent of sales including excise duty, but 6 per cent if duty is excluded. Promotional costs, such as the free samples sent by pharmaceutical firms to doctors, are similar in their nature to advertising, but are inevitably

excluded from these statistics; they might raise the proportions substantially in such trades.

53 Heavy advertising expenditures have been critically examined by the Monopolies Commission in their Reports, *Cigarettes and Tobacco* (1961), *Household Detergents* (1966) and *Breakfast Cereals* (1974).

54 'Rather than a shovelful of brown powder of uncertain origin' (D. H. Robertson, *Lectures on Economic Principles*, vol. I, London, Staples, 1957, p. 171).

55 Two weighted averages are available for 1963 for the general selection of products distinguished in the Census: 58·8 per cent based on 214 products for which there is comparable information for 1958, and 63·4 per cent based on 295 products for which there is comparable information for 1968 (see pp. 19–20 for details and sources).

56 In reality pharmaceutical firms often have speciality products protected by patents and the true average degree of concentration (if it could be calculated) is much higher than appears here. It seems likely that this 'aggregation bias' is greater for pharmaceuticals than for other products where patenting is of less importance.

57 A number of studies are reported in the literature, based on selected samples of commodities, some suggesting that the relation between advertising and concentration is 'unimpressive', and others that there is a clear and significant relation; see the articles by Telser (1964 and 1969); H. M. Mann, J. A. Henning and J. W. Meehan (Jr), 'Advertising and concentration: an empirical investigation', *Journal of Industrial Economics*, vol. 16, November 1967; R. B. Ekelund and C. Maurice, 'An empirical investigation of advertising and concentration: comment', *Journal of Industrial Economics*, vol. 18, November 1969; R. B. Ekelund and W. P. Gramm, 'Advertising and concentration: some new evidence', *The Antitrust Bulletin*, vol. 15, Summer 1970; H. M. Mann and J. W. Meehan (Jr), 'Advertising and concentration: new data and an old problem', *The Antitrust Bulletin*, vol. 16, Spring 1971. Much depends on the selection of commodities considered. For the United Kingdom in 1968 we examined the correlation between advertising and concentration for those product-groups for which comparable information on concentration was available for 1958–68 (the sample considered in earlier sections of this chapter); this selection process yielded forty-three observations with a correlation of only 0·20. If the observation for toilet preparations (a trade with very high advertising but low concentration) is omitted, the correlation rises to 0·27, which is just significant at the 5 per cent level. Much further work is needed before one can speak with precision on this relation.

58 See Blair, 1972, pp. 256 and 600; Scherer, 1970, pp. 99–100 and 129–30, and the American studies there quoted.

59 The comparison for the low-advertising trades is slightly clouded by a lack of comparability in the definition of two of these trades, but much the same rise emerges if those two trades are excluded from the average (see footnote *i* to table 4.4).

60 G. J. Stigler, 'The economies of scale', *Journal of Law and Economics*, vol. 1, October 1958, p. 66; indeed he found a low negative correlation – that is trades in his sample with high advertising had slightly smaller firm-sizes.

61 To avoid biasing the result we have deducted advertising expenditure from net output for the purposes of this comparison. If net output were taken as defined in the Census (gross of advertising), the difference between firm-sizes in high- and low-advertising trades would have been 40 per cent instead of the 20 per cent shown by the averages in the table.

62 The difficulty in doing anything more direct is that advertising expenditures are not published by the Census according to size of firm. Advertising expenditures in all manufacturing formed 2·7 per cent of net output, but when the proportions in each Order were reweighted by the industrial distribution of the hundred largest the weighted average was 3·2 per cent.

Notes to chapter 5 (pp. 87–136)

1 The nationalisation of a large company may in the extreme amount to little more than a transfer of its shares from the financial institutions to the government, and their replacement in the institutions' portfolios by government fixed-interest securities. The gain, or loss, from such a transaction is less obvious than is generally implied in popular discussion when such a course is suggested.

2 This may, however, involve some overstatement: duplication is possible where, for example, several directors are joint trustees in respect of a single holding, but where explicitly stated in the accounts we have excluded such double counting.

3 In technical terms – the distribution had a wide dispersion and was skewed to the right, so raising the arithmetic mean above the median.

4 A. Lumsden (in *The Times*, 9 September 1969) has previously drawn attention to the low holdings of the boards of the hundred largest companies, noting that they held an (arithmetic) average of $7\frac{1}{2}$ per cent of the aggregate voting capital in 1968. In a highly skewed and dispersed distribution such as this the arithmetic average does not perhaps give quite as useful a characterisation as the median.

5 There was some decline in the importance of A-shares in the hundred largest companies between 1968 and 1972, but as we have seen, this did not affect the median holding. Under a Companies Bill (introduced in December 1973, but not enacted because of the dissolution of Parliament in February 1974), it was proposed to make illegal any further issues of non-voting ordinary shares (s.21). The arguments for such a prohibition are not entirely clear-cut: A-shares make a take-over against the board's wishes less likely, but they also enable an entrenched and perhaps inefficient board to continue in office longer than is socially desirable.

6 Marshall (1923, p. 317) speaks of a third; writing about a later period Florence, (1972, p. 221) notes that a fifth was often considered adequate,

and that this was the fraction owned by the twenty largest shareholders in a sample of large companies in 1951 (ibid. p. 230). He also notes (p. 231) that the board itself held only 1–3 per cent, but this presumably refers to holdings in their own name only and ignores nominee holdings which were not disclosed before the 1967 Act. While the use of nominee shareholdings has previously made any very accurate analysis based on share-registers impossible, the trend for the largest holdings in major British companies to decline has nevertheless been apparent for some time. The divorce between ownership and control was the central theme of the classic work of Berle and Means (1932) relating to the United States; the only American analysis that can be compared to ours relates to 1939 and shows a median holding of 3·5 per cent by 'total management', and 2·3 per cent by 'non-officer' (non-executive) directors in the 115 largest industrial companies (R. A. Gordon, *Business Leadership in the Large Corporation*, Washington (DC), Brookings Institution, 1945, p. 27). A downward trend in the holdings of management in the subsequent thirty years may be inferred from the work of R. J. Larner ('Ownership and control in the 200 largest non-financial corporations', 1929 and 1963', *American Economic Review*, vol. 56, September 1966, and *Management Control and the Large Corporation*, New York, Dunellen, 1970), but the form of analysis used does not permit any direct comparison with results for the United Kingdom. The position in the two countries may not seem radically different in respect of the statistics of board shareholdings, but share-options are likely to be more important in America in ensuring that those who manage the firm have a stronger tangible incentive for its success.

7 Though, for simplicity, we speak of *the* Stock Exchange, it should be remembered that there were a number of provincial stock exchanges which were important in raising capital for local enterprises until recently (see W. A. Thomas, *The Provincial Stock Exchanges*, London, Frank Cass, 1974). The London Stock Exchange has, however, always been predominant; since 1973 all United Kingdom exchanges have been 'unified' and act as a single market.

8 The fall in prices of government securities has, of course, contributed substantially to the rise in the relative importance of industrials. Further information on the nominal values of securities for earlier years may be found in the work by E. V. Morgan and W. A. Thomas (*The Stock Exchange: its history and functions*, London, Elek Books, 1962, pp. 280–1), and on numbers of companies in the paper by Hart and Prais (1956, pp. 154 and 176). It should be noted that the latter relates to companies operating mainly in the United Kingdom.

9 The essential role played by financial elements in the growth of giant concerns becomes more evident if one asks whether the factors considered in the preceding chapter – the desire for market power, the lowering of communication costs and the growth of advertising – need necessarily lead to an increase in the number and size of large multi-plant firms. The growth of large retailing organisations purchasing from independent

manufacturers (often accompanied by own-branding) and of special marketing arrangements, such as franchising or patent licensing, show that many of the advantages of multi-plant operation can be obtained without numerous production units passing into the ownership of some single giant marketing enterprise. The fact that giant enterprises have arisen which *own* so many plants, and not merely have trading arrangements with them, indicates that financial factors affecting ownership and wealth-holding patterns have also been at work.

10 It has not been easy to order the various and rather complex factors treated in this chapter to meet the needs of all readers. There is little by way of general background reading that can usefully be taken as a starting point and to which the reader might be referred. See, however, J. F. Wright, 'The capital market and the finance of industry' in G. D. N. Worswick and P. H. Ady (eds.), *The British Economy in the Nineteen-Fifties*, Oxford, Clarendon Press, 1962, and, more generally, chapter 10 of Sir Alec Cairncross's *Introduction to Economics* (5th edn), London, Butterworth, 1973, pp. 137–50. Certain theoretical and factual developments are treated, the implications of which for industrial concentration have not previously been considered in much detail, and an attempt is made to bring together the results of a great many studies that fall under the general heading of risk-bearing and financing. The reader more interested in theoretical aspects may therefore prefer to spend his time on pp. 92–113 and then move to the summary on p. 135, while the reader who prefers a historical account of developments may wish to move at once to pp. 113–35 and return to the theoretical sections only after he has completed the chapter.

11 See J. Tobin's call in 'Comment on Borch and Feldstein', *Review of Economic Studies*, vol. 36, January 1969, to wanderers lost in the wilderness whilst searching for Generality.

12 We are here concerned solely with the implications of the substantially lower variability of returns in large companies, which has been confirmed in a great many studies, not with the slightly lower average rate of return which has sometimes been noticed for large companies. The reasons for the latter are considered on pp. 109–13.

The incentive to group together a number of firms into a single large enterprise is to some extent moderated by the foresight of investors who diversify their portfolios in a similar way, so raising the market-value of the constituent companies before their amalgamation; in the absence of transaction costs and in 'perfect' capital markets, certain academic commentators have said that all incentive for companies to amalgamate will have been exhausted by the prior action of investors in diversifying their portfolios. However, these assumptions (no transaction costs and 'perfect' markets) verge on begging the very questions in which we are interested; transactions costs cannot be ignored, and the knowledge available to the general investor cannot always be as expert as that of the directors of the merging concerns. The baker bakes his bread and the dairyman churns his butter; if no travelling costs were involved and consumers were skilled buyers of these commodities, the consumer would visit each in turn and there would be no incentive for grocers to set up a business from which the consumer could buy both his bread and butter at one visit, knowing that they were of reliable quality. Cf. Haim Levy and M. Sarnat, 'Diversification, portfolio analysis and the uneasy case for conglomerate mergers', *Journal of Finance*, vol. 25, September 1970, and J. Lintner, 'Expectations, mergers and equilibrium in purely competitive securities markets', *American Economic Association Papers and Proceedings*, vol. 61, May 1971.

13 The figures quoted in the text are taken from tables 5 and 6 of the study by J. M. Samuels and D. J. Smyth ('Profits, profits' variability and firm size', *Economica* (new series), vol. 35, May 1968, pp. 135–6); we have grouped two size-classes together because of the small number of firms in the sample. While variances are given in their table 6 for all years between 1954 and 1963, those for the earliest year are most relevant, since the size-grouping was determined by the size of the company in the initial year; by the last of the years shown the companies in each group are much less homogeneous in size, and the effect we wish to investigate is then less distinctly observable.

14 Earlier discussions of the square-root rule and other explanations of the observed decline in profit variability with size may be found in papers by S. S. Alexander ('The effect of size of manufacturing corporation on the distribution of the rate of return', *Review of Economics and Statistics*, vol. 31, August 1949), M. A. Adelman ('The Antimerger Act 1950–1960', *American Economic Association Papers and Proceedings*, vol. 51, May 1961), S. Hymer and P. Pashigian ('Firm size and rate of growth', *Journal of Political Economy*, vol. 70, December 1962, and 'Firm size and rate of growth: reply', *Journal of Political Economy*, vol. 72, February 1964), H. O. Stekler ('The variability of profitablity with size of firm', *Journal of the American Statistical Association*, vol. 59, December 1964), T. R. Dyckman and H. O. Stekler ('Firm size and variability', *Journal of Industrial Economics*, vol. 13, June 1965) and G. Whittington (*The Prediction of Profitability and Other Studies of Company Behaviour*, Cambridge University Press, 1971, p. 51). That an association between the constituent units modifies the operation of the rule is recognised in certain of these papers, but only in rather general terms. Once the existence of a correlation is accepted, there is no way of knowing from data for the whole firm whether large or small firms undertake riskier enterprises per unit of resources; it would require explicit information on the profitability of the constituents of large firms for that aspect to be clarified.

15 This relation may be derived by considering the variance of the mean of n correlated variables. In an obvious notation:

$$V(\Sigma x/n) = [nV(x) + n(n-1) C(x_i x_j)]/n^2 = \sigma^2/n + r\sigma^2(n-1)/n,$$

which may be rearranged to give the expression (1) in the text. A similar relation holds in terms of the coefficient of variation. This relation is used in the theory of portfolio selection as developed by H. M. Markowitz in *Portfolio Selection: efficient diversification of investments*, New York, Wiley, 1959, p. 109. The degree of subdivision of a group, that is the value of n, may depend on the purpose of the analysis, and corresponding variations take place in the other parameters, particularly r (this aspect is discussed further in note 19 below). The reader whose mind is tortured by the heresy of infinite variances raised in B. Mandelbrot's writings (for example, 'The variation of certain speculative prices', *Journal of Business*, vol. 36, October 1963), which has the implication that diversification does not reduce risk (see W. D. Nordhaus, *Invention, Growth and Welfare*, Cambridge (Mass.), MIT Press, 1969, p. 56, and F. M. Scherer, 'Firm size, market structure, opportunity and the output of patented inventions', *American Economic Review*, vol. 55, December 1965, but not in his 1970 treatise) may find comfort in the acerbic remarks of the great probability theorist W. Feller in *An Introduction to Probability Theory and its Application*, (2nd edn) vol. II, New York, Wiley, 1966, pp. 50, 52 and 172.

16 The case of negative correlations amongst constituent units is more complex than might appear, and is considered later.

17 This may be derived by putting the expression (1) equal to $1 \cdot 1 \sigma_1 \sqrt{r}$, and finding the value of r for which $n = 1$.

18 Stekler, 1964; the figures quoted from this study are particularly important since they include loss-making as well as profit-making corporations. If loss-making corporations are excluded the measured variability falls, especially for smaller concerns where the proportion making losses is greater (ibid. see table on p. 1187 for profitable concerns only; the graph on p. 1186 – reproduced here in chart 5.2 – is the only source that includes loss-makers). It is the greater variability of returns in small companies that leads to a greater frequency of losses, but this must not be taken as a reflection of their average profitability; American statistics indicate that small companies that are profitable (that is excluding those making losses) earn a higher rate of return than large companies, but if all small companies are considered (including those making losses) there is little difference in the average rate of return (ibid. p. 1188). Regrettably, no comparable British data are available.

19 The theoretical curve in chart 5.2 was derived by plotting the transformed variables σ^2 and $1/n$ on a graph (taking the basic unit of resources as \$1 million, that is n is measured in \$ millions) and fitting a straight line; the constant term of this line is $a = \sigma_1^2 r$, and its slope is $b = \sigma_1^2 (1 - r)$, as may be seen by comparison with equation (1) in the text. From these expressions one can easily derive an estimate of $r = a/(a+b)$, and of $\sigma_1 = \sqrt{(a+b)}$.

The equation of the theoretical curve in chart 5.2 is

$$\sigma = \sqrt{(77 + 30/n)} = 10 \cdot 34 \sqrt{(0 \cdot 72 + 0 \cdot 28/n)}.$$

The graph has been reproduced from Stekler's original paper, with the theoretical curve and the British data superimposed. The horizontal axis has a logarithmic scale, the marked intervals corresponding approximately to the mid-points of the ranges shown (the original publication is not entirely clear on this matter, but nothing substantial is involved). The opening interval is shown by Stekler as relating to the range $0–$25,000, but is better regarded as relating to $10–$25,000 in view of the logarithmic scale; we have treated it in the latter way in drawing the theoretical curve and it is not surprising that the first empirical observation (which presumably relates to $0–$25,000) lies above the theoretical curve.

The value of the unit of measurement (taken as $1 million in this case) influences the derived values of the constants; if we worked in terms of a smaller unit a lower correlation coefficient would be derived, compensated by a higher value of σ_1. This may seem surprising, but on reflection it will be seen that this is as it should be; if instead of considering an enterprise as being made up of ten arbitrary large units we supposed it to consist of a hundred small units, consistency requires that the correlation between the small units be lower than between the large units, and the random fluctuations larger. This arbitrariness can only be removed by working in terms of some objective basic unit, such as the plant, rather than an arbitrary monetary unit of resources. The fitted curve is however unaffected by units of measurement, and its asymptotic value $\sigma_1\sqrt{r}\,(=\sqrt{a})$ is also invariant. The value of the correlation coefficient can therefore only be understood with reference to the corresponding definitional unit of measurement. If the unit of measurement is increased by a factor λ, it can be shown that the measured correlation between the larger units rises by a multiple $1/[r+(1-r)/\lambda]$ of the correlation between the smaller units – for example, if $r = \frac{1}{2}$, the multiple is $2/(1+1/\lambda)$ – and as λ becomes larger the correlation between the larger units tends to unity. These are only formal matters, and do not affect the inferences drawn in the text.

20 The reader interested in paradoxes will notice that if A and B enjoy a perfect negative correlation it is not possible for C to be perfectly negatively correlated with both of them. For, if C has a perfect negative correlation with A, and A has a perfect negative correlation with B, it follows that C and B have a perfect positive correlation! The introduction of a third activity would thus increase the variability of the original group. In the general case of more than two activities a mildly negative correlation amongst all of them is conceivable, but a similar logic constrains the situation. If there are three activities of equal variance it can be seen, by setting equation (1) equal to zero, that the negative correlation cannot be lower than -0.5. In general, the correlation cannot be lower than $-1/(n-1)$, and as the number of activities increases the limiting value of the correlation tends to zero. In practice therefore a conglomerate may be satisfied to follow a working rule of seeking activities that are substantially independent. The treatment here has been simplified by considering the case where the correlations amongst the various activities can be regarded as all equal; if we allow for differing correlations amongst subgroups more interesting results are reached. For example, a working rule which is of some importance in practice is to expand a group in

terms of a limited number of 'divisions', such that the correlations amongst units *within* a division are highly positive, but *between* divisions they are as negative as possible; this leads to the multi-divisional form of an enterprise, other aspects of which have been examined by O. E. Williamson in *Corporate Control and Business Behavior*, Englewood Cliffs (NJ), Prentice Hall, 1970.

21 Recently the United States Federal Trade Commission in *Economic Report on Conglomerate Merger Performance*, Washington (DC), US Government Printing Office, 1973, examined in some detail nine large and rapidly put together diversified concerns; the report emphasises the information loss to the public, and the consequent difficulty of assessing correctly the value of the group and the terms on which capital should be supplied to it.

22 See R. H. Coase, 'The nature of the firm', *Economica* (new series), vol. 4, November 1937.

23 See S. J. Prais, 'Size, growth and concentration' in B. Tew and R. F. Henderson (eds.), *Studies in Company Finance*, Cambridge University Press, 1959, p. 116.

24 See Royal Commission on the Distribution of Income and Wealth [the Diamond Commission], *Report No. 2: Income from Companies and its Distribution*, Cmnd 6172, London, HMSO, 1975, p. 89; the ratios were calculated from the accounts of quoted companies compiled by the Department of Industry as a sequel to the earlier National Institute study (Tew and Henderson, eds., 1959) and now published in *Business Monitor. Miscellaneous series M3: company finance*. Bank loans have risen particularly sharply in the past decade.

25 The Diamond Commission (*Report No. 2*, p. 153) relied on a study of quoted companies by G. Meeks and G. Whittington, 'Financing of quoted companies in the United Kingdom', summarised in Appendix Q to *Report No. 2*, which included a division of the sample into three size-groups with equal numbers of companies in each group, but *excluded* the very smallest companies from the sample. For the period 1964–71 the proportion of debt in total issues varied only from 42 to 48 per cent, which seems rather narrow in comparison with the earlier results shown here in table 5.3; possibly the coarseness of the size-classification and the exclusion of the smallest companies is responsible. Nevertheless they write: 'Loan issues represented a much larger share of total sources of funds for larger companies than for smaller ones' (p.168), a view accepted by the Commission (para. 240).

26 Bolton Committee's *Report*, 1971, p. 13; but that sample was subject to serious reservations (p. 12, n. 1). In view of the important increases in borrowings in the last decade a new and fuller study of accounts is to be hoped for, including those of unquoted companies based on accounts filed at Companies House under the 1967 legislation.

27 We ignore the liability to make good arrears and assume simply that the interest is forgone if income is inadequate to cover it.

28 The mathematical principles governing the approach in the text and some further consequences may be set out here, as they differ from those to be

found in other theoretical writings (though I think they come closer to embodying the crux of the calculation carried out by the market). First, the formula from which the above proportions of debenture finance have been calculated may be derived. Let the mean and the standard deviation of the income-stream y before debenture interest of D, be μ and σ; then, after deducting debenture interest, we have a net income of $y - D$ with mean of $\mu - D$ and a standard deviation unchanged at σ. The coefficient of variation after deducting debenture interest is $c_D = \sigma/(\mu - D)$, which increases with D, and is of course greater than before that deduction, when $c = \sigma/\mu$. If y is normally distributed so is $y - D$, and the probability that the debenture interest is not covered can be found from normal tables by looking up the probability, ϕ, that a standard normal variable is less than $(\mu - D)/\sigma$. If investors are prepared to accept a risk of α that income is insufficient to cover dividends, we have $1 - \alpha = \phi\left[(\mu - D)/\sigma\right]$. It follows that $D/\mu = 1 - (\sigma/\mu)\phi^{-1}(1 - \alpha)$, which is the fundamental equation governing prior changes; it may be written more simply as

$$g = 1 - c\phi^{-1}(1 - \alpha) \tag{2}$$

where $g = D/\mu$ is the proportion of mean income taken by debenture interest,

       c is the coefficient of variation of the income-stream,

and $\phi^{-1}(p)$ is the inverse of the normal distribution function (it represents the number of standard deviations from the mean corresponding to a probability of p).

In the example above we took $\alpha = 0.03$, and $\phi^{-1}(0.97)$ is found from tables to be 1.881; the relation (2) thus reduces in this example to $g = 1 - 1.881c$, from which the proportions in the text may be derived.

Secondly, it will be noted that some companies are too risky to enable any debentures to be issued at all; the threshold level, c_t, is derived from (2) by setting $g = 0$, whence it follows that $c_t = 1/\phi^{-1}(1 - \alpha)$. In the example debenture holders were prepared to take a risk of 3 per cent; it follows that companies having an income-stream with a coefficient of variation in excess of 53 per cent are not able to issue debentures. Since small firms typically have very variable income-streams, we see at once why they do not often raise debenture finance.

Thirdly, if all companies able to issue debentures do so up to the limit given by (2), then their *net* income-stream (that is net of debenture interest) will show an increased coefficient of variation of $\sigma/(\mu - D)$, as already noted. An interesting consequence of the above rule governing debenture issues, if it applied strictly, is that the coefficient of variation of the *net* income of those companies issuing debentures would become the same, irrespective of the original variability of their income-streams – it would depend only on the degree of risk acceptable to debenture holders. (*Proof:* Using the definition of g and equation (2), we have $c_D = \sigma/(\mu - D) = c/(1 - g) = 1/\phi^{-1}(1 - \alpha)$. This is the same as the variability for the 'threshold company' considered in the preceding paragraph.) The market for securities thus tends to fall into three categories: debentures, to which there attaches a risk α of the interest not being covered; shares of companies issuing debentures, which all have a coefficient of variation of $1/\phi^{-1}(1-\alpha)$; shares of companies not issuing debentures because their income is more variable than that threshold level. Since companies' prospects change over time but their capital structure cannot be adjusted very frequently, this 'homogenisation' process works only imperfectly. The market's task is thus still concerned with the continuing assessment of changes in the risks of equities, though debenture issues help to constrain such variations.

Fourthly, the acceptable degree of risk on debentures (α) varies among investors, but certain modal degrees become conventionally associated with particular markets. We know that in some countries (Germany and Japan) banks take a much closer interest in the management of the companies to which they lend and provide a larger proportion of the capital employed in the form of loans. In the present terms this is consistent with a conventionally higher modal value of α and follows from equation (2); for example, if the degree of risk-acceptance were 10 per cent instead of 3 per cent as previously, debentures would be supplied to absorb 36 per cent of the income-stream instead of only 6 per cent.

It may, finally, be emphasised that the above account of the nature of gearing is very much a simplification (asset-cover is relevant, and so is cumulative interest and non-normality), but it embodies sufficient of the problem to bring out the heavy dependence of gearing on risk, and hence on size. Other aspects of company finance that may helpfully be explained using probability theory may be found in the recent work of R. C. Stapleton, *The Theory of Corporate Finance*, London, Harrap, 1970.

29 Whether it would be better to lower the rate of profits tax but to widen its base by bringing 'the interest on debenture stock into charge as profits' was, as far as I have been able to discover, a question only touched upon once by the Royal Commission on Taxation of Profits and Income (*Final Report*, Cmd 9474, London, HMSO, 1955) – this was in the course of Mr Kaldor's question no. 2535, addressed to representatives of the Issuing Houses Association. More attention was given to the related matter of exempting preference dividends from profits tax so as to bring them on to the same basis as debenture interest (ibid. p. 155; see also questions 2455 *et seq.* and 3910 *et seq.*, on the rise in debenture finance). But nothing has been done; with the consequence that preference issues have gradually disappeared and debentures have become increasingly important.

30 In examining real returns over periods of a year it would be preferable to look at yields on loans for a year (instead of on the twenty-year loans in table 5.4), but the conclusion derived would be much the same – that negative returns were almost universal in the period 1970–5. Strictly, also, one should refer to anticipated rather than actual rates of inflation, but these refinements are not worth pursuing here. A fuller analysis relating to medium-term government bonds and to industrial ordinary

shares has recently been published by N. Barr in 'Real rates of return to financial assets since the war', *The Three Banks Review*, no. 107, September 1975; this draws attention to average negative real net returns for both these assets for the period 1965–74, and for bonds in the 1950s.

31 The figures are quoted from A. T. K. Grant's, *A Study of the Capital Market in Britain from 1919–1936* (2nd edn), London, Frank Cass, 1967, p. 64.

32 See, for example, 'Lex' in the *Financial Times*, 4 December 1972. Under the advance Corporation Tax scheme yet a further tax-incentive has been provided for mergers: companies with largely overseas earnings benefit if they merge with local companies (this is discussed in detail in the *Economist*, 17 June 1972).

There has been a tedious debate in the American literature on whether gearing lowers the total cost of the firm's capital; it has been argued that as more debentures are issued the equity becomes more risky and so falls in value, but the total capital value of the firm remains unchanged. In other words, it is denied that anything is to be gained from a careful choice of financial structure. There are special circumstances under which this is conceivable, but it is clear from the discussion in the text that the proposition has no universal validity and no relevance in explaining what has been happening in the industrial capital market of the post-war period. For more recent studies attempting to assess the influence of gearing, see R. F. Wippern, 'Financial structure and the value of the firm', *Journal of Finance*, vol. 21, December 1966, and M. Davenport, 'Leverage and the cost of capital: some tests using British data', *Economica* (new series), vol. 38, May 1971.

33 Cf. Cairncross, 1973, pp. 121–2.

34 The earnings-yield can here be regarded as the earnings per share expressed as a percentage of the market price of that share, and equal to the reciprocal of the price–earnings (PE) ratio. Earnings are normally taken net of all company taxes; in practical calculations (for share-indexes, etc.) there are complications, since the amount of tax payable may vary with the dividend and certain conventions have to be adopted, but we need not be concerned with those complications here.

35 R. F. Henderson, *The New Issue Market and the Finance of Industry*, Cambridge, Bowes and Bowes, 1951, pp. 113 *et seq.*; Bolton Committee's *Research Report No. 4: Financial Facilities for Small Firms* by D. Lees *et al*, London, HMSO, 1971, p. 38; Fielding, Newsome-Smith & Co, *Company Share Quotations*, London, 1972, p. 19; E. W. Davis and K. A. Yeomans, *Company Finance and the Capital Market*, Cambridge University Press, 1974, pp. 19–20.

36 We ignore here the great variety of individual circumstances which affect issue costs, such as whether the company already has a quotation, whether new money is to be raised, whether the issue is to existing shareholders or to the public; these matters have been discussed in detail in Henderson's study (1951). The assessment of issue costs is complicated by the practice of fixing an initial issue price for the shares which usually

leads to an 'opening premium'; the average size of such premia is not clear (as we shall see below) and they have been omitted in most of the studies mentioned. It may be argued that planning for an opening premium limits the risk and therefore reduces the cost of underwriting; share issues by tender (a form of auction in which the underwriting risk is limited by a floor-price) also reduce underwriting costs; such issues became popular in the mid-1960s, in boom conditions on the Stock Exchange, when it became difficult to decide in advance on an issue price that would be fair to the company and to the investor, but subsequently this method of issue again became rare. Rather higher issue costs than those mentioned here were found in a study of the period 1958–63 by A. J. Merrett, M. Howe and G. D. Newbould (*Equity Issues and the London Capital Market*, London, Longmans, 1967); they suggested that conventional issue costs were in the region of 17 per cent for issues in the range £200,000–£300,000 and 6 per cent for issues in excess of £1 million; further, if the opening premium is included as part of the cost to the company raising the money, then total issue costs reached the extraordinary average of 35 per cent for the lower size-range and 14 per cent for the higher size-range. These costs are so very much higher than had been noted by earlier investigators that they would seem to require explanation. The study by Davis and Yeomans (1974) devotes much attention to opening premia (which they term 'revealed discounts') and to 'offers for sale'; they find averages in the region of 5 per cent for issues in the period 1968–71 (with much variability and rather higher values for 'placings'); these results thus also make one doubt the representativeness of the findings by Merrett *et al.* Possibly leading issue houses in the atmosphere of the 'bull' market of the years 1958–63 tended to under-price their issues to maintain their reputation in anticipation of a turn in the market. A more recent study of opening premia on issues made in the period 1970–2 suggested that, if the average premium is weighted by the sums subscribed, then it turns out to have been negligible in that period and only of the order of magnitude of the interest forgone on the cash advanced by way of subscriptions. A proper assessment of the efficiency of the new issue market must obviously make allowance for the fact that over-subscribed issues go at a premium but lead to low allocations to each investor, while under-subscribed issues go at a discount but are fully allotted (see J. Rothman's report, *An Analysis of New Issues* issued by Leopold Joseph & Sons Ltd, 1973, especially pp. 8–9; see also some statistics in appendix B of the study by Davis and Yeomans, 1974, p. 24). Because of the greater underwriting risk attached to issues of smaller companies, their opening premia may well be greater (even when weighted by subscriptions); while further study is needed before a definitive conclusion can be drawn on the average extent of opening premia, it would appear that their significance has been overstated in academic studies.

37 Because of the great range of individual circumstances it is difficult to be precise; the terms mentioned in the text can only be regarded as

approximate and illustrative of conditions in the period 1968–72. They are based on examinations of records at Companies House relating to the terms on which unquoted companies were acquired by large quoted companies, and on discussions with City institutions. Yields have, of course, altered following the collapse of the share market in 1973 and its subsequent volatility, but their ratios have probably not changed, so that the illustrative figures remain relevant.

38 See J. F. Turner, *Finding the Cash to Meet Estate Duty*, London, Estate Duties Investment Trust Ltd, 1970, p. 5.

39 E. V. Morgan and C. Taylor, 'The relationship between the size of joint stock companies and the yield on their shares', *Economica* (new series), vol. 24, May 1957.

40 Derived by fitting a double logarithmic equation to the seven grouped averages tabulated in the Morgan–Taylor paper, using weighted least-squares.

41 However, the coefficient was not very precisely determined, probably because of the small size of the sample; the calculation is based on unpublished data kindly made available by Professor J. M. Samuels and Mr A. D. Chesher of the University of Birmingham, which form part of the study reported in their paper, 'Growth, survival and size of companies 1960–9' in Cowling (ed.), 1972.

42 Some further details may be recorded here. For efficiency in estimating the regression slope we stratified the sample by size, putting rather more of the sample into the extremities of the size-range; twenty large companies with over £100 million in net assets were chosen from *The Times 1000* list of large companies for 1970 using random sampling (companies engaged mainly overseas or which were outside manufacturing were excluded); forty medium-sized companies with net assets in the range £1 million–£100 million were similarly chosen from that source, and twenty small quoted companies with assets under £1 million were chosen from the *Stock Exchange Official Year-Book*, by taking a random sample and omitting any companies that were too large. Earnings-yields were taken from the *Financial Times* of 27 September 1972 (as the reciprocal of the published price–earnings ratio); for the few companies that did not publish their prices in that paper, the price was taken from the *Stock Exchange Daily Official List* and earnings from the cards for *Moody's Industrials*. Loss-making companies were excluded from this regression calculation, as was general in the other studies referred to in this section; we note on p. 112 and in note 51 below, the results of an alternative treatment in which loss-making companies are included. Companies were classified into size-groups according to the book-value of net assets rather than the market valuation of their capital (as, for example, in the Morgan–Taylor study) and the regression was calculated on the basis of group means. This was done to avoid the suspicion of a bias: a high valuation of a company, that is, a low yield on its shares, due to factors independent of net assets would be sufficient to turn a large company into an even larger one, and so lead to a spurious correlation between market valuation and yields.

We wished to be sure that this factor was not responsible for the correlation between size and yield, and therefore measured size by net assets.

43 Derived by dividing the coefficients of the pooled regressions – the first equations on pp. 153-4 of Davenport's article (1971) – by the mean values of the cost of capital (ibid. p. 161) and dividing by a factor of 100 which, as the author kindly informed us, had inadvertently been omitted from the published article. This leads to elasticity estimates of −0·055 for chemicals, −0·071 for food and −0·046 for metal manufacturing, which were pooled to give the value noted in the text.

44 H. Benishay, 'Variability in earnings–price ratios of corporate equities', *American Economic Review*, vol. 51, March 1961.

45 S. H. Archer and L. G. Faerber, 'Firm size and the cost of externally secured equity capital', *Journal of Finance*, vol. 21, March 1966. This study posed difficult problems of interpretation. Two measures of size were included – total assets and size of stock issue – and these are obviously strongly collinear. A perverse positive coefficient is obtained for the former when the latter is included in the calculation, but if the latter is omitted the coefficient for total assets alone is duly negative. The regression excluding the collinear variable (stock issue) is not reported, but correlation coefficients including and excluding that variable are reported at +0·254 and −0·143 respectively (p. 80); from these it may be inferred that the required regression coefficient excluding the collinear variable is −1·60. To convert this semi-logarithmic gradient into an elasticity it is necessary to divide by the average yield (which we took as 10·1 per cent) and, since logarithms were to base 10 here, we multiplied by $\log_{10}e$.

46 Wippern, 1966, from which we took the coefficient of the pooled estimating equation (p. 623), which was in semi-logarithmic form, and divided by the earnings-yield averaged over the period (10·2 per cent, taken from the Dow–Jones index), so deriving an elasticity (although not specified in the text, Professor Wippern kindly informed us that natural logarithms were used in this analysis and there was no need for further adjustment).

47 H. Benishay, 'Market preferences for characteristics of common stocks', *Economic Journal*, vol. 83, March 1973.

48 The arithmetic in the example in the text may be worth outlining. If a given firm's yield is 10 per cent then, with an elasticity of −0·05, the yield of a firm ten times larger will be (10 per cent × $10^{-0.05}$) = 8·91 per cent. If the two firms merge (to form a firm eleven times the size of the smaller firm) the yield of the combined firm will be (10 per cent × $11^{-0.05}$) = 8·87 per cent. By taking reciprocals of these yields it will be seen that the capitalisation of the small firm is increased by 13 per cent and that of the larger firm is increased by ½ per cent of its original size – equivalent to 5 per cent of the size of the smaller firm. The combined gain is thus equivalent to 18 per cent of the original capitalisation of the small firm.

49 Attention is often drawn to the possibilities provided by take-over situations of unfairly swelling profits by taking capital profits to current account. Such practices are usually self-defeating after a few years, and

differ from the long-term and 'justifiable' sources of advantage outlined above.

50 For example, the Morgan–Taylor sample (1957) excluded loss-makers, and probably has a bias towards relatively successful firms since it was drawn from names mentioned in 'Company matters' articles in the *Financial Times*. The Davenport sample was, it was stated, 'biased towards "successful" firms through the elimination of those that had gone out of business or had been taken over in the course of the decade' (1971, p. 147).

51 The elasticity including loss-makers was estimated at -0.054 ± 0.039, compared with the estimate excluding loss-makers of -0.032 ± 0.004. Our calculations of sampling errors suggested that a sample of about 1000 companies would be needed for an adequate study which included loss-makers. Such a study would have to give careful attention to losses associated with liquidations, to the proceeds of amalgamations, etc.; it would be a major task, going far beyond the resources of the present inquiry.

52 In terms that may be more familiar to the economic theorist, one might say that the market reaches a short-term equilibrium position in supplying capital to large concerns at a preferential margin; but to understand long-term developments we must take into account, first, that this preferential margin depends on the rate of growth of those financial institutions and, secondly, that large concerns will be tempted to use those funds to take over smaller concerns and bid up their capitalisations. We are interested in developments over a period of ten or twenty years, during which the market is still seeking its 'long-term equilibrium'. The notion of a 'gap' in the financial spectrum of suppliers of risk capital is usually associated with the Macmillan Report (Treasury, *Report of the Committee on Finance and Industry*, Cmd 3897, London, HMSO, 1931), but in fact it was recognised in writing at the turn of the century – that is, from the time that the Stock Exchange's interests grew in industrial financing.

53 The three largest insurance companies each had assets in excess of £1500 million at book-values in 1973 and together accounted for over a quarter of all insurance companies' assets; in relation to the total market no single institution is of dominating importance, but a small group can exercise great power if it is so minded.

54 The Diamond Commission in its *Report No. 2*, pp. 6–19, brought together some of the more recent facts relating to institutional ownership of industrial capital, but we have here attempted a longer-term view of developments.

55 Despite the great fluctuation in Stock Exchange values in the years 1973–5, it appears that the relative sizes of the aggregates compared in this section have not altered appreciably; it was not therefore thought worthwhile revising the statistics and tables at proof stage to include the slightly later figures that had become available.

56 Some remarks on the statistical sources and their difficulties may be noted. The total market valuations of securities quoted on the Stock

Exchange are taken from the quarterly Stock Exchange 'Fact Book'. The funds in the hands of financial institutions are known with any accuracy only for the most recent years and, even then, there are qualifications because of the varying bases of valuation (see note 58 below on the adjustments that have been made to the officially published figures based on book and nominal values to bring them on to a comparable basis). It is to be regretted that market valuations are still not published for the holdings of most insurance companies, so making it necessary to rely on various approximations. For ease and consistency over time, we have assumed that the equity portfolios of insurance companies and of pension funds of the public sector are sufficiently similar to permit the published ratio of market-values to book-values for pension funds to be applied to insurance companies. J. Revell in *The Wealth of the Nation*, Cambridge University Press, 1967, p. 216, has used a more elaborate method which, for 1957–71 at least, gives a market valuation of ordinary shares that is higher by, perhaps, a tenth. Our calculations, therefore, possibly slightly understate the importance of the financial institutions' stake in ordinary shares. The recent survey by the Bank of England of the role of financial institutions ('The financial institutions', *Bank of England Quarterly Bulletin*, vol. 10, December 1970, and vol. 11, March and June 1971) also suffers from the lack of entirely reliable figures for insurance companies. The origin of this reticence to disclose figures, that must be readily available to the companies for their internal purposes, is to be found in the traditional belief that confidence in British insurance companies would be shaken if they published 'true and fair' accounts; a similar ideology governed the accounts of the clearing banks until they recently changed to normal accounting principles without ill consequence.

Some smaller qualifications on the coverage of the statistics have to be mentioned. The available figures for insurance companies relate to British companies; local subsidiaries of foreign companies are excluded. Lloyds also is not covered. The portfolio holdings managed by merchant banks, which in some respects have the characteristics of institutional holdings, are also excluded. Finally, there is a (probably small) amount of double counting, since insurance companies and (more especially) pension funds may hold the securities of investment and unit trusts.

57 As it happens, this is very close to the annual rates of increase that appear from the rough calculation in real terms shown in table 5·5. These are: 1952–62, 6·9 per cent; 1962–7, 6·1 per cent; 1967–72, 6·6 per cent. It is the real flow of new funds to the institutions rather than differential movements in prices of securities that has been responsible for the institutions' progress.

58 The published figures were converted from book and nominal values to approximate market-values by the following two adjustments. First, the book-values of ordinary shares were adjusted to market-values for 1962, 1967 and 1972 by multipliers of 1·65, 1·53 and 1·80 respectively (these multipliers are based on the relation between market- and book-values in these years for ordinary shareholdings of the superannuation funds of

public authorities as published by the Central Statistical Office in *Financial Statistics*, but as the earliest year for which this relation is published is 1963 we adjusted that value slightly by reference to movements in share prices to obtain an estimated multiplier for 1962). Secondly, British government securities, which are recorded at nominal (not book) values for insurance companies, were reduced to market-values by reference to the official index of long-dated government securities for 1962; for 1967 and 1972 (for which there is no official index) we prepared a similar index as the average of the following three securities – $6\frac{1}{2}$% funding loan 1985–7, $3\frac{1}{2}$% war loan and a Treasury stock ($6\frac{3}{4}$%, 1995–8 for 1967, and 8%, 2002–6 for 1972). The deflators for the three years are respectively 0·73, 0·88 and 0·76.

No doubt other adjustments ought also to be made (for example to property investments), but the above adjustments are probably the most important.

59 See G. Clayton, *British Insurance*, London, Elek Books, 1971, pp. 327–8; N. Macrae, *The London Capital Market*, London, Staples, 1955, p. 82. The proportions quoted are based on book-values, but these probably did not then differ much from market-values.

60 J. G. Blease, 'Institutional investors and the Stock Exchange', *District Bank Review*, no. 151, September 1964, p. 46.

61 The estimate is approximate. For unit and investment trusts figures are published by the Central Statistical Office in *Financial Statistics*. For insurance companies a division between home and foreign investment has been published in recent issues of the Department of Industry's *Business Monitor, Miscellaneous series M5: insurance companies and private pension funds*, though only on the basis of book-values. Some information on private pension funds is compiled by the Department of Industry.

62 Nominee holdings prevent any very precise inference from analyses of share-registers, though the sample inquiries reported in certain of the investigations referred to have yielded valuable approximations. The extent of cross-holdings between institutions also presents difficulties in deriving a grand total of quoted industrial share capital. We do not know, for example, the extent to which pension funds hold shares in investment companies, nor the extent of cross-holding among industrial companies (some industrial companies hold minority stakes in others; some have a majority stake in a quoted subsidiary and leave the public with a minority holding in that subsidiary). Simply taking the total number of quoted industrial shares issued therefore involves some double counting. Ideally we should like to compare the consolidated holdings of financial institutions with the consolidated share capital of industrial companies, but in practice we have to choose between two simple extremes. One is to make no omissions, that is to compare aggregate institutional holdings with the market aggregate – including in both aggregates the capital of investment companies and unit trusts (this is the method followed by the Bank of England in its survey, 'The financial institutions'); the argument for this is that, since numerator and

denominator are both exaggerated, the ratio may be near the truth. The alternative method (used by J. Moyle in *The Pattern of Ordinary Share Ownership 1957–1970*, Cambridge University Press, 1971, and by J. H. C. Leach in 'The role of the institutions in the UK ordinary share market', *The Investment Analyst*, no. 31, December 1971, and no. 32, May 1972) is to omit investment companies and unit trusts from the market total, thus avoiding an obvious piece of double counting, but to leave the numerator as it is in the hope that institutional cross-holdings are small. The former method gives a lower answer than the latter, the difference amounting to about 3 percentage points in 1970. We have followed the latter method in our calculations for 1972; it must not be thought that this necessarily gives too high an answer, for if industrial cross-holdings were eliminated (as they should be) from the denominator the estimate would be raised.

63 Blease (1964, p. 43) derived an estimate of 24 per cent for 1963, which is surprisingly close to Moyle's figure of 25 per cent bearing in mind the simpler method used.

Leach (1971, p. 33 and 1972, p. 37) gives a substantially higher estimate for 1970 – 39 per cent compared with 31 per cent by the Bank of England. This is partly because his figures relate to December (whereas the Bank's relate to March), but mainly because of his higher conversion factor for the valuation of insurance companies' investments in ordinary shares. That conversion factor was based on grossing-up the income from ordinary shares as reported by some of the larger insurance companies, using the market yield on ordinary shares, and comparing the resultant estimated market valuation with book-values (we are indebted to Mr Leach for a discussion on this matter). The method used by us for valuing ordinary shares (see note 58 on p. 270) leads to much the same result for this year as the 'perpetual inventory' method used by the Bank. R. J. Briston published an estimate of 36 per cent for 1970 – 'The impact of institutional investors on the London Stock Exchange' in *Institutional Investors and the London Stock Exchange*, London, British Accounting and Finance Association, 1972, p. 7.

The application of Mr Leach's method to 1972 would yield a figure in the region of 40 per cent, as compared with our estimate of 38½ per cent.

For 1973, the evidence submitted to the Diamond Commission by R. S. Allen, J. A. Miller, D. C. Damant and J. H. C. Leach (see 'Submission to the Royal Commission on the Distribution of Income and Wealth', *The Investment Analyst*, no. 41, May 1975) suggested 40·6 per cent; the Diamond Commission published their estimate of 40·8 per cent, but incorporated a number of compensating variations in method. The main differences are that Allen *et al* exclude investment and unit trusts from the grand total (to avoid double counting), and the Commission includes a 'public sector' category amongst the institutions.

64 Central Statistical Office, *National Income and Expenditure 1975*, p. 90; it should be kept in mind that these figures are in the nature of 'residual estimates' subject to large margins of error, see Central Statistical Office,

National Accounts Statistics: sources and methods (ed. R. Maurice), London, HMSO, 1968, pp. 428–9.

65 E. V. Morgan, 'Personal saving and the capital market', *District Bank Review*, no. 163, September 1967, p. 17.

66 Doubts on the calculation by Professor Morgan were raised by L. S. Berman writing in the official *Economic Trends* ('Role of the personal sector in the flow of funds in the United Kingdom', no. 193, November 1969, p. xiv). First, whereas Morgan relied on the Inland Revenue's estimate of £12,000 million for total personal holdings of company securities, Berman preferred to consider the higher estimate of £21,000 million from Revell's work (1967, p. 147). That higher figure arises mainly from the inclusion of unquoted securities; partly also from the use of a higher multiplier in grossing-up the estates passing at death (due to taking a more favourable view of the health of the wealthier classes). Secondly, Berman suggested that higher share-prices would offset personal sales of securities; nevertheless, in terms of the proportion of companies' capital in their hands, the holdings of persons would decrease. It was also said that the incorporation of hitherto unincorporated enterprises would provide fresh securities for personal holdings, but one may wonder whether this could be large enough to provide a substantial offset. What may be accepted from all this is that the notion of 'stripping the cupboard bare' by a certain date is not to be understood too literally.

67 The information for the 1950s is taken from G. Clayton and W. T. Osborn, *Insurance Company Investment*, London, George Allen & Unwin, 1965, p. 139, and is subject to the limitation of being based on book-values; cf. also Macrae, 1955, p. 82. From 1963 we have statistics of cash expenditure each year, following the improvements brought about by the Radcliffe Committee (Treasury, *Committee on the Working of the Monetary System*, Cmnd 827, London, HMSO, 1959). There are considerable year-to-year variations in the proportions invested in fixed-interest securities and ordinaries, and to speak of a break in policy may seem to the reader as being too simple. Nevertheless, it seems to be borne out by the following figures of the amounts put by insurance companies and pension funds into debentures and preference shares expressed as a proportion of investment in ordinaries: 1963–8 (average), 77 per cent; 1969, 72 per cent; 1970, 27 per cent; 1971, 22 per cent; 1972, 15 per cent; 1973, 15 per cent; 1974, 2 per cent. The change between 1969 and 1970 appears remarkably sharp. In reality the transformation was softened by the rise of convertible debentures in this period (these are securities that are initially debentures, but after a period of years are converted, or carry the option of conversion, into ordinary shares, so providing some protection against inflation). Such convertible issues are classified together with other debentures in the published statistics. There seems little doubt that institutional preferences were responsible for the evolution of this hybrid security.

68 According to estimates in the *Bank of England Quarterly Bulletin*, vol. 11, June 1971, p. 207–8, in 1970 the institutions owned 58 per cent of all

company fixed-interest securities outstanding, compared with 31 per cent of all ordinary shares.

69 An average of £280 million a year was invested by the institutions in company debentures in the years 1963–9, and £160 million a year in 1970–3.

70 For the sake of clarity we may recall (as noted on p. 105) that tax-avoidance legislation prevents a single company restructuring its own capital; as part of a take-over or reconstruction of two companies this inhibition does not apply.

71 The role of cheap money in promoting British expertise in property development during this period may also be noted here. The link between insurance companies and property developers often became formalised in jointly owned subsidiaries; an objective account for the period up to the early 1960s is given by Clayton and Osborn (1965, pp. 179–82). More recently the institutions have tended to participate directly in property development, partly because of tax advantages and partly to have fuller benefit from rising property values.

72 The fact that many institutions are gross funds meant that they were able to show a positive real return on fixed-interest securities while personal investors were suffering negative returns; the institutions' lag was therefore less obvious.

73 As appears to be the case at the time (end-1975) that this text was being corrected for publication.

74 The relative size of the 'unquoted sector' is not easy to assess in terms of capital. We know that in all United Kingdom manufacturing there were some 9 million employees in 1971, of which 5 million were recorded in the accounts of quoted manufacturing companies as being United Kingdom employees; this would put the unquoted sector at about 40 per cent in terms of employees, and rather lower – say a quarter – in terms of capital. In other branches of activity the unquoted sector would be greater.

75 Finance for oil tankers and property companies is mentioned by Revell (1967, p. 219). Where the investment is in an unquoted company, it is often in the nature of 'nursery' finance for a medium-sized company expecting to go public within five years. In the Bolton Committee's *Research Report No. 4*, pp. 31, 115, 128, it was estimated that the annual flow of funds from insurance companies and pension funds to 'small firms' (defined for the Bolton Committee as having less than 200 employees in manufacturing, with corresponding criteria for other sectors) was no more than £7 million. The development of investment companies and trusts specialising in investments in 'smaller' or 'provincial' companies is of interest, but it should be remembered that they are largely concerned with *quoted* smaller companies.

76 A sample of insurance company accounts for this period suggested that 3 per cent of their equity holdings were unquoted; this would correspond to about 1 per cent of all institutional holdings assuming that other institutions held negligible unquoted equity (I am grateful to the Bank of

England's Research Department for help on this point). The estimates by A. R. Roe (*The Financial Interdependence of the Economy, 1957–1966*, London, Chapman & Hall, 1971, pp. 85–91) lead to similar inferences.

77 Investment policies have apparently also changed over time: for example, the Prudential Assurance Company appears to have curtailed its investment in smaller companies and transferred its holdings in some fifty smaller companies to a specialist investment trust on the grounds of efficiency in investment management (Annual Report of the Prudential Assurance Co. Ltd for 1972, p. 9).

78 Moyle (1971) was able to distribute nominee holdings for all size-groups combined to various categories of beneficial ownership, but the corresponding information was not available for each size-group. We have here combined the two largest groups shown in the original publication because of their odd variability (perhaps attributable to the very largest sample group, which contains a number of companies with large overseas interests, and some with large public sector holdings).

79 A new official survey of shareholdings in United Kingdom companies listed on the Stock Exchange to estimate the distribution of ordinary shares at the end of 1975 between categories of holders is planned by the Department of Industry (see *Statistical News*, no. 31, November 1975, p. 40). It is proposed that this will include an analysis of the beneficial owners of nominee holdings, as in the survey for 1963 by J. Moyle, *The Owners of Quoted Ordinary Shares*, London, Chapman & Hall, 1966.

80 A note on the slightly different developments in the United States may be added here. Institutional ownership of shares has also grown there, and is so heavily focused on a small number of large quoted companies that one speaks of a 'two-tier' market. Much light has been cast on developments by the vast study by the Securities and Exchange Commission, *Institutional Investor Study Report*, Washington (DC), US Government Printing Office, 1971; 7 vols. 4806 pp.; the institutions there own a smaller proportion of all industrial shares than institutions here (24 per cent in 1968 including ownership by personal trusts, which are excluded from the estimate of 32 per cent for the United Kingdom in 1969, as given by Moyle, 1971, p. 18), but their portfolio turnover is more rapid, so that they have a much greater influence on current transactions.

81 Now published routinely by the Department of Industry in *Business Monitor. Miscellaneous series M5*.

82 For 1950 we were able to use the summary figures on the hundred largest companies previously published by the National Institute (*Company Income and Finance, 1949–53*, London, NIESR, 1956) for its inquiry into the finance of public companies. The work of standardising the annual accounts of large companies was subsequently carried on by the Board of Trade and the Department of Industry and, for the years 1960 and 1970, we are grateful to those concerned at Companies House for access to the work-sheets, on the basis of which we prepared summaries for the hundred largest companies.

83 Some of the smallest quoted companies are now no longer covered by this

analysis, but their omission has a negligible influence on this rise. Another interesting comparison is with the gross income of all manufacturing companies given in the Central Statistical Office's *National Income and Expenditure* 'Blue Books': in 1970 the income of all companies had risen to 2·3 times its 1950 level, whereas in 1970 the gross income of the hundred largest was 5·2 times that of the hundred largest in 1950 (it will be remembered that it is the largest companies in each year that are here compared and not the same companies throughout). The rapid rise in the profits of the hundred largest companies is, of course, just another aspect of the general rise in their importance, which was considered using other measures of their size in chapter 1.

84 This is not to deny that the behaviour of smaller quoted companies differed from that of their larger brethren, but these differences are not the concern of the present section.

85 There is no need to burden the reader with references to the many comparisons of gross company savings with gross capital expenditures, but he may find it instructive to contrast two recent official documents. The Diamond Commission, *Report No. 2*, p. 77, presents figures gross of depreciation and emphasises 'the predominant role of internally generated finance in total sources of funds'; in a rather lower key (Appendix P, p. 147) it recognises that in measuring company growth depreciation needs separate treatment, but stock appreciation is not mentioned. A report by the National Economic Development Office, *Finance for Investment. A study of methods available for financing investment*, London, NEDO, 1975, pp. 39–41, on the other hand, draws up a table deducting stock appreciation from retentions, and notes the 'marked drop during 1974 in the funds internally available to companies for financing fixed capital formation'; but capital consumption is not deducted in that study. See also the paper by M. A. King, 'The United Kingdom profits crisis: myth or reality?', *Economic Journal*, vol. 85, March 1975, and the recent article, 'Structure of company financing' by J. L. Walker in *Economic Trends*, no. 263, September 1975, which shows net retentions after deducting capital consumption and stock appreciation as having fallen to zero in 1974 for industrial and commercial companies as a whole (p. 101).

The misleading nature of company accounts in inflationary times has long been understood in general terms and the need for some adjustment became pressing in the early 1970s when inflation accelerated. A draft proposal, *Accounting for Changes in the Purchasing Power of Money*, was published by the Accounting Standards Steering Committee in 1973 (document ED8) and was adopted as a provisional standard in 1974. An application of these proposals to the accounts of 137 large quoted companies for 1971 indicated that historical earnings were overstated by a median value of 20 per cent and that the most important reason for this was the valuation of stocks (the calculations related to 137 companies accounting for 75 per cent of the market-value of United Kingdom quoted equities apart from investment trusts; see R. S. Cutler and

C. A. Westwick, 'The impact of inflation accounting on the stock market', *Accountancy*, March 1973, pp. 15–24). The Economic Development Council ('little Neddy') for mechanical engineering produced a study, *Inflation and Company Accounts in Mechanical Engineering*, London, NEDO, 1973, indicating the illusory nature of retentions as shown in the accounts of 126 quoted engineering companies in the years 1965–71: retentions totalling £124 million were recorded in the accounts of those companies, but after adjusting for inflation the total is reduced to a mere £10 million (see pp. 30–3 of the study)! Even this figure, it may be argued, is an exaggeration since, in adjusting for inflation, credit was taken *on income account* for the decline in real value of debenture and preference shares (the amount credited in respect of the latter items totals some £40 million; if this is omitted, the net amount retained out of current earnings is negative). In adopting this procedure the Neddy study followed the draft recommendations of ED8, but that is not entirely helpful on this point (see N. Pilkington, 'Inflation accounting – treatment of monetary items', *The Investment Analyst*, no. 39, September 1974). The prime purpose of correcting for inflation is to show as far as possible earnings as they would be if transactions were recorded at stable prices; to introduce as part of income the gain to ordinary shareholders which arises in inflation at the expense of preference shareholders and debenture holders seems to me to run counter to the prime object of the exercise. Such a transfer undoubtedly arises, but it is better treated in a 'below the line' reckoning.

The government appointed a committee on inflation accounting in January 1974, which submitted a lengthy report in September 1975 (Treasury, *Inflation Accounting. Report of the Inflation Accounting Committee*, Cmnd 6225, London, HMSO, 1975). It remains to be seen what the government will extract from it by way of amendments to the definition of company profits for purposes of taxation. In the meantime the need to exempt stock appreciation from taxation was recognised in the budgets of 1974–6.

86 For other purposes there is no doubt much to be said for the conventional treatment of interest as a deduction *before* computing profits and dividends as a distribution *out* of profits, but in view of the switch to debenture financing, it is of interest to see how total distributions have changed, irrespective of whether they are taken at a fixed or a variable rate. Debenture interest is normally shown in published company accounts gross of income tax, and for most of this twenty-year period (that is except for 1967–73) dividends have normally been shown net of tax. To make the figures comparable they have here been adjusted on to a net basis throughout.

87 A small reduction in ordinary dividends did in fact take place: the Central Statistical Office's 'Blue Book' shows that ordinary dividends of industrial and commercial companies rose until 1965, but in the subsequent seven years they were below that level even in money terms.

88 Both dividends and retentions are now subject only to Corporation Tax

in the company's hands; dividends are subject to higher rates of personal tax in the recipient's hands, but not, as in the years 1965–73, to a further charge to income tax at the standard rate or its equivalent (we need not concern ourselves here with the changes in tax-nomenclature that have accompanied these cavortings).

89 See the *Economist*, 3 April 1971, and the Treasury White Paper, *Reform of Corporation Tax*, Cmnd 4955, London, HMSO, 1972. In the budget of March 1974 an additional advance payment of half the advance Corporation Tax on dividends was imposed – to discourage dividend payments again.

90 Investment grants are not shown explicitly in the summaries published in the Department of Industry's *Business Monitor*, but are grouped under 'other capital receipts' and credited to current account. This grouped item rises from a negligible £5 million at the beginning of the 1960s to nearly £300 million at the end of the decade; substantially the whole of the item may be assumed to represent investment grants insofar as they were explicitly published in the underlying accounts for individual companies.

91 That new issues play a relatively greater part in fast-growing companies has often been shown; see R. F. Henderson, 'Capital issues' in Tew and Henderson (eds.), 1959, p. 66, and Diamond Commission, *Report No. 2*, Appendix Q, p. 169.

92 The available figures for 1949–53 relate to the 105 (rather than 100) largest companies, 53 per cent of which issued new capital at some time in that five-year period (see Henderson, 1959, table 5.4, p. 69). It is not easy to convert this proportion to an annual basis because of 'duplication'; if those companies making issues did so repeatedly in each of the five years we would conclude that half the companies were making an issue each year, but this seems an extreme and unlikely assumption. The other extreme is to assume that each company making an issue did so only once in that five-year period; this would lead to the conclusion that one in ten companies made an issue each year at that time. An average between these extremes leads to the view that there has been an approximate doubling in the frequency of recourse to the new issue market in the ensuing twenty years.

93 This appears from a valuable analysis carried out by the Board of Trade, 'Acquisitions and amalgamations of quoted companies, 1962–1963', *Economic Trends*, no. 145, November 1965, p. xxiv. For the 1374 unquoted companies acquired by quoted companies in the years 1962–3 70 per cent of the consideration was in cash, but for the 139 quoted companies acquired in those years only 23 per cent of the consideration was in cash.

94 An earlier Board of Trade analysis for 1954–61 showed that the ninety-eight largest companies acquired nearly a third of all quoted companies that were taken over in that period, but these large companies acquired only 7 per cent of the unquoted companies that were taken over ('Acquisitions and amalgamations of quoted companies, 1954–1961', *Economic Trends*, no. 114, April 1963, p. vi).

95 The same treatment is adopted in the list of the fifty largest mergers recorded annually in *The Times 1000* lists of large companies, where the consideration is shown as being for the 'equity not already owned'. According to these lists, in 1972–3 the proportion of debentures reached 36 per cent of the total consideration as a result of two very highly geared and large take-overs: Grand Metropolitan's bid for Watney Mann (of which £380 million – 55 per cent – was in convertible debentures) and the Imperial Group's bid for Courage (of which £258 million – 52 per cent – was in debentures, mostly convertible). The role of convertible debentures in these large acquisitions and their ultimate holders deserve further study; though they are customarily grouped together with other debentures, there is much to be said for the view that they are more nearly akin to equity.

96 Growth was measured from the 'sources and uses of capital funds account' and excluded revaluations.

97 The component standard deviations are not directly additive, but the *squares* of the total can be partitioned into the squares of the components plus twice their covariance terms; the covariance terms, as it turned out, were negative and relatively small and none of the correlations between the components were significant, making the interpretation of the result easier. Squaring the components given in the text gave

$$51 = 19 + 19 + 20 - 7,$$

where the last item represents the covariance terms.

98 The results of an attempt to estimate more directly the impact of mergers on the recent rise in the share of the hundred largest enterprises may be mentioned here. We wished to calculate by how much the sharp rise in the share of the hundred largest manufacturing companies in the six years to 1970 would have been moderated if all of the 122 largest acquisitions and mergers (those of more than £5 million) in which the hundred largest had been involved in that period had been prohibited. The answer depended crucially on what other resources (in place of those acquisitions) could reasonably be assumed to accrue to those companies in that period; if the same total resources had accrued but were expended in other ways, such as on the creation of new plants rather than on acquisitions of existing businesses, it appears that the rise in share of the hundred largest would have been reduced very slightly, by only about 5 per cent of the actual rise; if no additional resources had accrued to replace the assets taken over (that is, if we are prepared for a moment to forget – in patent contrast to the facts – that retentions and cash issues contributed resources to take-overs and would remain available for expansion in other ways), the rise in the share of the hundred largest would have been very small. The more realistic assumption to be made, consistent with the analysis in the text, would seem to be that a third of additional resources were the result of exchanges of paper on acquisition and the remainder the results of retentions and cash issues; on that basis, we would deduce that the rise in the share of the hundred largest would be

reduced by a third. Calculations of this kind are thus very difficult to carry out in a useful way and are much dependent on the assumptions made (cf. Aaronovitch and Sawyer, 1974).

An earlier National Institute study (Hart and Prais, 1956, pp. 168–9) attributed a rather small role to mergers in the general rise of concentration up to 1950. There seems little doubt that mergers have become more important since then; but, as will be clear from the present discussion, the contribution of mergers is not as easy to assess as might be thought. See the studies by A. Singh, (*Take-overs, their relevance to the stockmarket and the theory of the firm*, Cambridge University Press, 1971), Kuehn (1974) and Hannah (forthcoming) for other aspects of mergers. Hannah's researches attach very much more importance to mergers in the inter-war period than did our earlier (1956) study, but his method of assessing the role of mergers (by examining a sample of companies chosen at the end of a period) necessarily contributes to his result.

Notes to chapter 6 (pp. 137–62)

1 In some countries each legal entity, that is each subsidiary company, is obliged to make a Census return, but in others grouped returns are accepted and there is an unknown degree of consolidation of subsidiaries, possibly changing over time, irrespective of the real situation.

2 Directives concerned with the 'harmonisation' and improvement of accounting practices have been issued by the Commission of the European Communities, but the latest (the fourth, issued at the beginning of 1974 with a view to implementation in 1978) still does not make consolidated accounts obligatory. Germany and France have in recent years made some progress: the former introduced consolidation requirements in 1965, excluding however any requirement on foreign subsidiaries, and the latter made consolidation obligatory from 1973 (see R. C. Morris, *Corporate Reporting Standards and the 4th Directive*, London, Institute of Chartered Accountants in England and Wales, 1974).

3 The problems of defining the statistical unit in Censuses of production were discussed in a document issued by the United Nations Economic and Social Council, *The Statistical Unit in Economic Inquiries*, New York, 1960; they were, however, glossed over in the recent recommendations produced in connection with the 1973 world programme of industrial statistics (United Nations Statistical Office, *Statistical Papers M54*, Part III: *Organization and Conduct of Industrial Censuses*, New York, 1972). Regrettably the Statistical Office of the Commission of the European Communities has accepted as standard practice for its members in conducting industrial Censuses the definition of an 'enterprise' which excludes subsidiaries (*Coordinated Annual Inquiry into Industrial Activity in the Member States of the European Communities*, Luxembourg, 1972, and 'Council directive of 6 June 1972 concerning coordinated annual surveys of industrial activity', *Official Journal of the European Communities*, 10 June 1972, p. 523).

　　Even within a single country there are difficulties in maintaining consistent definitions between successive Censuses in consequence of the growth of multi-plant enterprises. The flow of goods between plants in a group is generally recorded in quantity terms, but it is not always valued; hence output statistics cannot be computed in precisely the same detail as previously. An account of these and other difficulties is given in the context of the British Census of Production by Fessey and Browning in *Statistical News*, no. 13, May 1971. However, perhaps because of a greater cost consciousness in the United States, large industrial corporations there tend increasingly to draw up accounts at a more detailed level as a 'management tool' (see United Nations Economic and Social Council, 1960, p. 21, n. 13).

4　For the sake of clarity the reasons for this choice may be spelled out. Since the EEC Census statistics on 'enterprises' do not group subsidiary companies together with their parent concerns, it is not possible to rely on them for information on the largest firms; we have instead used company reports. On the other hand, for the smallest concerns it seems reasonable to suppose that they are mainly independent and the Census statistics have therefore been relied upon. We have, however, no information on the number of enterprises (in our sense, including their subsidiaries) of intermediate size and fuller comparisons of the size-distributions (as for the United States) are thus not possible.

　　It was originally intended also to include in this chapter a comparison of plant-sizes between Britain and Europe. But a proper treatment requires a careful investigation of the differences in definitions of 'local units' and 'establishments', which did not prove possible within the limits of the available resources. It is hoped to repair this deficiency in future work.

5　The United States Census authorities publish these figures correct only to the nearest percentage point, so that we cannot know for certain whether there have been any minor changes (possibly up to 1 point) in recent years. By interpolating with the help of the other published observations (relating to the 50, 150 and 200 largest enterprises), one may tentatively infer that here has probably been a very slight rise, of the order of 0·5 points, between 1963 and 1970 in the share of the hundred largest.

6　Earlier studies of whether concentration is on average higher in the United States or the United Kingdom have reached different conclusions; that now seems less surprising in the light of the reversal in the 1950s suggested by the calculations reported here. Florence (1972, p. 157) quotes a number of comparisons of frequency distributions of industry concentration ratios from which he concludes that British industry is somewhat more concentrated, but he notes that the greater geographical distances in America temper the significance of that conclusion. G. Rosenbluth ('Measures of concentration' in National Bureau of Economic Research, *Business Concentration and Price Policy*, Princeton University Press, 1955, pp. 74–6) concluded that British concentration levels tended to be higher in 1935. On the other hand, J. S. Bain (*Inter-*

national Differences in Industrial Structure, New Haven, Yale University Press, 1966, p. 76) concluded from a comparison of thirty-two industries relating to the years 1951–4 that the United Kingdom 'evidences a tendency towards approximately the same or a slightly lesser degree of concentration'. W. G. Shepherd's study ('A comparison of industrial concentration in the United States and Britain', *Review of Economics and Statistics*, vol. 43, February 1961), also based on the 1950s, suggested 'a rough similarity' and perhaps lower concentration on average in the United Kingdom, but this conclusion was criticised by B. P. Pashigian ('Market concentration in the United States and Great Britain', *Journal of Law and Economics*, vol. 11, October 1968), who concluded that British concentration was higher, mainly because of the smaller market here. The studies referred to in this note are sometimes based on samples of industries which are fairly comparable in their definitional scope but with the sample not necessarily representative of all industry, and sometimes on samples wider in representiveness but with the industries less comparable in their definitions; in any event they differ from the present study, which takes a single measure of aggregate concentration. The main point to be noted, however, is that if there has been a crossing of trend lines in the two countries the date of the comparison makes a great difference, and so may the precise sample of industries compared. If this is taken into account, a consistent thread can perhaps be traced through the various studies.

7 See G. C. Means, 'Statistical Appendix' in Berle and Means (eds.), (rev. edn), 1968, p. 345; Scherer, 1970, p. 42; Blair, 1972, p. 67.

8 An important strengthening of American law took place in 1950 which particularly inhibited mergers by the largest enterprises. Until 1950 the acquisition of the shares of a competing corporation was governed by section 7 of the Clayton Act of 1914 prohibiting acquisitions which 'substantially lessen competition or tend to create a monopoly', but this was interpreted by the Courts as applying only to acquisitions of shares and as being intended to prevent hidden control – the open acquisition of the assets (as distinct from the shares) of another corporation was regarded as permissible. This interpretation was reversed by the Celler–Kefauver amendment of 1950, which prohibited also the acquisition of the assets of another corporation. The Courts have interpreted the amendment with increasing severity (in 1966 a Court went as far as preventing the third largest retailer in a single area acquiring the sixth largest, even though combined they would have had under a tenth of that area's sales) and they consider it to include also acquisitions which reduce 'potential competition', and 'conglomerate' acquisitions. Though the amendment was passed in 1950 its full effects may well not have been felt until the 1960s. In 1968 the Department of Justice issued its 'Merger Guidelines' setting out the criteria in terms of market shares under which it would ordinarily challenge mergers; for example, in a concentrated market where the four largest firms account for three-quarters of the total, any acquiring firm already accounting for over 4 per cent of the

market might not acquire another firm accounting for 4 per cent and, if the acquiring firm already accounted for 15 per cent, it might not acquire a firm accounting for even 1 per cent. Stricter criteria still are applied to markets which have shown a rising trend in concentration over the previous five to ten years. A full account of these matters is given by A. D. Neale in *The Antitrust Laws of the U.S.A.* (2nd edn), Cambridge University Press, 1970, pp. 180–200, and the 'Guidelines' are reproduced on pp. 494–505 of that book.

9　Certain aspects noted in this section (and in the immediately following section on plant-sizes) have already been observed by Florence (1972, pp. 40–4) and M. Metwally ('A comparison between representative size of plant in manufacturing industries in industrialised and less-industrialised countries', *Yorkshire Bulletin of Economic and Social Research*, vol. 17, November 1965) on the basis of the Censuses of 1963 and earlier years. The present account includes the Censuses of 1967–8 and examines the extremes of the size-distribution more closely.

10　The detailed size-distributions (ranked by size of employment) for United States enterprises published by the Bureau of the Census in *Enterprise Statistics 1967*, Part I, include any non-manufacturing establishments belonging to those enterprises that are classified in manufacturing according to their predominant activity; they are thus not comparable with United Kingdom Census data, which exclude any non-manufacturing establishments belonging to enterprises predominantly engaged in manufacturing. For the 200 largest manufacturing enterprises there is a special tabulation for the United States which is comparable with United Kingdom data; these 200 are chosen according to size of value added in manufacturing alone. Whether non-manufacturing establishments are included makes a considerable difference to the figure for the largest concerns, since about a seventh of the employment of all manufacturing enterprises is outside manufacturing (for the smallest enterprises – those employing under 1000 – the difference may be ignored, but for those employing over 2500 it appears that over a third of their employment is outside manufacturing). In addition, certain size-distributions are published by the United States Department of Commerce, Bureau of the Census in *Census of Manufactures 1967. Special Report: concentration ratios in manufacturing*, Part I, Washington (DC), US Government Printing Office, 1970; this shows employment according to a coarser size-grouping of enterprises, but the *numbers* of enterprises in each group are regrettably not given! Some care is thus required in comparing American and British statistical sources.

11　The comparison cannot be made with great precision from the published data, which are that the value added by the fifty largest manufacturing enterprises in the United States, when ranked by net output, totalled some $66,000 million in 1967 (to be inferred from the Bureau of the Census, *Concentration Ratios in Manufacturing*, Part I, which shows 25 per cent of total net output produced by the fifty largest), and that United Kingdom total net output in all manufacturing was £16,700 million (from the 1968 Census). Using a purchasing power parity exchange rate, which, as shown below, may be taken at approximately \$3·1 to the £ in 1968 (rather than the official rate of \$2·4), we may convert the American figure to an approximate British equivalent of £21,300; it appears therefore that the fifty largest enterprises in the United States produced more than all United Kingdom manufacturing. By extrapolating a Pareto line from the four published observations relating to the 50, 100, 150 and 200 largest enterprises, it can be estimated that approximately twenty-eight United States enterprises produce the equivalent of the British total. If we were content to use official exchange rates it would appear that the output of the twenty largest United States manufacturing enterprises exceeds that of all United Kingdom manufacturing.

The purchasing power parity exchange rate mentioned above was derived as follows. We started from the detailed comparison of output and productivity in the United Kingdom and the United States by D. Paige and G. Bombach (Organisation for European Economic Co-operation, *A Comparison of National Output and Productivity*, Paris, 1959, p. 21), which suggested a rate of exchange for manufacturing in 1950 of between \$4·1 and \$3·6 to the £ according to whether a British or American weighting was used; for present purposes we took the geometric mean of \$3·8. Prices rose rather more rapidly in the United Kingdom than in the United States in the period 1950–68 (in the United Kingdom the index of wholesale prices of manufactured products rose by 64 per cent, in the United States that of finished goods rose by 30 per cent), which leads to a lower rate of exchange for 1968 at \$3·1. We have thus assumed in our calculations that American prices were some 28 per cent higher in 1968 than would be given by the official exchange rate. I. B. Kravis, Z. Kenessy, A. Heston and R. Summers in *A System of International Comparisons of Gross Product and Purchasing Power*, Baltimore, Johns Hopkins University Press, 1975, p. 9, estimate a very similar purchasing power parity exchange rate of \$3·2 in respect of gross domestic product in 1970; their work became available after these calculations had been completed.

12 The Department of Economic Affairs' White Paper, *The Industrial Reorganisation Corporation*, Cmnd 2889, London, HMSO, 1966, spoke of 'the need for more concentration' to promote the 'international competitiveness of British industry'; it is not clear whether this was regarded as a limitless need. It seems likely that those who drafted that document were unaware of the facts relating to the role of smaller enterprises and plants in the United States considered here. Subsequent reports of the Industrial Reorganisation Corporation are more cautious in tone: we learn that 'size in itself is no solution' (*Report and accounts for the year ended March 31, 1969*); 'indeed size has absolute disadvantages where it increases managerial problems and lengthens lines of communication. The spur of competition can also be blunted' (*Report and accounts for the year ended March 31, 1970*). In October 1970 the government announced that the Corporation was to be wound up, but by 1975 a National Enter-

prise Board was set up in which the same confused spirits thrash about.

13 To avoid misunderstanding it is perhaps worth repeating that these figures of employment are based on the largest companies ranked by their net output; the published ranking by employment cannot be used here for the reason indicated in note 10 above.

14 In fact our calculation suggested 1 percentage point higher for the United Kingdom than for the United States, but this may be ignored in view of the approximations that had to be adopted to derive the comparison. The only satisfactory distributions for this comparison are, again, those ranking enterprises by size of net output; by interpolating from the published distributions it appears that the 110 largest United States enterprises and the forty largest United Kingdom enterprises (both numbers are approximate) are those with over 20,000 employees. Both numbers have been derived in the same complex and indirect way from the published distributions ranked by net output (the lower limit of employment in each size-class was derived with the help of the textbook formula relating to the Pareto curve; the average size of the largest N firms divided by the Pareto slope being equal to the lower size-limit of those N firms). In this way a number of points can be derived showing the proportion of total employment in firms above certain sizes and, by further interpolation, the proportions quoted in the text were reached. Until international co-ordination of Census work improves, such round-about and approximate methods are regrettably inevitable for answering even the simplest questions.

15 The greater median-size of enterprise in Britain when measured in terms of employment was already apparent in 1958; cf. Florence, 1972, p. 41. The values quoted in the text were obtained by graphical interpolation. It appears that a United States size-distribution of enterprises in the 1967 Census has not been published on the same basis as for 1958 and 1963 (that is excluding non-manufacturing subsidiaries, which would permit comparison with later British figures), but it would be of great interest in view of the very sharp rise in enterprise-size in the subsequent five years – in Britain the median-size rose by nearly half to 4200 employees.

16 An estimate based on the assumption that all 'unsatisfactory returns' relate to small enterprises; if these are excluded the share is reduced to 14 per cent.

17 Calculated from the number of employees in enterprises with under a hundred employees (3·48 million as given in Bureau of the Census, *Enterprise Statistics 1967.* Part I, p. 168) divided by total employment in all manufacturing establishments (18·49 million from the main Census tabulations). The validity of the calculation depends on small enterprises having a negligible proportion of their employment in non-manufacturing establishments; this seems to be so, since only 2 per cent of their employment is in multi-industry companies.

18 L. Rostas (*Comparative Productivity in British and American Industry*, Cambridge University Press, 1948, pp. 60 and 72), as part of his investigation

of productivity differences between the two countries before the war, compared the sizes of plants for some thirty trades on the basis of the Censuses of 1935–9, but was not able to find any support for the popular view that larger plant-sizes in America were related to higher productivity there. In a similar study of the immediate post-war Censuses of 1947–8, M. Frankel (*British and American Manufacturing Productivity*, Urbana, University of Illinois Press, 1957, especially p. 60) correlated the ratio of output per worker in the two countries with the ratio of their plant-sizes in thirty-four selected industries, but was also unable to establish any significant relation ($r = -0.12$).

19 Calculated at an effective exchange rate of $3·1 to the £ (see note 11 above).

20 The rise in American plant-sizes that apparently occurred between 1963 and 1967 is so sharp that one may suspect some change in compilation procedures, for example a greater acceptance of combined returns, but we have been unable to obtain confirmation from the Bureau of the Census on this possibility. Preliminary results of the 1972 American Census which became available at proof stage show a return to the size-distribution of 1963; the 1967 results thus appear anomalous.

21 United States Department of Commerce, Bureau of the Census, *Census of Manufactures 1963. Special Report: concentration ratios in manufacturing*, Part II, Washington (DC), US Government Printing Office, 1967, table 23, gives 8028 as the number of establishments controlled by the 200 largest enterprises; information of this kind is not available for other years. If allowance is made for central administrative offices serving manufacturing establishments, it appears that the total is raised to just over 9000 establishments (thanks are due to the Industry Division of the Bureau of the Census for help on this point).

22 The size-distributions of plants in America are published only on a rather coarse grouping, the top group relating to those with over 2500 employees (whereas the British Census has a top group at over 10,000 employees). Estimates for the hundred largest plants have here been made by fitting Pareto curves to the distribution and extrapolating; the individual results cannot be treated too precisely, but the general impression they yield is unlikely to be far from the truth.

23 The 420 industry groups distinguished in the United States Census of Manufactures were grouped to correspond with the fourteen Industrial Orders distinguished in the British Census; further details are given in appendix E.2.

24 It perhaps needs emphasising at this point that what is produced in a large plant may be far removed from what is produced in a small plant that is classified in the same 'industrial group' even in the same country. The above comparisons must therefore be construed broadly. If we had approached these industrial comparisons more simply by considering only the arithmetic average employment per plant, it would be found that plants were smaller in America in all industrial groups (except for clothing); this is the result of the great preponderance in the number of

small plants there. Some, but only some, of the true complexity becomes apparent on considering also the dispersion of plant-sizes, as has been attempted here.

25 The greater distances in America would be one factor leading to smaller plants there, particularly for perishable goods such as bread. But others are more difficult to attach to economic realities; it is perhaps the appalling taste for sweets in Britain which has encouraged large-scale plants in that branch of manufacture (thus, 56 per cent of employment in cocoa, chocolate and sugar confectionery in Britain is in plants of over 1000 employees, compared with only 23 per cent in America, and the median plant-sizes in this trade are 1300 in Britain and 300 in America). Britain also has larger biscuit factories (connected originally with the special suitability of British wheat for biscuit baking). Tobacco plants in America include a greater proportion at the earlier stages – stemming and re-drying – which are small. The differences just mentioned are related to the natural conditions of the two countries, but others are related to the state of technological development and training of the work-force; thus instrument engineering, and particularly the production of photographic and document copying equipment and supplies, is carried out on a much larger scale in America than here (in Britain employment in the production of photographic equipment, etc., is entirely in plants of under 2500 employees, whereas in America 57 per cent of employment is in plants above that size).

26 It may also be said that earlier writings which encouraged that notion are not as conclusive as might appear, in particular the choice of a summary measure of plant-size has caused difficulties. Bain (1966, pp. 34 and 49), in his study of international differences in industrial concentration, takes as his measure the average number of employees in the twenty largest plants in each country; that same number of plants is taken for each country irrespective of the country's size. One must expect, as pointed out by Florence amongst others, that 'a smaller country is almost bound to have a lower number of employees in the twenty largest (plants) than a large country' (1972, p. 30), and Bain's conclusion that British plant-sizes are only 78 per cent of the size of American plants is misleading. The reader should also be warned that the pre-war American Censuses classify plants by number of wage-earners only and exclude salaried staff and proprietors; the published size-distributions thus require adjustment in comparisons with later years as indicated in footnote *e* to table 6.1. Florence's table (ibid. p. 38) thus slightly exaggerates the long-term rise in the share of employment in plants employing over 500, which he puts as increasing in the period 1909–63 from 28 to 43 per cent, instead of from 31 to 43 per cent when an allowance is made for other staff.

27 Some of the technical details relating to our comparison may be recorded here. The most recent five-year period for which the relevant statistics were available when this exercise was carried out was 1967–72. Figures of United Kingdom employment were required to be published

by British companies following the Companies Act of 1967 and it was hoped to use them as a measure of size in addition to a capital measure. However, not enough companies published figures for their 1967 employment and it thus proved necessary to base the British employment calculations on a period commencing one year later, 1968–73. The British figures were taken from the lists published by *The Times* (the lists for 1968–9 were taken as relating to accounting periods ending mainly in 1967, and similarly for later years); capital employed, as shown there, was taken as the capital measure – it is defined as 'total tangible assets less current liabilities (other than bank loans and future tax)'; the number of employees could not always be taken directly from these lists because for some companies overseas employment was included (and sometimes included for one year and excluded in another). By going to the original published company accounts, and when necessary contacting the companies, an attempt was made to obtain a list that consistently referred to domestic employment for both years. Unquoted companies and foreign subsidiaries were excluded. The American figures were taken from the lists published in *Fortune* in 1968 and 1973; 'invested capital' (later termed 'stockholders' equity') is tabulated there and was taken as the capital measure – though this is not quite the same as the British concept, in that debentures and bank loans are excluded. The number of employees was taken as published in the *Fortune* lists.

28 These were Sinclair Oil (by Atlantic Richmond), Jones and Laughlin Steel (by Ling Temco Vought, subsequently collapsed) and Sunray DX (merged with Sun Oil). If the list was chosen according to the number of employees rather than by capital, the same number of firms lost their independence, but they were the following: Jones and Laughlin Steel (as in the previous list), Glen Alden (taken over by Rapid American) and Armour (taken over by Greyhound).

29 Associated Electrical Industries, Watney Mann and Leyland Motors were taken over by GEC, Grand Metropolitan and BMC. The other companies taken over in this period that were in the top hundred in 1967 were English Electric (by GEC), Gallaher (American Tobacco), Courage (Imperial Tobacco), International Publishing (Reed International), Wiggins Teape (British-American Tobacco), Schweppes (Cadbury), Viyella (ICI), Carreras (Rothman's), Carrington and Dewhurst (ICI via Viyella), Parsons (Reyrolle), Cerebos (Rank-Hovis-McDougall).

30 For the sake of clarity it may be noted that the capital of the three companies that were taken over amounted to double that proportion – 1·9 per cent – but in accounting for changes in our measure of concentration only the sizes of the smaller three that replace them are relevant.

31 It should be emphasised that this statement relates strictly to merger activity amongst the very largest concerns (where, of course, it is easier for public policy to be implemented and to have a noticeable effect on aggregate concentration). As far as the total number of reported mergers in manufacturing is concerned, there is less obvious disparity between the

two countries when allowance is made for the different sizes of their economies.

It might be asked whether it is correct to compare the number of take-overs in the hundred largest in America and in Britain, given the different sizes of the two countries. An alternative procedure might be to compare the fifty largest in Britain with the hundred largest in America, since they account for the same share, 33 per cent of manufacturing net output, in their respective countries. But the contrast in the rate of take-over activity is then slightly increased because of the preponderance of very large take-overs in Britain. Eight of the fifty largest were taken over in Britain and, following the same calculation as in the text, would account for a 1·7 points rise in the share of the fifty largest in net output (instead of 1·4 points for the hundred largest).

32 It will be remembered that the American Census publishes the share of the hundred largest only to the nearest percentage point.

33 These are surveyed in appendix D; one of the studies mentioned there has a wider coverage still, being based on the Census of Production.

34 There is little point in carefully raking over the heap of misunderstandings to be found in the American writings in this field, but the student of that literature will wish to have the following two points in mind. First, rank correlations are often employed, but these are sometimes misleading. The extent to which firms change their size-ranking between two dates depends, amongst other things, on how close they are together in size at the initial date (a simple enough point, but its implications have apparently been overlooked in certain writings). If rank correlations change over time it does not necessarily mean that there is any change in the size-mobility of firms in the sense of a change in the dispersion of their percentage rates of growth; the ordinary product-moment correlations are more relevant, particularly the correlations between the logarithms of size. Secondly, there is confusion between the correlation coefficient (a unit-free measure of goodness of fit) and the regression coefficient (a measure of the magnitude of the dependence of one variable upon another). The American papers in this field (N. R. Collins and L. E. Preston, 'The size structure of the largest industrial firms, 1909–1958', *American Economic Review*, vol. 51, December 1961; D. Mermelstein, 'Large industrial corporations and asset shares' and 'Large industrial corporations and asset shares: reply', *American Economic Review*, vol. 59, September 1969, and vol. 61, March 1971; S. E. Boyle and J. P. McKenna, 'Size mobility of the 100 and 200 largest U.S. manufacturing corporations: 1919–1964', *The Antitrust Bulletin*, vol. 15, Fall 1970; S. E. Boyle, 'Large industrial corporations and asset shares: comment', *American Economic Review*, vol. 61, March 1971) must therefore be read critically; though they follow the earlier work on Britain by Hart and Prais (1956), they are not fully in tune.

35 The standard deviations of the growth-rates measured in terms of employment were also very similar: 5·9 percentage points for America, 5·6 points for Britain.

36 See appendix D, where studies are quoted for 1951–60 by Samuels (1965) and for 1954–65 by Utton (1971). These indicate residual standard deviations, after allowing for Regression, of 0·69 and 0·58 respectively in terms of natural logarithms of net assets. To transform this result into units comparable with those used in the text the following steps are necessary. First, we add the small variance removed by the Regression, so that we have, as strictly required, the variance of the logarithm of the change in size. Using the notation of appendix D this is given by $s^2 + c^2 V(x_{t-1})$; however, since $c \simeq$ 0·1, and $V(x)$ is only about 7, even for the whole Census population, the effect of this adjustment is almost negligible – it would raise the values given above to 0·76 and 0·65 respectively, or say to 0·70. Secondly, we have to convert to annual rates of change from the decennial changes; this requires taking a tenth-root, that is dividing the logarithmic change by ten, yielding a value of 0·07, corresponding to a standard deviation of 7 per cent a year. A. Singh and G. Whittington in *Growth, Profitability and Valuation*, Cambridge University Press, 1967, p. 78, quote a directly calculated standard deviation of 5·5 percentage points for four selected industries in the period 1948–60, which is of the same order of magnitude. Finally, we have to allow for the different periods of measurement. A five-year period formed the basis for our comparison for 1967–72, whereas approximate decades were covered in the studies just mentioned. If we standardise our 1967–72 study on to a ten-year period, the variability would fall to approximately $5·7/\sqrt{2} = 4·1$ points (this assumes independence between successive periods, which is approximately justified). Singh and Whittington (1967, p. 109) quote a correlation of $r^2 = 0·02$ between growth in successive six-year periods; if we nevertheless wished to take this correlation into account we would adjust by $\sqrt{(1 + r)}$ yielding 4·3 points. Thus, our study relating to the hundred largest companies yields a value of the variability of growth-rates rather lower than that for all quoted companies; this is without doubt because the latter group includes smaller companies which have a greater variability.

37 This appears from Collins and Preston, 1961, p. 992, table 2, row 2d; the standard deviation of growth-rates in percentage points for the various periods were as follows: 1909–19, 5·3; 1919–29, 4·6; 1929–35, 3·6; 1935–48, 2·7; 1948–58, 3·2. The periods are not quite of the same length and prevent a precise comparison; an adjustment on to a common period of a decade would lower the value for 1929–35 and raise that for 1935–48, bringing them both closer to 3 per cent. It may perhaps be mentioned again here that the measured degree of variability depends on the length of the time-period in a non-proportional way, there being a partial offsetting of random movements between sub-periods; measurements of variability can be compared directly only if they relate to an identical time-period, otherwise some adjustment is required (along the lines described in appendix D). The increasing stability appears also in the other studies referred to. Mermelstein (1969, p. 538, table 6 and also his preceding tables) takes the story forward to include the period

1958–64 using a somewhat different approach (see note 42 below); one may infer from his *correlations* (not from the regressions, on which point there is some theoretical confusion) that firm-sizes stabilised further in that period.

38 The bias arises because the American studies are based on those companies that were included in the hundred largest both at the beginning and at the end of the period considered; any companies that were in that group at the beginning but had declined out of it by the end of the period, even though they were still alive (for example, a company ranked 99th in 1948 and 101st in 1958), would be excluded. This reduces the measured degree of variability and biases the regression coefficient; the conclusion drawn as to the direction of change in dispersion is perhaps still valid, but one cannot be sure that the extent of the change is properly reflected in the figures; there is clearly need for further research in this area. The correct method is to follow through the fate of the largest companies chosen in the opening year of the period and not to exclude any simply because they have declined too much in size (this was the procedure followed in our special comparison for 1967–72). See S. J. Prais, 'The statistical conditions for a change in business concentration', *Review of Economics and Statistics*, vol. 40, August 1958, for a general exposition of this problem, and Boyle, 1971, p. 164, for an analogous worry in this context.

39 See chapter 2, p. 36. A slightly lower value would apply for America, since the dispersion of enterprise-sizes is slightly greater there, but the difference is too small to warrant comment given the approximations that have to be assumed.

40 The Regression slope was -0.04 for America and $+0.01$ for Britain, but the standard errors were about ±0.04 in each case.

41 See note 38 above.

42 Mermelstein (1969, pp. 535 and 538) correlated the 'shares' at the beginning and end of a period of time of each of the hundred largest surviving companies, the 'share' being defined as the ratio of a company's assets to the total assets of the sample. The approach thus differs from ours both in not taking logarithms, so giving relatively greater weight to the very largest companies, and in being confined to the hundred largest companies, whereas the British studies relate to a sample from the full size-range of quoted companies. For 1948–58 he finds $c = +0.11$ (±0.03) for all survivors (p. 535, tables). This is altered to $+0.04$ (±0.03) after making some adjustments (p. 538, table 6) to show what might have happened if there had been no changes in industrial structure and no 'trust-busting', but these adjustments he regards with 'skepticism' (p. 539).

43 The choice of 40,000 employees as the criterion was determined by the available published lists, which generally relate to the 300 or 500 largest companies, but are arranged by value of sales rather than employment. The lower that one sets the criterion in terms of employment the greater the risk of omitting a firm that should be included; it also

seems likely that the lists are less complete at lower sizes. Employment seems a better criterion than sales for present purposes, since national totals (needed for comparative purposes) of the sales of all enterprises combined are not available for some countries; further, sales are less satisfactory because they suffer from an element of duplication (part of the sales of one enterprise form the purchases of another – this is the familiar reason for the use of net rather than gross output in Censuses of Production).

44 Based on employment in 1969, as given by H. W. de Jong ('Concentration in Benelux' in Arndt (ed.) 1971, p. 43). The example may not seem entirely fair since the first two concerns are of joint Dutch–British nationality – a problem discussed further in appendix F.2 (in table 6.3 'dual nationality' concerns have been apportioned to each country as noted in that appendix); however, even Philips – which is not subject to this problem – has three-quarters of its total employment outside its home country.

45 That Britain and the United States stand close together as generators of employment in large enterprises was noted on p. 143 on the basis of Census returns. In 1968 about 27 per cent of manufacturing employees within each country were accounted for by manufacturing enterprises with over 20,000 employees; a similar inference is to be drawn here from table 6.3 in relation to enterprises of double that size.

46 Interesting distinctions can be drawn between the legal home of a company, the home of its headquarters and its tax domicile, but in practice – for these largest companies – the difference is not all that significant. A glance at the names of the large concerns listed in table F.1 is sufficient to show that these large companies are centred in all respects in the countries to which they are allocated (the few exceptions are the true multinationals, such as Unilever).

47 The world employment accounted for by the four Dutch giants (even if we consider only the Dutch portions of Unilever and Royal Dutch–Shell) totals 0·75 million, compared with an employment of 1·2 million in the Netherlands by all manufacturing concerns; an index for the Netherlands calculated as in the final column of table 6.3 would show large firms 1·9 times as frequent there as in Britain.

48 Cf. de Jong, 1971, p. 66.

49 Apart from the Netherlands if considered alone.

50 There are now only a handful of British quoted companies with 'Imperial' as the first word of their title, whereas twenty years ago forty were listed in the *Stock Exchange Official Year-Book* (and there has been no compensating increase in 'Commonwealth'-named companies; on the contrary, these too have decreased in number).

51 Lists of the hundred largest German concerns and their employment which are published annually by the *Frankfurter Allgemeine Zeitung* and by *Die Zeit* (Hamburg) differ slightly; the former list includes the names of major subsidiaries. These lists also differ slightly from those published by *Fortune* and *The Times*. Jane's handbook, *Major Companies of Europe*,

and Hoppenstedt's, *Handbook of Large Enterprises in Germany*, have also been found useful in drawing up the present comparisons.

52 See United States Senate, *Hearings: Economic Concentration* (Part 7); the text of Professor Arndt's statement is on p. 3490 and includes percentages for the period 1959–66. A list of company names for 1966 is reproduced from the *Frankfurter Allgemeine Zeitung* on pp. 3817–19. Professor Arndt is Director of the Institute for Research on Concentration, Berlin.

53 Commission of the European Communities, *Proposal for a Regulation (EEC) of the Council on the Control of Concentration between Undertakings*, Brussels, 1973. Earlier calculations for 1954 and 1960 were reported in a German parliamentary inquiry into concentration (Deutscher Bundestag, *Bericht über das Ergebnis einer Untersuchung der Konzentration in der Wirtschaft*, Drucksache IV/2320, Bonn, 1964, p. 15); from the limited description of the method of calculation given there it appears that the figures do not rely on any official Census, but are based on similar lists of large companies (there is a curious reference to total sales by the hundred largest enterprises of DM260 million, whereas Arndt in United States Senate, *Hearings: Economic Concentration*, (Part 7), quotes DM110 million for that year; the outside observer hesitates to comment on such discrepancies).

54 Manufacturing establishments classified in 'Handwerk' employed 1·7 million persons in 1967 (according to the German *Statistical Yearbook* for 1972, p. 239), and a similar number were employed in building and construction; these establishments are not covered in most of the German statistics relating to 'Industrie', the employment of which in that year totalled 7·8 million in establishments with ten or more employees (ibid. p. 199). The 1963 German Census, carried out in co-ordination with the Statistical Office of the European Communities, related to 'Industrie' and 'Handwerk' together and showed a manufacturing employment of 9·2 million in establishments of all sizes. There appears to be no information on the number employed in establishments with fewer than ten employees in 'Industrie'. One can therefore speak only approximately of the proportion of total industrial sales excluded from the calculations referred to in the text.

55 The comparison given in the text is, however, very crude and not nearly as satisfactory as that made with America on the basis of Censuses in each country. For example, it ignores the problem posed by steel (excluded as a nationalised industry from the British total, but included in the German total). Further, the sales of the hundred largest British enterprises as noted relate to industrial companies operating mainly in Britain (any companies operating mainly abroad or engaged in distribution, services, etc. are excluded; if they were not the British ratio would be higher still).

56 For example, K. D. George and T. S. Ward in *The Structure of Industry in the EEC*, Cambridge, Department of Applied Economics, 1975, p. 17, note that in 1963 the average of the four-firm concentration ratios for

forty-one industries was 30 per cent in the United Kingdom and 19 per cent in Germany.

57 Commission of the European Communities, Statistical Office, *Industrie-zensus 1963*, Luxembourg, 1969.

58 Though the EEC Censuses were carried out according to a central plan, there remain important differences in scope. To improve the comparability of the results, we made the following adjustments to the published EEC data (NICE reference numbers are given in brackets) because in some countries only parts of the relevant trades were included in the Censuses. Meat slaughtering (201), milk (202), grain milling etc. (205), bread, biscuits etc. (206), were excluded from the food industry (20). Millinery (237) and other textile industries (239) were excluded from the textile industry (23). The clothing industry (24) was excluded except for mechanical production of footwear (241) and leather and fur (245). The rubber, plastic and synthetic products industry (30) was excluded except for plastics (302). Car repairers (384) and other transport (389) were excluded from transport construction (38). Manufacture and repair of clocks (394), of musical instruments (396) and of toys and sports equipment (397), and other manufacturing (399) were excluded from miscellaneous manufacturing (39). Corresponding adjustments were made to the British and American Censuses for the comparisons in table 6.4. The proportion of Census employment so excluded amounts to about a fifth of the total (varying from 15 per cent in Britain to 28 per cent in the Netherlands).

It makes negligible difference in practice whether we take European statistics of 'enterprises' or of 'local units'; table 6.4 was based on the latter, since we wished to analyse these statistics in greater detail for other purposes.

59 A short discussion of current differences in European capital markets, with particular reference to their effects on gearing, is given by J. H. Coates and P. K. Woolley in their article, 'Corporate gearing in the EEC', *Journal of Business Finance & Accounting*, vol. 2, Spring 1975. See also J. M. Samuels, R. E. V. Groves and C. S. Goddard, *Company Finance in Europe*, London, Institute of Chartered Accountants in England and Wales, 1975.

60 It would not be right to conclude without a word on the pioneering international comparisons by Bain (1966). Two important differences in approach have to be noted. First, he is concerned with the share of a given number (for example, the eight largest firms) in selected industries in each country. Not surprisingly, in a smaller economy a given number of firms will account for a greater share of the total than in a larger country; thus he finds (p. 96) Italy more concentrated than France, and France more concentrated than the United States. On our approach in table 6.3 an attempt is made to allow for the size of the country by considering the employment in large firms in relation to total employment. Secondly, his approach is based on individual industries; this might seem superior to our aggregative approach, but this is not necessarily so,

since the industries for which he is able to obtain statistics tend to be those that are more concentrated and not necessarily representative of all industry.

Notes to chapter 7 (pp. 163–71)

1 It is known, for example that the great mass of small firms in Germany that come into the 'Handwerk' category provide a disproportionately large amount of the systematic training that is obligatory there for all 15–18 year olds, many of whom subsequently move into larger firms. It is also noteworthy that their training courses on technical subjects include instruction in the elements of business accounting, so that the needs of business are more widely appreciated.

2 A caution is perhaps in order here. Our analysis has been based mainly on data for Britain; were comparable data available for other countries it is conceivable that a similar model might be found to apply, but with different coefficients reflecting a different balance of forces.

3 See the chapter on industrial policy in the National Institute's forth-coming study of British economic policy since 1960.

4 There are some small exceptions, such as the denationalisation of the travel agents, Thos. Cook, and the Carlisle Brewery, but they do not really bear on the issue.

5 But neither should one overestimate the ability of a small body, such as a Monopolies Commission, to master the intricacies of the trades into which it is called to inquire and to find time to supervise the multitude of technicalities that are involved. For example, the manufacture of light bulbs was considered twice by the Commission (in 1951 and 1968) and on both occasions the limited length of the life of lamps was raised; eventually a mathematical argument was produced by the trade to justify limiting the life of lamps to 1000 hours. This was accepted by the Commission; yet it contained a mathematical error, and if this is cor-rected the optimum length of life may well be much greater (S. J. Prais, 'Economic life of incandescent lamps for domestic lighting', *Lighting Research & Technology*, vol. 6, no. 2, 1974, and 'The electric lamp mono-poly and the life of electric lamps', *Journal of Industrial Economics*, vol. 23, December 1974). Public control of a monopolistic industry cannot be expected to achieve the same results as open competition. The time available to a public supervisory body is inevitably too limited to permit a deep investigation of details such as this, though the public interest is as much affected by quality – in this case, length of life – as by price. The present position on this case is that there is no way of bringing about an alteration of the lamp industry's agreed standard on the life of a light bulb short of a third Monopolies Commission inquiry and, given the many other calls on the time of the Commission, it is not surprising that this matter is at present in limbo.

6 The size-brackets suggested here by way of illustration are chosen so as to leave the total yield of Corporation Tax roughly unchanged. About

200 companies would come into the top tax-rate and these are the companies that have had particularly easy access to the capital market. The majority of private companies, which have virtually no access to the new issue market for additional risk capital, would fall into the bottom tax-rate. The 1972 Finance Act provided lower rates of Corporation Tax where profits fell below £15,000 (with tapering relief up to £25,000); this measure was intended to avoid an excessive tax penalty for incorporation (many companies would otherwise have done better to give up limited liability and be taxed as partnerships) – it did not have in mind the long-term structural objectives considered here.

7 Exemptions from higher tax-rates might also be accorded in relation to those parts of a company's assets where technology demands a large plant, for example for plants employing more than 10,000 persons (but these are very rare – only fourteen were reported in the 1968 Census).

8 A similar problem arose in the United States: in 1969 a Tax Reform Act provided that interest ceased to be allowable as a deduction for tax when it related to large convertible debenture issues made in connection with a merger (see P. O. Steiner, *Mergers: motives, effects, policies*, Ann Arbor, University of Michigan Press, 1975, p. 87).

9 The Bolton Committee rejected the need for a preferential source of funds for small firms, but it took a narrow view. Perhaps a different conclusion would have been reached if greater weight had been given to the long-term trends in the supply of risk capital and the implications for the distribution of firm-sizes as a whole (that is to say, if rising concentration had been considered in the same general context).

10 The great pressure in the United States for even stricter controls is apparent in Senator P. A. Hart's proposals for a new Industrial Reorganization Commission to 'restructure' oligopolised trades; see 'Restructuring the oligopoly sector: the case for a new Industrial Reorganization Act', *Antitrust Law and Economics Review*, vol. 5, Summer 1972, and vol. 6, Fall 1972.

11 See p. 134. For the United States, Steiner (1975, pp. 288 *et seq.*) suggests that large mergers account for only about a tenth of the growth of giant enterprises.

Notes to appendix A (pp. 172–84)

1 See appendix E for references regarding the United States; for the United Kingdom, see Prais, 1957.

2 For a discussion of these matters in the American context see M. A. Adelman, 'The measurement of industrial concentration', *Review of Economics and Statistics*, vol. 33, November 1951, especially pp. 272–8.

3 See, for example, the comparisons in the Bolton Committee's *Report*, 1971, pp. 40–3, based on Census information.

4 This is based on a study of the 1951 Census which tabulates wages by establishment-size (regrettably not by enterprise-size); we assume that the differential found there for establishments employing over 500 corresponds to that for the hundred largest enterprises in 1963.

5 See G. W. Nutter, *The Extent of Enterprise Monopoly in the United States: 1899–1939*, University of Chicago Press, 1951; Berle and Means, 1932, pp. 343–4.

6 The rule regarding the overlap between manufacturing and non-manufacturing is set out, for example, in footnote (g) to *Census 1968*, vol. 158, p. 12, table 42; line 4 of footnote (b) to that table is inconsistent with the rule, but should be ignored.

7 Board of Trade, *Company Assets and Income in 1957*, London, HMSO, 1960.

8 Estimate based on *Census 1963*, vol. 131, p. 52 and vol. 132, p. 6.

9 Size-distributions of *firms* are available for each trade and for all factory trades combined, but these are not relevant here (it will be recalled that in the Census usage of those days a firm was a collection of establishments trading under the same name; it thus bore no necessary relation to an enterprise with all its subsidiaries).

10 *Census 1935. Final Summary Tables*, p. 5.

11 This includes an estimate for firms employing not more than ten persons, based on their employment and an assumed net output of £200 a head (see *Census 1935. Final Summary Tables*, p. 3).

12 From the 1958 Census (the one nearest to 1935 with the relevant information) it appears that the share of the hundred largest in net output, on a ranking by net output, exceeds by $3\frac{1}{2}$ per cent the same share when taken from the hundred largest ranked by employment (the shares are 32·5 and 31·4 per cent respectively).

13 To be precise, we interpolated between Hart's figures for 1924 and 1938 to obtain an estimate on the profits basis for 1935, and used that as the link. It was assumed that, for these large companies at any rate, the degree of consolidation of the accounts of subsidiaries did not change materially over the relevant periods. Accountants will be familiar with the subtle change brought about by the 1948 Companies Act between accounts that merely gave a 'true and correct' view and those that give a 'true and fair' view of the company's state; for our purposes we must hope that these early accounts were throughout consistently 'true' enough in aggregate not to distort the present comparisons.

14 Later estimates of profits of all manufacturing companies in this period are available in C. H. Feinstein's *National Income, Expenditure and Output of the United Kingdom, 1855–1965*, Cambridge University Press, 1972, and G. D. N. Worswick and D. G. Tipping's *Profits in the British Economy, 1909–1938*, Oxford, Blackwell, 1967. These series could have been used instead of those published in Hart's original article, but the net effect is slight and reduces the estimates for 1909 and 1924 given in the text by about 1 percentage point. We have preferred to rely on Hart's series to provide the link for the present study, since his work was primarily concerned with concentration, and we did not wish to lose the benefits of any adjustments he made to ensure consistency between the various figures for this purpose. I have benefited from correspondence with Dr L. Hannah (University of Essex) on this aspect.

15 The 'gross true income' of British firms operating abroad amounted to 15 per cent of that of all British firms in 1909, but to only 9 per cent by 1938; however, for predominantly manufacturing companies the shares would have been smaller (see Worswick and Tipping, 1967, pp. 86–7).

16 The profits of the hundred largest companies were taken from the Board of Trade's published lists (*Company Assets and Income in 1957*, and *Company Assets, Income and Finance in 1963*, London, HMSO, 1960 and 1965) which give gross incomes for 1957 and 1961–3; to make the results as comparable as possible with the Census, they were adjusted with respect to date by interpolation.

Notes to appendix B (pp. 185–90)

1 This section relies on the Interdepartmental Committee's *Guides to Official Sources: no. 6*, especially pp. 23 *et seq.*

2 Ibid. provides invaluable help in the comparison of the various Censuses; see also a recent article by E. Primorac, 'Censuses of production in the United Kingdom 1924–1958: an attempt at reconciliation', *Journal of the Royal Statistical Society* (series A), vol. 134, part 1, 1971.

3 A discussion of further details is given in the paper by Fessey and Browning in *Statistical News*, no. 13, May 1971. See also the relevant paragraphs in the 'Notes' published in the Census volumes for 1970–2.

Notes to appendix C (pp. 191–9)

1 The illustrative statistics for 1963 quoted in this appendix are taken from the revised figures published in the *Census 1968*, vol. 158, p. 10.

2 The latter term in this context is due to Aitchison and Brown (1957).

3 The Pareto curve also has some useful and simple relations between the original and the first-moment distributions but, as will be familiar, that curve is relevant only to the upper tail of a distribution.

4 In view of the many misunderstandings in the academic literature a further remark on goodness of fit may, however, be in order. In considering the general shape of frequency distributions we have, of course, in mind the properties of a large number of observations, and we would hardly expect to say anything very precise about, for example, only the four largest observations in a sample of a hundred, even if it were known that the sample came from a population that was precisely log-normal. In practice, since there are deviations from theoretical purity, a curve fitted to the central bulk of observations will be especially prone to exhibit deviations in the tails. I. H. Silbermann in 'On lognormality as a summary measure of concentration,' *American Economic Review*, vol. 57, September 1967, carried out a number of 'tests' of this type on American enterprise-size distributions and, not surprisingly, found that there were 'statistically significant' deviations from log-normality; regrettably we are not told in that study whether the deviations are of a size that would make them of economic or other practical significance, or whether they

are practically insignificant though detectable by refined tests. We are also not told how the theoretical curves were fitted in that study, a matter that is of some importance in evaluating the results.

5 The various transitions between common and natural logarithms may appear unnecessarily involved, but experience indicates that errors are reduced if the calculations are carried out as described.

Notes to appendix D (pp. 200–8)

1 The table was compiled on the basis of a full count for all enterprises having over 2000 employees, and on a sample basis for smaller enterprises as follows: 1 in 3 of enterprises with 500–2000 employees, 1 in 20 of those employing 100–500 and 1 in 50 of those employing 25–100. Size was measured according to employment in 1958. Special thanks are due to the Business Statistics Office for permission to reproduce this table here.

2 One could possibly estimate the missing frequencies by fitting a symmetrical distribution to the truncated data available, but the results would hardly be convincing. It is to be hoped that the Census authorities will continue compiling two-way size distributions, but it would be an advantage if in future the basis of the sample was the initial rather than the final year of the period, so as to permit the full information to be used in this analysis.

3 Singh and Whittington, 1967, p. 108; I. M. D. Little and A. C. Rayner, *Higgledy-piggledy Growth Again*, Oxford, Blackwell, 1966; A. C. Rayner, 'Effect of the length of the time period on serial correlation,' *Review of Economics and Statistics*, vol. 51, February 1969.

4 A recent paper by J. L. Eatwell, 'Growth, profitability and size' in R. Marris and A. Wood (eds.), *The Corporate Economy*, London, Macmillan, 1971, contains a useful bibliography of earlier studies in this field.

5 See the discussion of the alternative measures of the share of the largest firms in terms of employment, profits and net output in appendix A.

6 For the benefit of students who may otherwise be puzzled by the basic table on p. 58 of Utton's paper (1971), it may be noted here that the row headed 'zero' relates to births of firms and the column so headed relates to deaths.

7 S. J. Prais, 'The formal theory of social mobility,' *Population Studies*, vol. 9, July 1955.

8 I. G. Adelman, 'A stochastic analysis of the size distribution of firms,' *Journal of the American Statistical Association*, vol. 53, December 1958.

9 J. Steindl, *Random Processes and the Growth of Firms: a study of the Pareto law*, London, Griffin, 1965; D. G. Champernowne, *Uncertainty and Estimation in Economics*, Edinburgh, Oliver and Boyd, 1969.

10 J. S. Cramer, *Empirical Econometrics*, Amsterdam, North-Holland, 1969.

Notes to appendix E (pp. 209–15)

1 But another source, Bureau of the Census, *Enterprise Statistics 1967*, is not comparable, in that non-manufacturing plants are included if they are owned by a group predominantly engaged in manufacturing; that approach is, however, of interest from other points of view.

2 Taken from United States Department of Commerce, Bureau of the Census, *Historical Statistics of the United States: Colonial times to 1957*, Washington (DC), US Government Printing Office, 1960, p. 413, series P137, which is derived from Census returns.

3 From Kaplan, 2nd edn, 1964, p. 120, and allowing for the small change in the proportion of non-incorporated businesses.

4 Using W. F. Mueller's compilations of asset totals in United States Senate, *Hearings: Economic Concentration* (Part 1) pp. 120–1; quoted in Means, 1968, p. 354.

5 Federal Trade Commission, *Economic Report on Corporate Mergers*, Washington (DC), US Government Printing Office, 1969, p. 173.

6 An interesting discussion of the relative merits of these two measures appears in the United States Senate, *Hearings: Economic Concentration* (Part 1) on a paper by Means (pp. 25 *et seq.*), but the matter is not central to our interests here and did not seem worth pursuing in the light of other uncertainties.

7 The slightly greater rise in concentration in the period 1929–62 that is implied by Means' calculation is attributed by the Federal Trade Commission (1969, p. 174) to an increase in the extent of consolidation of subsidiaries in the accounts examined by Means; this presumably has been allowed for in the Federal Trade Commission's figures.

Virtually the same estimate (24 per cent) for 1929 is reached on using an alternative link, provided by Kaplan's lists of the hundred largest industrial companies for 1929 and 1960 (Kaplan, 1964, p. 120 *et seq.*) and the Census estimate for 1960.

8 D. Creamer, S. P. Dobrovolsky and I. Borenstein, *Capital in Manufacturing and Mining: its formation and financing*, Princeton University Press, 1960; the main results now appear in Bureau of the Census, *Historical Statistics of the United States*, series P14.

9 As given in Bureau of the Census, *Enterprise Statistics 1967*, Part I, p. 326, industry 33A.

Notes to appendix F (pp. 216–24)

1 This section is included here only because of the difficulty I had in finding any summary account of these matters in the literature. I hope it will not be found too superficial. For a fuller discussion on Europe generally the student may turn to H. J. Habakkuk and M. M. Postan (eds.), *The Industrial Revolutions and After* (2 vols.) Cambridge University Press, 1965, and M. M. Postan *An Economic History of Western Europe, 1945–64*, London, Methuen, 1967; for France and Germany there is J. H. Clap-

ham's *The Economic Development of France and Germany, 1815–1914* (4th edn), Cambridge University Press, 1945; for Sweden, E. F. Heckscher's *An Economic History of Sweden* (transl. G. Ohlin), Cambridge (Mass.), Harvard University Press, 1954; for Britain and Germany, D. S. Landes' 'The structure of enterprise in the nineteenth century: the cases of Britain and Germany' in *Rapports*, vol. 5, Uppsala, Comité International des Sciences Historiques, 1960; for Benelux, de Jong, 1971. More recent developments may be gleaned from the United States Senate, *Hearings: Economic Concentration* (Part 7).

2 H. A. Shannon, 'The coming of general limited liability', *Economic History*, vol. 2, January 1931.

3 See de Jong, 1971, pp. 48–51. The groups he mentions are Société Générale, Launoit (Cofinindus and Brufina), d'Anvers and Petrofina, Solvay-Jansen, Lambert and some smaller ones. The largest groups just named are all related in some way to the Société Générale and it is not clear how many independent groups there really are. Only the Solvay group's interests appear in the large concerns summarised in table 6.3. I have not been able to find any recent and reliable measure of the size of the Société Générale's interests (*Fortune* does not list any Belgian companies with over 40,000 employees aside from Solvay; four other Belgian companies are mentioned with between 900 and 37,000 employees), but cf. P. Readman, *The European Money Puzzle*, London, Michael Joseph, 1973, pp. 98–9, where some information is given on its assets (at nominal values?).

4 Marshall (1919, pp. 343 and 568), basing himself on the investigations of Calwer and Riesser, noted that the seven large German banks had representatives on the boards of 350 large industrial companies.

5 The further information here suggested as relevant was, however, possibly available to the Commission producing that report. A further governmental inquiry into the banks and their relations with industry is in progress and is due to report in 1977 (see an article by P. Norman in *The Times*, 13 January 1976). Information on equity stakes of more than 25 per cent are now made public and could be analysed further. S. Schattmann (in *The Times*, 20 January 1976) looked at the hundred largest companies and found that the banks had stakes in twenty-one of them. Heavy bank borrowings by industry are, no doubt, of even more significance in ensuring that the banker's voice is clearly heard at the industrialist's table.

6 Cf. Landes, 1960, p. 114.

7 See Postan, 1967, pp. 215–725, where a fuller account is given of postwar developments.

8 See Postan, 1967, p. 220, and Bernini's statement in the United States Senate, *Hearings: Economic Concentration* (Part 7), pp. 3552–64.

9 Ibid. p. 3557.

10 Ibid. p. 3562.

LIST OF WORKS CITED
IN FIRST IMPRESSION

I. BOOKS, ARTICLES AND PERIODICALS

AARONOVITCH, S. and SAWYER, M. C. 'The concentration of British manufacturing', *Lloyds Bank Review*, no. 114, October 1974, p. 14.

Accounting Standards Steering Committee. *Accounting for Changes in the Purchasing Power of Money*, London, 1973.

ADELMAN, I. G. 'A stochastic analysis of the size distribution of firms', *Journal of the American Statistical Association*, vol. 53, December 1958, p. 893.

ADELMAN, M. A. 'The measurement of industrial concentration', *Review of Economics and Statistics*, vol. 33, November 1951, p. 269.

— 'The Antimerger Act, 1950–1960', *American Economic Association Papers and Proceedings*, vol. 51, May 1961, p. 236.

Advertising Quarterly, London, Advertising Association.

AITCHISON, J. and BROWN, J. A. C. *The Lognormal Distribution*, Cambridge University Press, 1957.

ALEXANDER, S. S. 'The effect of size of manufacturing corporation on the distribution of the rate of return', *Review of Economics and Statistics*, vol. 31, August 1949, p. 229.

ALLEN, R. S., MILLER, J. A., DAMANT, D. C. and LEACH, J. H. C. 'Submission to the Royal Commission on the Distribution of Income and Wealth', *The Investment Analyst*, no. 41, May 1975, p. 4.

ARCHER, S. H. and FAERBER, L. G. 'Firm size and the cost of externally secured equity capital', *Journal of Finance*, vol. 21, March 1966, p. 69.

ARMSTRONG, A. and SILBERSTON, A. 'Size of plant, size of enterprise and concentration in British manufacturing industry, 1935–58', *Journal of the Royal Statistical Society* (series A), vol. 128, part 3, 1965, p. 395.

ARNDT, H. (ed.) *Die Konzentration in der Wirtschaft*, Berlin, Duncker and Humblot, 1971.

ASHTON, T. S. 'The growth of textile businesses in the Oldham district, 1884–1924', *Journal of the Royal Statistical Society*, vol. 89, May 1926, p. 567.

ASHTON, T. S. and CHAPMAN, S. J. 'The size of businesses, mainly in the textile industries', *Journal of the Royal Statistical Society*, vol. 77, April 1914, p. 469.

BAIN, J. S. *Barriers to New Competition: their character and consequences in manufacturing industries*, Cambridge (Mass.), Harvard University Press, 1956.

— *International Differences in Industrial Structure: eight nations in the 1950s*, New Haven, Yale University Press, 1966.

BANNOCK, G. *The Juggernauts*, London, Weidenfeld and Nicholson, 1971.

BARKER, T. C. *Pilkington Brothers and the Glass Industry*, London, George Allen & Unwin, 1960.

BARR, N. 'Real rates of return to financial assets since the war', *The Three Banks Review*, no. 107, September 1975, p. 23.

BENISHAY, H. 'Variability in earnings–price ratios of corporate equities', *American Economic Review*, vol. 51, March 1961, p. 81.

— 'Market preferences for characteristics of common stocks', *Economic Journal*, vol. 83, March 1973, p. 173.

BERLE, A. A. and MEANS, G. *The Modern Corporation and Private Property*, New York, Macmillan, 1932 (rev. edn, 1968).

BLACKABY, F. T. (ed.) *British Economic Policy since 1960*, Cambridge University Press (forthcoming).

BLAIR, J. M. 'Technology and size', *American Economic Association Papers and Proceedings*, vol. 38, May 1948, p. 121.

— *Economic Concentration: structure, behavior and public policy*, New York, Harcourt, Brace & World, 1972.

BLANK, D. M. 'Television advertising: the great discount illusion or Tony-pandy revisited', *Journal of Business*, vol. 41, January 1968, p. 10.

— 'Tonypandy once again', *Journal of Business*, vol. 42, January 1969, p. 104.

BLEASE, J. G. 'Institutional investors and the Stock Exchange', *District Bank Review*, no. 151, September 1964, p. 38.

BORDEN, N. H. *The Economic Effects of Advertising*, Chicago, Irwin, 1942.

BOYLE, S. E. 'Large industrial corporations and asset shares: comment', *American Economic Review*, vol. 61, March 1971, p. 163.

BOYLE, S. E. and McKENNA, J. P. 'Size mobility of the 100 and 200 largest U.S. manufacturing corporations: 1919–1964', *The Antitrust Bulletin*, vol. 15, Fall 1970, p. 505.

BRISTON, R. J. 'The impact of institutional investors on the London Stock Exchange' in *Institutional Investors and the London Stock Exchange*, London, British Accounting and Finance Association, 1972.

British Bureau of Television Advertising. 'Costing the television commercial', *BBTA Bulletin*, no. 18, January 1973, p. 7.

CABLE, J. 'Market structure, advertising policy and inter-market differences in advertising intensity' in Cowling (ed.), 1972, q.v.

CAIRNCROSS, A. K. *Introduction to Economics* (5th edn), London, Butterworth, 1973.

CHAMPERNOWNE, D. G. *Uncertainty and Estimation in Economics*, Edinburgh, Oliver and Boyd, 1969.

CHANDLER, A. D. (Jr) *Strategy and Structure: chapters in the history of the industrial enterprise*, Cambridge (Mass.), MIT Press, 1962.

CLAPHAM, J. H. *The Economic Development of France and Germany, 1815–1914* (4th edn), Cambridge University Press, 1945.

CLAYTON, G. *British Insurance*, London, Elek Books, 1971.

CLAYTON, G. and OSBORN, W. T. *Insurance Company Investment*, London, George Allen & Unwin, 1965.

COASE, R. H. 'The nature of the firm', *Economica* (new series), vol. 4, November 1937, p. 386.

COATES, J. H. and WOOLLEY, P. K. 'Corporate gearing in the EEC', *Journal of Business Finance & Accounting*, vol. 2, Spring 1975, p. 1.

COHEN, R. 'The abortive combine, 1906' in P. L. Cook and R. Cohen (eds.), *Effects of Mergers*, London, George Allen & Unwin, 1958.

COLLINS, N. R. and PRESTON, L. E. 'The size structure of the largest industrial firms, 1909–1958', *American Economic Review*, vol. 51, December 1961, p. 986.

Commission of Inquiry into Advertising. 'Report' (mimeographed), Labour Party, 1966.

COWLING, K. (ed.) *Market Structure and Corporate Behaviour: theory and empirical analysis of the firm*, London, Gray-Mills, 1972.

CRAMER, J. S. *Empirical Econometrics*, Amsterdam, North-Holland, 1969.

CREAMER, D., DOBROVOLSKY, S. P. and BORENSTEIN, I. *Capital in Manufacturing and Mining: its formation and financing*, Princeton University Press, 1960.

CRITCHLEY, R. A. *UK Advertising Statistics*, London, Advertising Association, 1972.

CUTLER, R. A. and WESTWICK, C. A. 'The impact of inflation accounting on the stock market', *Accountancy*, March 1973, p. 15.

DAVENPORT, M. 'Leverage and the cost of capital: some tests using British data', *Economica* (new series), vol. 38, May 1971, p. 136.

DAVIS, E. W. and YEOMANS, K. A. *Company Finance and the Capital Market: a study of the effects of firm size*, Cambridge University Press, 1974.

DE JONG, H. W. 'Concentration in Benelux' in Arndt (ed.), 1971, q.v.

Les Dossiers de l'Entreprise, Clichy, Société D'Études et De Publications Économiques (two-monthly).

DOYLE, P. 'Economic aspects of advertising: a survey', *Economic Journal*, vol. 78, September 1968, p. 570.

DU BOFF, R. B. 'The introduction of electric power in American manufacturing', *Economic History Review* (second series), vol. 20, December 1967, p. 509.

DYCKMAN, T. R. and STEKLER, H. O. 'Firm size and variability', *Journal of Industrial Economics*, vol. 13, June 1965, p. 214.

EATWELL, J. L. 'Growth, profitability and size: the empirical evidence' in R. Marris and A. Wood (eds.), *The Corporate Economy: growth, competition and innovative potential*, London, Macmillan, 1971.

EKELUND, R. B. and GRAMM, W. P. 'Advertising and concentration: some new evidence', *The Antitrust Bulletin*, vol. 15, Summer 1970, p. 243.

EKELUND, R. B. and MAURICE, C. 'An empirical investigation of advertising and concentration: comment', *Journal of Industrial Economics*, vol. 18, November 1969, p. 76.

ELLIOTT, D. and GRIBBIN, J. D. 'The abolition of cartels and structural change in the United Kingdom' (forthcoming).

EMMETT, B. P. 'The television and radio audience in Britain' in D. McQuail (ed.), *Sociology of Mass Communications. Selected readings*, Harmondsworth, Penguin, 1972.

EVELY, R. and LITTLE, I. M. D. *Concentration in British Industry*, Cambridge University Press, 1960.

FEINSTEIN, C. H. *National Income, Expenditure and Output of the United Kingdom, 1855–1965*, Cambridge University Press, 1972.

FELLER, W. *An Introduction to Probability Theory and its Application* (2nd edn), vol. II, New York, Wiley, 1966.

Fielding, Newsome-Smith & Co. *Company Share Quotations*, London, 1972.

FITZGERALD, P. *Industrial Combination in England* (2nd edn), London, Pitman, 1927.

FLORENCE, P. SARGANT. 'The size of the factory: a reply', *Economic Journal*, vol. 64, September 1954, p. 625.

— *The Logic of British and American Industry: a realistic analysis of economic structure and government* (3rd edn), London, Routledge and Kegan Paul, 1972.

Forbes, New York, Forbes Inc. (twice monthly)

Fortune, Chicago, Time Inc. (monthly)

FRANKEL, M. *British and American Manufacturing Productivity*, Urbana, University of Illinois Press, 1957.

GALTON, F. *Hereditary Genius*, London, Macmillan, 1869 (reprinted 1925).

GEORGE, K. D. 'Changes in British industrial concentration, 1951–1958', *Journal of Industrial Economics*, vol. 15, July 1967, p. 200.

GEORGE, K. D. and WARD, T. S. *The Structure of Industry in the EEC: an international comparison*, Department of Applied Economics, Cambridge University, 1975.

GIBRAT, R. *Les Inégalités Économiques*, Paris, Sirey, 1931.

GLOVER, K. F. 'Statistics of the transport of goods by road', *Journal of the Royal Statistical Society* (series A), vol. 123, part 2, 1960, p. 107.

GORDON, R. A. *Business Leadership in the Large Corporation*, Washington (DC), Brookings Institution, 1945.

GRANT, A. T. K. *A Study of the Capital Market in Britain from 1919–1936* (2nd edn), London, Frank Cass, 1967.

GRIBBIN, J. D. 'The conglomerate merger', *Applied Economics*, vol. 8, March 1976, p. 19.

GRILICHES, Z. and RINGSTAD, V. *Economies of Scale and the Form of the Production Function*, Amsterdam, North-Holland, 1971.

HABAKKUK, H. J. and POSTAN, M. M. (eds.) *The Industrial Revolutions and After: incomes, population and technological change* (2 vols.), Cambridge University Press, 1965.

HALDI, J. and WHITCOMB, D. 'Economies of scale in industrial plants', *Journal of Political Economy*, vol. 75, August 1967, p. 373.

HANNAH, L. 'Managerial innovation and the rise of the large-scale company', *Economic History Review* (second series), vol. 27, May 1974, p. 252.

— *The Corporate Economy* (forthcoming).

HART, P. A. 'Restructuring the oligopoly sector: the case for a new Industrial Reorganization Act', *Antitrust Law and Economics Review*, vol. 5, Summer 1972, p. 32, and vol. 6, Fall 1972, p. 47.

HART, P. E. 'Business concentration in the United Kingdom', *Journal of the Royal Statistical Society* (series A), vol. 123, part 1, 1960, p. 50.

— 'Concentration in the United Kingdom' in Arndt (ed.), 1971, q.v.

HART, P. E. and CLARKE, R. *Concentration in Manufacturing Industries in the United Kingdom, 1958–68*, Cambridge University Press (forthcoming).

HART, P. E. and PRAIS, S. J. 'The analysis of business concentration: a statistical approach', *Journal of the Royal Statistical Society* (series A), vol. 119, part 2, 1956, p. 150.

HART, P. E., UTTON, M. A. and WALSHE, G. *Mergers and Concentration in British Industry*, Cambridge University Press, 1973.

HECKSCHER, E. F. *An Economic History of Sweden* (transl. G. Ohlin), Cambridge (Mass.), Harvard University Press, 1954.

HENDERSON, R. F. *The New Issue Market and the Finance of Industry*, Cambridge, Bowes & Bowes, 1951.

— 'Capital issues' in Tew and Henderson (eds.), 1959, q.v.

Hoppenstedt. *Handbook of Large Enterprises in Germany* (annual).

HYMER, S. and PASHIGIAN, P. 'Firm size and rate of growth', *Journal of Political Economy*, vol. 70, December 1962, p. 556.

— 'Firm size and rate of growth: reply', *Journal of Political Economy*, vol. 72, February 1964, p. 83.

JACQUEMIN, A. P. and DE JONG, H. W. (eds.) *Markets, Corporate Behaviour and the State*, The Hague, Nijhoff, 1976.

Jane's Major Companies of Europe, London (annual).

JEWKES, J. 'The size of the factory', *Economic Journal*, vol. 62, June 1952, p. 237.

KALDOR, N. 'The economic aspects of advertising', *Review of Economic Studies*, vol. 18, no. 1, 1949–51, p. 1

KALDOR, N. and SILVERMAN, R. *A Statistical Analysis of Advertising Expenditure and of the Revenue of the Press*, Cambridge University Press, 1948.

KALECKI, M. 'On the Gibrat distribution', *Econometrica*, vol. 13, April 1945, p. 161.

KAPLAN, A. D. H. *Big Enterprise in a Competitive System*, Washington (DC), Brookings Institution, 1954 (2nd edn, 1964).

KING, M. A. 'The United Kingdom profits crisis: myth or reality?', *Economic Journal*, vol. 85, March 1975, p. 33.

KLEMM, F. *A History of Western Technology* (transl. D. W. Singer), London, George Allen & Unwin, 1959.

KRAVIS, I. B., KENESSY, Z., HESTON, A. and SUMMERS, R. *A System of International Comparisons of Gross Product and Purchasing Power*, Baltimore, Johns Hopkins University Press, 1975.

KUEHN, D. *Takeovers and the Theory of the Firm. An empirical analysis of the United Kingdom 1957–69*, London, Macmillan, 1974.

LANDES, D. S. 'The structure of enterprise in the nineteenth century: the cases of Britain and Germany' in *Rapports*, vol. 5, Uppsala, Comité International des Sciences Historiques, 1960.

LARNER, R. J. 'Ownership and control in the 200 largest nonfinancial corporations, 1929 and 1963', *American Economic Review*, vol. 56, September 1966, p. 777.

— *Management Control and the Large Corporation*, New York, Dunellen, 1970.

LEACH, J. H. C. 'The role of the institutions in the UK ordinary share market', *The Investment Analyst*, no. 31, December 1971, p. 33, and no. 32, May 1972, p. 37.

LEAK, H. and MAIZELS, A. 'The structure of British industry', *Journal of the Royal Statistical Society* (series A), vol. 108, parts 1–2, 1945, p. 142.

LEONARD, W. N. 'Network television pricing: a comment', *Journal of Business*, vol. 42, January 1969, p. 93.

LEVY, Haim and SARNAT, M. 'Diversification, portfolio analysis and the uneasy case for conglomerate mergers', *Journal of Finance*, vol. 25, September 1970, p. 795.

LEVY, Hermann. *Monopoly and Competition, a study of English industrial organisation*, London, Macmillan, 1911.

LINTNER, J. 'Expectations, mergers and equilibrium in purely competitive securities markets', *American Economic Association Papers and Proceedings*, vol. 61, May 1971, p. 101.

LITTLE, I. M. D. and RAYNER, A. C. *Higgledy-piggledy Growth Again: an investigation of the predictability of company earnings and dividends in the UK, 1951–1961*, Oxford, Blackwell, 1966.

MACRAE, N. *The London Capital Market: its structure, strains and management*, London, Staples, 1955.

MACROSTY, H. W. *The Trust Movement in British Industries*, London, Longmans, 1907.

MANDLEBROT, B. 'The variation of certain speculative prices', *Journal of Business*, vol. 36, October 1963, p. 394.

MANN, H. M., HENNING, J. A. and MEEHAN, J. W. (Jr) 'Advertising and concentration: an empirical investigation', *Journal of Industrial Economics*, vol. 16, November 1967, p. 34.

MANN, H. M. and MEEHAN, J. W. (Jr) 'Advertising and concentration: new data and an old problem', *The Antitrust Bulletin*, vol. 16, Spring 1971, p. 101.

MARKOWITZ, H. M. *Portfolio Selection: efficient diversification of investments*, New York, Wiley, 1959.

MARQUAND, H. A. *The Dynamics of Industrial Combination*, London, Longmans, 1931.

MARRIS, R. 'Why economics needs a theory of the firm', *Economic Journal*, vol. 82, March 1972 (supplement), p. 322.

MARSHALL, A. 'Some aspects of competition', Presidential Address to the Economic Science and Statistics section of the British Association, Leeds, 1890 (quoted in A. C. Pigou, *Memorials of Alfred Marshall*, London, Macmillan, 1925).

— *Principles of Economics* (6th edn), London, Macmillan, 1910 (8th edn, 1920) (9th *variorum* edn, ed. C. W. Guillebaud, 1961).

— *Industry and Trade*, London, Macmillan, 1919 (4th edn, 1923).

MEANS, G. C. 'Statistical Appendix' in Berle and Means (eds.), rev. edn, 1968, q.v.

MEEKS, G. and WHITTINGTON, G. 'Financing of quoted companies in the United Kingdom' (report to the Diamond Commission, summarised as Appendix Q to Diamond Commission, *Report No. 2*, q.v.)

MERMELSTEIN, D. 'Large industrial corporations and asset shares', *American Economic Review*, vol. 59, September 1969, p. 531.

— 'Large industrial corporations and asset shares: reply', *American Economic Review*, vol. 61, March 1971, p. 168.

MERRETT, A. J., HOWE, M. and NEWBOULD, G. D. *Equity Issues and the London Capital Market*, London, Longmans, 1967.

MERRIMAN, J. H. H. 'Engineering innovation in a service industry: Post Office telecommunications', *Proceedings of the Institution of Electrical Engineers*, vol. 122, January 1975, p. 1.

METWALLY, M. 'A comparison between representative size of plant in manufacturing industries in industrialised and less-industrialised countries', *Yorkshire Bulletin of Economic and Social Research*, vol. 17, November 1965, p. 139.

MORGAN, E. V. 'Personal saving and the capital market', *District Bank Review*, no. 163, September 1967, p. 3.

MORGAN, E. V. and TAYLOR, C. 'The relationship between the size of joint stock companies and the yield on their shares', *Economica* (new series), vol. 24, May 1957, p. 116.

MORGAN, E. V. and THOMAS, W. A. *The Stock Exchange: its history and functions*, London, Elek Books, 1962.

MORRIS, R. C. *Corporate Reporting Standards and the 4th Directive*, London, Institute of Chartered Accountants in England and Wales, 1974.

MOYLE, J. *The Owners of Quoted Ordinary Shares: a survey for 1963*, London, Chapman & Hall, 1966.

— *The Pattern of Ordinary Share Ownership 1950–1970*, Cambridge University Press, 1971.

National Institute of Economic and Social Research. *Company Income and Finance, 1949–53*, London, 1956.

NEALE, A. D. *The Antitrust Laws of the U.S.A.* (2nd edn), Cambridge University Press, 1970.

NELSON, R. L. *Concentration in the Manufacturing Industries of the United States: a midcentury report*, New Haven, Yale University Press, 1963.

NIEHANS, J. 'An index of the size of industrial establishments', *International Economic Papers*, no. 8, 1959, p. 122.

NORDHAUS, W. D. *Invention, Growth and Welfare*, Cambridge (Mass.), MIT Press, 1969.

NUTTER, G. W. *The Extent of Enterprise Monopoly in the United States: 1899–1939*, University of Chicago Press, 1951.

OLIVER, J. L. *The Development and Structure of the Furniture Industry*, Oxford, Pergamon, 1966.

PASHIGIAN, B. P. 'Market concentration in the United States and Great Britain', *Journal of Law and Economics*, vol. 11, October 1968, p. 299.

PAYNE, P. L. 'The emergence of the large-scale company in Great Britain 1870–1914', *Economic History Review* (second series), vol. 20, December 1967, p. 519.

PEN, J. *Income Distribution*, London, Allen Lane, 1971.

PETERMAN, J. L. 'The Clorox case and the television rate structures', *Journal of Law and Economics*, vol. 11, October 1968, p. 321.

PIGOU, A. C. 'Marshall's "Industry and Trade"', *Economic Journal*, vol. 29, December 1919, p. 443.

PILKINGTON, N. 'Inflation accounting – treatment of monetary items', *The Investment Analyst*, no. 39, September 1974, p. 30.

POSTAN, M. M. *An Economic History of Western Europe 1945–64*, London, Methuen, 1967.

PRAIS, S. J. 'The formal theory of social mobility', *Population Studies*, vol. 9, July 1955, p. 72.

— 'The financial experience of giant companies', *Economic Journal*, vol. 67, June 1957, p. 249.

— 'The statistical conditions for a change in business concentration', *Review of Economics and Statistics*, vol. 40, August 1958, p. 268.

— 'Size, growth and concentration' in Tew and Henderson (eds.), 1959, q.v.

— 'Economic life of incandescent lamps for domestic lighting', *Lighting Research & Technology*, vol. 6, no. 2, 1974, p. 101.

— 'A new look at the growth of industrial concentration', *Oxford Economic Papers*, vol. 26, July 1974, p. 273.

— 'The electric lamp monopoly and the life of electric lamps', *Journal of Industrial Economics*, vol. 23, December 1974, p. 153.

PRATTEN, C. F. *Economies of Scale in Manufacturing Industry*, Cambridge University Press, 1971.

PRIMORAC, E. 'Censuses of production in the United Kingdom 1924–1958: an attempt at reconciliation', *Journal of the Royal Statistical Society* (series A), vol. 134, part 1, 1971, p. 39.

Prudential Assurance Co. Ltd. *124th Annual Report and Statement of Accounts, 1972*, London.

PRYOR, F. L. 'Size of establishments in manufacturing', *Economic Journal*, vol. 82, June 1972, p. 547.

RAYNER, A. C. 'Effect of the length of the time period on serial correlation', *Review of Economics and Statistics*, vol. 51, February 1969, p. 107.

READMAN, P. *The European Money Puzzle*, London, Michael Joseph, 1973.

REVELL, J. *The Wealth of the Nation, the national balance sheet of the United Kingdom, 1957–1961*, Cambridge Universiy Press, 1967.

ROBERTSON, D. H. *The Control of Industry*, London, Nisbet, and Cambridge University Press, 1923 (rev. edn with S. R. Dennison, 1960).

— *Lectures on Economic Principles*, vol. I, London, Staples, 1957.

ROE, A. R. *The Financial Interdependence of the Economy 1957–1966*, London, Chapman & Hall, 1971.

ROSENBLUTH, G. 'Measures of concentration' in National Bureau of Economic Research, *Business Concentration and Price Policy*, Princeton University Press, 1955.

ROSTAS, L. *Comparative Productivity in British and American Industry*, Cambridge University Press, 1948.

ROTHMAN, J. *An Analysis of New Issues*, London, Leopold Joseph & Sons Ltd, 1973.

SAMUELS, J. M. 'Size and growth of firms', *Review of Economic Studies*, vol. 32, April 1965, p. 105.

SAMUELS, J. M. and CHESHER, A. D. 'Growth, survival and size of companies 1960–9' in Cowling (ed.), 1972, q.v.

SAMUELS, J. M., GROVES, R. E. V. and GODDARD, C. S. *Company Finance in Europe*, London, Institute of Chartered Accountants in England and Wales, 1975.

SAMUELS, J. M. and SMYTH, D. J. 'Profits, profits' variability and firm size', *Economica* (new series), vol. 35, May 1968, p. 127.

SAMUELSON, P. A. 'Rational theory of warrant pricing' in P. Cootner (ed.), *The Random Character of Stock Market Prices*, Cambridge (Mass.), MIT Press, 1964.

SAWYER, M. C. 'Concentration in British manufacturing industry', *Oxford Economic Papers*, vol. 23, November 1971, p. 352.

SCHERER, F. M. 'Firm size, market structure, opportunity and the output of patented inventions', *American Economic Review*, vol. 55, December 1965, p. 1097.

— *Industrial Market Structure and Economic Performance*, Chicago, Rand McNally, 1970.

— 'The determinants of industrial plant sizes in six nations', *Review of Economics and Statistics*, vol. 55, May 1973, p. 135.

— 'The determinants of multi-plant operation in six nations and twelve industries', *Kyklos*, vol. 27, fasc. 1, 1974, p. 124.

SCHMALENSEE, R. *The Economics of Advertising*, Amsterdam, North-Holland, 1972.

SCHNABEL, M. 'A note on advertising and industrial concentration', *Journal of Political Economy*, vol. 78, September/October 1970, p. 1191.

SHANNON, H. A. 'The coming of general limited liability', *Economic History*, vol. 2, January 1931, p. 267.

SHEPHERD, W. G. 'A comparison of industrial concentration in the United States and Britain', *Review of Economics and Statistics*, vol. 43, February 1961, p. 70.

— 'Changes in British industrial concentration 1951–1958', *Oxford Economic Papers*, vol. 18, March 1966, p. 126.

SILBERMANN, I. H. 'On lognormality as a summary measure of concentration', *American Economic Review*, vol. 57, September 1967, p. 807.

SILBERSTON, A. 'Economies of scale in theory and practice', *Economic Journal*, vol. 82, March 1972 (supplement), p. 390.

SIMON, J. L. *Issues in the Economics of Advertising*, Urbana, University of Illinois Press, 1970.

SINGH, A. *Take-overs, their relevance to the stock market and the theory of the firm*, Cambridge University Press, 1971.

SINGH, A. and WHITTINGTON, G. *Growth, Profitability and Valuation*, Cambridge University Press, 1967.

STAPLETON, R. C. *The Theory of Corporate Finance*, London, Harrap, 1970.

STEINDL, J. *Random Processes and the Growth of Firms: a study of the Pareto law*, London, Griffin, 1965.

STEINER, P. O. *Mergers: motives, effects, policies*, Ann Arbor, University of Michigan Press, 1975.

STEKLER, H. O. 'The variability of profitability with size of firm', *Journal of the American Statistical Association*, vol. 59, December 1964, p. 1183.

STIGLER, G. J. 'Monopoly and oligopoly by merger', *American Economic Association Papers and Proceedings*, vol. 40, May 1950, p. 23.

— 'The statistics of monopoly and merger', *Journal of Political Economy*, vol. 64, February 1956, p. 33.

— 'The economies of scale', *Journal of Law and Economics*, vol. 1, October 1958, p. 54.

Stock Exchange. *Statistics Relating to Securities Quoted on the London Stock Exchange*, London (quarterly).

Stock Exchange Official Year-Book, Croydon, Thomas Skinner and Co.

SWANN, D., O'BRIEN, D. P., MAUNDER, W. P. and HOWE, W. S. *Competition in British Industry: restrictive practices legislation in theory and practice*, London, George Allen & Unwin, 1974.

TELSER, L. G. 'Advertising and competition', *Journal of Political Economy*, vol. 72, December 1964, p. 541.

— 'On the regulation of industry: a note', *Journal of Political Economy*, vol. 77, December 1969, p. 937.

TEW, B. and HENDERSON, R. F. (eds.) *Studies in Company Finance*, Cambridge University Press, 1959.

THOMAS, W. A. *The Provincial Stock Exchanges*, London, Frank Cass, 1974.

The Times 1000, London, Times Newspapers Ltd (annual).

TOBIN, J. 'Comment on Borch and Feldstein', *Review of Economic Studies*, vol. 36, January 1969, p. 13.

TORNQUIST, G. *Contact Requirements and Travel Facilities*, Department of Geography, Lund University, 1973.

TORNQUIST, G., NORDBECK, S., RYSTEDT, B. and GOULD, P. *Multiple Location Analysis*, Department of Geography, Lund University, 1971.

TURNER, J. F. *Finding the Cash to Meet Estate Duty*, London, Estate Duties Investment Trust Ltd, 1970.

UTTON, M. A. 'The effect of mergers on concentration: UK manufacturing industry, 1954–65', *Journal of Industrial Economics*, vol. 20, November 1971, p. 42.

— 'Some features of the early merger movements in British manufacturing industry', *Business History*, vol. 14, January 1972, p. 51.

— 'Aggregate versus market concentration', *Economic Journal*, vol. 84, March 1974, p. 150.

WALKER, G. *Road and Rail: an enquiry into the economics of competition and state control*, London, George Allen & Unwin, 1942.

WALSHE, G. *Recent Trends in Monopoly in Great Britain*, Cambridge University Press, 1974.

WHITTINGTON, G. *The Prediction of Profitability and Other Studies of Company Behaviour*, Cambridge University Press, 1971.

WILLIAMSON, O. E. *Corporate Control and Business Behavior: an inquiry into the effects of organizational form on enterprise behavior*, Englewood Cliffs (NJ), Prentice Hall, 1970.

WIPPERN, R. F. 'Financial structure and the value of the firm', *Journal of Finance*, vol. 21, December 1966, p. 615.

WORSWICK, G. D. N. 'On the benefits of being denied the opportunity to "go shopping"', *Bulletin of the Oxford University Institute of Statistics*, vol. 23, August 1961, p. 271.

WORSWICK, G. D. N. and TIPPING, D. G. *Profits in the British Economy, 1909–1938*, Oxford, Blackwell, 1967.

WRIGHT, J. F. 'The capital market and the finance of industry' in G. D. N. Worswick and P. H. Ady (eds.), *The British Economy in the Nineteen-Fifties*, Oxford, Clarendon Press, 1962.

II. OFFICIAL PUBLICATIONS

(There are a great many general references to the United Kingdom Censuses of Production and the United States Censuses of Manufactures, but the various volumes quoted are not included in these lists.)

(a) *United Kingdom*

Bank of England. 'The financial institutions', *Bank of England Quarterly Bulletin*, vol. 10, December 1970, p. 419; vol. 11, March 1971, p. 48, and June 1971, p. 199.

British Transport Commission. *Annual Report*.

Central Statistical Office. *Standard Industrial Classification*, London, HMSO, 1958 and 1968.

— 'Acquisitions and amalgamations of quoted companies, 1954–1961', *Economic Trends*, no. 114, April 1963, p. vi.

— 'Acquisitions and amalgamations of quoted companies, 1962–1963', *Economic Trends*, no. 145, November 1965, p. xx.

— *National Accounts Statistics: sources and methods* (ed. R. Maurice), London, HMSO, 1968.

— 'Role of the personal sector in the flow of funds in the United Kingdom' by L. S. Berman, *Economic Trends*, no. 193, November 1969, p. ix.

— 'The statistical unit in business inquiries' by M. C. Fessey and H. E. Browning, *Statistical News*, no. 13, May 1971, p. 1.

— 'Structure of company financing' by J. L. Walker, *Economic Trends*, no. 263, September 1975, p. 96.

— 'The development of a central register of businesses' by D. R. Lewis, *Statistical News*, no. 31, November 1975, p. 7.

— *Economic Trends* (monthly).

— *Financial Statistics* (monthly).

— *Monthly Digest of Statistics*.

— *National Income and Expenditure* (annual).

— *Statistical News* (quarterly).

Department of Economic Affairs. *The Industrial Reorganisation Corporation* Cmnd 2889, London, HMSO, 1966.
— *Industrial Reorganisation Corporation. Report and accounts for the year ended March 31, 1969*, London, HMSO, 1969.
Department of Industry. *Business Monitor, Miscellaneous series:*
   M3: company finance (annual).
   M5: insurance companies and private pension funds (quarterly).
Interdepartmental Committee on Social and Economic Research. *Guides, to Official Sources: no. 6, Census of Production Reports*, London, HMSO, 1961.
Monopolies [and Mergers] Commission. *Report on the Supply of Cigarettes and Tobacco, and of Cigarette and Tobacco Machinery*, London, HMSO, 1961.
— *Household Detergents. Report on the supply of household detergents*, London, HMSO, 1966.
— *Breakfast Cereals. A report on the supply of ready cooked breakfast cereals*, London, HMSO, 1974.
— *Boots Company Limited and the House of Fraser Limited. Report on the proposed merger*, London, HMSO 1974.
National Economic Development Office:
   Mechanical Engineering EDC. *Inflation and Company Accounts in Mechanical Engineering*, London, 1973.
— *Finance for Investment. A study of methods available for financing investment*, London, 1975.
Royal Commission on Taxation of Profits and Income. *Final Report*, Cmd 9474, London, HMSO, 1955.
Royal Commission on the Distribution of Income and Wealth [the Diamond Commission]. *Report No. 2: Income from Companies and its Distribution*, Cmnd 6172, London, HMSO, 1975.
Ministry of Technology. *Industrial Reorganisation Corporation. Report and accounts for the year ended March 31, 1970*, London, HMSO, 1970.
Board of Trade. *Company Assets and Income in 1957*, London, HMSO, 1960.
— *Company Assets, Income and Finance in 1963*, London, HMSO, 1965.
Department of Trade and Industry. *Report of the Committee of Inquiry on Small Firms* [the Bolton Report], Cmnd 4811, London, HMSO, 1971.
   Research Report No. 1: The Small Firm in the Road Haulage Industry by B. T. Bayliss, London, HMSO, 1971.
   Research Report No. 4: Financial Facilities for Small Firms by D. Lees *et al.*, London, HMSO, 1971.
   Research Report No. 16: A Postal Questionnaire Survey of Small Firms. An analysis of financial data by M. Tamari, London, HMSO, 1972.
— *Trade and Industry* (weekly).
Treasury. *Report of the Committee on Finance and Industry* [the Macmillan Report], Cmd 3897, London, HMSO, 1931.
— *Committee on the Working of the Monetary System. Report* [the Radcliffe Report], Cmnd 827, London, HMSO, 1959.
— *Reform of Corporation Tax*, Cmnd 4955, London, HMSO, 1972.
— *Inflation Accounting. Report of the Inflation Accounting Committee* [the Sandilands Report], Cmnd 6225, London, HMSO, 1975.

(b) *United States*

Department of Commerce, Bureau of the Census. *Historical Statistics of the United States: Colonial times to 1957*, Washington (DC), US Government Printing Office, 1960.
— *Census of Manufactures 1963. Special Report: concentration ratios in manufacturing*, Part II, Washington (DC), US Government Printing Office, 1967.
— *Census of Manufactures 1967. Special Report: concentration ratios in manufacturing*, Part I, Washington (DC), US Government Printing Office, 1970.
— *Enterprise Statistics 1967. Part I: General Report on Industrial Organization*, Washington (DC), US Government Printing Office, 1972.
Executive Office of the President, Office of Management and Budgets. *Standard Industrial Classification Manual*, Washington (DC), US Government Printing Office, 1967.
Federal Trade Commission. *Economic Report on Corporate Mergers*, Washington (DC), US Government Printing Office, 1969.
— *Economic Report on Conglomerate Merger Performance*, Washington (DC), US Government Printing Office, 1973.
Department of Justice. 'Merger Guidelines' (issued 1968).
Securities and Exchange Commission. *Institutional Investor Study Report*, Washington (DC), US Government Printing Office, 1971.
Senate Committee on the Judiciary, Subcommittee on Antitrust and Monopoly. *Hearings: Economic Concentration* (Parts 1–7), Washington (DC), US Government Printing Office, 1964–8.

(c) *West Germany*

Deutscher Bundestag. *Bericht über das Ergebnis einer Untersuchung der Konzentration in der Wirtschaft*, Drucksache IV/2320, Bonn, 1964.
Statistisches Bundesamt. *Statistiches Jahrbuch*.

(d) *International*

Commission of the European Communities:
   Statistical Office. *Industriezensus 1963*, Luxembourg, 1969.
   — *Coordinated Annual Inquiry into Industrial Activity in the Member States of the European Communities*, Luxembourg, 1972.
   — 'Council directive of 6 June 1972 concerning coordinated annual surveys of industrial activity', *Official Journal of the European Communities*, 10 June 1972, p. 523.
   — *Proposal for a Regulation (EEC) of the Council on the Control of Concentration between Undertakings*, Brussels, 1973.
International Labour Office. *Yearbook of Labour Statistics*.
Organisation for European Economic Co-operation. *A Comparison of National Output and Productivity* by D. Paige and G. Bombach, Paris, 1959.

United Nations:
  Economic and Social Council. *The Statistical Unit in Economic Inquiries*,
  New York, 1960.
  Statistical Office. *Statistical Papers M54: Recommendations for the 1973 World
  Programme of Industrial Statistics*. Part III: *Organization and Conduct of
  Industrial Censuses*, New York, 1972.
  — *Monthly Bulletin of Statistics*.

INDEX

RECENT PUBLICATIONS FOR THE NATIONAL INSTITUTE OF ECONOMIC AND SOCIAL RESEARCH BY THE CAMBRIDGE UNIVERSITY PRESS

ECONOMIC AND SOCIAL STUDIES

XXVI *Urban Development in Britain: Standards, Costs and Resources, 1964–2004*
By P. A. STONE. Vol. I: *Population Trends and Housing*. 1970. pp. 436. £14.75 net.

XXVII *The Framework of Regional Economics in the United Kingdom*
By A. J. BROWN. 1972. pp. 372. £15.00 net.

XXVIII *The Structure, Size and Costs of Urban Settlements*
By P. A. STONE. 1973. pp. 304. £12.00 net.

XXIX *The Diffusion of New Industrial Processes: An International Study*
Edited by L. NABSETH and G. F. RAY. 1974. pp. 346. £13.50 net.

XXXI *British Economic Policy 1960–74*
Edited by F. T. BLACKABY. 1978. pp. 710. £24.00 net.

XXXII *Industrialisation and the Basis for Trade*
By R. A. BATCHELOR, R. L. MAJOR and A. D. MORGAN. 1980. pp. 372 £17.50 net

OCCASIONAL PAPERS

XXV *The Analysis and Forecasting of the British Economy*
By M. J. C. SURREY. 1971. pp. 120. £5.25 net.

XXVI *Mergers and Concentration in British Industry*
By P. E. HART, M. A. UTTON and G. WALSHE. 1973. pp. 190. £7.25 net.

XXVII *Recent Trends in Monopoly in Great Britain*
By G. WALSHE. 1974. pp. 156. £6.75 net.

XXVIII *Cyclical Indicators for the Postwar British Economy*
By D. J. O'DEA. 1975. pp. 184. £8.10 net.

XXIX *Poverty and Progress in Britain, 1953–73*
By G. C. FIEGEHEN, P. S. LANSLEY and A. D. SMITH. 1977. pp. 192. £8.50 net.

XXX *The Innovation Process in the Energy Industries*
By G. F. RAY and L. UHLMANN. 1979. pp. 132. £7.50 net.

XXXI *Diversification and Competition*
By M. A. UTTON. 1979. pp. 124. £6.95 net.

XXXII *Concentration in British Industry, 1935–75*
By P. E. HART and R. CLARKE. 1980. pp. 178. £10.00 net.

NIESR STUDENTS' EDITION

1 *Growth and Trade* (abridged from *Industrial Growth and World Trade*)
By A. MAIZELS. 1970. pp. 312 £4.75 net.

2 *The Antitrust Laws of the U.S.A.* (2nd edition, unabridged)
By A. D. NEALE. 1970. pp. 544. £7.25 net.

4 *British Economic Policy, 1960–74: Demand Management*
(abridged from *British Economic Policy, 1960–74*)
Edited by F. T. BLACKABY. 1979. pp. 472. £7.50 net.

REGIONAL PAPERS

1 *The Anatomy of Regional Activity Rates* by JOHN BOWERS, and *Regional Social Accounts for the United Kingdom* by V. H. WOODWARD. 1970. pp. 192. £5.50 net.

2 *Regional Unemployment Differences in Great Britain* by P. C. CHESHIRE and *Interregional Migration Models and their Application to Great Britain* by R. WEEDEN. 1973. pp. 118. £5.50 net.

3 *Unemployment, Vacancies and the Rate of Change of Earnings: A Regional Analysis* by A. E. WEBB, and *Regional Rates of Employment Growth: An Analysis of Variance Treatment* by R. WEEDEN. 1974. pp. 114. £5.50 net.

Published by

HEINEMANN EDUCATIONAL BOOKS

AN INCOMES POLICY FOR BRITAIN

Edited by FRANK BLACKABY. 1972. pp. 260. £4.00 net.

THE UNITED KINGDOM ECONOMY

By the NIESR. 4th edn. 1979. pp. 128. £1.80 net.

DEMAND MANAGEMENT

Edited by MICHAEL POSNER. 1978. pp. 256. £4.50 (paperback) net.

DE-INDUSTRIALISATION

Edited by FRANK BLACKABY. 1979. pp. 282. £9.50 (hardback), £5.50 (paperback) net.

BRITAIN'S TRADE AND EXCHANGE-RATE POLICY

Edited by ROBIN MAJOR. 1979. pp. 240. £9.75 (hardback), £5.50 (paperback) net.

Available from booksellers

———————————

THE NATIONAL INSTITUTE OF ECONOMIC AND
SOCIAL RESEARCH

publishes regularly

THE NATIONAL INSTITUTE ECONOMIC REVIEW

A quarterly analysis of the general economic situation in the United Kingdom and the world overseas, with forecasts eighteen months ahead. The last issue each year contains an assessment of medium-term prospects. There are also in most issues special articles on subjects of interest to academic and business economists.

Annual subscriptions, £25.00 (home), and £35.00 (abroad), also single issues for the current year, £7.00 (home) and £10.00 (abroad), are available directly from the NIESR, 2 Dean Trench Street, Smith Square, London, SW1P 3EH.

Subscriptions at the special reduced price of £10.00 p.a. are available to students in the United Kingdom and Irish Republic on application to the Secretary of the Institute.

Back issues for the years 1959–79 and reprints of issues which have gone out of stock are obtainable from Wm Dawson & Sons Ltd, Cannon House, Park Farm Road, Folkestone, Kent. Microfiche copies for the years 1959–79 are available from EP Microform Ltd, Bradford Road, East Ardsley, Wakefield, WF3 2JN, Yorkshire.